G. WILSON KNIGHT
COLLECTED WORKS

G. WILSON KNIGHT
COLLECTED WORKS

VOLUME XI

BYRON AND SHAKESPEARE

London and New York

First published 1966 by Routledge & Kegan Paul Ltd

This edition published 2002 by Routledge
2 Park Square, Milton Park, Abingdon, Oxon OX14 4RN

Simultaneously published in the USA and Canada
by Routledge
270 Madison Avenue, New York, NY 10016

Routledge is an imprint of the Taylor & Francis Group

Transferred to digital printing 2010

© 1966 by G. Wilson Knight

Typeset in Times New Roman by
Keystroke, Jacaranda Lodge, Wolverhampton

British Library Cataloguing in Publication Data
A catalogue record for this book is available from the British Library

Library of Congress Cataloging in Publication Data
A catalog record for this book has been requested

ISBN 978-0–415–27896–6 (Set)
ISBN 978-0–415–29080–7 (Volume XI) (hbk)
ISBN 978-0–415–60669-1 (Volume XI) (pbk)

Publisher's Note
The publisher has gone to great lengths to ensure the quality of this
reprint but points out that some imperfections in the original book
may be apparent.

BYRON
and
SHAKESPEARE

by

G. WILSON KNIGHT

ROUTLEDGE & KEGAN PAUL
London

Statue of Lord Byron in the Library of Trinity College, Cambridge; by Bertel Thorvaldsen (photo: Edward Leigh)

For
PATRICIA M. BALL

PREFACE

THE notes on which this book is based were taken down over fifteen years ago. I have now put them into shape. The task has been rendered difficult by the superabundance of analogies between Byron and Shakespeare. The more I have read of, or about, Byron, the more they have multiplied, and I have had to leave many of my later reference notes in the volumes of my Byron shelf unconsulted for fear of too great an expansion.

My chapter 'A Regency Hamlet' is a longer version of a lecture 'Byron and Hamlet' delivered at the John Rylands Library, Manchester, and published in their *Bulletin* of September 1962 (Vol. 45, No. 1).

A recent article by Mr. Geoffrey Strickland 'Stendhal, Byron et John Cam Hobhouse' which appears in an offprint entitled 'Extrait de Stendhal Club' (Lausanne; 28; 15 July 1965) argues against the reliability of Stendhal's accounts of Byron; and it might seem that my own use of them should have been modified. In such matters I try, in this so critical age of ours, to preserve caution. Though Teresa Guiccioli, Medwin and Lady Blessington have been frequently distrusted, yet their reports of Byron's conversations chime so closely in factual detail, turn of thought, and style of expression with what a sympathetic Byronist knows from other sources, that I follow them without anxiety. Stendhal may be less trustworthy than are those. However, my references to him concern mainly Byron's response to music, and on this Mrs. Langley Moore has given us reason to suppose that his repeated emphasis may have been correct (*The Late Lord Byron*, 379).

As my 'List of authorities' shows, I have not always followed the editions used in my previous studies. Where it is likely to prove helpful I have given the numbers of pages contained, so that in looking up a reference a rough calculation in a different edition may be possible.

For Byron's narrative poems my numerals signify canto and stanza. A difficulty arises in quoting Byron's poetry. Hartley Coleridge, presumably following manuscripts, prints Byron's capitals, italics, and dashes; but these are reduced in the current Oxford text, which generally, though with deviations, follows the one-volume edition published and reprinted during the last century by Murray. Byron's mannerisms are helpful as directions for reading aloud, and for the reading aloud of Byron see p. 37 below, note; but some are hard on the critical eye. To print them all might be unwise, and yet many are of sharp intellectual significance. I have accordingly taken my own course, collating the texts.

After years of confusion, caused originally by my following the Globe Shakespeare, I nowadays in quoting Shakespeare's poetry follow the Oxford Shakespeare in printing '-ed' at the end of verbs whenever the syllable is to be sounded, but when it is not to be sounded replacing the 'e' with an apostrophe: "d'. I only occasionally, when misunderstanding would be particularly unfortunate, accent an 'e' to ensure pronunciation. Now, though Hartley Coleridge's text uses accents for the pronounced syllable and avoids the abbreviation, the Oxford Byron, following the Murray text, is as inconsistent as the Globe Shakespeare (or the text of Tennyson's plays), using or not using the abbreviation when the syllable is—as in Byron it nearly always will be—slurred, according to no apparent system. For my present purpose, involving quotations from both poets, standardization was obviously forced, and I have accordingly used the same system of abbreviations for Byron as I use for Shakespeare.

A problem has arisen regarding the 1965 reissue of my book *Laureate of Peace: on the Genius of Alexander Pope*, which includes a long section on Byron's praise of his favourite poet, leading to a number of references in my present study. Since I was asked to substitute a clearer title high-lighting the poet's name, I agreed to *Alexander Pope: Laureate of Peace*. The book has now appeared with nothing in the preliminary pages to inform the public of its status as a corrected edition rather than a simple reprint, and without my 1965 addition to the preface where its nature was explained; together with a title-page reading, when punctuated, *The Poetry of Pope:*

Laureate of Peace, an inapposite title trespassing on that of Prof. Geoffrey Tillotson's *On the Poetry of Pope* and itself neither rhythmically nor syntactically, since 'Laureate' *sounds* as in apposition to 'Poetry', satisfying. Moreover the cover and spine, though not the title-page, of the new and simultaneously published *paper-back* edition read: *The Poetry of Alexander Pope*, with cover sub-title *Laureate of Peace*. Since confusion is bound to arise in bibliographies and library catalogues in regard to the paper-back, I herewith name as its correct title, for technical purposes: *The Poetry of [Alexander] Pope: Laureate of Peace*.[1] When the book is again, in either form, reissued, whether during or after my life, I direct that this explanation be repeated and that it shall bear the originally agreed, new, title: *Alexander Pope: Laureate of Peace*.

Two Byron essays referred to in the following pages, 'The Two Eternities' from *The Burning Oracle* and my Byron Foundation Lecture *Byron's Dramatic Prose*, are to be grouped with an abbreviated version of my *Chariot of Wrath* (on Milton, 1942) to make part of a new volume soon to be published by Messrs. Methuen & Co. under the title *Poets of Action*.

Once again I record my gratitude to Dr. Patricia M. Ball for checking a large proportion of my many quotations from Byron's prose and poetry, and for compiling the Index of Names and Titles. I am also indebted to Mr. Keith Walker for bringing scholarship and accuracy to bear on my references to other works.

I have to thank my friend Mr. Oliver Campion for presenting me with a copy of the picture by Théodore Géricault which I use in this volume. It is generally supposed, though without certainty, to be a study of Byron. Géricault did a number of illustrations for French editions of Byron's poems. Whatever the truth, the portrait has a depth relevant to my present purpose, and I am grateful to the Musée Fabre of Montpellier for permission to reproduce it.

Acknowledgments in regard to my other illustrations are given on p. xv.

G. W. K.

Exeter, February 1966

1. A full bibliography of my writings is being prepared by Dr. John E. Van Domelen for publication, probably, in the Bulletin of the New York Public Library.

LIST OF AUTHORITIES

This is not an official bibliography. The editions noted are simply those actually used by me for my present purposes. These include more convenient editions of Teresa Guiccioli's *Recollections* and Lady Blessington's *Conversations* than those used in my previous studies. To facilitate calculation for those using different editions I have, where it seemed helpful, noted the number of pages in the volumes to which I refer. Abbreviated designations used in my text are given in brackets.

The Works of Lord Byron: Poetry: ed. E. Hartley Coleridge; 7 vols., 1898–1904 (P).

The Poetical Works of Lord Byron: Oxford Edition; 1926. N.B. For narrative poems my two numerals refer to (i) Canto and (ii) Section or Stanza.

The Works of Lord Byron: Letters and Journals: ed. R. E. Prothero, Lord Ernle; 6 vols., 1898–1901 (LJ).

Lord Byron's Correspondence: ed. John Murray; 2 vols., 1922 (C).

Byron; A Self-Portrait: letters, ed. Peter Quennell; 2 vols., 1950 (SP).

Letters and Journals of Lord Byron, with notices of his life: Thomas Moore; 2 vols., 1830; single vol. edn., entitled *Byron's Life, Letters and Journals,* with chapter divisions, 1860 (Moore). N.B. I give references to both editions, my numerals indicating volume and page for the one and chapter and page for the other.

Memoirs, Journal and Correspondence of Thomas Moore: ed. Lord John Russell; 8 vols., 1853–6.

The Life of Lord Byron: John Galt; 1830 (Galt).

Recollections of the Life of Lord Byron: R. C. Dallas; 1824 (Dallas).

My Recollections of Lord Byron and those of Eye-Witnesses of his Life: Countess Guiccioli; single volume translation, 1869. 25 chapters and 'Reflections, etc.' (the two-volume edition, used in my previous studies, numbers its chapters separately), 499 pages (Teresa).

The Last Attachment: The story of Byron and Teresa Guiccioli as told in their unpublished letters and other family papers: Iris Origo; 1949 (Origo).

Conversations of Lord Byron: Thomas Medwin; octavo edn., 1824 (1824 editions exist with varying pagination). 351 pages and appendix (Medwin).

A Journal of the Conversations of Lord Byron with the Countess of Blessington: Lady Blessington; revised, with chapter divisions, 1893. 369 pages (Blessington).

Conversations on Religion with Lord Byron and others: James Kennedy; 1830 (Kennedy).

A Narrative of Lord Byron's Last Journey to Greece: Pietro Gamba; 1825 (Gamba).

The Last Days of Lord Byron: William Parry; 1825 (Parry).

Memoirs of the Affairs of Greece; . . . with Various Anecdotes relating to Lord Byron and An account of his Last Illness and Death: Julius Millingen; 1831 (Millingen).

Records of Shelley, Byron and the Author: E. J. Trelawny; Routledge edn., 1905 (?—Editions are confusing), 26 chapters and appendix, 264 pages (Trelawny).

Byron; The Last Phase: Richard Edgcumbe; 1909 (Edgcumbe).

Astarte: Lord Lovelace; enlarged, ed. Lady Lovelace; 1921 (Lovelace).

The Byron Mystery: Sir John C. Fox; 1924.

Byron, The Last Journey: Harold Nicolson; 1924 (Nicolson).

The Pilgrim of Eternity: John Drinkwater; 1925 (Drinkwater).

The Life and Letters of Anne Isabella, Lady Noel Byron: Ethel Colburn Mayne; 1929.

Byron: André Maurois; 1950 English reprint (Maurois).

Byron: a Biography: Leslie A. Marchand; 3 vols., 1957 (Marchand).

The Late Lord Byron: Doris Langley Moore; 1961 (Mrs. Moore).

Lord Byron's Wife: Malcolm Elwin; 1962 (Elwin).

The following Byron works of my own are also referred to:

Lord Byron: Christian Virtues; 1952 (LBCV).

Lord Byron's Marriage; 1957 (LBM).

Laureate of Peace, on Pope; 1954; reissued under a new title (see p. viii), 1965. Contains a long section on Byron.

'The Two Eternities' in *The Burning Oracle;* 1939. See p. ix.

Byron's Dramatic Prose: Byron Foundation Lecture, 1953. See p. ix.

All page references are given without the letter 'p.' except for those applying to my present volume, for which I use it.

My Shakespearian numerals apply to the Oxford Shakespeare.

xii

CONTENTS

ILLUSTRATIONS

For information regarding the frontispiece and illustration 2 see, respectively, Marchand, I, 178 and III, 1256. For illustration 6 see p. ix of the present volume.

Grateful acknowledgments are recorded for permission to reproduce the following pictures: for the frontispiece, to the Master and Fellows of Trinity College, Cambridge; for 3 and 5, to Sir John Murray; for 4, from a photograph kindly loaned by Sir John Murray, to the Marchesa Origo; and for 6, to the Musée Fabre, Montpellier.

I

INTRODUCTION

I

Iɴ the Eton and Harrow match of 1805 Lord Byron went in
directly after a boy named Shakespeare. Shakespeare was
stumped for 8 and Byron caught for 7. In the second innings
their runs were respectively 5 and 2. How far these figures
should be regarded as symbolically relevant will perhaps be determined by my present study: I would not agree that they do Byron
justice (for the scores, see LJ, I, 70, note).

Shakespeare and Byron are alike in that each bestrides, as do none
of their contemporaries, two cultural periods. Byron is as notable for
his synthesis of the Augustan and the Romantic, which corresponds
roughly to the aristocratic and the revolutionary, as was Shakespeare
for his interfusing of the Medieval and the Renaissance. In neither
Shakespeare nor Byron can we say that one term of the opposition
is wholly favoured and the other repudiated: the total effect is nearer
marriage than conflict, though many conflicts are contained. It is
a marriage made of conflicts. It is by reason of this more inclusive
comprehension that Shakespeare and Byron out-span their contemporaries.

Within the framework of this general similarity we shall find a
number of detailed correspondences, and in the following pages I
trace some of the more interesting. Of these correspondences we can
say this: that what in Shakespeare is given a full poetic realization
and embodiment, and remains to that extent veiled, tends in Byron
not only to be rendered more *intellectually* explicit and purposive but
also to demand, and in his own life to be expressed in, action. The
only Shakespearian play that shows a similar kind of direct and
purposive statement is *Timon of Athens*; and it is interesting to find

I

Professor Allardyce Nicoll calling it, in respect to this very quality, 'Byronic' (*Shakespeare*, 1952, 61). The uncompromising and forthright style of Byron's challenge may even seem to draw nearer to Marlowe than to Shakespeare, and yet its true nature was less Marlovian than Shakespearian. The only biographer to my knowledge who has come near to observing this is André Maurois. Maurois goes sadly astray on the matter of Byron's marriage, but in noting that in 1813 and 1814 Byron *lived* Shakespeare, he makes a valid point. He writes:

> *King Lear, Hamlet, Macbeth*—his evenings were passed in seeing Shakespeare. He knew Shakespeare by heart. He lived Shakespeare. He made frequent mention in his journal of the Prince of Denmark's brusque tone.[1] And in that winter of 1814 life itself was Shakespearian. The drama of the Empire was rising to the climax of its last act.   (Maurois, 198)

Maurois is thinking of Byron's comments on the defeat of Napoleon. Here is the first, in his Journal for Saturday 9 April 1814, using quotations from *Hamlet* (II, ii, 174), *Antony and Cleopatra* (III, xi, 31) and *Macbeth* (V, iii, 49):

I mark this day!

Napoleon Buonaparte has abdicated the throne of the world. 'Excellent well.' Methinks Sylla did better; for he revenged and resigned in the height of his sway, red with the slaughter of his foes—the finest instance of glorious contempt of the rascals upon record. Dioclesian did well too—Amurath not amiss, had he become aught except a dervise—Charles the Fifth but so so— but Napoleon, worst of all. What! wait till they were in his capital, and then talk of his readiness to give up what is already gone!! 'What whining monk art thou—what holy cheat?' 'Sdeath!—Dionysius at Corinth was yet a king to this. The 'Isle of Elba' to retire to!—Well—if it had been Caprea, I should have marvelled less. 'I see men's minds are but a parcel of their fortunes.' I am utterly bewildered and confounded.

I don't know—but I think *I*, even *I* (an insect compared with this creature), have set my life on casts not a millionth part

---

1. Should he not have written: 'frequent comments, or quotations, in his journal *in* the Prince of Denmark's brusque tone'? There appears to be an error in translation.

2

of this man's. But, after all, a crown may be not worth dying for. Yet, to outlive *Lodi* for this!!! Oh that Juvenal or Johnson could rise from the dead! *Expende—quot libras in duce summo invenies?* I knew they were light in the balance of mortality; but I thought their living dust weighed more *carats.* Alas! this imperial diamond hath a flaw in it, and is now hardly fit to stick in a glazier's pencil:—the pen of the historian won't rate it worth a ducat.

Psha! 'Something too much of this.' But I won't give him up even now; though all his admirers have, 'like the thanes, fallen from him.' (LJ, II, 409)

'What whining monk . . .' comes from Otway's *Venice Preserved.*

On 10 April Byron records the composition of his *Ode to Napoleon Buonaparte* and on 19 April, finding his hopes of man and superman shattered, concludes with a pregnant entry drawing on *Macbeth* (v, v, 22), *Romeo and Juliet* (III, iii, 56) and *King Lear* (II, iv, 289):

There is ice at both poles, north and south—all extremes are the same—misery belongs to the highest and the lowest only, to the emperor and the beggar, when unsixpenced and unthroned. There is, to be sure, a damned insipid medium—an equinoctial line—no one knows where, except upon maps and measurement.

'And all our *yesterdays* have lighted fools
The way to dusty death.'

I will keep no further journal of that same hesternal torchlight; and, to prevent me from returning, like a dog, to the vomit of memory, I tear out the remaining leaves of this volume, and write, in *Ipecacuanha*—'that the Bourbons are restored!!!'—'Hang up philosophy.' To be sure, I have long despised myself and man, but I never spat in the face of my species before—'O fool! I shall go mad.' (LJ, II, 411)

In these passages we watch European history attaining a dramatic condensation within the protagonist consciousness of Byron. Shakespeare is the natural voice and Byron the natural speaker. We begin to understand what Shakespeare, what all great drama, is *for*: it

3

exists for a human, and more than human, purpose, of which Byron is the exemplar.

But it was not only in 1814 that Byron lived Shakespeare. He was always doing it.

How far Shakespeare himself can be said to have lived what he wrote it would be rash to assert. He obviously cannot, in his quiet and well organized life, be supposed to have done it to anything like the extent that Byron did.

An objection may be raised. Shakespeare appears to be a strong supporter of royalty, whereas Byron is famed as a revolutionary. We shall, of course, be aware, that each has, as we have noted, the opposites always in mind and in sympathy; and we shall obviously take note of a natural shift in emphasis demanded by the periods of composition. Even so, is it not strange, if I am right in claiming that they are so alike in both depth and surface, that their at least superficial reputations in regard to those affairs of state with which both were so deeply engaged should appear so widely to diverge?

Well, we can remind ourselves that Byron honoured Britain's 'ancient and honourable aristocracy' (p. 326 below), and even the Regent in so far as he acted nobly; politically he stood always for a *middle* path; and he took a considerable pride in his claim to a royal descent (see variously pp. 93, 109, 202, 333-8; below). But what of Shakespeare? Even though Byron can be shown to have sympathies with the traditional order, can we suppose that Shakespeare had in him any revolutionary impulses? Can he in any way be aligned with the revolutionary principle that was to expand so violently in subsequent generations?

Shakespeare's patron was the Earl of Southampton, friend of the Earl of Essex. Essex, a man of Byronic daring and sensitivity, became dangerous and even insurrectionary, was tried, and executed. Southampton, his supporter, was imprisoned. Shakespeare honoured Essex in one of the Chorus prologues in *Henry V*; and since he so consistently avoided such gestures, the salute is significant. Prof. J. Dover Wilson has argued that *Hamlet* may be related to Essex's personality. Two recent biographers, Dr. A. L. Rowse and Mr. Peter Quennell, have laid emphasis on its probable importance to Shakespeare. Both underline, for what it is worth, the evidence of

4

Henry Chettle's *England's Mourning Garment* that Shakespeare's muse appears to have been strangely silent, when so many others were vocal, at the great Queen's death.

If we find a contemporary meaning in *Hamlet*, we shall naturally do so in *Julius Caesar* too, equating Brutus, as did Byron thinking of himself ('Brutus, thou sleep'st'; Journal, 18 Feb. 1814; LJ, II, 384), with the poet's own political instincts. Shakespeare clearly could not make any too obvious references; but that such parallels could be suspected is clear from the fortunes of *Richard II*. The Abdication lines were omitted from the two editions published during the Queen's lifetime and the supporters of Essex commissioned a performance of what seems to have been the full text on the eve, 7 February 1601, of Essex's rebellion. The Queen herself is reported to have referred to the incident in the words 'I am Richard II, know ye not that?' (Peter Alexander, *Shakespeare*, 1964; 185–6). But all Shakespeare's dramas are characterized by a fine balancing of sympathies; he never as a dramatist whole-heartedly supports revolution as against rulers, nor rulers against revolution. What we can say is, that his interest in current events, perhaps emotionally impregnated by his connection with Southampton—I am not referring to the Sonnets—gave him at the turn of the century some raw but rich material for more universal creations.

Whether we dare say more than that is doubtful. The trouble is, that if Hamlet could be seen as Essex, then Claudius at once corresponds to Elizabeth I; and even if my view of Claudius as a far from obvious villain could be supposed, as it probably cannot, to have been the contemporary view of him, the implication would have been extremely dangerous, if not professionally suicidal. Moreover, the murder of Hamlet's father would now inevitably correspond to the execution of Mary Queen of Scots by Elizabeth; and just as Mary was, as a Catholic, a personified symbol of the old order, so was, in a different fashion, the old King Hamlet. Southampton was a Catholic. The pattern fits only too well. But could Shakespeare want any of this to be recognized? Was he even aware of the correspondence? Was it not, at the most, a pushing through of certain general feelings, such as those which made the Milton of *Paradise Lost* create the vanquished Satan and his followers on the pattern, which he himself would scarcely have acknowledged, of the Cromwellian party? Such relations may be admitted; but they are of so complex a nature that they raise all the well-known questions attending the study of poetry; and the relation of poetry to biography, except when we are dealing with a Byron in whom poetry and biography are so often identical, is as yet obscure.

As for Catholicism, many have thought that Shakespeare had strong Catholic sympathies. Mrs. Alan Keen, writing of his relations with Sir John Salusbury, to whom *Love's Martyr* was dedicated, regards them as a determining element in his life.[1] If he did have such sympathies, however, we must suppose that they were to a large extent masked, for Shakespeare seems to have had the worldly wisdom of a Polonius, and was a cautious man. Besides, such sympathies would scarcely have in him taken an extreme form, because he would simultaneously be recognizing—he had personally every reason to—all that was good in Protestantism and the reign of Elizabeth. Once again, he was, like Byron, comprehensive. Byron also had Catholic sympathies. The ancestral ghost of Newstead Abbey descended from the time of the dissolution of the monasteries under *Henry VIII* and is poetically treated in the concluding cantos of *Don Juan*:

> Amundeville is lord by day
> But the Monk is lord by night.
>
> (XVI, 40)

Byron's natural daughter Allegra was given a Catholic education, for Byron regarded Catholicism 'as the best religion, as it is assuredly the oldest of the various branches of Christianity' (Hoppner, 3 April 1821; LJ, V, 264). One of Byron's speeches in the Lords was vigorous in support of Catholic emancipation (LJ, II, App. ii, 431–43; LBCV, 131–4). In both Shakespeare's day and Byron's, Catholicism had dual pointings. It could be (i) respected as part of a long tradition and an older order; but it was also (ii) suppressed, largely for political reasons, as a danger, and to that extent itself revolutionary.

1. I have a broad-sheet of hers entitled *Phoenix*, printed by the Favil Press, Kensington, Oct. 1957. See my letter in *The Times Literary Supplement*, 26 December 1963, 1072.

In every age revolution is likely to claim that it is harking back to tradition; Protestantism itself did so, as Milton so clearly emphasized. But the ramifications of Medievalism and Renaissance criss-crossed variously by the different opposition of Catholicism and Protestantism are inexhaustible. The works of Shakespeare were born from a period which, as Patrick Cruttwell has argued in *The Shakespearean Moment* (1954), enjoyed a unique balance of Church and State, corresponding within a limited field to the balance of Pope and Emperor striven for in the Middle Ages. Shakespeare, in his own fashion, reflects this balance, which in artistic terms becomes more than a balance, drawing near to integration. For this very reason analysis plunges us into a mass of complexities and paradoxes. In any comprehensive survey in which conflicts are, as they are in Shakespeare and Byron, harmonized, we must be prepared when inspecting any particular constituent to find it turning into its antithesis. All we can be reasonably sure about is that both Shakespeare (p. 68 below) and Byron (pp. 46, 92, 307–8) had a strong sense, in Byron rising to a mystique, of the ancestral past, and that this sense inevitably contained a respect for Catholicism; but that Shakespeare could be, in fact, as Cranmer's prophecy at the conclusion to *Henry VIII* shows, a supporter of Elizabeth I, as a Protestant monarch; and that Byron was always ready to accept and honour the ruling powers of his country in so far as they acted graciously (pp. 109–10, 203, 332, 336).

Neither Shakespeare nor Byron were levellers. Both repudiated extremes of revolution and distrusted demagogues (pp. 202–3). Both labour to steer a middle course between tyranny or ineffectual rulers on the one side and mass revolution on the other. Even so, the revolutionary principle that broke out so fiercely during the Civil War, and was to become so widespread in Byron's day and Byron's thought, had been written into Shakespeare's dramas: *Richard II* is a vivid forecast of what was to happen later, the contrast of cultural superiority against practical efficiency in Richard and Bolingbroke prefiguring neatly the contrast of Charles I and Cromwell, and their respective parties. In my *Chariot of Wrath* (see p. ix above) I compared the puritanical severity of Milton to Shakespeare's Brutus (33, 63–4, 91, 94).

7

And we can go deeper. Despite his massive moral stability Shakespeare's tragedies derive their central appeal not from the moral framework, which sometimes seems little more than that, nor from statements of 'order', but, as I have often emphasized (e.g. *The Shakespearian Tempest*, edn. of 1953, vii–viii; *The Sovereign Flower*, 'Some Notable Fallacies', 245–55), from the clash of some Dionysian or even nihilistic force against the established order, against even the cosmos itself, the two terms of the opposition being excellently defined in the arguments of Nestor and Ulysses in *Troilus and Cressida* (see *The Wheel of Fire*, enlarged 1949, 49–52). Shakesperian tragedy accordingly points ahead on a metaphysical level to the revolutionary impetus that was to follow; it *is* itself perhaps in part the origin of that impetus. There were, of course, others: Rabelais, Marlowe, Molière, Milton's Satan. All these, and Shakespeare preeminently in Falstaff and the tragedies, point on to what was later to be made of the Faust and Don Juan myths; to Gothic Drama and Romantic poetry; to Shelley's *Prometheus Unbound*; to Byron as anarch and Satanist, for so he was often regarded by his contemporaries; to Ibsen, Nietzsche and Shaw. The whole vast movement is contained, embryonically, within Shakespeare. Shakespeare, it is true, controls it all magnificently and finally includes it within the serenities and contemporary acceptances of *Henry VIII*, making peace as it were with the conditions under which his challenges had been composed (p. 317 below); but challenges they were, and are, and *Timon of Athens* the clearest example. Byron, as we shall see, traced an analogous course concluding with a not-dissimilar acceptance.

If nevertheless it were again advanced that Byron did not, his whole life and work considered, show the serenity and balance of a Shakespeare, this was inevitable; he was tracing the same course in a more tumultuous and more tormented age, and developing the various themes concerned into both doctrine and action. His universe, the world of his contemplation, was superficially at least far larger and more confusing than Shakespeare's; but what he did about it was, in both sweep and detail, Shakespearian.

How comes it then, we may ask, that he consistently refused to take Shakespeare as a literary model? He regarded Shakespeare as 'though the most extraordinary of writers', yet the 'worst of models' (Murray, 14 July, 1821; LJ, v, 323).

Byron's own dramas were given a different, more 'classic', style.[1] Why was this? The answer is easy.

It was just because Byron had so much Shakespearian and other drama in him as a man that he regarded Shakespeare as a danger; and it was precisely because he had so Shakespearian a universe to control, that he preferred Alexander Pope as an exemplar. Of his admiration of Pope and its reasons I have given a full account in my *Laureate of Peace* (1954; reissued as *The Poetry of Pope*, see p. viii above, 1965). Pope at a moment of cultural stability succeeded miraculously in pointing the Shakespearian and Renaissance aware-ness towards a harmony. Conflicts there were, but they were per-sonal, and the major tumults stilled: they were conflicts within a peace. After the insecure balance of Elizabethan and Jacobean England, forces had tugged apart. The Puritan revolution followed; thought was being split into more and more specializations; our modern chaos was beginning to show itself in society and—the pro-cess is described at the conclusion of Pope's *Dunciad*—in thought. But for a short while a new stability was made and held, or all but held, under a newly 'constitutional' monarchy and a powerful and cultured aristocracy in what we call the 'Augustan' age, of which Pope was the voice. Logically enough Byron, enduring in his vast consciousness the Shakespearian and more than Shakespearian tumult, and all the new chaos which Pope had predicted, and him-self caught up moreover in the necessities of *action*, being as a man

1. Much valuable work has been, and is being, done on Byron's dramas. Standard works are William Gerard, *Byron Restudied in his Dramas*, 1886, and Samuel C. Chew, *The Dramas of Lord Byron*, 1915. My own approaches have appeared in *The Burning Oracle*, 1939; *T.L.S.*, 3 February 1950 (article) and 20 February 1959 (correspond-ence); '*Byron's Dramatic Prose*', Byron Foundation Lecture, 1953 (pub. 1954); and 'Shakespeare and Byron's Plays', *Shakespeare-Jahrbuch*, 1959. We now have also John W. Klein, 'Byron's Neglected Plays', *Drama*, Winter 1961 (New Series, 63) and Bonamy Dobrée, *Byron's Dramas,* Byron Foundation Lecture, 1962. The follow-ing University theses should be noted: B. Taborski, Bristol, 1952; Patricia M. Ball, Leeds, 1953; Zahava Karl Dorinson, Roosevelt University, Chicago, 1963; O. P. Mathur, Agra, 1963; M. S. Kushwaha, Lucknow, in preparation.

Chew's study (published in 1915 at both Göttingen and Baltimore) includes an appendix on Shakespearian echoes in *Marino Faliero*.

simultaneously both playwright and protagonist on a world-stage wider than any Shakespeare had envisioned—logically enough, he sought his star not in the poet of Dionysian tumult but in the Laureate of Peace, Alexander Pope. Shakespeare was too close. Byron *was* Shakespearian drama incarnate; but what he reached for was a poet in whom ideals and passion, society and religion, state and church, could be felt in harmony. Pope was the exemplar he wanted; his life's task was to adjust contemporary Europe and contemporary man, through his own tumultuous self, to the works of Pope. Pope was his New Testament; the Old Testament he loved but the New Testament, lacking or seeming to lack a contemporary political and sexual relevance, meant less to him. So his faith was planted in Pope, the 'Christianity of English poetry' and 'Book of Life' (*Laureate of Peace*, see p. viii above; 132, 153; LJ, IV, 486; V, 590).

After reporting a conversation in which Byron had been criticizing Shakespeare and elevating Pope, Lady Blessington writes:

Byron is so prone to talk for effect, and to assert what he does not believe, that one must be cautious in giving implicit credence to his opinions. My conviction is, that, in spite of his declarations to the contrary, he admires Shakespeare as much as most of his countrymen do; but that, unlike the generality of them, he sees the blemishes that the freedom of the times in which the great poet lived led him to indulge in his writings, in a stronger point of view, and takes pleasure in commenting on them with severity, as a means of wounding the vanity of the English. I have rarely met with a person more conversant with the works of Shakespeare than was Byron. I have heard him quote passages from them repeatedly; and in a tone that marked how well he appreciated their beauty, which certainly lost nothing in his delivery of them, as few possessed a more harmonious voice or a more elegant pronunciation than did Byron. Could there be a less equivocal proof of his admiration of our immortal bard than the tenacity with which his memory retained the finest passages of all his works? When I made this observation to him he smiled, and affected to boast that his memory was so retentive that it equally retained all that he read; but as I had seen many proofs to the contrary, I persevered in affirming what I have never ceased to believe, that, in despite of his professions to the reverse, Byron was in his heart a warm admirer of Shakespeare. (Blessington, XIII, 323)

There is here a strange admixture of true reporting and false deduction. The charge of insincerity is off the mark.

Lady Blessington could not see how Byron's obvious *kinship with* Shakespeare could be assimilated to his *preference for* Pope. And yet the one was the direct cause of the other; for it was precisely the Shakespeare in Byron that reached out in self-dissatisfaction to Pope, rather as Hamlet envied the mastery of passion in Horatio. Byron's love of Pope was in direct proportion to his Shakespearian identity.

II

Byron's stature has been quite amazingly missed, in England especially. He has been handed over either to the biographers who have been comically misled by Lady Byron's propaganda; or to the literary critics who write from an irrelevant standpoint. The errors of biography in dealing with Byron's marriage I have discussed elsewhere. On literary criticism a few words may here be helpful.

Our critics want Byron to have written a kind of poetry alien to his nature and to the task he had before him. In his *Essay on Criticism* Pope has warned us against those who 'write dull receipts how poems may be made'. Can we not take the hint? Can we not, when a great writer is before us, be ready to substitute *interpretation* for *criticism*—'criticism' being surely the least profitable of all approaches to Byron's extraordinary attainment. For example, carelessness may be imputed for occasional freedoms of a sort readily allowed to Shakespeare and the moderns, simply because they jar his Augustan manner; so that, handling a poetic world of unprecedented amplitude, he ends by being blamed for his will to clarity and control.

Our literary values are all wrong; they are deceptive and self-deceptive; they go askew. Here is a typical example. Recently I read a review of a book on D. H. Lawrence noting without a murmur of disapproval that the author had no room for Lawrence's novels of 'leadership' such as *Kangaroo* and *The Plumed Serpent*. I do not suppose that any readers of this review observed anything strange;

it was all exactly the kind of thing we expect and accept. But consider: is not the proper aim of a book on Lawrence the facing and exposition of what Lawrence himself was driving at? True, the critic has every right to his own, personal, views; but so have we all; and it is for each of us to make our own judgments, as we please, regarding the validity of Lawrence's views. This we shall, in any case, do. The book in question merely records the critic's judgments; and who wants these? If he is presuming to know better than Lawrence what Lawrence's created world should be, he is in effect putting himself forward as a creative writer; and he has every right to do this. But why then not write his own original book? Why tie it up with bits and pieces, chosen arbitrarily, of Lawrence? There is one only reason for doing this that has any justification: he knows that by acting as a parasite his own ideas will reach a public that they could not reach in any other way. The reason is a sound and practical reason enough; but we should all realize what he is doing.

I have always liked this passage from Mazzini's essay 'Byron and Goethe':

> Certain travellers of the eleventh century relate that they saw at Teneriffe a prodigiously lofty tree, which, from its immense extent of foliage, collected all the vapours of the atmosphere; to discharge them, when its branches were shaken, in a shower of pure and refreshing water. Genius is like this tree, and the mission of criticism should be to shake the branches. At the present day it more resembles a savage striving to hew down the noble tree to the roots.   (*Life and Writings, etc.*; VI, 94)

Every age can produce similar complaints; it is no new problem; and we seem to advance not at all. And yet there is today hope, because now, for the first time, in the various works which I have been called upon to write, there is apparent a consistent, reasoned, and fruitful approach to the dimension of what we call 'genius' that is throughout dispassionately interpretative. Genius traffics with the imponderables; it outspaces all simple categories; and once recognized by our own imaginations *as* 'genius', it immediately has sovereign rights. Observe that our own imaginations first recognize the powers in question; and what is next needed is to attune our ratiocinative faculties to our own imaginative insights. But what if

12

our critic says that his imagination does *not* ratify the works and life of Byron? All we can then say is that the wider, racial, imagination *has* so ratified them, and that he is in a dangerous, if not a ludicrous, minority. Turn up the immense bibliography under 'Byron' in the catalogue of the British Museum. Does that mean nothing? I do not expect contemporary critics of my own generation to be affected by anything that I say; but I would ask the younger ones among my readers whether, in view of the massive and still increasing outpouring of works on Byron, our twentieth-century critics are *likely* to be right? I ask this young reader, with his career before him, and thinking of his own personal and professional, long-range, advantage, to avoid the constricting poverties of tendentious criticism and decide instead to invest his talents where a rich yield is certain.

While the iron is hot, let me adduce a concrete example. I offer for consideration the famous anthology piece *The Destruction of Sennacherib* (1815):

The Assyrian came down like the wolf on the fold,
And his cohorts were gleaming in purple and gold;
And the sheen of their spears was like stars on the sea,
When the blue wave rolls nightly on deep Galilee.

Like the leaves of the forest when Summer is green,
That host with their banners at sunset were seen:
Like the leaves of the forest when Autumn hath blown,
That host on the morrow lay wither'd and strown.

For the Angel of Death spread his wings on the blast,
And breath'd in the face of the foe as he pass'd;
And the eyes of the sleepers wax'd deadly and chill,
And their hearts but once heav'd, and for ever grew still!

And there lay the steed with his nostril all wide,
But through it there roll'd not the breath of his pride;
And the foam of his gasping lay white on the turf,
And cold as the spray of the rock-beating surf.

And there lay the rider distorted and pale,
With the dew on his brow, and the rust on his mail:

And the tents were all silent, the banners alone,
The lances unlifted, the trumpet unblown.

And the widows of Ashur are loud in their wail,
And the idols are broke in the temple of Baal;
And the might of the Gentile, unsmote by the sword,
Hath melted like snow in the glance of the Lord!

Are we to pass this by as a school-boy exercise to be denigrated by 'mature' minds as an out-dated piece of rhetoric?[1] Let us first see what it contains.

We are made aware of imperial and military glory, of its flash and ambition, its pride and fall. The Assyrian host challenges the stars and sea, man as against the cosmos, its co-equal and rival. But it is, nevertheless, of earth; subject like leaves to the rhythm of the seasons, summer and autumn, life and death.

Death is shown. That engine of proud life, the war-horse, is so fearful in death-agony that his very death seems to define the life-power it is killing; but this death is 'cold', vast, inhuman, like the vast otherness of a great sea's infinitude foaming on the rocks of life; the foam is the mysterious meeting place of sea and rock, of death and life, infinitude and earth. The rider's face, once mobile, is now 'distorted' and 'pale', but the sweet 'dew' of nature is on the 'brow' which cannot be so distorted and which suggests what is humanly or spiritually permanent; and it is as though the dew were blessing it, and forgiving. That the word 'dew' has such poetic connotations may be seen from the line 'To dew the sovereign flower and drown the weeds' in *Macbeth* (v, ii, 30); and 'brow', in Shakespeare and Byron (pp. 49, 50, 70, 109, 173, 259), radiates power. But there is no blessing on the soldier's iron 'mail', on which the dew acts as a curse, rusting it. That is the kind of exactitude and depth carried often by the minutiae of Byron's poetry. The still and silent tents, banners and trumpets, are nerveless symbols of what is, and yet is not. We return to the external facts: the bereaved families, the false religion that has not availed, the power of the true God.

1. The poem is finely rhetorical, and demands exact vocal projection. It is included in my tape-recording *Byron's Rhetoric*, published by *Sound Seminars*, 3402 Clifton Avenue, Cincinnati, U.S.A.

14

Much of Byron, apart from his humour, is here compacted: his love of the stellar universe, of the sea, of animal vigour; his sense of human endeavour in magnificence and crime; the repudiation of militarism, coupled with the soft feeling in 'dew' and 'brow', the forgiveness (as at *Don Juan*, III, 109, on Nero); his life-long devotion to the Old Testament; and his sense of an overruling—to use his favourite term—'Deity'.[1]

The poem must be read aloud, the voice modulated within the poetic beat to dramatize each separate gem of apprehension in terms of vocal sound: grandeur, pathos, wonder, terror; each emotion must be lived and expressed by the reader.

Byron is a great tragic poet, directing us to a sense of (i) human magnificence; (ii) its inevitable tragedy; and to (iii) a supervening acceptance. To point Byron's superlative power in tragic apprehension I adduce two brilliantly compact, lightning-like, poetic marvels, both of which I quoted in my first main essay on Byron in *The Burning Oracle*. Here is the first:

> Oh! o'er the eye Death most exerts his might,
> And hurls the Spirit from her throne of light.
>
> (*The Corsair*, III, 20)

That is best judged, if 'judged' it must be, by someone who has recently known a loved-one's death. All the mystery of life and all the mystery of death is in it. The doctor looks first at the *eye*. Each verb and noun of the second line must be exactly received: the meaningless cruelty of 'hurls', the concretely apprehended reality of 'the Spirit', conceived as a sovereign, the amazing and potent personality that was, but now is not there, a second ago *ruling* the body, the eye its 'throne'; and 'light' basic to life here on earth, perhaps in death. Is the Spirit itself light? No: the Spirit is more than light, which was its temporary 'throne'.[2] And beyond? We are not told. The royal spirit is gone. We are not told where, or whether it still exists. We are not told that it does not exist. This is the pure tragic apprehension.

1. For Byron's beliefs see my *Lord Byron; Christian Virtues*, Index A, xvi, Religion; 'The Deity', etc; also Teresa Guiccioli's chapter 'His Religious Opinions'.
2. The thought is typically Byronic, corresponding to thoughts elsewhere of the Sun and Stars as representative symbols or the 'abodes' of divinity (*Manfred*, III, ii, 14–16; *Sardanapalus*, II, i, 259–62; *Cain*, I, i, 499–500).

Our second example is this. Byron writes of the mists above the Falls of Terni, in which there is a rainbow like 'Hope upon a death bed' or 'Love watching Madness with unalterable mein' (*Childe Harold*, IV, 72). 'Hope' is felt to penetrate, 'serene' in turmoil, *beyond* death. It has been said that love can stand anything. I do not know. One would have thought that love would only make the suffering more poignant. But it is true that when nursing a loved but disjointed mind, not only does the old love help but a *new* love may be conjured into being of a quality not known before that seems to raise the occasion to a higher, more bearable, plane And yet more is involved than an assuagement; a positive and new power is born from the tragic occasion, to be valued in its own right. Byron's line recalls Cordelia and Lear, and Pericles' lines on Marina as 'Patience gazing on kings' graves and smiling extremity out of act' (p. 286 below). Still more, to me, it recalls that statement with which I started, that love can endure *anything*; for love *in this sense* is a new power; and that is why Byron did not write 'unaltered'. 'Unaltered' would mean that the old love was so strong that it could endure; 'unalterable' means that a new love, born of tragedy, has come into being that is somehow a solution, an answer, and is accordingly, though for reasons that cannot be explained, impregnable.[1]

It is on matters of this high order that Byron, whenever he needs to, writes with a compression, a clarity, and an authority, in my own literary experience unsurpassed.

III

Our concern here is as much a concern with Byron the man as with Byron the poet or prose writer. It is sometimes complained that Byron has suffered from an over-emphasis on biography and a corresponding neglect of his poetry. The complaint cannot justly be

1. That these latter judgments hold a certain experiential validity may be supposed from the fact that the passage was written while in November 1964 I was at Frenchay visiting twice daily my brother who, before he passed from us on 4 December, was for the last six weeks suffering from a physical disorder extending to the brain which left his talk, though active, yet quite random and irrational, and beyond verbal communication.

levelled against my own Byronic commentaries, which started with the eighty-page survey of his poetry entitled 'The Two Eternities' in *The Burning Oracle* in 1939; an essay which will be reprinted (see p. ix). There is, however, a good reason for our interest also in Byron's life. With most poets it may be very dangerous to mix up biographical detail, often of a dubious sort, with the results of their poetic genius. Poetic success exists on a different plane from normal thinking and normal behaviour. We may well find a discontinuity between the poetry and what we take to be 'the man'. The artist composes under the compulsions and the illuminations of the creative mood; and this comes and goes, as it will, and exactly how we cannot say. Nevertheless, in practice we find it far from easy to keep our poetic understanding pure; and it is perhaps fortunate that we know so little of Homer and Shakespeare. Had we a set of notes composed on Shakespeare after his death by the Dark Lady of the Sonnets, we might be tempted to regard Shakespeare as a scandalous person; worse—we might be tempted, for all we know, to regard him as a weak and ineffectual person; and though this ought not to affect our reception of the dramas, it would, very likely, do so.

Now with Byron our problem is different. Not only have we masses of information, variously trustworthy and deceptive, regarding his own life, but the details of his life, his personal relationships and prose thinking, are all so entangled with his poetry that it is difficult to keep them apart. Nor indeed should we want to, and for a reason quite easy to define. The danger of mixing up poetry with biography comes from the risk of reducing the authoritative poetry to the lesser order of the poet's apparent life. I say 'apparent', because we can never be sure what that life was; but for all practical purposes it is clear that the great passages of *The Prelude* bear little relation to what we happen to know, or think we know, of Wordsworth as a man. We receive more from *Kubla Khan* as an anthology piece than we do from regarding it as a milestone in Coleridge's life, perhaps the readiest way to reduce its importance. But with Byron everything is different. Any one of his greater poems can, like all poetry, be read in and as itself alone; but if we choose to relate it to his life there is no danger whatsoever of reducing it to a lower order since *his life itself exists in the poetic dimension,* and is itself poetically authoritative. That is the great, yet simple, difference. As a result the poetry, already great, becomes yet greater when related to his life; and his life and poetry together make something for which we have no name of staggering importance.

Naturally, we have to be careful in regard to the biographical evidences. The worst dangers I have already countered in my *Lord Byron's Marriage,* where I have shown how and why Lady Byron's propagandist accounts of the marriage break are untrustworthy; and we shall, I hope, henceforth give them the exact degree of authority, and no more, that the evidence I have adduced permits. I say 'I hope', since there is still a fair amount of confused thinking on the matter (see my Appendix, 'The Marriage Separation'). This is not to suggest that we blame Lady Byron for the marriage's failure. The material presented in the following pages is so extraordinary that we shall probably agree that to live on intimate terms with Byron, who was by turns or simultaneously Hamlet, Puck, Macbeth, Falstaff, Antony, Timon and Prospero, must have been not merely distracting but tormenting; and never more so than during the crucial period of 1815–1816, the period of Napoleon's fall. Byron was kaleidoscopic; he was good and evil, violent and childlike, worldly and fey; and yet a single, recognizable man. Each of these qualities were aspects only; the man himself, behind or within, might well have seemed terrifying.

What we find in Byron is an amazing comprehensiveness in strict correspondence to the main themes and persons of Shakespearian drama. Literary genius naturally tends towards variety, dramatist or novelist being what they are through the capacity to live temporarily in other life-forms than their own. They may even seem to have no settled life of their own. On 22 November, 1817, Keats wrote to Benjamin Bailey:

> Men of Genius are great as certain ethical chemicals operating on the Mass of neutral intellect—but they have not any individuality, any determined Character—I would call the top and head of those who have a proper self Men of Power.

Tolstoy was on the same problem when he complained that scholars

18

praised Shakespeare for creating in Hamlet the character of a man who 'has no character' ('Shakespeare and the Drama' in *Tolstoy on Art*, trans. Aylmer Maud, O.U.P. undated; 434). And yet we do recognize in Hamlet a unity, despite his variations; and so too, though Lady Blessington and others were baffled by what they called Byron's 'mobility' and all the play of *opposites* which it contained, yet we cannot, any more than when thinking of Hamlet, deny that we are always in the presence of a single man; every different aspect of Byron remains 'Byronic'; and he must accordingly be ranged also among what Keats calls the 'men of power'. As we read and reread his prose and poetry, his own journals and letters and the reports of his conversations, we are not aware of any real disparity between the ascetic and the debauchee; between the bluff man-of-action and the Adonis of effeminate sensibility; between the anarch who terrified London and the kindly humorist; between the ineffectual dandy and the greatest legendary figure in Europe's political and literary history; between, finally, the satanist and the saint. They are all Byron. Perhaps only Teresa Guiccioli, by strength of love's insight, came near to understanding Byron not only as a compendium but also, quite simply, as a man.

And yet he was no ordinary man. He was a man of some new order, as yet unrecognized. His ancestry may be traced to Greek tragedy, especially the *Prometheus Bound*; to what in *The Golden Labyrinth* I have called Shakespeare's 'dramatic supermen'; and to all those who have tried to inject literary genius into the world of politics and action, such as Dante, Milton and Swift. Byron sums and surpasses the great figures of the past and is a hinge towards the future, pointing on to Ibsen and Nietzsche, both of whom had sense of a new kind of man in process of creation; and both were influenced by Byron.[1] Bernard Shaw, writing in the same tradition, regarded Byron as the 'best brain' in the England of his day (*Every-body's Political What's What*, 1944; XXXVII, 323).

But more is involved than intellect, literary genius, and politics. Byron exerted a magic, which his contemporaries recognized but which we today find it less easy to recapture. We can however find

1. See my *Ibsen*, Writers and Critics Series; Edinburgh and London, and also New York, Grove Press; 1962; 107. For Nietzsche, see my note below, p. 20.

evidences of it in the more occult and spiritualistic intuitions embedded in his poetry, which are far more widespread, exact, and authoritative than has yet been recognized. In comparing Byron with Shakespeare's heroes, it is as easy to equate him with Prospero as with Hamlet. He had the reputation of being what is called 'superstitious'; he was probably clairvoyant; and some of his greater works, *Childe Harold, Manfred* and *Cain* are saturated in occult perception.[1] All this forms part of a personality famed for its practical, down-to-earth, physical, prowess. The comprehensiveness is indeed baffling. The truth is, Byron was the nearest personality we know of to what Nietzsche envisioned in his 'over-man'; he was probably, in part, behind Nietzsche's vision;[2] he is modern Europe's attempt at an evolutionary advance.

Such categories are hard to discuss, and harder still to explain and defend. The trouble is, that whereas negatives are easily handled, a new positive conception, as St. Paul's brilliantly confused Epistles so abundantly witness, is in any period notoriously difficult to put across. My own inability to find a better word than 'interpretation' for the *new type* of literary exegesis in which I have now for forty years been engaged is a modern example. Any hint of some new *power* will be regarded as either stupid or wicked. Especially do those like Byron who *in their own persons* appear to be bearers of such a power incur mockery and reviling, their reputations sullied by slander. Byron knew all about it and describes the process in commenting on a man of lesser genius—though he may have been thinking of others too, Pope pre-eminently, and of himself—in his *Monody on the Death of Sheridan* (1816):

Hard is his fate on whom the public gaze
Is fix'd for ever to detract or praise;
Repose denies her requiem to his name,
And Folly loves the martyrdom of Fame.

1. Those who are interested primarily in this aspect of Byron will find relevant passages on pp. 39, 54–5, 76–87, 275, 283, 298–316, below.
2. In his introduction to the Everyman (1933) translation of *Thus Spake Zarathustra* Ernest Rhys writes 'In his Pforta years Nietzsche was much affected by Byron's heroes, who first gave him the idea of those Promethean poets who 'compressed the God within them and rejoined the stars', and of one who should be 'the new Prometheus of new men' (Introduction, viii; for Byron's words, see p. 344 below).

The secret enemy whose sleepless eye
Stands sentinel, accuser, judge, and spy,
The foe, the fool, the jealous, and the vain,
The envious who but breathe in others' pain,
Behold the host! delighting to deprave,
Who track the steps of Glory to the grave,
Watch every fault that daring Genius owes
Half to the ardour which its birth bestows,
Distort the truth, accumulate the lie,
And pile the pyramid of Calumny!

Society is not all to blame: there *is* a problem, because evil, or what at least seems evil, generally what has hitherto been regarded as evil but is not necessarily and in essence evil, may be involved. John Milton, writing of Truth in his *Doctrine and Discipline of Divorce*, has an apposite passage:

> Though this ill hap wait on her nativity, that she never comes into the world but like a Bastard, to the ignominy of him that brought her forth: till Time the Midwife rather than the Mother of Truth, have washed and salted the Infant, declared her legitimate; and churched the Father of his young Minerva, from the needless causes of his purgation.

The thought was echoed by Nietzsche in *Thus Spake Zarathustra* when, thinking of truth and poetry, he noted that all new birth is necessarily accompanied by dirt (IV, 73). 'Who ever', wrote Milton in the *Areopagitica*, 'knew Truth put to the worse in a free and open encounter?' True: but the encounter is rarely free and open; all the forces of society combine, like Pharoah, to stifle the new, miraculous, birth.

Goethe recognized Byron's stature, and so did Shelley, writing in a Sonnet 'Lift not the painted veil . . .' which very clearly refers to Byron (see p. 349 below):

> Through the unheeding many he did move,
> A splendour among shadows, a bright blot
> Upon this gloomy scene, a spirit that strove
> For truth, and like the Preacher found it not.

'Truth' again; but the concept must not be limited to mental truth;

it designates rather wholeness and sincerity. Such was Byron's impact on a famous contemporary. A similar report appears to shine through some passages of Walter Scott's *The Pirate*, in which Cleveland, speaking in terms that recall Byron's attempt to adjust himself to society, says that he has gained mastery over his pirate band by assuming strength, whereas his softer qualities 'made them envy and hate me as a being of another species' (XXII). The thought occurred earlier (XIX) for another person associated with Cleveland: 'A stranger, Minna, a fatal stranger—full of acts unknown to us, and graces which to the plain manners of your father were unknown. Yes, he walked, indeed, among us like a being of another and of a superior race' (XIX). Whether or not Scott was thinking of Byron— and we are inevitably reminded of Conrad in *The Corsair*—these phrases are for our immediate purpose apposite. For in Byron too we are aware of a softness which was forced to assume a mask, a vizard, if only to battle in its cause (LBC, 97–8).

Our concentration will be limited to Byron's Shakespearian qualities. I omit those which might be compared with Dante, Marlowe, Milton, Swift and Pope. To Byron's relations with Pope I have already devoted an extended discussion in my *Laureate of Peace* (p. 9 above). Much more might be said too of Byron's Biblical and Hebraic affinities, on which I touch only briefly (p. 207). Byron may be called a dramatic incarnation of the European imagination as it had in his period matured; and he prophetically forecasts what was to follow. This is what I had in mind when in my *Lord Byron: Christian Virtues* I called Byron 'the next Promethean figure in Western history after Christ'. The remark registered as a severe shock to our religious-minded and reverent age. But I have never been in the habit of putting forward opinions without evidence or engaging in abstract pleasantries. I would ask this:—Could any test for such a claim be more reasonable than that the new Messiah should, in our Renaissance era, be an incarnation, involving, *as our religion does not*, both sex and politics, of Shakespearian drama? That is what I show Byron to have been.

A sympathetic contemporary, Thomas Mulock (p. 185 below), once wrote that Byron 'seems to himself to be a fated voyager upon an ocean untracked by any other keel'. 'Untracked', yes; but not entirely unknown. Byron was on a course linking Shakespeare to Ibsen and Nietzsche which, though newly self-conscious, was not uncharted, since it was precisely the charting that Shakespeare had done. Shakespeare made the map; Byron was the explorer; Ibsen and Nietzsche established lines of communication with home. It is for us to civilize the place, and mine its wealth.

II

SONNETS AND SERAPHS

I

O SCAR WILDE, being questioned during his trial as to the meaning of a sonnet by Lord Alfred Douglas containing the cryptic words 'Love that dare not speak its name', replied to the judge

The 'Love that dare not speak its name' in this century is such a great affection of an elder for a younger man as there was between David and Jonathan, such as Plato made the very basis of his philosophy, and such as you find in the sonnets of Michelangelo and Shakespeare. It is that deep, spiritual affection that is as pure as it is perfect. It dictates and pervades great works of art like those of Shakespeare and Michelangelo, and those two letters of mine, such as they are. It is in this century misunderstood, so much misunderstood that it may be described as the 'Love that dare not speak its name', and on account of it I am placed where I am now. It is beautiful, it is fine, it is the noblest form of affection. There is nothing unnatural about it. It is intellectual, and it repeatedly exists between an elder and a younger man, when the elder man has intellect, and the younger man has all the joy, hope and glamour of life before him. That it should be so the world does not understand. The world mocks at it and sometimes puts one in the pillory for it.

(H. Montgomery Hyde, *The Trials of Oscar Wilde*, 1948; 236)

This love Wilde proceeded, under question, to distinguish from his more disreputable engagements; it was an experience such as one has 'once in one's life, and once only' (241). The passage may serve as an introduction to a comparison of Shakespeare's Sonnets and Byron's amatory life. In both we find a balance of homosexual idealism against engagements, which may be either heterosexual or homosexual, of a less ideal order.

Shakespeare's Sonnets, whatever the date and circumstances of their composition, have a reasonably clear pattern. The main body of them is addressed to a beautiful young man and ranges from flattery to criticism. They record considerable suffering, sometimes caused by the Friend's apparent unkindness and sometimes, towards the end, by the passing of the youth's adolescent charm. Part of the trouble comes through the interruption of a lady for whom the poet was simultaneously experiencing a powerful sexual passion and with whom the young man also became involved, so arousing in the poet a kind of dual jealousy besides the torment of seeing his ideal desecrated by a woman of loose behaviour. The young man is himself attacked for licentiousness and untruth. As for the fading of the youth's adolescent charm, the poet keeps his eye firmly on the original vision, which he regards, in Platonic terms, as a vision of some ultimate perfection possessing eternal sanction, whatever its apparent physical, or other, failures. The general situation is defined by Sonnet 144:

> Two loves I have, of comfort and despair,
> Which, like two spirits, do suggest me still:
> The better angel is a man right fair,
> The worser spirit a woman, colour'd ill.
> To win me soon to hell, my female evil
> Tempteth my better angel from my side,
> And would corrupt my saint to be a devil,
> Wooing his purity with her foul pride.
> And whether that my angel be turn'd fiend,
> Suspect I may, but not directly tell;
> But being both from me, both to each friend,
> I guess one angel in another's hell:
>   Yet this shall I ne'er know, but live in doubt,
>   Till my bad angel fire my good one out.

The sonnet neatly symbolizes a universal balance of idealism and lust. The sexes are correctly used since, as Byron tells us, 'all passions in excess are female' (*Sardanapalus*, III, i, 381).

Shakespeare's narrative poems *Venus and Adonis* and *The Rape of*

Lucrece, describing respectively an approved love for a male and a criminal lust for a female, are to this extent of the same stuff as the Sonnets. In Shakespeare's public dramas love is necessarily for the most part heterosexual, though the girls are often disguised as boys. In *The Two Gentlemen of Verona* sexual love is sacrificed on the altar of friendship and in *The Merchant of Venice* and *Twelfth Night* we have strong examples of homosexual devotion. In the first the depth of Antonio's love for Bassanio is central; and in *Twelfth Night* the other Antonio's passion for Sebastian gives us a little side-drama that bears resemblance to the Sonnets and *Othello*. In *Troilus and Cressida* the loves of Achilles and Patroclus come, as one might expect in this play, under as sharp a criticism as everything else.

Apart from all externals, it is easy to relate the Sonnets to the recurring emphases on jealousy and betrayal in Shakespeare's tragedies; and though these are mostly given a normal expression, it is noteworthy that they culminate in the far from normal *Timon of Athens*, which both reads as a peculiarly personal and deliberated exposition of earlier themes, and in its sharp contrast of idealized male friendships against the heterosexual disgust of Timon's curses might be called an expansion of the Sonnets, the falsity of Timon's friends finding an obvious place in the comparison.

It is my purpose to show that Byron's life and writings bear evidence of a sexual balance close to Shakespeare's. The horror of sexual lust written into *Hamlet, Troilus and Cressida, Othello, King Lear* and *Timon of Athens* is given a condensed expression in one of the Sonnets (129), on the Dark Lady:

> The expense of spirit in a waste of shame
> Is lust in action; and till action, lust
> Is perjur'd, murderous, bloody, full of blame,
> Savage, extreme, rude, cruel, not to trust;
> Enjoy'd no sooner but despised straight;
> Past reason hunted; and, no sooner had,
> Past reason hated, as a swallow'd bait
> On purpose laid to make the taker mad.
> Mad in pursuit, and in possession so;
> Had, having, and in quest to have, extreme;

A bliss in proof, and, prov'd, a very woe;
Before, a joy propos'd; behind, a dream.
> All this the world well knows; yet none knows well
> To shun the heaven that leads men to this hell.

By this we may place a stanza from *Childe Harold*:

'Tis an old lesson—Time approves it true,
And those who know it best deplore it most;
When all is won that all desire to woo,
The paltry prize is hardly worth the cost;
Youth wasted—minds degraded—honour lost,
These are thy fruits, successful Passion! these!
If, kindly cruel, early hope is crost,
Still to the last it rankles, a disease,
Not to be cur'd when Love itself forgets to please.

(II, 35)

A more compacted statement occurs in *Cain*, where sexual union is called a 'sweet degradation' and 'most enervating and filthy cheat' to lure man into procreation (*Cain*, II, i, 56).

Byron's love-life shows vivid Shakespearian correspondences. Here is Shakespeare inveighing against his Dark Lady for being false to her marriage vows:

In loving thee thou know'st I am forsworn,
But thou art twice forsworn, to me love swearing,
In act thy bed-vow broke, and new faith torn
In vowing new hate after new love bearing . . .

(152)

Here is Byron's version (1814) addressed to Lady Caroline Lamb:

Remember thee! Remember thee!
    Till Lethe quench life's burning stream
Remorse and shame shall cling to thee,
    And haunt thee like a feverish dream!

Remember thee! Ay, doubt it not.
    Thy husband too shall think of thee:
By neither shalt thou be forgot,
    Thou *false* to him, thou *fiend* to me!

(P, III, 59)

Shakespeare could see his Lady as almost an evil spirit without denying the magnetic spell which she exerted on him. Apart from his boy-love for Mary Chaworth and his enigmatic relationship to his half-sister, Augusta Leigh, Byron was never before his association with Teresa Guiccioli, and perhaps not even with her, sexually enslaved to any one woman; yet he was enslaved to sexual relationships in a more general way; he asserted that he had been a martyr to women (p. 230 below); and many of them, Lady Caroline Lamb and Clare Clairmont pre-eminently, became a torment.

Now against this succession of variously unrestful sexual engagements stands the different emotions aroused in Byron by male youth.

At Harrow Byron had many friendships of various degrees and kinds, and of these he has written in *Childish Recollections,* contained in his early collection of poems *Hours of Idleness.* These early poems are redolent of ideals and heroism. To Byron youth, as Lady Blessington (XIII, 312) records, always remained in his mind the age of unsullied insight and valuation. Though in himself and others the early perfection was destined, in various ways and from various causes, to be desecrated, he throughout remained true to this world of ardent friendship, self-sacrifice, and heroism. It was a world of classic, Greek, tone. As good an expression of it as any is Vergil's story of Nisus and Euryalus in the *Aeneid* (IX); a translation of it is among Byron's youthful poems.[1]

Of Byron's more important male loves our first is the Cambridge chorister, John Edleston, for whom he felt 'a violent, though *pure,* love and passion', probably the most ideal in his experience, coming at 'the most romantic period' of his life (Journal, 12 Jan. 1821; LJ, v, 169). When Byron first met him at Cambridge, Edleston was

1. In Vergil dark female powers, Juno and the war-stirring fury Allecto, are contrasted with such idealism as the heroic comradeship of Nisus and Euryalus and the pathos of the young Pallas, avenged by Aeneas at the *Aeneid's* conclusion. Shakespeare's sense of slaughtered youth in *Henry VI* and *Richard III* (*The Mutual Flame,* 109–10) is Vergilian. Behind the *Aeneid* are the *Eclogues,* as the Sonnets behind Shakespeare's dramas.

In a striking paragraph my brother long ago grouped together Vergil's idealizing of tragic youth, the Amazonian warrior-maiden Camilla, and the vision of Venus disguised as a young huntress, so covering the whole area of what I have since termed the 'seraphic' intuition (pp. 50–53, below). See W. F. Jackson Knight, *Roman Vergil,* 1944, etc., IV, 113–14; Peregrine edn., 1966; IV, 146.

fifteen. He gave Byron a Cornelian heart, referred to in Byron's poems *The Cornelian* (1806: P, I, 66) and *Pigus Amoris* (c. 1806: P, I, 231–3) and *The Adieu* (1807). On Byron's return to England in 1811 he heard that Edleston had died.

I shall quote next from the group of 1811 and 1812 lyrics best designated 'the *Thyrza* poems', *To Thyrza* being the first, written after his hearing of Edleston's death on Byron's return from Greece. The use of a female name and female pronouns must be accepted as a necessary mask.[1]

Thyrza aroused in Byron intimations of some higher state of being. His love—I use the male pronoun—was such on earth that 'it fain would form my hope in Heaven' (*To Thyrza*). Its delicate magic is well expressed in *Away, Away, ye Notes of Woe*:

> Away, away, ye notes of woe!
>   Be silent, thou once soothing strain,
> Or I must flee from hence—for, oh!
>   I dare not trust those sounds again.
> To me they speak of brighter days—
>   But lull the chords, for now, alas!
> I must not think, I may not gaze,
>   On what I am—on what I was.
>
> The voice that made those sounds more sweet
>   Is hush'd, and all their charms are fled:
> And now their softest notes repeat
>   A dirge, an anthem o'er the dead!
> Yes, Thyrza! yes, they breathe of thee,
>   Beloved dust! since dust thou art;
> And all that once was harmony
>   Is worse than discord to my heart!
>
> 'Tis silent all!—but on my ear
>   The well remember'd echoes thrill;
> I hear a voice I would not hear,
>   A voice that now might well be still.

---

1. The relation of these poems to John Edleston is now generally accepted. My own arguments are set out in *Lord Byron's Marriage*, I, 33–38; and see Marchand, I, 302, note.

Yet oft my doubting soul 'twill shake;
Even slumber owns its gentle tone,
Till consciousness will vainly wake
To listen, though the dream be flown.

Sweet Thyrza! waking as in sleep,
Thou art but now a lovely dream;
A star that trembled o'er the deep,
Then turn'd from earth its tender beam.
But he who through life's dreary way
Must pass, when heaven is veil'd in wrath,
Will long lament the vanish'd ray
That scattered gladness o'er his path.

In *One Struggle More and I am Free* Thyrza is naturally associated
with the heavenly lights:

On many a lone and lovely night
It sooth'd to gaze upon the sky;
For then I deem'd the heavenly light
Shone sweetly on thy pensive eye:
And oft I thought at Cynthia's noon,
When sailing o'er the Ægean wave,
'Now Thyrza gazes on that moon'—
Alas, it gleam'd upon her grave!

Euthanasia, though grouped with the others, seems not to be a
Thyrza poem since one of its lines 'In her who lives, in him who
dies' suggests a living person.[1] In it Byron would have 'no friends' or
'maiden with dishevell'd hair' attend his death-bed:

Yet Love, if Love in such an hour
Could nobly check its useless sighs,
Might then exert its latest power
In her who lives, and him who dies.

1. *Euthanasia* is not among the *Thyrza* MSS. referred to at P, III, 32, note; but the
earlier one volume Murray edition of Byron's poems (my copy dated 1837), on which
the Oxford edition appears to be based, in noting that 'The five following pieces are
all devoted to *Thyrza*' (550 note), accepts it as a *Thyrza* piece. If Edleston was not
intended, 'my Psyche' may be Mary Chaworth.

'Twere sweet, my Psyche! to the last
  Thy features still serene to see:
Forgetful of its struggles past,
  E'en Pain itself should smile on thee.

There is no such doubt concerning the person addressed in *And Thou art Dead as Young and Fair*, wherein Byron, in close accord with those Shakespearian sonnets burdened with anxiety at the Fair Youth's passing beauty, finds solace in knowing that Edleston's youthful charm has not suffered 'decay':

The flower in ripen'd bloom unmatch'd
  Must fall the earliest prey;
Though by no hand untimely snatch'd,
  The leaves must drop away:
And yet it were a greater grief
  To watch it withering, leaf by leaf,
Than see it pluck'd to-day;
Since earthly eye but ill can bear
To trace the change to foul from fair.

I know not if I could have borne
  To see thy beauties fade;
The night that follow'd such a morn
  Had worn a deeper shade.
Thy day without a cloud hath pass'd,
And thou wert lovely to the last;
  Extinguish'd, not decay'd;
As stars that shoot along the sky
Shine brightest as they fall from high.

The thought is that of Shakespeare's Sonnet 104:

Ah, yet doth beauty, like a dial hand,
Steal from his figure, and no pace perceiv'd.

In Shakespeare's later Sonnets the poet is felt labouring to maintain his love, despite the inevitable change (*The Mutual Flame*, 84, 113–14, 122–4, etc.). The conclusion to *If Sometimes in the Haunts of Men* haloes Edleston with terms divine:

For well I know, that such had been
Thy gentle care for him, who now

Unmourn'd shall quit this mortal scene,
Where none regarded him, but thou:
And, oh! I feel in *that* was given
A blessing never meant for me;
Thou wert too like a dream of Heaven
For earthly Love to merit thee.

The *Thyrza* poems belong to that great tradition of homosexual elegy to which so much of our poetry on such idealized relationships belongs: in ancient literature, in Milton's *Lycidas*, Arnold's *Thyrsis* and Tennyson's *In Memoriam*; and in the general tenour of Gray's *Elegy* and Housman's *A Shropshire Lad*. The experience, as Byron found, is hard to maintain; time, as both Shakespeare and Byron knew, tends to sully its perfection; and death may be the proper home for what was, in essence, 'a dream of Heaven'.

Byron's homosexual instincts were not confined to purity and Platonism. In going to Greece he expected to experience physical engagements, and did. His love here was Nicolo Giraud, one of a number of boys or, as Byron called them 'sylphs', at a convent school near Athens, with whom Byron enjoyed a riotous and amatory companionship. Byron taught Nicolo to swim and Nicolo taught Byron Italian (Hobhouse, 23 Aug. 1810; C, I, 14–17; LBM, 179). The relationship seems, from Byron's letters (as explained in my note 'Byron's Marriage' in *Essays in Criticism*, Oct. 1958; VIII, 4; see Appendix, p. 351), to have been an uninhibited and carefree association without psychological or moral unrest. Byron was young and a stranger in a land and climate where actions were possible that in England would have aroused in him a sense of unease, if not sin. It is likely that he was thinking of these carefree experiences when he told Trelawny that Greece was the only place where he had ever been 'contented' (Trelawny, 15 June 1823; LJ, VI, 224).

That Edleston was Byron's social inferior only increased the element of care and protectiveness in Byron's affection; with Nicolo the relation had, on both sides, an educational element; and for another boy, Robert Rushton, Byron's servant, Byron's affection was blended with a strong sense of responsibility (LBCV, 73–4) not unlike that of Shakespeare's Brutus for Lucius. There was in general a parental quality in play, such as we find in Byron's regular concern for his servants and for all who were in any way oppressed, including oppressed communities and nations. In Shakespeare's Sonnets, as in his treatment of tragic youth in the early dramas (p. 28 above, note), we find a similarly parental note; the poet is angered at the thought of any taint of corruption, or ill repute, sullying his ideal. There are differences. Byron seems to have responded most warmly to boys of about fifteen, whereas Shakespeare's Fair Youth sounds older than that, though the attraction certainly depended on the peculiar charm of adolescence as defined in *A Lover's Complaint* (92–8). Moreover, the social relationship is reversed, the young man being here the one of high birth—though that is not to say that he was a peer—and suggesting as a comparison Wilde's love for Lord Alfred Douglas rather than anything in Byron. But these are superficial differences: the love of Shakespeare's Sonnets was conditioned by the young man's adolescence, and at the earliest signs of maturity it was in danger (e.g., Sonnets 22, 100, 104, 108, 115; *The Mutual Flame*, 114, 122–4); and as for social status, it seems that a difference may often help to give a sense of breaking through into a certain otherness corresponding to the otherness of heterosexual engagements; but that it may work either way.

Whether the relationship of the Sonnets remained independent of physical contact cannot be known. At least two editors, Samuel Butler and Martin Seymour-Smith, think that it did not. Though in the much quoted Sonnet 20 the poet regrets that physical intercourse has been rendered by nature impossible, yet the phrase 'thee of me defeated' certainly implies desire. We cannot assert that Shakespeare was guiltless of the moral charges that may be levelled against Byron and Wilde: we just do not know. After his returning from Greece in 1811 we have no evidence of homosexual indulgence during Byron's life in England, but there may have been occasions of it and the propensity played its part, as I have shown throughout *Lord Byron's Marriage*, among the causes leading to the Separation. Among Byron's Venetian excesses after the Separation extreme forms of vice with both sexes appear to have been included (Quennell, *Byron*, Selections, 1959; 53); and though Byron told Shelley that he disapproved, he added, significantly, that he 'endures'

(Shelley to Peacock, 22 Dec. 1818; LJ, IV, 259–60, note). Like Macbeth according to A. C. Bradley, he seems to have undertaken what was morally reprehensible as some sort of a duty ('appalling duty', *Shakespearian Tragedy*, edn. of 1932; IX, 358; and see, variously, pp. 41, 62–3, 340–1 below).

He experienced ideal and 'pure' loves for women; for Mary Anne Chaworth, the 'Starlight' of his 'Boyhood' (*The Dream*, 1816; viii), and for his half-sister Augusta, as a 'solitary star' and 'seraph's eye', a love of which he strongly emphasized the 'purity' (*Stanzas to Augusta*, 1816, first poem (P, III, 544); *Epistle to Augusta*, 1816; *Childe Harold*, III, 55; and see LBM, 119–20). The concept of 'purity' in such passages indicates rather a wholeness than any deficiency. It was applied, as we have seen (p. 28), to Byron's love for Edleston, whom in 1812 he called 'the only human being that ever loved me in truth and entirety' (Hodgson, 16 Feb. 1812; LJ, II, 100). He was one 'who lov'd me for myself alone' (*Pignus Amoris*; P, I, 232); that is, for my deepest, most real, and therefore whole, self; meaning a love such as Coleridge in *To William Words- worth*, called 'Love for the human being's absolute self'. There are states where the whole physical being is so suffused by feeling that it is not sexually located and therefore not felt as desire.[1]

Byron's obsession with boy loves such as John Edleston, Nicolo Giraud, Robert Rushton, William Harness (LBCV, 68–74), and many, no doubt, of whom we know nothing, remained to the end. Augusta was afraid of what boy servants or servant might be attracting him after he left London in 1816 (LBM, 130). These loves were conditioned by youth; we are not arguing that they could remain at pressure for long; on his return to England in 1811 Byron made a will leaving Nicolo a large legacy, but it was omitted from subsequent wills, and there is evidence, which I cannot at the moment trace, that Byron was subsequently unresponsive to Nicolo's letters.

A similar failure is written into some of Shakespeare's later Sonnets (e.g., 100, 101, 103, 109, 117, 119, 120, 122; *The Mutual Flame*, 112–28). These experiences are probably nearer *vision* than *love*; or perhaps not so much love as the visionary state of being *in*

1. Examples are discussed in my study of John Cowper Powys, *The Saturnian Quest*: 40, 50; also Index C, Sexology, etc.

34

love; and the vision fades as the youthful, pre-sexual, harmony matures into manhood.

To such attractions Byron at Missolonghi was still susceptible. He took with him from Cephalonia a boy Loukas Chalandritsanos, of what William Parry called 'a most prepossessing appearance' (Parry, I, 16), whose family was among the many displaced persons whom Byron had helped (LBM, 216). We have a poem recording his care for Loukas when threatened at sea first by Turks and later by storm, and narrating how he had nursed him in fever and planned for his safety when there was an earthquake. The prevailing note, and it is characteristic of what such love meant to Byron—his acquaintance with Edleston started with his saving the boy from drowning (LJ, I, 130-1, note)—is that of *care*. From Harrow onwards, Byron's protective, almost maternal, instincts were a driving force. Once he wrote that his love for children persisted when all other emotions had grown cold (*Childe Harold*, III, 54; for Byron and children, see LBCV, 75-85.) The Missolonghi poem, which has been posthumously given the not wholly satisfying title '*Love and Death*', is not as poetry strong; it has a weakness perhaps born of Byron's own ill-health at Missolonghi and all the distracting anxieties of the time, and also perhaps the weakness of over-much, immediate, emotional involvement, lacking artistic serenity. The two concluding stanzas—there are six—run:

And when convulsive throes denied my breath
    The faintest utterance to my fading thought,
To thee—to thee—e'en in the gasp of death
    My spirit turn'd, oh! oftener than it ought.

Thus much and more; and yet thou lov'st me not,
    And never wilt! Love dwells not in our will.
Nor can I blame thee, though it be my lot
    To strongly, wrongly, vainly love thee still. (P. VII, 85)

'Death' refers to one of the severe attacks to which Byron's health succumbed during the last weeks. We have other, more powerful, lines entitled *Last Words on Greece*:

What are to me those honours or renown
    Past or to come, a new-born people's cry?

35

Albeit for such I could despise a crown
  Of aught save laurel, or for such could die.
I am a fool of passion, and a frown
  Of thine to me is as an adder's eye
To the poor bird whose pinion fluttering down
  Wafts unto death the breast it bore so high;
Such is this maddening fascination grown,
  So strong thy magic or so weak am I.

(P, VII, 85)

The attraction here is more than Platonic and yet the carefree indulgence experienced in 1811 with Nicolo is no longer possible.
The power is best defined as 'magnetic' and corresponds closest to
certain lines of Shakespeare's Sonnet 147, addressed to the Dark
Lady:

> My love is as a fever, longing still
> For that which longer nurseth the disease;
> Feeding on that which doth preserve the ill,
> The uncertain sickly appetite to please.

And

> Past cure I am, now reason is past care,
> And frantic-mad with evermore unrest . . .

That our comparison should come from a heterosexual sonnet is
not strange. This is, in fact, the point: a desire more proper to sexual
differentiation has got entangled with what is more readily placed as
a Platonic vision. This may appear a too facile solution, but it is
one which Byron, at this period, would probably have approved,
as our poems witness. There is a third poem, the famous *On this
day I complete my Thirty Sixth Year*. This, which was composed
before *Love and Death*, on Byron's birthday (22 January 1824), has
the completed artistry lacking to the later poem. It has a stronger
beat, and an athletic force. Its very theme is self-transcendence, for in
it Byron registers his will to inject personal desire into public service.
Despite the two subsequent poems, written under stress, he did, in
fact and in act, accomplish this. From his early youthful and heroic
poems onwards personal love and public service were aspects of
the same instinct; the one was the heart of the other; and this noble
lyric, which we shall quote later (p. 69), shows the transition.

II

Byron's 'violent' though 'pure' love-passion for Edleston coming at the 'most romantic' period of his life (p. 28), together with the early poems of idealized friendship and heroism, may stand as the heart of his life's story. His life's problem was to expand this instinct or vision to meet (i) his own sexual being and (ii) the society of his day. There is throughout a give-and-take, a reciprocity, between his more spiritual intuitions and their human setting. I use the word 'spiritual' advisedly, and shall now proceed to a few notes on the Third and Fourth Cantos of *Childe Harold* as records of an interaction between personal instincts and aspirations on the one side and objective reality on the other; the continual switch from inward meditation and personal torment to concern for places, nations, and history *corresponding to the relation of Shakespeare's Sonnets to his Dramas*. We shall mark a steady will towards the fusing of vision and society, the link being poetry and the arts, and the key, or solution, in both cantos, Love. After discussing *Childe Harold* we shall return to a further comparison of Byron's boy-loves with Shakespeare's Sonnets, driving home their relation both to what I call 'the seraphic intuition' and to Shakespeare's and Byron's wider, dramatic and social, gospels.

Childe Harold is of a poetic *genre* that needs reading aloud, at least as a first introduction. The alternation of rhetorical grandeur and personal talk; the dramatic passion; the variation in speed within the line or from one line to another; the kaleidoscope of vocal tones required; all this can be demonstrated only by a vocal projection.[1] In his own, different, poetic terms the Byronic use of variation is as consummate as Shakespeare's; and, like Shakespeare's dramatic poetry, it is simultaneously attuned to ear and intellect. *Childe Harold* contains a visionary metaphysic, and when we have had our say about diction and rhetoric, we have still to consider the meanings which they serve. Or perhaps we should put it the other way round, since without an inward and intellectual appreciation the performer will do scant justice to the externals.

1. These qualities I have pointed in readings of Byron broadcast by the B.B.C. Third Programme on 8 June and 19 December 1964. They are also now available on tapes published by *Sound Seminars*, Cincinnati, U.S.A. See p. 14 above, note.

The Third Canto (1816) was written under great personal stress: 'I was half mad', Byron tells us, during the writing of it (Moore, 28 Jan. 1817; LJ, IV, 49). It is as though his recent experiences had shattered surfaces to reveal depths before only half glimpsed; the language of these depths is poetry, which is here a major theme: the poem is, like *The Prelude*, a work of poetic self-consciousness. Two modes inter-shift. We have (i) Byron speaking direct of his own troubles and aspirations and (ii) Byron trying to objectify himself as the shadowy Childe Harold on his travels surveying, objectively and historically, the scenes of his passage. There is however no rigid distinction, and as the poem unfolds the mask becomes less important.

The link between the subjective mind and the world of its experience is poetry:

> He, who grown aged in this world of woe,
> In deeds, not years, piercing the depths of life,
> So that no wonder waits him; nor below
> Can love or sorrow, fame, ambition, strife,
> Cut to his heart again with the keen knife
> Of silent, sharp endurance—he can tell
> Why thought seeks refuge in lone caves, yet rife
> With airy images, and shapes which dwell
> Still unimpair'd, though old, in the soul's haunted
> cell.   (III, 5)

Of this stanza, which neatly balances Byron's prose definition of poetry as 'the dream of my sleeping passions' and a kind of 'somnambulism' (Murray, 2 Jan. 1817; LJ, IV, 43), there is much to say.

The poet is, like the Shakespeare of the Sonnets (Sonnets 22, 62, 63; *The Mutual Flame*, 9–10), old beyond his years, having penetrated to a non-temporal, vertical dimension (for 'depths of life' compare Keats's 'the depth of things', *The Fall of Hyperion*, I, 304–5). The mind is forced by suffering into a world of ethereal entities, 'airy' suggesting height, in contrast to 'below'. 'Shapes' are envisaged, a word chosen for its non-committal quality, like the 'Shapes' of the banquet scene in *The Tempest* (III, iii, 17; direction). They are simultaneously old yet ever fresh, archetypal and immortal. The final phrase beautifully defines and realizes what we today crudely call the 'unconscious mind' by use of the numinous or spiritualistic word 'haunted' and the religious connotations of 'cell'. This single stanza compacts as much human, tragic, aesthetic, and psychological wisdom as any poetry of my experience; and yet there is no taint of obscurity; it can be received by a listener. This is poetry beyond praise.

But we are not left with subjective insight; there follows that swerve to objectivity so necessary and natural to Byron. We continue:

> 'Tis to create, and in creating live
> A being more intense that we endow
> With form our fancy, gaining as we give
> The life we image, even as I do now.
> What am I? Nothing: but not so art thou,
> Soul of my thought! with whom I traverse earth,
> Invisible but gazing, as I glow
> Mix'd with thy spirit, blended with thy birth,
> And feeling still with thee in my crush'd feelings dearth.

(III, 6)

Either 'fancy' is in apposition to 'form', or 'that' in the second line must be read not as a relative but as a conjunction, meaning 'in that' or 'so that'.[1] Creation gives 'form' to the soul-sight, and in this act of creation we attain a new intensity, which is simultaneously a giving out and a self-enrichment. In imagining Harold Byron transcends his normal ego, projecting his consciousness into a kind of travelling spirit-personality—'soul of my thought'—which, though itself invisible, yet has sight. That such spirit-selves exist is known, and their voyaging is sometimes called 'astral travelling' or 'astral projection'; and that Byron is thinking in such concrete terms is witnessed by the word 'glow', because if seen, as the soul-self, the astral or etheric body, sometimes is, it does just that.[2] We have evidence that Byron himself was once actually seen astral travelling,

---

1. There is a manuscript variant, but it leaves the question open. See P, II, 219, note.

2. See the account of Powys's soul-projection, with the phrase 'pale white glow', as reported in my study of Powys, *The Saturnian Quest*, IX, 128 (p. 311 below); also for Powys's many discussions of soul-travelling, Index C. Powys raises the issue of Byron's 'invisible but gazing', noting that the disembodied soul somehow uses the body's senses (*The Saturnian Quest*, V, 75; VI, 88).

during a fever (pp. 312–13); and, as we have seen, he regarded poetry as 'the dream of my sleeping passions' (p. 38). But again, the sense of union and creation in 'mix'd' and 'birth' is also primary; in poetic creation the daylight ego is not lost, but joined to the soul-self, as in sleep it would not be. The last line asserts that in identifying his ordinary self with his soul-self Byron enjoys the more athletic feelings of his fictional person in place of an egocentric despair ('dearth'). Though Harold obviously *is* Byron in a far closer sense than that in which Hamlet is Shakespeare, yet by at least pretending to himself to be creating an objective person, Byron jerks himself into the dispassionate artistry and lucid thinking of an impersonal dramatic creation.

The poem shows repeated alternations from ego to object. Byron can enjoy the stars like a Chaldean, temporal humanity forgotten:

> Could he have kept his spirit to that flight
> He had been happy; but this clay will sink
> Its spark immortal, envying it the light
> To which it mounts, as if to break the link
> That keeps us from yon heaven which woos us to its
> brink.   (III, 14)

Here the spirit-categories and aspiring thought of our third Canto touch the immortal 'light'. Like the fleshly 'dungeon' of Marvell's *A Dialogue between the Soul and Body* (i), 'clay' muffles the soul's 'spark immortal' which by instinct 'mounts' towards the higher plane, or dimension, of light.

We next swerve to objective comment in the famous description of Waterloo, with comments on the death of young Howard, and on all the families that mourn, yet still live on and even smile, like broken mirrors that reflect even more images for their breaking (III, 33; Byron may have been thinking of *Richard II*, IV, i, 276–88); as though the very breaking were an enlargement. Despite all torment, Byron's thinking—we shall find many examples (pp. 271–7 below) —*consistently regards suffering as creative*:

> There is a very life in our despair,
> Vitality of poison—a quick root
> Which feeds these deadly branches; for it were

As nothing did we die; but Life will suit
Itself to Sorrow's most detested fruit,
Like to the apples on the Dead Sea's shore,
All ashes to the taste.   (III, 34)

Here is a deeper mystery than the mystery of evil; the mystery of evil,
at least of suffering, as even while 'detested' a *vitalizing* force; the
force that has made Byron's poetry in this Canto attain, through his
recent sufferings, a new dimension.

We pass to Napoleon. The following compacted stanzas contain
as profound a psychological analysis of the power-quest as one might
demand from a full-length drama. Once, asked by Murray for an
epic poem, Byron answered, with a characteristic concomitance of
scorn and claim:

If one's years can't be better employed than sweating poesy, a
man had better be a ditcher. And works, too!—is *Childe Harold*
nothing? You have so many '*divine*' poems, is it nothing to have
written a *Human* one? without any of your worn-out machinery.
Why, man, I could have spun the thoughts of the four cantos
of that poem into twenty, had I wanted to book-make, and its
passion into as many modern tragedies.

(6 April 1819; LJ, IV, 284)

The claim is true; stanza after stanza contains enough thought for a
major essay, or volume; and the human and historic delineations are
a succession of miniature yet explosive dramas. We should observe
how precisely *Childe Harold* corresponds to the relation of Shakespeare's dramas to his Sonnets. In both we are aware of a personal
self-communing *expanded* into objective creation; the heart of the
Shakespearian process from sonnets to dramas being that explained
in my chapter 'The Expansion', in *The Mutual Flame*. If it were no
more, and it is very much more, *Childe Harold* would be the best
commentary on the nature of Shakespeare's total art conceivable.

Human ambition, such as Napoleon's, is woven of light and
darkness. There is, as in Dryden's Achitophel, an unceasing inner
dynamism and aspiration, a more than corporeal soul-fire, demanding expression:

But quiet to quick bosoms is a hell,
And *there* hath been thy bane; there is a fire

41

And motion of the soul which will not dwell
In its own narrow being, but aspire
Beyond the fitting medium of desire;
And, but once kindled, quenchless evermore,
Preys upon high adventure, nor can tire
Of aught but rest; a fever at the core,
Fatal to him who bears, to all who ever bore.

This makes the madmen who have made men mad
By their contagion; Conquerors and Kings,
Founders of sects and systems, to whom add
Sophists, Bards, Statesmen, all unquiet things
Which stir too strongly the soul's secret springs,
And are themselves the fools to those they fool;
Envied, yet how unenviable! what stings
Are theirs! One breast laid open were a school
Which would unteach mankind the lust to shine or rule.

(III, 42–3)

Such are the torments, and the dangers, of genius. A truer 'Wisdom'
would keep them content 'within its own creation', or in Nature's
(III, 46); that is, within a self-making such as that which Wordsworth defined in his *Recluse* fragment (Preface to *The Excursion*,
1814; discussed in my *The Starlit Dome*, 1; and *The Saturnian Quest*,
1). These are the poets of Byron's *Prophecy of Dante* (IV) who, instead
of writing, 'compress'd the god within them', the more blessed for
their lack of ambition.

We pass to description of the Rhine, its castles and their history,
and its people. There is again a swerve from inward diagnosis to
external description.

But aspiration is not stilled. Men of genius, we have been told,
are as mountain peaks:

He who ascends to mountain-tops, shall find
The loftiest peaks most wrapt in clouds and snow;
He who surpasses or subdues mankind
Must look down on the hate of those below.

(III, 45)

So now the Alps are as 'Eternity', made of 'all that expands the
spirit', objective witnesses that 'Earth may pierce to Heaven' (III, 62).

Byron's more personal spirit-aspirations are related to memory of those others who in the past acted sacrificially, fine souls who suffered for good, and live beyond death like the Alpine heights 'imperishably pure' (III, 67). He keeps returning to the political and communal past of the places seen, and to memory of great patriots; and yet he remains himself un-at-home among men. He identifies himself with the mountains; he is as 'a link reluctant in a fleshly chain', a 'soul' which, set among 'creatures', craves rather the sky, peak, plain, ocean and stars, all that is vast and elemental; striving to 'remount'—as to its *real* home—with 'fresh pinion' on 'delighted wing', spurning 'the clay-cold bonds' which 'cling' around our 'being' (III, 72-3):

> And when, at length, the mind shall be all free
> From what it hates in this degraded form,
> Reft of its carnal life, save what shall be
> Existent happier in the fly and worm—
> When elements to elements conform,
> And dust is as it should be, shall I not
> Feel all I see, less dazzling, but more warm?
> The bodiless thought? the Spirit of each spot?
> Of which, even now, I share at times the immortal lot?
>
> (III, 74)

That is our firmest statement of Byron's drive for the spirit dimension. Even so, it is not independent of earth; it is as a seeing of 'each spot' as from a new dimension; and this is precisely what his poetry, himself as Harold, even now is doing. The thought corresponds to Socrates' reading of the life-beyond-death as a new dimension of earth life in Plato's *Phaedo*; and we may recall Byron's view of himself-as-Harold ranging over earth like a spirit in astral travel (p. 39).

'But this is not my theme . . .' (III, 76): again, the recurring alternation. Now he loses himself in writing of Rousseau; it is a process of continual self-negation, re-realizing himself in objective poetry. Rousseau was afire with love; in his 'burning page' we find 'ideal beauty', such beauty, we may suggest, as Byron saw in Edleston —for there is authority for the association of Edleston with Byron's social gospel (p. 65 below)—taking on 'existence'; and from him as

43

a 'Pythian oracle' the world was set 'in flame' (III, 78, 81). The
terrible revolution with all its horrors was loosed; but reconciliation
will come (III, 82–4). In contrast Lake Leman is placid. The stars,
the poetry of heaven', look down on human confusions, and

> . . . 'tis to be forgiven
> That in our aspirations to be great,
> Our destinies o'erleap their mortal state,
> And claim a kindred with you . . .
>
> (III, 88)

By night's infinitude, though solitary, we are not 'alone'; a 'truth'
transfuses to purify us from the 'self;' its 'tone' is 'the soul and source
of music' revealing 'the eternal harmony' and disarming 'the spectre
Death' (III, 90). The early Persians were right to put their altars on
mountains, seeking there the great 'Spirit' (III, 91). But Byron, never
for long among the placidities, delights to imagine the thunder-storms
leaping from crag to crag, for these are as himself (III, 92–3). His
'own spirit, and all that he has to say, might be expressed in the one
word 'lightning' (III, 97).

The oppositions in our poem of tumult and peace, of inward
thought and external comment, are crowned by description of
Clarens, by the Lake of Geneva, honoured as a place sacred to the
'god' of Love. The mountains are steps for his 'heavenly feet'. Trees,
snows, glaciers rosy at sunset, the flowers and all things are 'of *him*'
(III, 99–101). Here nature is a spirit-land:

> A populous solitude of bees and birds,
> And fairy-form'd and many-colour'd things,
> Who worship him with notes more sweet than words,
> And innocently open their glad wings,
> Fearless and full of life . . .
>
> (III, 102)

All, with water-falls and rustling branches, mingle, made by Love,
'unto one mighty end' (III, 102). It is a momentary intuition in
earthly terms of that 'mighty end' for which all earth's torments exist.
Byron's thought here resembles Tennyson's in *In Memoriam*—a poem
inspired by a seraphic love recalling those of Shakespeare and
Byron—where, despite nature's manifold horrors, Love as 'creation's

44

final law' points on—however waveringly—to that 'far off divine event to which the whole creation moves' (56, 131; for 'seraphic', 109). For Byron, his most perfect love was, so far as his expressed records tell us, that of the *Thyrza* poems, on his love for Edleston, and that, or some similar love, is present here:

> He who hath lov'd not, here would learn that lore,
> And make his heart a spirit; he who knows
> That tender mystery, will love the more;
> For this is Love's recess, where vain men's woes,
> And the world's waste, have driven him far from
> those,
> For 'tis his nature to advance or die;
> He stands not still, but or decays, or grows
> Into a boundless blessing, which may vie
> With the immortal lights, in its eternity!
>
> (III, 103)

The 'tender mystery' makes the 'heart' into a 'spirit': love opens the spirit-world. Here at Clarens, the scene of Rousseau's *Nouvelle Héloïse*, is a place fit for 'the mind's purified beings'; here 'Love', that is Eros, was joined with 'Psyche' (III, 104). In *Euthanasia* (p. 31) the loved one is addressed as 'my Psyche'; that is, 'my soul'.

Byron has an extended note on Clarens:

> But this is not all; the feeling with which all around Clarens, and the opposite rocks of Meillerie, is invested, is of a still higher and more comprehensive order than the mere sympathy with individual passion; it is a sense of the existence of love in its most extended and sublime capacity, and of our own participation of its good and of its glory: it is the great principle of the universe, which is there more condensed, but not less manifested; and of which, though knowing ourselves a part, we lose our individuality, and mingle in the beauty of the whole.—If Rousseau had never written, nor lived, the same associations would not less have belonged to such scenes.

The thought is again of *expansion*; of a widening of individual passion to some grand universal. This third Canto contains a precise metaphysic. We follow Byron living a poetic expansion from inner unrest to external apprehension. Simultaneously, helped by the mountains around, he feels himself on the edge of a new dimension to which his soul responds. Over-viewing man's historic and present convulsions, sharing in them, aware above all of the torments of genius, himself a living thunder yet delicately tuned to a spirit-life beyond mortal bounds, he finds at Clarens a visionary spot where earth is spirit-land and Love reigns.

Canto IV (composed 1817) has a different mood. In place of mountains, aspiration and spirit-intimations we have at first-sight a less optimistic and levelled concentration on Venice, Florence and Rome; on the tragic lives of literary genius, on works of art, on tombs and ruins. Poetry such as Byron's cannot remain for long content with any too obvious a spirit-apprehension; it returns to fuse the higher or deeper powers with a human and horizontal, concrete, expression: this forces a more tragic concentration, reaching its best fulfilment in the arts of design, in architecture and sculpture.

Venice has been made for ever magical by *The Merchant of Venice*, *Othello* and *Venice Preserved*. Such 'beings of the mind', we are told, are of an 'immortal' essence that illuminates and fertilizes our 'mortal bondage' (IV, 4, 5). Byron claims to have experienced a reality beyond poetry by direct vision (IV, 6, 7; see p. 315), and imagines his 'unbodied' 'spirit' returning to England after death (IV, 9); but more characteristic of our mood here are thoughts of the 'mind' attaining the strength of a vast storm-withstanding tree; and of animal and human endurance, darkly toned, though defined also in terms of bitter-sweet memories, and lightning (IV, 20–4; pp. 220, 275). Man's destiny is to strive with God or demons, even though melancholy sometimes makes of earth a 'tomb' or 'hell' (IV, 33–4). By the tomb of a Roman lady the poet derives a mysterious and 'solemn' comfort like 'dying thunder' that inspires him with the will to live, and fight on (IV, 104–5). Great writers, Petrarch, Tasso, Ariosto, Dante, Boccaccio, attune us to a tragic nobility, perhaps a tragic conquest, poetically defined by the thought of Ariosto's bust rendered sacred by the stroke of lightning (IV, 41).

Byron invokes Rome as 'skeleton' of a 'Titanic' past and Italy as 'Mother of Arts' and 'Parent of our religion' (IV, 46–7). The Falls of Terni are made marvellously symbolic of tragic endurance and a Cordelia-like conquest (IV, 69–72; p. 285). Then we return to Rome as 'Niobe of nations', 'childless', 'crownless' and 'voiceless' in her 'woe', (IV, 79), reduced by repeated disasters to a 'chaos of ruins' (IV, 79, 80). But she lives in her great writers, Cicero, Vergil, Livy; and in her great men, Brutus, Sylla, Pompey (IV, 82–5). Descriptions of Rome pile up: she is the protagonist of this canto, as a vast presence, concretely apprehended in ruins, tombs and sculptures. There is a sublimity felt in the very pathos; the tragic is somehow the soul; in the ruins of the Coliseum, Time is 'the beautifier of the dead' (IV, 130). But the living St. Peter's, 'Christ's mighty shrine', is honoured in great stanzas, equally rich in architectural analysis and religious awe (IV, 153–9; *Laureate of Peace*, see p. viii above; 87). Byron's more concrete and tragically toned mood in Canto IV searches for solution in either the actuality of historic religion within its architectural home, or in idealized sculptures.

Byron could write slightingly of painting and sculpture, or anyway of his own appreciation of them, in comparison with nature (Murray, 14 April 1817; LJ, IV, 107); but from a gallery in Florence he returned 'drunk with beauty'; here he saw 'sculpture and painting which for the first time at all gave me an idea of what people mean by their *cant*' (Murray, 26 April 1817; LJ, IV, 113). In Italy a new art was unveiled for him.

The tragic yet heroically enduring mood of Canto IV naturally responded to the Laocoön group at the Vatican blending 'a father's love and mortal's agony' with 'an immortal's patience' (IV, 160). Pompey's statue is honoured:

> And thou, dread Statue! yet existent in
> The austerest form of naked majesty—
> Thou who beheldest, 'mid the assassins' din,
> At thy bath'd base the bloody Caesar lie . . .
>
> (IV, 87)

Within the human form itself a certain sublimity or significance is apprehended. Our Fourth Canto approaches supernal meaning within man; man not as spirit opposed to 'clay' (III, 14), but rather as spirit-in-clay, almost as clay made through form into spirit, as when Coleridge writes of the body as 'Eternal Shadow of the finite

Soul' and 'the Soul's self-symbol' (Fragment 22, *Poetical Works*, ed.
E. H. Coleridge, 1912). This is logically the kind of high-light
which in this humanistic canto we need; and the arts of Italy provide
it.

We have an extended passage on the Medici *Venus* of Florence.
Naturally enough, Byron's sculptural idealism finds its most perfect
expression in figures of love. Though he deliberately refuses 'the
paltry jargon of the marble mart' (IV, 50), he in purely general terms
describes the figure's effect on him:

> Glowing, and circumfus'd in speechless love,
> Their full divinity inadequate
> That feeling to express, or to improve,
> The gods become as mortals, and man's fate
> Has moments like their brightest; but the weight
> Of earth recoils upon us;—let it go!
> We can recall such visions, and create,
> From what has been, or might be, things which grow
> Into thy statue's form, and look like gods below.
>
> (IV, 52)

'Glowing' and 'circumfus'd' give a sense of spirit-aura (cp. 'glow' on
p. 39 above); but it is concretely embodied, the divine in mortal
form. Man has equivalent 'moments', presumably moments not here
of direct spirit-vision (as, it would seem, at IV, 6–7; p. 46 above,
315 below), but of the divine felt in a human being, though the
experience is hard to capture and maintain; and it is from such
moments that the sculptor's art is created. For Byron art is here
regarded as less a matter of invention or vision than as a capturing in
permanent form of what can be, on choice occasions, glimpsed in
life.

In Byron's experience such occasions appear to have been most
perfect with his early love of Edleston and the torture of Loukas'
beauty at Missolonghi. We have at least no Byronic poetry like his
lines on the delicate perfection of the one or the transfixing magic of
the other. It is accordingly natural that our finest statue description
should be of a male figure, the Apollo Belvedere in the Vatican:

> Or view the Lord of the unerring bow,
> The God of life, and poesy, and light—

48

The Sun in human limbs array'd, and brow
All radiant from his triumph in the fight;
The shaft hath just been shot—the arrow bright
With an immortal's vengeance; in his eye
And nostril beautiful disdain, and might
And majesty, flash their full lightnings by,
Developing in that one glance the Deity.

But in his delicate form—a dream of Love,
Shap'd by some solitary nymph, whose breast
Long'd for a deathless lover from above,
And madden'd in that vision—are exprest
All that ideal beauty ever bless'd
The mind with in its most unearthly mood,
When each conception was a heavenly guest—
A ray of immortality—and stood
Starlike, around, until they gather'd to a god!

And if it be Prometheus stole from Heaven
The fire which we endure, it was repaid
By him to whom the energy was given
Which this poetic marble hath array'd
With an eternal glory—which, if made
By human hands, is not of human thought;
And Time himself hath hallow'd it, nor laid
One ringlet in the dust—nor hath it caught
A tinge of years, but breathes the flame with which
'twas wrought.

(IV, 161–3)

The Sun, the most concrete possible symbol for the divine, and obviously suited to Apollo, is here clothed in human limbs; as near as may be the body-spirit dualism is healed; the terms, as this canto demands, *coalesce*. To Byron the figure naturally suggests Love, since in such forms he had experienced keenest love, and so, in a usual poetic manner (e.g. so much of Shakespeare's best dramatic love-poetry, Pope's *Eloisa to Abelard*, etc.), he imagines the subjective viewer as a girl. It is not all happy; the vision maddens, as Loukas maddened Byron. The 'unearthly mood' recalls that 'most romantic period' of his young life when Byron knew Edleston (p. 28). Note too the typically Byronic thought of our tragic destiny being at root *caused by our own exquisite apprehensions*. Lightning is Byron's symbol for tragedy, and tragedy is for him a positive (pp. 271–7 below). Such experiences are too keen; as Shakespeare puts it, 'tun'd too sharp in sweetness' for our 'ruder powers' (*Troilus and Cressida*, III, ii, 23).

A fine passage on sculpture and painting occurs in *The Prophecy of Dante* (IV):

> But thus all they
> Whose intellect is an o'ermastering power
> Which still recoils from its encumbering clay
> Or lightens it to spirit, whatsoe'er
> The form which their creations may essay,
> Are bards; the kindled marble's bust may wear
> More poesy upon its speaking brow
> Than aught less than the Homeric page may bear;
> One noble stroke with a whole life may glow,
> Or deify the canvas till it shine
> With beauty so surpassing all below,
> That they who kneel to idols so divine
> Break no commandment, for high heaven is there
> Transfus'd, transfigurated . . .

With 'glow' compare the 'glowing' in 'speechless love' of the Venus in *Childe Harold*—'glow' designates a state of love elsewhere (III, 54) —and Byron's use of 'glow' for the travelling spirit-body (p. 39 above); for love, art, and spirit are interrelated. After this passage Byron as Dante proceeds to honour the *Moses* of Michelangelo.

The excellence cannot be referred to without some kind of physical-material dualism; even with art-works, those most relevant are of deities, and description uses the word 'divine'. In writing of such loves as Shakespeare's for his Fair Youth or Byron's for Edleston, I have found it necessary to follow the poets themselves in the use of some supernal term. Shakespeare's 'cherubins' and 'angel' (Sonnets, 114, 144), besides being too saturated in religious orthodoxy, cannot since the nineteenth century help suggesting respectively a child and a woman; whereas a boy or youth is needed. The most suitable terms are 'seraph' and 'seraphic'. Seraphs were in the traditional hierarchies known as love-experts, and the word has a general poetic validity, as in Coleridge's use of it for man's state beyond death in *The Ancient Mariner*, and *To an Infant*; and as adoring powers in *Religious Musings* (see *The Starlit Dome,* 87, 119, 135). Seraphs are love-powers in Pope's *Eloisa to Abelard* (218, 320); Shelley in the Fragments relating to *Epipsychidion* sees a Platonic love as giving birth to 'a naked Seraph' (145); and Tennyson wrote of the young Hallam's 'seraphic intellect' (*In Memoriam*, 109). My full discussion of the problems involved is presented in the material added to *The Christian Renaissance,* under the title 'The Seraphic Intuition', in 1962. We pass now to a key Byronic love-passage where the word 'seraph' is central.

In Canto III of *Childe Harold* spirit categories were freely used; in Canto IV architecture, majestic ruins, tombs and the plastic arts replace them. But both cantos find Love their centre and positive: in Rousseau and Clarens in the one, and in the Venus and the Apollo in the other; and in yet another passage, pre-eminently, on a Grotto devoted by some lover to the goddess-nymph Egeria, a place 'haunted by holy Love—the earliest oracle'. Here a 'celestial' was once blended with a 'human' heart. Byron's life-long problem is here posed: how to match 'the purity of heaven' with 'earthly joys', how to—in a marvellously pregnant line—'expel the venom and not blunt the dart' (IV, 119); a line in which enough erotic and spiritual wisdom is contained to fill many volumes; if indeed it does not sum, once and for all, man's destiny on earth. Our moral and spiritual teachings inevitably *blunt the dart;* and for this reason religion throughout the ages remains what it is, ancillary and not primary. Can the heavenly be blended with earthly love? Such an ideal Byron had, once at least, glimpsed. Our passage continues:

> Alas! our young affections run to waste,
> Or water but the desert; whence arise
> But weeds of dark luxuriance, tares of haste,
> Rank at the core, though tempting to the eyes,
> Flowers whose wild odours breathe but agonies,
> And trees whose gums are poisons; such the plants
> Which spring beneath her steps as Passion flies
> O'er the world's wilderness, and vainly pants
> For some celestial fruit forbidden to our wants.

51

Oh Love! no habitant of earth thou art—
An unseen Seraph, we believe in thee—
A faith whose martyrs are the broken heart—
But never yet hath seen, nor e'er shall see
The naked eye, thy form, as it should be;
The mind hath made thee, as it peopled Heaven,
Even with its own desiring phantasy,
And to a thought such shape and image given,
As haunts the unquench'd soul—parch'd, wearied,
    wrung, and riven.

Of its own beauty is the mind diseas'd,
And fevers into false creation:—where,
Where are the forms the sculptor's soul hath seiz'd?
In him alone. Can Nature show so fair?
Where are the charms and virtues which we dare
Conceive in boyhood and pursue as men,
The unreach'd Paradise of our despair,
Which o'er-informs the pencil and the pen,
And overpowers the page where it would bloom again?

Who loves, raves—'tis youth's frenzy—but the cure
Is bitterer still, as charm by charm unwinds
Which robed our idols, and we see too sure
Nor worth nor beauty dwells from out the mind's
Ideal shape of such; yet still it binds
The fatal spell, and still it draws us on,
Reaping the whirlwind from the oft-sown winds;
The stubborn heart, its alchemy begun,
Seems ever near the prize—wealthiest when most undone.

We wither from our youth, we gasp away—
Sick—sick; unfound the boon, unslak'd the thirst,
Though to the last, in verge of our decay,
Some phantom lures, such as we sought at first—
But all too late—so are we doubly curst.
Love, fame, ambition, avarice—'tis the same,
Each idle, and all ill, and none the worst—

For all are meteors with a different name,
And Death the sable smoke where vanishes the flame.

(IV, 120–4)

The passage is deeply important.

'Young affections' such as those recorded in Byron's early poems and attaining a supreme fulfilment in his love for Edleston are subsequently either wasted or breed poisons. There may be a reference to physical indulgence with Nicolo in Greece, though Bryon's letters at the time (pp. 32, 351) show no sense of sin; perhaps later on, in England, there was. These last stanzas were composed when Byron's life-story was drawing towards its period of extreme dissipation at Venice.[1] It is typical of Byron's thought that evil appears to spring from good; the 'celestial fruit' is 'forbidden'; but it *is* celestial.

The thought attains expansion in Byron's *Heaven and Earth* (composed 1821), on the Hebrew legend of the love of divine beings, the angels Samiasa and Azaziel, called 'seraphs' in the text (I, iii, 445, 457, 509, 631, 714), for earthly women. Though they, as divine beings, 'should be passionless and pure' (I, iii, 715), they remain true to their loves. The union is simultaneously honoured and regarded as wrong: the relevance to Byron's own life is clear. Love for Byron is, in essence, just such a seraph love. So in our *Childe Harold* passage it is called an 'unseen Seraph' of the mind's phantasy, for some equivalent of whom we search in vain. The quest is religious: we are its 'martyrs'; it comes from the same 'phantasy' as originally 'peopled heaven'; yet we thirst for it as a needed reality. If it be 'false' the 'mind' is 'diseased' by its own highest apprehension ('beauty'). This love-quest is behind the sculptor's art, out-doing Nature. The point is, that sculpture need not submit to the temporal attrition and chances of human life, whereby what we conceived in 'boyhood' is for ever after an 'unreach'd Paradise', the more tormenting through our recognition of 'youth's frenzy' as a deception; so that the 'cure'— exactly as in Marvell's *Dialogue between the Soul and Body* (28)—is worse than the disease. But despite the ideal's admitted subjectivity,

1. They were among the additional stanzas sent to Murray during the autumn of 1817 (P, II, 313), about a year before what is generally supposed to be the period of dissipation at the Palazzo Mocenigo.

its power remains unabated. Our souls are at their richest ('wealth-iest') when most near their inevitable failure ('undone').

Whether or not the youthful vision was true, from youth onwards we 'wither'. But even to the last the 'phantom' which 'we sought at first' lures us; a neat forecast of Loukas at Missolonghi.

Byron's conclusion is that *something is wrong:*

> Our life is a false nature: 'tis not in
> The harmony of things—this hard decree,
> This uneradicable taint of Sin,
> This boundless Upas, this all-blasting tree,
> Whose root is earth, whose leaves and branches be
> The skies which rain their plagues on men like dew—
> Disease, death, bondage—all the woes we see,
> And worse, the woes we see not—which throb through
> The immedicable soul, with heart-aches ever new.
>
> (IV, 126)

There follows a determination to apply our human prerogative of 'reason'; 'from our birth' the 'faculty divine' may be, in various ways, constricted; perhaps 'the unprepared mind' is not yet ready for the 'truth'; but the 'beam pours in', and 'time and skill' can 'couch' (i.e. remove a cataract from) 'the blind'. We may compare Byron's thought in an earlier stanza that social 'opinion' so impinges that we are afraid lest our own 'judgments' should bring 'too much light' to mankind (IV, 93).

III

Though their normal poetic instinct is to rely on symbols, Shake-speare and Byron can both think freely in direct spirit-terms, when they choose. Sonnet 146, 'Poor soul, the centre of my sinful earth', is a firm enough statement regarding the 'soul'. Shakespeare's Sonnets contain thought of mind-travel similar to Byron's (p. 39). The poet regrets that 'the dull substance' of his 'flesh' cannot like 'thought' traverse 'space' to join his love:

> For nimble thought can jump both sea and land
> As soon as think the place where he would be.

54

But, ah! thought kills me that I am not thought,
To leap large lengths of miles when thou art gone . . .
(Sonnet, 44)

Being made so largely of 'earth and water', he cannot do this, but
in Sonnet 45 he asserts that the elements of 'air' and 'fire' in him,
that is 'thought' and 'desire', are less limited: 'these present-absent
with swift motion glide'. The designation of telepathic ubiquity is
clever; and there is no sharp distinction between it and astral
travelling. 'Present-absent' asserts the paradox, faced likewise by
Byron and Powys (p. 39 above and note), of the projected soul's
apparent use of the body's senses. Shakespeare works it all out very
exactly. His lighter elements gone off on their 'embassy of love', the
poet is left heavy with gloom; but on their return, bringing news of
his loved one's health, his 'composition' is restored and he is, for a
while, happy (Sonnet 45). 'Air and fire' are the etheric or astral body,
which actually goes a journey, sees the loved one, and returns with
news. Either may do it. Seeing the other's image by night the poet
asks, in Sonnet 61:

> Is it thy spirit that thou send'st from thee
> So far from home, into my deeds to pry?

Such suggestions are directly in line with what is known of astral
projection (p. 313 below, note).

However both Shakespeare and Byron usually rely for poetic
purposes on more traditionally accepted, and therefore apparently
more concrete, even though perhaps more fictional, terms. Shakespeare has his cherubins and angels. 'Such cherubins as your sweet
self resemble' occurs in Sonnet 114, and the word is used by Lorenzo
in the music-and-love scene of *The Merchant of Venice* (v, i, 62).
Angels and beautiful young men are regularly in Shakespeare
associated. Imogen disguised as a boy is an 'angel':

> By Jupiter, an angel, or, if not,
> An earthly paragon! Behold divineness
> No elder than a boy!   (III, vi, 42)

Juliet may be compared to a 'bright angel', but the 'winged messenger
of Heaven' concerned is itself male (*Romeo and Juliet*, II, ii, 26–8).

Shakespeare's angels are imagined as active, often athletic, youths. The matter is fully discussed in the second appendix of *The Wheel of Fire* (enlarged; 1949, etc.). As we have seen (p. 25), in Sonnet 144 Shakespeare compares the Fair Youth to a good angel four times with the Dark Lady as the poet's 'worser spirit', the one 'saint' and the other 'devil' and 'fiend'. We have already quoted Byron's use of such terms as 'a dream of Heaven' and 'sylphs' (p. 32). The *Thyrza* poems are essays in 'seraphic' apprehension.

Let us enquire more closely into the nature of such seraphic loves as those of Michelangelo's and Shakespeare's sonnets, of Byron, Gray, Tennyson, Wilde, and many another.

Byron can help us. 'Of its own beauty', he wrote, 'is the mind diseas'd' (p. 52). Coleridge once urged man to leap into his own 'light'[1]. Parallels in mystical writers abound. Now for many minds this light may be kindled most readily by male youth. Perhaps our clearest expression of the result occurs in a play by Massinger and Dekker called *The Virgin Martyr* in which a persecutor of Christians is reformed—I quote from my book *The Golden Labyrinth* (118)—by 'being shown a vision of Paradise by the heroine's mysterious page Angelo, a "delicate" and "young lad" upon whose eyes "dance" a thousand "blessings"'. He addresses Angelo:

It is, it is, some angel! Vanish'd again!
Oh, come back, ravishing boy! Bright messenger!
Thou hast, by these mine eyes fix'd on thy beauty,
Illumin'd all my soul.

(v, i)

Angelo turns out to be a real angel, manifesting as a boy: the significance is clear, and bears a direct relation to those many instances in our dramatic tradition when a boy or a girl-disguised-as-a-boy is accorded seraphic status. One such in Nat Lee's *Caesar Borgia* bears the name 'Seraphino'. Relevant examples are given throughout *The Golden Labyrinth*.

Girls in male disguise may be called 'bisexual', and a similar quality may be carried by young male figures, blending as they do

---

1. I cannot now trace the reference. Coleridge's minor poetry is rich with relevant thought and imagery, especially 'light': see *The Starlit Dome*, 97–143.

grace with strength. Shakespeare describes his loved youth in bi-sexual terms:

A woman's face with Nature's own hand painted
Hast thou, the master-mistress of my passion . . .
(Sonnet 20)

As a dramatist, he relied continually, as did other dramatists, on the accepted convention of disguise, so that girls could be shown in, as Lorenzo puts it, 'the lovely garnish of a boy' (*The Merchant of Venice*, II, vi, 45). That last phrase must have appealed to Byron. One of his early girl-loves used to dress as a boy, and he took her to Newstead sometimes passing her off as his brother; and when the passionate Lady Caroline Lamb visited Byron in a page's dress, she probably expected the disguise to increase her attraction (LBM, 7, 17, 44, 205). In Byron's narrative poem *Lara* the page Kaled, who turns out to be a girl, is alone in the hero's confidence, and of central importance. The wit and wisdom of Shakespeare's girl heroines have been often praised, but it is less often recognized that, as I have argued in *The Golden Labyrinth,* they *only speak their best wisdom when in sexual disguise.*

To all these bisexual figures the lover's soul responds because it is itself bisexual; it is also immortal, and as 'soul' or 'spirit' eternally young. Now the more nearly a man approaches integration with his own soul the more likely he is to show signs of bisexuality. Instances from the annals of genius are abundant (discussed at LBM, 255–60, 281–2; *The Mutual Flame,* 30–4; *The Christian Renaissance,* 1962; 269–325). Hobhouse's feeling for Byron was such as might be felt for a 'froward sister'; there was a strong feminine strain in him (LBCV, 81). Byron's male qualities tend to go into his prose, the more female ones into his poetry; and much of his life was given to trying to fuse the two principles; rather as the bisexual and visionary Tiresias is conceived as the fusing medium of the sexes in Eliot's *The Waste Land.*

It is all very difficult. We could say that perfected love, *as love,* must be bisexual, and that the state of 'being in love', with all its age-old romantic accompaniments, is a bisexual state; otherwise the barrier could not be surpassed from the 'you', or 'thou', to the magical identification, or near-identification, of the two 'I's. This state cannot easily be *maintained;* and for a neat balancing of the bi-sexuality of love against the necessities of sexual differentiation, dis-cussing man and woman 'when their state of being-in-love no longer lifts them out of themselves into that magic mutual world created by the super-senses of the ideal man-woman', I would point to John Cowper Powys's *The Art of Happiness* (1935; III, 101, 103; IV, 179). But since differentiation implies limitation, we may certainly suppose that the more fully integrated and inclusive man will be the less in need of a sexual partner. Shakespeare's own phraseology helps us, as when Rosalind says of a man late for a lovers' meeting 'I'll warrant him heart-whole' (*As You Like It,* IV, i, 51). There are weightier implications when the Duke in *Measure for Measure* rebuffs any suggestion of love with the words:

> Believe not that the dribbling dart of love
> Can pierce a complete bosom.

> (I, iii, 2)

If the Duke, as it seems, is to marry Isabella at the conclusion, we may suppose it to be a union of 'married chastity' such as that celebrated in *The Phoenix and the Turtle.* Perfect love and normal sex-uality are, paradoxically, opposed. The saint, always enjoying a perpetual state of 'being in love', is to that extent likely to be barred from sexual experience.[1]

An interesting superiority to love as ordinarily understood is implied when Antonio meets a similar suggestion that he is in love with 'Fie, fie!' (*The Merchant of Venice,* I, i, 46). But Antonio loved Bassanio. Such integrated, or near-integrated, men need some objec-tive equivalent to their own soul-state: their *fulness* demands ex-pression in the external world (compare our passages quoted on pp. 62–3, 340–1); and they may find what they need in persons of their own sex. As Shakespeare puts it:

> The beauty that is borne here in the face
> The bearer knows not, but commends itself
> To others' eyes: nor doth the eye itself—

1. For John Cowper Powys's rejection of normal sexuality in favour of what he calls a more 'diffused' love, see *The Saturnian Quest,* Index C, 'Sexology'.

That most pure spirit of sense—behold itself,
Not going from itself; but eye to eye oppos'd
Salutes each other with each other's form;
For speculation turns not to itself
Till it hath travell'd and is mirror'd there
Where it may see itself.
                    (*Troilus and Cressida*, III, iii, 103)

The lines are spoken by Achilles, lover of Patroclus. The Sonnets
provide obvious correspondences: one, Sonnet 24, is devoted to a
complex analysis of the process (*The Mutual Flame*, 40–1). *The
Phoenix and the Turtle* condenses the experience neatly:

So between them love did shine,
That the Turtle saw his right
Flaming in the Phoenix' sight,
Either was the other's mine.

The last line means more than 'each belonged to the other'. Rather,
each *was* the other's inmost, subjective, 'I am'; as when Cathy in
Wuthering Heights says 'I *am* Heathcliff'.

We can accordingly place without difficulty the loves of poet-
seers for youth. They may themselves be ugly, like Socrates; or feel
old, like the Shakespeare of the Sonnets 'bated and chopp'd with
tann'd antiquity' (Sonnet 62), or Byron in *Childe Harold, Manfred,*
and the *Thirty-Sixth Year* (pp. 38, 216, 69). But what they see in the
adored is nevertheless a reflection of their soul-selves:

My glass shall not persuade me I am old,
So long as youth and thou are of one date;
But when in thee Time's furrows I behold,
Then look I death my days should expiate.
For all that beauty that doth cover thee
Is but the seemly raiment of my heart,
Which in thy breast doth live, as thine in me.
How can I then be elder than thou art?
                                    (Sonnet 22)

'My spirit is thine', the poet writes, 'the better part of me' (74). Again:

As easy might I from myself depart
As from my soul, which in thy breast doth lie.
                                    (Sonnet 109)

The dramas contain similar thoughts: 'It is my soul', says Romeo of Juliet, 'that calls upon my name' (*Romeo and Juliet*, II, ii, 164). These soul-selves are whole, young, and beautiful. They are also, we may suppose, to be regarded as bisexual. Unity is glassed in unity.

Were the soul-selves fully realized, there would presumably be no unrest: there appears to have been none in Socrates, or in Christ in regard to the Beloved Disciple, John (as discussed in *The Christian Renaissance*, 1962; 301–10). But with poets, though *at the moment of composition* the creative, which is the bisexual, state, is, as Shelley says in his *Defence of Poetry*, beyond all 'base desire' (we need not linger to question the word 'base'), yet man's sexual physiology remains active, with resulting unrest. Some kind of physical reciprocity is desired; but for what Shakespeare's Duke calls a 'complete bosom', differentiation is not relevant; and what is therefore sought is a self-reflection. The Narcissus myth expresses the need and its dangers. Much of Byron's *Don Juan* and his *Deformed Transformed* is in a narcissistic vein; and Shelley's too, when he writes of himself as 'a pard-like Spirit beautiful and swift' in *Adonais* (xxxii); and we may compare Powys's attribution to Christ *as a natural characteristic of divinity*, of 'majestic lovableness and a magnetic passion for being loved' (*The Pleasures of Literature*, 63). Or some form of self-resemblance in a familial love may be sought; in a mother, as in the *Oedipus* story; or a sister. Shakespeare's Sonnet 143 to the Lady reflects a desire for maternal love:

> So run'st thou after that which flies from thee,
> Whilst I, thy babe, chase thee afar behind;
> But if thou catch thy hope, turn back to me,
> And play the mother's part, kiss me, be kind.

Hamlet is a central Shakespearian figure and his main emotional concentration is on his mother; and Byron's childhood relations with his mother were close and fierce. Wordsworth and Byron drew strength respectively from a sister's and a half-sister's love. 'That love was pure', wrote Byron, thinking of Augusta (*Childe Harold*, III, 55); 'pure' meaning something like 'whole'. Literature and myth-ology, and the royal practices of ancient Egypt and the Incas of Peru, provide relevant examples of sister-love. But of all such self-reflections male youth, for a male subject, on the meeting place of strength with grace, male with female, sex with soul, appears to awake the keenest and most fiery physical-spiritual apprehensions. How far these apprehensions can or should be physically expressed it is beyond my purpose or authority to decide. A distinction appears to have been drawn both by the ancients and by Renaissance moralists between kisses and other types of union (*The Mutual Flame,* 89, 199, notes; *The Christian Renaissance,* 1962; 305, note). Shakespeare, in Sonnet 20, felt thwarted by the young man's sex. Byron, who was nothing if not comprehensive, experienced homosexual loves (i) idyllic with Edleston, (ii) carefree and physical with Nicolo, and (iii) tormented and accompanied by self-condemnation with Loukas at Missolonghi.

It seems that Byron as he grew older found himself unable to match his seraphic intuitions to any satisfying line of action or thought. Shelley saw him as an 'eagle spirit' blinded 'by gazing on its own exceeding light' (*Julian and Maddalo,* 52); and he himself, as we have seen, interprets human torment in terms of some supreme good, seen but unreachable. Something has gone wrong:

> Our life is a false nature: 'tis not in
> The harmony of things—this hard decree,
> This uneradicable taint of sin . . .
>> (*Childe Harold,* IV, 126)

The only assuagement offered for 'the immedicable soul' is that there *is* an answer in terms of man's thought, what Shakespeare called his 'capability and god-like reason' (*Hamlet,* IV, iv, 38), if only man's thought be allowed freedom:

> Though from our birth the faculty divine
> Is chain'd and tortur'd—cabin'd, cribb'd, confin'd,
> And bred in darkness, lest the Truth should shine
> Too brightly on the unprepared mind,
> The beam pours in, for time and skill will couch the blind.
>> (*Childe Harold,* IV, 127)

Men are 'pale' with fear lest their own unfettered 'judgments' might become so brilliant that earth has 'too much light' (*Childe Harold,*

IV, 93). As I have shown in *Lord Byron's Marriage* (127–8), the central love-symbol of *Manfred,* Astarte, is an ambivalent symbol of (i) love and (ii) desecration. The problem is, how to 'expel the venom and not blunt the dart' (*Childe Harold,* IV, 119).

Byron's meaning may be elucidated by analogies in both Nietzsche and Shakespeare. In my *Christ and Nietzsche* I wrote of 'The Night-Song' in *Thus Spake Zarathustra* as follows:

All but complete, he cannot quite accept his completeness; he has no object, and, being himself light, cannot 'suck at the breasts of light'. Living in his own hard brilliance, drinking the flames that break from himself, he cannot know the 'happiness of the taker' . . . He thirsts not for drink, but for thirst itself: he is chaste through his own plenitude . . . It is a testing moment at which he, replete with virtue, tired of giving, hungers for its opposite, for 'wickedness', in order to make contact, to 'touch' the 'souls' of others.

(*Christ and Nietzsche,* V, 178)

Byron, like Manfred a 'Croesus in creation', endured this lonely fulness; and he not only hungered inwardly to touch others, but 'plung'd amidst mankind' (*Manfred,* II, ii, 142, 145), in action. His Venetian dissipation was a rebound from virtues and visions that had from his youth been thwarted.

Both Byron and Nietzsche's Zarathustra endure a too-great abundance, or perfection. Shakespeare's Sonnets express a similar experience. The poet is said to be 'incapable of more', being 'replete' with his love (113):

Like as, to make our appetites more keen,
With eager compounds we our palate urge;
As, to prevent our maladies unseen,
We sicken, to shun sickness, when we purge;
Even so, being full of your ne'er cloying sweetness,
To bitter sauces did I frame my feeding;
And, sick of welfare, found a kind of meetness
To be diseas'd, ere that there was true needing.
Thus policy in love, to anticipate
The ills that were not, grew to faults assur'd,

And brought to medicine a healthful state,
Which, rank of goodness, would by ill be cur'd;
But thence I learn, and find the lesson true,
Drugs poison him that fell so sick of you.

(Sonnet 118)

This is not to be read as a record of satiation: the sweetness does not
'cloy'. The meaning's essence is in the twelfth line, corresponding to
Byron's 'Of its own beauty is the mind diseas'd' in *Childe Harold*
(IV, 122). Shakespeare's vision had attuned him temporarily to what
for a similar purpose is called by other poets of Shakespeare's day
'perfection'; its symbol being the Phoenix (*The Mutual Flame*, discussing the Phoenix poems in *Love's Martyr*; 183–4). In such experiences the male and female elements in the lover are fused in
contemplation of the male-female quality in what Shakespeare
calls his 'master-mistress' (Sonnet 20; and see *A Lover's Complaint*,
92, 100). Unity is glassed in unity; but since such a perfection is hard
to maintain the sexual centres may reawake to create an unrest
for which there is no easy fulfilment; and in desperation the soul
plunges low, if only for relief.

Of his Venetian period Byron wrote:

I sometimes think that I should have written the *whole* as a
lesson, but it might have proved a *lesson* to be *learnt* rather than
avoided; for passion is a whirlpool, which is not to be viewed
nearly without attraction from its vortex.

(*Detached Thoughts*, 1821; 75; LJ, v, 447)

He told Medwin that his Memoirs would be as a lesson to young men
in treating of 'the fatal consequences of dissipation'. In Venice he
distracted his mind from the city's 'desolation' and his own 'solitude'
—as so often in Byron public and personal anxieties coalesce—by
'plunging into a vortex that was anything but pleasure' (Medwin,
34; 56). To this descent we shall return (pp. 136–8, 340–1).

Like the Shakespeare of the Sonnets, Byron admits to an extreme
of dissipation, but with neither can we be sure whether the extreme indicated is heterosexual, homosexual or both. We can,
however, state a tension between (i) the ideal seen most keenly in

Platonic-homosexual terms and (ii) physical debauchery, whatever the sex. Byron describes the resultant agony:

> It is an awful chaos—light and darkness—
> And mind and dust—and passions and pure
> thoughts,
> Mix'd and contending without end or order.
>
> (*Manfred*, III, i, 164)

The references here, though quite general and basic enough to human nature, are such as are most poignantly endured by men in whom their whole selves are in, or near, a full consciousness.

To return to the moment of perfect insight, or being, which is also the finest essence of love, on which all else depends. In *The Adieu* (1807) Byron wrote, with reference to Edleston:

> And thou, my Friend! whose gentle love
> Yet thrills my bosom's chords,
> How much thy friendship was above
> Description's power of words!
> Still near my breast thy gift I wear
> Which sparkled once with Feeling's tear,
> Of Love the pure, the sacred gem.
> Our souls were equal, and our lot
> In that dear moment quite forgot;
> Let Pride alone condemn!

'Our souls were equal': that is a quiet, yet final, phrase. It is a union of like with like in terms of 'soul', on the exact wave-length of *The Phoenix and the Turtle*. That kisses were involved is clear from the poem *To Thyrza;* but in the great days of Platonism in the Renaissance a distinction was drawn between kisses and the more sexual contacts (p. 61).

The relating of such experiences of 'perfection'—the 'perfection' of the Phoenix poems in *Love's Martyr*—into normal terms is so difficult that we find such loves most readily expressed in tragic terms, leading to the many famous elegies already noted (p. 32). These may be called 'tragic' loves provided that we allow 'tragic' to cover the optimism of our seraphic and heavenly connotations. On all visionary-mystical occasions the vision may (i) be expressed in tragic and other-worldly terms, and (ii) be expanded and extended socially. For (i) our quotations have already shown the tragic and mystical qualities of the *Thyrza* poems, and to these we shall return. For (ii), much of Byron's life shows the will to expand his ideal experience into selfless and social action. His early poems concentrate on his youthful friendships and—with the sacrificial heroism of Nisus and Euryalus (p. 28, note) as a link—on the will to public fame, burning to emulate in honour the names of Chatham and Fox (*Lines addressed to the Rev. J. T. Becher etc.*; LBCV, 234–5). We have recently found him making little distinction between the plight of Venice and his own loneliness. The close relation of Byron's seraphic loves to his public service is suggested by the imagery of one of those bold anonymous poems of his in the cause of French liberty published in 1816. It is called *On the Star of The Legion of Honour* and, though designated 'From the French', was Byron's own writing. Here is the French 'tricolor':

> Before thee rose, and with thee grew,
> A rainbow of the loveliest hue
> Of three bright colours, each divine,
> And fit for that celestial sign;
> For Freedom's hand had blended them,
> Like tints of an immortal gem.

> One tint was of the sunbeam's dyes;
> One, the blue depth of Seraph's eyes;
> One, the pure Spirit's veil of white
> Had rob'd in radiance of its light:
> The three so mingled did beseem
> The texture of a heavenly dream.
>
> (P, III, 437)

'Immortal gem'. Edleston gave Byron a Cornelian heart, referred to in the lyric *The Cornelian* (1806; P, I, 66), and this is the 'sacred gem' of *The Adieu* (1807; and see *Pignus Amoris*, c. 1806; P, I, 231–3). 'Seraph' corresponds to love as the 'unseen seraph' of *Childe Harold* (p. 52). 'Heavenly dream' recalls Edleston as 'a dream of Heaven' (p. 32). 'Celestial' is in *To Thyrza* (p. 282) and the love-passage in

Childe Harold (p. 51). Byron's use of it matches Shakespeare's (*The Crown of Life*, 190–1).

Byron's instincts for protection and care were not limited to such as Edleston and Nicolo and Loukas; they were also apparent in his relation to the unprepossessing charwoman, Mrs. Mule (LBCV, 74), and the host of others for whose good he was active; and for society, and nations. What was happening is perfectly expressed in two of Shakespeare's Sonnets:

> Since I left you, mine eye is in my mind;
> And that which governs me to go about
> Doth part his function and is partly blind,
> Seems seeing, but effectually is out;
> For it no form delivers to the heart
> Of bird, of flower, or shape, which it doth latch:
> Of his quick objects hath the mind no part,
> Nor his own vision holds what it doth catch;
> For if it see the rud'st or gentlest sight,
> The most sweet favour or deformed'st creature,
> The mountain or the sea, the day or night,
> The crow or dove, it shapes them to your feature:
>   Incapable of more, replete with you,
>   My most true mind thus maketh mine untrue.

> Or whether doth my mind, being crown'd with you,
> Drink up the monarch's plague, this flattery?
> Or whether shall I say, mine eye saith true,
> And that your love taught it this alchymy,
> To make of monsters and things indigest
> Such cherubins as your sweet self resemble,
> Creating every bad a perfect best,
> As fast as objects to his beams assemble?
> O! 'tis the first, 'tis flattery in my seeing,
> And my great mind most kingly drinks it up:
> Mine eye well knows what with his gust is 'greeing,
> And to his palate doth prepare the cup:
>   If it be poison'd, 'tis the lesser sin
>   That mine eye loves it and doth first begin.
>   (Sonnets, 113 and 114)

The importance of these two sonnets can scarcely be over-emphasized. In the first the poet regards himself as blind, since he sees nothing properly. Instead of ugly forms he sees the one beauty. This comes from the *fulness* ('replete with you'; the 'most full flame' of Sonnet 115) which we have already discussed. The paradox is driven home: his 'most true mind', the mind of ultimate vision, has in effect led him into a seeming deception ('untrue'). This paradox is discussed in the second sonnet. Which is true? Is there some valid 'alchemy' at work, making 'cherubins' of 'monsters'? Though the poet decides that there must be some deception, that the sight makes the mind see what it *wants* to see, yet the final couplet states a reservation It means that if, in Byronic terms, the 'mind' is indeed 'diseas'd' by its own 'beauty' (*Childe Harold*, IV, 122; p. 52)—Byron and Shakespeare are thinking in identical terms—then the 'disease' or 'sin' is the less in that the 'eye' did actually experience this 'alchemy'; it did in fact see perfect beauty within the apparently ugly.

The alternation of introspective and personal agonies and external and communal concerns which we noted in *Childe Harold* corresponds to the expansionary movement within Shakespeare's Sonnets of which these two form the heart. In my chapter entitled 'The Expansion' in *The Mutual Flame* I argued that the last sequence of Fair Youth sonnets showed a gradual transition from the first vision to a more explicitly Platonic concentration on *the essence behind* rather than *the fact of* the loved one's excellence. The Youth's beauty fading, the poet looks back to what it was; he swears that he *will* be true to his love. He now sees this love-beauty everywhere; he claims that his love is now greater, not less (*The Mutual Flame*, 122–3). His 'most full flame' (Sonnet 115) has expanded, flooding the world's stage. The relation to Shakespeare's dramas is obvious; for in them all humanity, including Richard III, Iago, Lady Macbeth and Caliban, bears, as it were, the impress of its divine creator. Shakespeare is reporting the expansion of personal love to dramatic creation.

Therefore it is not strange that the sequence, apart from the final *envoi*, concludes with three sonnets (123, 124, and 125) of weighty and objective reference. In the first the poet opposes his love to the grandest monuments of the past; in the second to state affairs; in the third to high place. In all there is the will to assert his love's pre-eminence; but the co-presence of personal love and external grandeurs is none the less meaningful. When he writes

> It fears not policy, that heretic,
> Which works on leases of short-number'd hours,
> But all alone stands hugely politic,
> That it nor grows with heat, nor drowns with
>   showers   (124)

love is being momentarily *identified* with the political order. For a poetic instant it *is* state affairs, and that, throughout his life, is just what Byron, as in his *On the Star of The Legion of Honour,* tried to make it.

We have stated that the seraphic experience must be expressed either in tragical-visionary or in social-political terms. In Sonnet 123, where the poet asserts his love's power against great monuments, we have a sense of the eternal corresponding to Byron's different but related use of tombs and architectures in *Childe Harold* IV. But poetry is needed too:

> Not marble, nor the gilded monuments
> Of princes, shall outlive this powerful rhyme.
>   (Sonnet 55)

Rhyme: as in *Childe Harold* (pp. 37–9), poetry is the language of the higher, which is the tragic, dimension. Tragedy involves the past. The past is alive throughout the Sonnets; it, with its keywords 'antique' and 'antiquity,' is a prevailing theme (*The Mutual Flame,* 82). A numinous aura is conjured into being, whatever the explicit reasoning—which in the Sonnets is often subsidiary to a richer pur-pose—for which we have no better parallel than Byron's life-long concentration on the mystique of the past, in *Childe Harold* and else-where. Byron might be said to have written expansions, again and again, of this Shakespearian theme. The Sonnets, in their sense of beauty passing, in the haunting line 'bare ruin'd choirs where late the sweet birds sang' (Sonnet 73), in their attacks on time, are tragic documents; but in their conjuring up of great monuments as time's rivals and their sense of the yet greater powers of love's vision and poetry as its voice, they touch the eternal, the Youth living despite apparent death within the dimension to which poetry is a sure, if only provisional, approach:

> When wasteful war shall statues overturn,
> And broils root out the work of masonry,
> Nor Mars his sword nor war's quick fire shall burn
> The living record of your memory.
> 'Gainst death and all-oblivious enmity
> Shall you pace forth; your praise shall still find room
> Even in the eyes of all posterity
> That wear this world out to the ending doom.
>
> (Sonnet 55)

As I have shown in *The Mutual Flame* (85–6, 101–2) the reverbera-tion of such lines cannot be limited to their rational content, to the simple thought that future readers will hear of the poet's adoration. The 'living record' must be felt rather as a record of *what lives*. 'Pace forth': the youth's adolescent beauty comes before us as a vast, numi-nous, presence, with the accompaniment of the most terrible associa-tions ('the ending doom') that man may conceive. Nowhere else can we better attune ourselves to the fearful powers, despite its apparent fragility, of the seraphic intuition.

Such thought may serve as an introduction to Byron's greatest short poem, *On this Day I complete my Thirty-Sixth Year*, written at Missolonghi, for his birthday on 22 January 1824.[1] In it he describes a move from personal love to public service, and death. The tragic overtones natural to seraphic poetry attain a sharp, sacrificial drama-tization, all our relevant themes being contained:

> 'Tis time this heart should be unmov'd,
>   Since others it hath ceas'd to move:
> Yet, though I cannot be belov'd,
>   Still let me love!
>
> My days are in the yellow leaf;
>   The flowers and fruits of Love are gone;
> The worm, the canker, and the grief
>   Are mine alone!

1 The poem is included in my tape 'Byron's Rhetoric' published by *Sound Seminars*, Cincinnati (p. 14 above, note).

The fire that on my bosom preys
  Is lone as some volcanic isle;
No torch is kindled at its blaze—
  A funeral pile.

The hope, the fear, the jealous care,
  The exalted portion of the pain
And power of love, I cannot share,
  But wear the chain.

But 'tis not *thus*—and 'tis not *here*—
  Such thoughts should shake my soul, nor *now*,
Where glory decks the hero's bier,
  Or binds his brow.

The sword, the banner, and the field,
  Glory and Greece, around me see!
The Spartan, borne upon his shield,
  Was not more free.

Awake! (not Greece—she *is* awake!)
  Awake, my spirit! Think through *whom*
Thy life-blood tracks its parent lake,
  And then strike home!

Tread those reviving passions down,
  Unworthy manhood!—unto thee
Indifferent should the smile or frown
  Of Beauty be.

If thou regrett'st thy youth, *why live?*
  The land of honourable death
Is here:—up to the field, and give
  Away thy breath!

Seek out—less often sought than found—
  A soldier's grave, for thee the best;
Then look around, and choose thy ground,
  And take thy rest.

The transcendence of personal passion in the thought is accompanied by an impersonal artistry in the expression; and in both this poem is far superior to the subsequent, and less serene, *Love and Death;* while the tormented fragment *Last Words on Greece,* though powerful, is little more than a poetic spasm. The order of composition (p. 36) need not here concern us. It was natural that, beset by anxieties and his health failing, Byron should not in all moods have been able to maintain the control. His *Thirty-Sixth Year* correctly records what his total self willed and what in fact happened.

Nor does it apply only to Missolonghi. The poem is a tight condensation of Byron's will to expand the seraphic experience into noble action. In this it corresponds to what I have in *The Mutual Flame* called 'the expansion' recorded in Shakespeare's later Sonnets. The poetic modes may be different, and Shakespeare's aim was drama, whereas Byron's was life itself; but the comparison is valid. Byron's stanzas develop Shakespearian themes: the poet's age, felt as in Shakespeare's Sonnets, with in 'sere' a *Macbeth* (v, iii, 23) reminder together with a sense of loneliness and desertion corresponding to the Shakespearian lines; the tragic apprehension; the transition or expansion to state-affairs, and—as in *Hamlet*—to a martial end, here sacrifice for Greece, the land so well tuned both through its ancient culture and Byron's early experiences at Athens to Byron's central instincts. Rather strangely, because in so modern a vein, Byron regards these instincts as 'unworthy manhood', as harking back, perhaps, to school, or undergraduate, days; and it is true that he often appears to the biographer to be trying to prove himself to be sexually normal. The repudiation must, however, be read as no more than a needed step in the transition from personal desire to public service, corresponding to Shakespeare's sense, in Sonnet 115, of his early love as a 'babe' becoming mature through the 'full growth' of the expansion. But the original is not, somehow, lost; it is still active, within, as Shakespeare makes abundantly clear. Byron looked back to his youth, honouring its emotions. The 'heart of man' at 'eighteen' was at its best (Blessington, XIII, 312). In *Detached Thoughts,* in 1821, he remembers how sad he was to leave school. At Cambridge 'I was so completely alone in this new world that it half broke my spirits.' The remembrance is ratified by the mature Byron:

I mingled with, and dined and supped, etc., with them; but, I know not how, it was one of the deadliest and heaviest feelings of my life to feel that I was no longer a boy. From that moment I began to grow old in my own esteem; and in my esteem age is not estimable.

(72; LJ, V, 445)

It was as though he were being severed from his soul; the soul of man *is* young, and youth reflects it. In another of his *Detached Thoughts* (118) is the famous lyric starting

Oh! talk not to me of a name great in story,
The days of our Youth are the days of our Glory,
And the myrtle and ivy of sweet two and twenty
Are worth all your laurels, though ever so plenty.

(LJ, V, 466)

And yet this very recognition, which again burns so strong in the anguished *Last Thoughts on Greece,* together with Byron's emphasis on young lovers in *Don Juan* and *The Island,* and his own, on occasion, light-hearted, boy spirits at Missolonghi, show that he did, in fact, remain young. For such as he there is no progress; there is only eternity; and within that ever-youthful eternity, which is also death, he knew that he, as—to use Shelley's brilliant phrase for him in *Adonais*—'the Pilgrim of Eternity', was already moving. Our story begins with the youthful poems of ideal friendship and herosim in *Hours of Idleness* and his love for Edleston, and at its conclusion Byron could have said with Shakespeare's Cassius, 'Where I did begin, there shall I end' (*Julius Caesar,* V, iii, 24). At Missolonghi the wheel comes full circle.

III

A REGENCY HAMLET

I

REFERRING TO what he had omitted from his Memoirs, Byron wrote that they were 'like the play of Hamlet— "the part of Hamlet omitted by particular desire" ' (Murray, 29 Oct. 1819; LJ, IV, 369). This seemingly careless witticism suggests a line of investigation of some importance, since the correspondences between Byron's life and Shakespeare's play may be used to enrich our understanding of both.

The fatherless Byron grew up in close association with a mother as difficult as himself, each enduring a dramatic interplay of antagonism and affection. As a youth Byron was anxious to break free from 'this maternal bondage' under a 'domestic tyrant'. He could be violently critical: she whom he should revere as his 'guide and instructor' shows a 'perversion of temper' corrupting his own, her 'harshness' being varied by 'ridiculous indulgence' (Augusta, 18 Aug. 1804; 6 Nov. 1805; Hanson, 13 Dec. 1805; LJ, I, 31, 81, 90). Byron's youthful criticisms correspond to Hamlet's at a slightly later age: each demands of his mother virtues she does not possess and suffers agonies of revulsion. And yet Byron wrote home regularly on his early travels: we must hold in mind both the affection, on which John Galt lays a heavy emphasis (Galt, XXV, 162), and the antagonism. After his Mother's death Byron's entanglement in family emotions was maintained through his association with his half-sister, Augusta Leigh. Hamlet's maternal obsession has been often enough stressed, and given the usual 'Oedipus' connotations. Without attempting any too precise a definition, we can say that both Hamlet and Byron show strong 'familial' tendencies.

Byron was by nature lonely and melancholy. Despite school and

73

university friendships and early love-affairs an autobiographical truth is conveyed by the stanzas 'to Inez' in *Childe Harold:*

> It is that settled, ceaseless gloom
> The fabled Hebrew wanderer bore;
> That will not look beyond the tomb,
> But cannot hope for rest before.

The supposed hero's life is blighted, like Hamlet's, by 'the Demon Thought' (*Childe Harold,* after 1, 84). Hamlet could, he says, 'be bounded in a nutshell and count myself a king of infinite space, were it not that I have bad dreams' (*Hamlet,* 11, ii, 264). Byron's experience was of the same nature. He tells us in *Childe Harold* of

> demons who impair
> The strength of better thoughts, and seek their prey
> In melancholy bosoms, such as were
> Of moody texture from their earliest day,
> And lov'd to dwell in darkness and dismay,
> Deeming themselves predestin'd to a doom
> Which is not of the pangs that pass away;
> Making the sun like blood, the earth a tomb,
> The tomb a hell, and hell itself a murkier gloom.
>
> (IV, 34)

Byron felt himself 'an isolated being on the earth' (Long, 16 April 1807; LJ, 11, 19, note), and despite his happier tendencies his wife, years later, was not far out in saying 'at heart you are the most melancholy of mankind; and often when apparently gayest' (*Detached Thoughts,* 1821; 73; LJ, v, 446). Sir Walter Scott thought that the 'proper language' of his features 'was that of melancholy' (quoted LJ, IV, 73, note). It was the romantic, Gothic, Byron so well described by John Galt as withdrawn, silent and wrapped in a mysterious gloom (Galt, VIII, 63), that first impressed itself on his contemporaries.

These tendencies were fearfully accentuated by bereavement. Hamlet lost his father and was shocked by his mother's hasty remarriage. On his return from his early travels, Byron was staggered by a succession of bereavements. His mother and some of his nearest friends, C. S. Matthews, J. Wingfield and John Edleston, were

74

dead. 'Some curse', he wrote, 'hangs over me and mine. My mother lies a corpse in this house; one of my best friends is drowned in a ditch.' This was Matthews who had 'perished miserably in the muddy waves of the Cam'. The various sorrows fell on him, as on Hamlet, 'within a month', this last phrase, together with 'one little month' in another letter, and the word 'muddy', all recalling *Hamlet*. Byron realizes, as the Queen and Claudius remind Hamlet, that we 'shall all one day pass along with the rest—the world is too full of such things, and our very sorrow is selfish'; but Hamlet's bitter 'Ay, madam, it *is* common', balancing Byron's 'too full', is the prevailing note (Scrope Davies; Hobhouse; Dallas; 7, 10, 12, Aug. 1811; LJ, I, 324–7; C, I, 44; *Hamlet*, I, ii, 145, 147; IV, vii, 184 ('muddy'); I, ii, 74). Though Byron had for long lived close to death, meditating in a graveyard at Harrow and keeping four skulls in his room at Newstead (Dallas, 12 Aug. 1811; LJ, I, 327), the corruption that had once been his mother remained 'incomprehensible'. Even so, like Hamlet after the experience of communing with his father's ghost, he can engage in 'a kind of hysterical merriment' which he cannot understand, and even laugh 'heartily', wondering the while at himself; and he engages in athletic exercise (Hobhouse, 10 Aug. 1811; C, I, 44).

Hamlet's loss of his father and grief at his mother's betrayal corresponds to Byron's loss of his single remaining parent and his friends, especially Matthews, whom, using a phrase from *Romeo and Juliet* (II, ii, 114), he calls the 'god' of Hobhouse's 'idolatry' (Hodgson, 22 Aug. 1811; LJ, I, 338). Hamlet's father was one on whom 'every god did seem to set his seal' (III, iv, 61–2). He was what human creation is always aiming at, but seldom achieves:

> He was a man. Take him for all in all
> I shall not look upon his like again.
>
> (I, ii, 187)

The thought is that of Antony over Brutus:

> His life was gentle, and the elements
> So mix'd in him that Nature might stand up
> And say to all the world, 'This was a man'.
>
> (*Julius Caesar*, V, v, 73)

Such intuitions are summed up in Hamlet's speech on man as a wondrous 'piece of work' in the creative scheme, angelic in 'action' and god-like in 'apprehension' (II, ii, 323-8). So too Matthews bore 'the stamp of immortality' as one 'created to display what the Creator *could make* his creatures'; and this man was now 'gathered into corruption' (Dallas, 7 Sept. 1811; LJ, II, 29). Later Byron was to praise William Windham as 'a man of action', seeing him as Mercutio or Hamlet's father, both conceived, if we remember Mercutio's aspersions on the new duelling, as persons of an *older order* of manliness: so an action of heroism, he writes, quoting from *Romeo and Juliet,* has sent 'that gallant spirit to aspire the skies'; he is gone, and Time 'shall not look upon his like again' (Journal, 24 Nov. 1813; LJ, II, 342-3; *Romeo and Juliet,* III, i, 123; *Hamlet,* I, ii, 188).

Hamlet sees his father's ghost and Byron thought on one occasion that he saw Matthews', soon after his death: 'I nearly dropped, thinking that it was his ghost'; but it turned out to be his brother (Murray, 9 Nov. 1820; LJ, V, 116). Byron was strongly aware of ghostly presences: 'Such a dream!—but she did not overtake me. I wish the dead would rest, however. Ugh! how my blood chilled . . .' (Journal, 23 Nov. 1813; LJ, II, 334; also 341). This was presumably his Mother. Hamlet too had 'bad dreams' (II, ii, 266).

Byron saw ghosts. In the year 1803 he saw one at Newstead. Moore writes:

> He used, at first, though offered a bed at Annesley, to return every night to Newstead, to sleep; alleging as a reason that he was afraid of the family pictures of the Chaworths—that he fancied 'they had taken a grudge to him on account of the duel, and would come down from their frames at night to haunt him'. At length, one evening, he said gravely to Miss Chaworth and her cousin, 'In going home last night I saw a *bogle*';—which Scotch term being wholly unintelligible to the young ladies, he explained that he had seen a *ghost,* and would not therefore return to Newstead that evening. From this time he always slept at Annesley during the remainder of his visit. . . .
>
> (Moore, I, 54 or III, 27)

The half-ruined Newstead was a ghostly place enough, with an aura of wronged sanctity lingering from the dissolution of the mona-

steries under Henry VIII. In 1814 Byron writes: 'The ghosts, however, and the gothics, and the waters, and the desolation, make it
very lively still' (Moore, 13 Aug. 1814; LJ, III, 126). As a gloss on
this letter Moore writes:

> It was, if I mistake not, during his recent visit to Newstead, that
> he himself actually fancied he saw the ghost of the Black Friar,
> which was supposed to have haunted the Abbey from the time
> of the dissolution of the monasteries . . . It is said that the
> Newstead ghost appeared, also, to Lord Byron's cousin, Miss
> Fanny Parkins, and that she made a sketch of him from memory.
>
> Moore, I, 576–7 or XXII, 262; notes)

As Moore notes, the experience was recaptured in *Don Juan*. But it,
or something very like it, was reflected earlier in *Lara* (1814).

In *Lara* the hero communes with the dead while his retainers hint
and gossip about those who are

> 'too discreetly wise
> To more than hint their knowledge in surmise;
> But if they would—they could'.
>
> (*Lara*, I, 9)

The correspondence with Hamlet's warning to his friends not to let
slip hints such as 'we could an if we would' (*Hamlet,* I, v, 176) is
exact. Lara undergoes ghostly experiences. He is in his Hall, by
night, surrounded by Gothic windows and pictured saints of more
than 'mortal' life. His own 'bristling locks' are themselves like those
of a 'spectre' with a grave-like 'terror'. Ghostly impressions pile up.
A shriek wakes his retainers, who find him unconscious, sabre half-
drawn, having fainted 'in more than nature's fear' (I, 11–13).

Afterwards Byron re-worked his Newstead memories into the
description of Norman Abbey in *Don Juan*. Through its ruins
sweeps an unearthly music of unknown cause which Byron claims
to have heard 'once perhaps too much' (XIII, 64). The Black Friar
appears to Juan. Byron prefaces its appearance by defending, with
reference to his personal experience, the reality of such phenomena
(XV, 95–6; XVI, 4–7; p. 303 below). His Ghost here has an authority
not unlike that of the Ghost in *Hamlet*. Each comes as an accusing
power, the one royal and the other ecclesiastical. Each has been

hideously dispossessed of his rights, each belongs to an older order
challenging from death the usurpation of the new. Here it is:

It was no mouse, but lo! a monk, array'd
　In cowl and beads, and dusky garb, appear'd,
Now in the moonlight, and now laps'd in shade,
　With steps that trod as heavy, yet unheard;
His garments only a slight murmur made;
　He mov'd as shadowy as the sisters weird,
But slowly; and as he pass'd Juan by,
Glanc'd, without pausing, on him a bright eye.

Juan was petrified; he had heard a hint
　Of such a spirit in these halls of old,
But thought, like most men, there was nothing in't
　Beyond the rumour which such spots unfold,
Coin'd from surviving superstition's mint,
　Which passes ghosts in currency like gold,
But rarely seen, like gold compar'd with paper.
And did he see this? or was it a vapour?

Once, twice, thrice pass'd, repass'd—the thing of air,
　Or earth beneath, or heaven, or t'other place;
And Juan gaz'd upon it with a stare,
　Yet could not speak or move; but, on its base
As stands a statue, stood: he felt his hair
　Twine like a knot of snakes around his face;
He tax'd his tongue for words, which were not granted,
To ask the reverend person what he wanted.

The third time, after a still longer pause,
　The shadow pass'd away—but where? the hall
Was long, and thus far there was no great cause
　To think his vanishing unnatural:
Doors there were many, through which, by the laws
　Of physics, bodies, whether short or tall,
Might come or go; but Juan could not state
Through which the spectre seem'd to evaporate.

He stood—how long he knew not, but it seem'd
　An age—expectant, powerless, with his eyes

78

Strain'd on the spot where first the figure gleam'd,
  Then by degrees recall'd his energies,
And would have pass'd the whole off as a dream,
  But could not wake; he was, he did surmise,
Waking already, and return'd at length
Back to his chamber, shorn of half his strength.

(XVI, 21–5)

We have a ballad on the ghost:

Amundeville is lord by day,
  But the Monk is lord by night . . .

(XVI, 40; v)

The enigma presses on Juan's distraught mind:

They little knew, or might have sympathis'd,
  That he the night before had seen a ghost,
A prologue which but slightly harmonis'd
  With the substantial company engross'd
By matter, and so much materialis'd,
  That one scarce knew at what to marvel most
Of two things—how (the question rather odd is)
Such bodies could have souls, or souls such bodies.

(XVI, 90)

When at the long poem's conclusion Juan is again confronted by night, beneath portraits mystically alive from the past, by what seems a ghost, and the conclusion takes a humorous twist, *this* ghost —though the earlier appearance was genuine enough—turning out to be an amorous duchess, every element of numbing terror has nevertheless again been given its poetry.

It is not surprising that phrase-reminders from the Ghost scenes of *Hamlet* occur in 'List, oh list', and 'Alas, poor ghost', though the context is trivial (XIII, 97; *Hamlet*, I, v; 22, 4); nor that Aurora Raby is soon after the real Ghost's appearance specifically designated as 'Shakespearian' (XVI, 48) in respect to her more than earthly insights (p. 287 below).

Juan's ghostly experience recaptures Byron's dating back to his youth at Newstead and setting the tone for his life-long concentration on the mystique of the past, on the ghostly, on death and on what

79

lies within or beyond death. Writing of Byron's belief in supernatural appearances, Lady Blessington said that 'he assumes a grave
and mysterious air when he talks on the subject, which he is fond of
doing, and has told me some extraordinary stories relative to Mr.
Shelley, who, he assures me, had an implicit belief in ghosts'. He
also told her that 'Shelley's spectre had appeared to a lady, walking
in a garden' (Blessington, II, 36–7). Of Hamlet I once, in *The Wheel
of Fire,* wrote that, after his first meeting with Death he moves
through the rest of the drama 'aureoled in its ghostly luminance'. The
statement would be equally true of Byron.

On the young Byron Newstead Abbey with all its past and
ancestral associations weighed heavily, exerting on him a kind of
paternal authority. Once he seems to have thought that his own
recent experiences of bereavement had reawakened the slumbering
dead. Of his old servant he wrote to Hobhouse on 15 December,
1811:

Joe Murray has been frightened by dreams and ghosts; it is
singular that he never superstitized for seventy-six years before.
All my affairs are going on very badly, and I must rebel too, if
they don't mend. I shall return to London for the meeting of
Parliament.

(C, I, 67)

The transition in thought may perhaps be allowed to suggest a
typically Byronic association of the occult and the political. Newstead and its pre-Reformation ghost, the Black Friar, symbolized the
authority of an older order; and throughout his life the past existed
as a semi-supernatural power variously countering and impelling his
revolutionary course.

If Byron was, as we are so often told, superstitious, his superstitions, like Shakespeare's, empower much of his greatest poetry; as
in his sense of a numinous past throughout *Childe Harold;* the ghosts
on the beleaguered battlements of Rome in *The Deformed Transformed;* the Doge's communing with the ancestral dead on the eve of
revolution in *Marino Faliero;* and the hero's nightmare contact with
his forbears in *Sardanapalus.* Byron was never himself for long free
from such over-watching presences. The philosophy of it is written

into *Manfred,* where the protagonist searches out death's meaning from study of graves and skulls, is able, like Lara, to commune with the dead, and is shown doing it (*Manfred,* II, ii, 79–83, 177; II, iv, 82–98; III, i, 34–9). Manfred, the 'enlightener of nations' (III, i, 107), is under the spell of

> The dead, but sceptred, Sovereigns, who still rule
> Our spirits from their urns.
>
> (III, iv, 40).

Among Byron's last works is *Cain,* patterned closely on *Hamlet.* The ruling thought throughout both is that of death. More—both dramas are dominated not only by the thought, but also by the *presence* of death. Cain visits the world of the dead.

We open with a scene showing Cain standing apart from his family's ceremonial of prayer and thanksgiving in which he cannot join because he is more sensitive than they to his parents' fall and the *new law of death.* His parents are disturbed:

> But thou, my eldest born? art silent still?
>
> (I, i, 26)

Cain's answers are curt as Hamlet's. Abel's 'Why wilt thou wear this gloom upon thy brow?' (I, i, 53) and Adah's 'Wilt thou frown even on me?' (I, i, 56) balance the Queen's

> Good Hamlet, cast thy nighted colour off,
> And let thine eye look like a friend on Denmark...
>
> (I, ii, 68)

Cain is, like Hamlet, half-paralyzed by a situation arising from his elders' sin, and in a state recalling the young Byron's 'Indeed the blows, followed each other so rapidly that I am yet stupid from the shock' (Hodgson, 22 Aug. 1811; LJ, I, 338); and to Hamlet's after his father's death, his mother's marriage, and his subsequent meeting with the Ghost. Cain's encounter with the supernatural follows his first appearance among his relatives in a manner distinctly reminiscent of Hamlet.

He meets Lucifer, a majestic figure—Bradley called the ghost in *Hamlet,* as indeed does Shakespeare, majestic—but with a bearing, again like Shakespeare's ghost, of 'sorrow' (*Cain,* I, i, 95; *Hamlet,* I, ii, 231). Like the old Hamlet, Lucifer has been overthrown by an opponent, though the circumstances were very different. He offers to initiate Cain into some of the mysteries of existence. Adah, Cain's wife, is disturbed, like Hamlet's companions, Horatio and Marcellus. Cain's 'Let him say on; him will I follow' and 'Lead on' (I, i, 525, 533) balance Hamlet's 'Then will I follow it' and 'Go on, I'll follow thee' (I, iv, 63, 79). The exit of Cain and Lucifer has on the stage the exact impact of the exit in *Hamlet,* the anxious Adah being left behind like Hamlet's similarly anxious companions. Hamlet's subsequent 'Whither wilt thou lead me?' (I, v, i) is matched by Lucifer's earlier 'Follow where I will lead thee' and Adah's anxious 'Whither?' (I, i, 322, 526).

There is in both incidents a sense of some great danger, the danger of the unknown. Shakespeare, in his usual manner, keeps as near as may be within concretely normal terms:

> What if it tempt you toward the flood, my lord,
> Or to the dreadful summit of the cliff
> That beetles o'er his base into the sea,
> And there assume some other horrible form,
> Which might deprive your sovereignty of reason,
> And draw you into madness? Think of it.
> The very place puts toys of desperation,
> Without more motive, into every brain
> That looks so many fathoms to the sea
> And hears it roar beneath.
>
> (I, IV, 69)

Cain will soon be introduced to appalling heights, and to a sea. In *Hamlet* these were just what we call 'part of the poetry'; it did not actually happen. In *Cain* it does. And yet, what is in Shakespeare concrete and particularized is also by Byron expanded and universalized. There is a process of interpretation: that is the easiest way to see what is happening.

Cain is taken on a metaphysical excursion which includes (i) space travel, which we shall discuss later (p. 307) and (ii) the past, living within a ghostly ocean. He had been asked by Lucifer 'Darest thou look on Death?' (I, i, 250), and in accepting the challenge shows the courage of Hamlet's decision to visit the battlements of Elsinore:

> I'll speak to it, though Hell itself should gape
> And bid me hold my peace.
>
> (I, ii, 244)

Cain's visit to Hades we shall also discuss later (p. 307). On his return his mental state serves as a valuable commentary on Hamlet's after the Ghost scenes. We have another, and peculiarly neat, example of Byron's relation to Shakespeare. What in Shakespeare is embedded in a human story and embodied in the opacities of a highly wrought poetic language is in Byron universalized and rationalized in a lucid and transparent diction. Think of Hamlet's address to the Ghost:

> What may this mean,
> That thou, dead corse, again in complete steel
> Revisit'st thus the glimpses of the moon,
> Making night hideous; and we fools of nature
> So horridly to shake our disposition
> With thoughts beyond the reaches of our souls?
>
> (I, iv, 51)

Cain's more universalized experience on his visit to Hades is again and again in his long dialogues with Lucifer conceived as an experience straining his uttermost comprehension. On his return he tells Abel of it:

> Abel   Where hast thou been?
> Cain: I know not.
> Abel: Nor what thou hast seen?
> Cain: The dead—
> The Immortal—the Unbounded—the Omnipotent—
> The overpowering mysteries of space—
> The innumerable worlds that were and are—
> A whirlwind of such overwhelming things,
> Suns, moons, and earths, upon their loud-voic'd spheres
> Singing in thunder round me, as have made me
> Unfit for mortal converse: leave me, Abel!

Abel: Thine eyes are flashing with unnatural light—
Thy cheek is flush'd with an unnatural hue—
Thy words are fraught with an unnatural sound—
What may this mean?
Cain: It means—I pray thee, leave me.

(III, i, 176)

This helps us to understand what is behind Hamlet's appearance to
Ophelia 'as if he had been loosed out of Hell to speak of horrors' (II,
i, 83). Cain's 'I pray thee, leave me', springs from a mind-state
corresponding to Hamlet's in his 'nunnery' scene with Ophelia.
There are, of course, differences in tone and detail, but both Hamlet
and Cain are rendered 'unfit for mortal converse' through an other-
worldly initiation.

Both, too, are forced into bloody actions by their very virtues.
Hamlet becomes distracted, anti-social, and murderous. Cain's
quarrel with Abel arises from his horror of the blood-law, the death-
law, in a tyrant god's creation, and his consequent refusal to engage
with Abel in a blood-sacrifice.

The ruling impression throughout both is Death, starting with
the death of Hamlet's murdered father and the punishment of death
pronounced on mankind through the sins of Cain's parents, Adam
and Eve; personal in the one and universal in the other, but of
similar impact on the hero.

Byron's *Manfred* (1817) is preluded by the quotation of Hamlet's

There are more things in heaven and earth, Horatio,
Than are dreamt of in your philosophy.

(I, v, 166)

The heading would have been even more apt for *Cain*. The lines
condense very exactly the gist of Lucifer's conversations with Cain.

Cain is a later work, but the experience behind it is the experience
of the young Byron at the Harrow graveyard and the ghostly Newstead. From then on his story resembles Hamlet's. His journals are
used as Hamlet uses soliloquy to 'unpack' his 'heart' with 'words'
(*Hamlet*, II, ii, 622):

This journal is a relief. When I am tired—as I generally am—
out comes this, and down goes every thing.

(6 Dec. 1813; LJ, II, 366)

They are full of Shakespearian reminiscence. Here are some from *Hamlet:*

> I am now six-and-twenty; my passions have had enough to cool them; my affections more than enough to wither them— and yet—and yet—always *yet* and *but*—'Excellent well, you are a fishmonger'—'Get thee to a nunnery'—'They fool me to the top of my bent.'
>
> (18 Feb. 1814; LJ, II, 383; *Hamlet*, II, ii, 174; III, i, 144; III, ii, 408)

Death is a favourite theme. In a letter to Francis Hodgson on 3 September 1811 he had opposed immortality, introducing an argument with 'argal' and saying 'I argue like the Gravedigger' (LJ, II, 21; *Hamlet*, V, i, 13, 20, 53); though he does not question the existence of God (Gifford, 18 June 1813; LJ, II, 221-2). In his 1813-1814 Journal he quotes from *Hamlet:*

> My restlessnes tells me I have something 'within that passeth show'. It is for Him, who made it, to prolong that spark of celestial fire which illuminates, yet burns, this frail tenement; but I see no such horror in a 'dreamless sleep', and I have no conception of any existence which duration would not render tiresome.
>
> (27 Nov. 1813; LJ, II, 351-2; *Hamlet*, I, ii, 85; III, i, 60-8)

Do we not all love 'a sleep without dreams, (*Don Juan*, XIV, 4)? Thinking no doubt of Hamlet's 'country from whose bourne no traveller returns' (III, i, 79)—to which he refers in *Don Juan* (VIII, 41) as that 'somewhat misty bourne which Hamlet tells us is a pass of dread'—he wonders:

> Is there anything beyond?—*who* knows? *He* that can't tell. Who tells that there *is*? He who don't know. And when shall he know? Perhaps when he don't expect, and generally when he don't wish it.
>
> (Journal, 18 Feb. 1814; LJ, II, 385)

Later he grew more positive, concluding that mind is immortal and able to affect matter directly (pp. 303-4 below). Again and again

Byron probes the problem of death in the mood of Hamlet's famous soliloquy. In *Don Juan* he records how he saw the corpse of a murdered military commander. He 'thought or said'

> 'Can this be Death? then what is Life or Death?
> Speak!' but he spoke not: 'wake!' but still he slept—
> But yesterday, and who had mightier breath? . . .
>
> (v, 36)

Byron tells us that he

> gaz'd (as oft I have gaz'd the same)
> To try if I could wrench aught out of Death
> Which should confirm, or shake, or make a faith.
>
> (v, 38)

Like Hamlet, he is baffled:

> But it was all a mystery. Here we are,
>   And there we go:—but *where*? five bits of lead,
> Or three, or two, or one, send very far!
>   And is this blood, then, form'd but to be shed?
> Can every element our elements mar?
>   And Air—Earth—Water—Fire live—and we dead?
> *We*, whose minds comprehend all things? No more.
> But let us to the story as before.
>
> (v, 39)

'No more' is from Hamlet's 'To be or not to be' soliloquy (III, i, 61). Once as an example of the 'fulness' of Shakespeare's finest passages he chose this soliloquy, which in its interweaving of the themes of being, action, death and suicide was certainly the perfect example for his purpose. (Note to *Childe Harold,* IV, 75.) Shakespeare's phrase 'to be' fascinated him:

> 'To be or not to be?'—Ere I decide,
>   I should be glad to know that which *is being*.
> 'Tis true we speculate both far and wide,
>   And deem, because we *see*, we are *all-seeing*:
> For my part, I'll enlist on neither side,
>   Until I see both sides for once agreeing.
> For me, I sometimes think that Life is Death,
> Rather than Life a mere affair of breath.
>
> (*Don Juan,* IX, 16)

These thoughts all go back to Byron's youth. Looking in 1811 on his dead mother he had doubted 'whether I *was,* or whether she *was not*' (Hobhouse, 10 Aug. 1811; C, I, 44).

Like Hamlet, Byron thinks from time to time of suicide, the thought occurring as early as his boyhood letters to Augusta. After his ghostly nightmare he threatened to try 'whether *all* sleep has the like visions', the suicide-thought following Hamlet's 'for in that sleep of death what dreams may come' (Journal, 23 Nov. 1813; LJ, II, 335; *Hamlet,* III, i, 66). He knew Hamlet's fear that 'the last sleep' might contain nightmare (Blessington, VII, 165). His wife feared that he might commit suicide during the troubles leading to the separation. He was near suicide in 1816:

> I should, many a good day, have blown my brains out, but for the recollection that it would have given pleasure to my mother-in-law; and even *then,* if I could have been certain to haunt her . . .
>
> (Moore, 28 Jan. 1817; LJ, IV, 49)

He repeated the thought, saying that he also feared a verdict of lunacy from—thinking of *Hamlet* (V, i, 23)—the 'Crowner's Quest' (Murray, 9 April 1817; LJ, IV, 98).

In both there is a turning inward, as from life itself, expressed in Byron by his strong anti-physical tendencies. He is a mind at war with his body. His diet was generally vegetarian (Mrs. Byron, 25 June; Hobhouse, 17 Nov.; Hodgson, 8 Dec.; 1811; LJ, I, 311; C, I, 61; LJ, II, 87; Galt, VIII, 62). Often he lived on tea or soda-water and biscuits and then a normal dinner upset him (Journal, 5 and 6 Dec. 1813; 10 April 1814; LJ, II, 360–1, 366, 411). He was afraid of obesity (Long, also Pigot; April, 1807; LJ, II, 19; I, 127, 290, with notes), but another motive was the belief that meat aroused dangerous passions (Journal, 17 Nov. 1813; LJ, II, 327–8). These habits, to which we shall return (p. 127 below), continued, with intermittent exceptions, throughout his life, and caused anxiety to his friends on his last expedition to Greece. He was a spiritualized, intellectual, type. 'By starving his body', wrote E. J. Trelawny, 'Byron kept his brains clear' (Trelawny, VI, 44). William Parry said that he lived more on 'thought' than on 'food', and regarded him as

'more a mental being' than 'any man I ever saw' (Parry, v, 107).
Byron could resent the dependence of intellect on food (*Don Juan*,
v, 32).

There was in him, as in Hamlet, a strong moralizing, puritanical,
strain, perhaps derived from his Calvinistic upbringing (Gifford,
18 June 1813; LJ, II, 222), and directed against both himself and
others. He could no more 'trust' himself than others with a 'good
motive'; if he is slandered, 'Am I not in reality much worse than
they make me?' (Lady Melbourne, 28 Sept. 1813; March 1814; C, I,
183, 247). His view of human nature—'Curse on Rochefoucault for
being always right!' (Journal, 1 Dec. 1813; LJ, II, 359)—corresponds
to Hamlet's 'Use every man after his desert, and who should 'scape
whipping?' (II, ii, 561), and

> I am myself indifferent honest; but yet I could accuse me of such
> things that it were better my mother had not borne me. I am
> very proud, revengeful, ambitious; with more offences at my
> beck than I have thoughts to put them in, imagination to give
> them shape, or time to act them in. What should such fellows
> as I do crawling between heaven and earth? We are arrant
> knaves all; believe none of us.
>
> (III, i, 125)

'Crawling': Byron too could see himself as an 'insect'; he has long
'despised' both himself and mankind (Journal, 9 and 19 April 1814;
LJ, II, 409, 412). Moore refers to 'the perverse fancy he had for
falsifying his own character, and even imputing to himself faults the
most alien to his nature' (Moore, II, 272 or XXXVI, 422).

He was a severe critic of society. His disapproval of the new
waltzing on moral grounds makes an early poem *The Waltz* (1813),
which includes a satiric description of the Prince Regent reminding
us of Hamlet's criticism of the drinking and dancing in Claudius'
court:

> The King doth wake tonight and takes his rouse,
> Keeps wassail, and the swaggering up-spring reels;
> And as he drains his draughts of Rhenish down,
> The kettle-drum and trumpet thus bray out
> The triumph of his pledge.
>
> (I, iv, 8)

From youth on, Byron makes bitter comments on contemporary morals, seeing the literary and social worlds as, in Hamlet's phrase, 'penetrable stuff' to his thrusts (*English Bards and Scotch Reviewers,* 1050; *Hamlet,* III, iv, 36). He could never 'share in the commonplace libertinism' of Cambridge 'without disgust'; he may himself fall, but he 'hates' it; he takes no pleasure in 'fashionable dissipation'; his friends' amours repel him; sickened by vice, he learns the value of love (*Detached Thoughts,* 1821; 72; Hanson, 23 Nov. 1805 and 18 Nov. 1808; Harness, 15 Dec. 1811; Hoppner, 2 July 1819; LJ, V, 446; I, 85; I, 199; II, 91; IV, 326).

After Byron's return from the East, 'no anchorite', wrote Moore, was more averse to sensuous allurements than he (Moore, I, 202 or IX, 95). Though that does not tell the whole truth of Byron, it tells a part, and the strain persisted, rising to fierce moral denunciation in the *Ode on Venice* and the conclusion of *Marino Faliero.* Though Byron was, as he readily admitted, himself guilty, Hamlet was probably no saint either. He could attack Ophelia and his mother with neurotic frenzy, but himself appears to have been a full-blooded Renaissance man, normally assiduous at athletic exercise (II, ii, 315; V, ii, 221) and ready enough to engage in bawdy talk (as at II, ii, 243–4; III, ii, 126); and perhaps Laertes had reason to warn Ophelia against his advances.

II

Both Hamlet and Byron are happy in male companionship. Mixed parties Byron rejects with a Hamlet reminiscence: 'I'll none of it' (Journal, 10 March 1813; and see 12 Dec. 1813 and 20 March 1814; LJ, II, 398–9, 374, 402; *Hamlet,* III, i, 155). But Hamlet's welcoming of Horatio and afterwards of Rosencrantz and Guildernstern show a friendliness exactly Byronic. John Cam Hobhouse was a devoted university friend, Byron's Horatio; intellectual, yet steady, almost stolid, more scholar than poet, of advanced politics and conventional morals, he recalls Hamlet's high praise of Horatio, and if he does not quite deserve it, it is likely that Horatio did not either. Byron, rocked by diverse impulses, must often throughout his life have admired, and relied on, Hobhouse as a man of 'judgment' who 'is not

passion's slave' (*Hamlet*, III, ii, 74, 77). In gayer moods Thomas
Moore suited him better, or the 'dashing vivacity' of Scrope Davies,
always so 'full of pleasaunt mirth' (Dallas, 7 Sept.; Hobhouse,
15 Dec.; 1811; LJ, II, 29; C, I, 66). Scrope was Byron's Yorick:

> I have solaced myself moderately with such 'flagons of Rhenish'
> as have fallen in my way, but without our Yorick they are
> nothing.
> (Hobhouse, 16 May 1816; C, II, 7–8; *Hamlet*, V, i, 196)

Once, comparing him with a dull man of sterling virtue, as 'the life
and soul of me, and everybody else' Byron concludes with the words
of that precursor of Hamlet the melancholy Jaques, 'Motley's the
only wear'; and when Scrope is gone he comments, like Hamlet over
Yorick's skull, 'I shall never hear such jokes again' (Hobhouse, 20
Sept. 1811; 11 May 1820; C, I, 47; II, 148; *As You Like It*, II, vii,
34). We remember: 'Where be your jibes now? your gambols? your
songs? your flashes of merriment, that were wont to set the table on a
roar?' (*Hamlet*, V, i, 207).

Elsewhere, writing to Lady Melbourne on 18 September 1812,
Byron inexactly quotes from Jaques:

> O that I were a fool, a motley fool;
> I am ambitious of a motley coat.
> (C, I, 81; *As You Like It*, II, vii, 13, 42–3)

Jaques wanted motley as a medium for social attack. So was it, often
enough, with Byron; and here we must widen our discussion.
Byron's resentment at maternal tyranny widened to a life-long campaign against political tyrannies. *Lara* is a study in personal anguish,
but the hero is also a political revolutionary. Byron's mental torment
has its political extensions and implications. He was bitterly critical
of current politics. Three times (1812–13) in the House of Lords he
attacked the ruling powers, arousing their hostility and mistrust,
and being the more dangerous for his rank and the success of *Childe
Harold*. However, he was quickly dissatisfied by the ineffectuality of
speeches. Life was out-of-joint:

> A king who *can't*, a Prince of Wales who *don't*,
> Patriots who shan't, and Ministers who *won't*,

What matters who are *in* or *out* of place,
The *Mad*, the *Bad*, the *Useless* or the *Base*?
(Lady Melbourne, 21 Sept. 1813; C, I, 182)

Of these discontents, the Prince Regent was the obvious symbol and in 1812 Byron published in the *Morning Chronicle* an anonymous eight-line attack on him, 'Weep, daughter of a royal line . . .' Soon after the Regent made a point of meeting the young and popular poet. Though Byron was impressed by his courtesy, he deliberately reprinted his attack under his own name, appending it to the second edition of *The Corsair* in 1814, with explosive effect (LBCV, III, 138–40). Byron's refusal to respond to the kindly approaches of royalty from sense of a deep-seated iniquity that could not be veiled by manners matches Hamlet's relations with Claudius.

And yet, like Hamlet, he was impotent. Disillusion regarding 'parliamentary mummeries' (Journal, 14 Nov. 1813; LJ, II, 318) had left him limp, unable to 'stimulate' himself to help a petitioner:

Ah, I am as bad as that dog Sterne, who preferred whining over 'a dead ass to relieving a living mother'—villain—hypocrite—slave—sycophant! but *I* am no better . . . Curse on Rochefoucault for being always right!
(Journal, 1 Dec. 1813; LJ, II, 359)

We remember Hamlet's soliloquy 'Now I am alone'—Byron often itches for aloneness in his library (e.g. Journal, 10 April 1814; LJ, II, 410)—with its self-accusations 'Am I a coward?' and 'Who calls me villain?' (*Hamlet*, II, ii, 606–7). In society Byron had outbursts of unnatural hilarity like the hysteria he observed in himself at the time of his bereavements. When, soon after the hornet's nest aroused by the admission of his attack on the Prince Regent, he went to dinner with the Princess of Wales, he records that 'The "damnable faces" (as Hamlet says) of the whole party threw me into a convulsion of uncourtly laughter', which he had to strangle with his handkerchief (Lady Melbourne, 25 April 1814; C, I, 252; *Hamlet*, III, ii, 267).

Byron shows a mixture of impudence and self-accusation, of pride and humility. To intimates he is open, but for the world he adopts, as did Hamlet in putting on an 'antic disposition' (*Hamlet*, I, v, 172), a mask: 'I have', he wrote, 'a part to play'; his 'insolence'

91

—like Hamlet's semi-mad behaviour—was only in part deliberate and 'almost natural' (Lady Melbourne, 29 April 1814; C, I, 254). Despite violent opposition he refused compromise. His lampoon was to be discussed in the House of Lords:

To complete the farce, the Morning Papers this day announce the intention of some zealous Rosencrantz or Guildernstern to 'play upon his pipe' in our house of hereditaries.
(Lady Melbourne, 11 Feb. 1814; C, I, 243; Hamlet, III, ii 373)

Press attacks leave him inactive. He has, quoting Hamlet, 'that within me' that is unafraid; 'All these externals are nothing to *that within*'; and he takes no pleasure 'in torturing earwigs', a phrase to be compared with Hamlet's use of 'water-fly' for Osric (Lady Melbourne, 11 Feb. and March 1814; C, I, 243–4, 247; *Hamlet*, I, ii, 85, v, ii, 84; for 'externals', *Richard II*, IV, i, 296).

The political relationship to *Hamlet* is closer than might be supposed. Byron's earliest poems are tuned to an old-world, classic heroism. The Newstead ghost represented a pre-Reformation order. Byron was deeply imbued with the mystique of the past and had enduring sympathies with Catholicism. To him England under the new constitutional monarchy may well have seemed, like the Queen in *Hamlet*, to have left a past greatness for a decadent present under pigmy kings controlled by dangerous cliques. Claudius' virtues include manners as fine as the Regent's, a pacific diplomacy and a constitutional reliance on the 'better wisdoms' of his advisers (I, ii, 15); there would appear to be an advance on the fierce old warrior-king in his 'angry parle' smiting 'the sledded Polacks on the ice' (I, i, 62); and yet the new regime secretes a deception, an evil. Nor is religious help available. Claudius' useless prayer of repentance is conceived—as is Laertes' attack on the Priest (v, i, 262–4)—in what might be called 'Protestant' terms in contrast to the more traditional eschatology of Hamlet's following speech on damnation (III, iii, 36–98) and the Catholic toning of the Ghost scenes. Since the new British order was based on the blood of Stuart royalty Hamlet's

Almost as bad, good mother,
As kill a king and marry with his brother . . .
(III, iv, 28)

might be Byron addressing his country. Byron was descended from the royal family of the Stuarts (pp. 334–5, 338, below). Charles I, he once said, was 'the greatest *king* (that is, villain) that ever lived'; and his own 'bad blood' he attributed to those 'bastards of Banquo' (Lady Melbourne, 7 April 1813; C, I, 147). Charles I had at least been a real king: that is the point, developed by Byron later in his study of the fiery warrior-Doge in *Marino Faliero*, chafing under the control of a vicious oligarchy. After thinking of the proposed strictures on him in the House of Lords, Byron remembers his 'pedigree' (Journal, 18 Feb. 1814; LJ, II, 382). On his departure from England he left a ring containing the hair of a royal ancestor— according to Merchand (II, 599) Charles I's—for his child (Lady Byron, April 1816; LJ, III, 281). Southey and Wordsworth he re- garded much as Hamlet regarded Rosencrantz and Guildernstern, men who 'sponge'-like soak up the new king's 'favours' (*Hamlet*, IV, ii, 15). Of Southey he wrote;

> I was born of the aristocracy, which he abhorred; and am sprung, by my mother, from the kings who preceded those whom he has hired himself to sing.
>
> ('*Blackwood's* Defence'; LJ, IV, App. ix, 483)

To the last he remembered 'through whom' his 'life-blood' traced its descent (*On this Day I complete my Thirty-Sixth Year*). Byron was no propagandist for royalty, but he knew that it had once held a validity to which contemporary monarchs offered no real equivalent; and something of the old essence he felt active in himself. While rejecting the suave exteriors of their respective societies and yet ill- tuned to violence, both Hamlet and Byron are trying to focus some new and finer order in descent from religious tradition and the heroic past.

Byron's ambitions were unique. Hamlet complained that he lacked 'advancement', though in other moods he could be 'bounded in a nutshell' and count himself 'king of infinite space' were it not that he had 'bad dreams' (*Hamlet*, III, ii, 361; II, ii, 264). Once Byron told Hobhouse that he had 'no ambition left'; ambition might awake him; as it is, 'I merely start in my sleep' (Hobhouse, 23 Aug. 1819; C, II, 124). But that was not the whole truth. He could also write, 'I have no ambition; at least, if any, it would be *"aut Caesar aut nihil"* ' (Journal, 23 Nov. 1813; LJ, II, 338–9). That, tersely, was the truth.

Britain's monarchy was only one among a number of effete monarchies throughout Europe, and Byron thought and felt as a European. His 'detestation of all existing governments' and desire for a 'universal republic' (Journal, 16 Jan. 1814; LJ, II, 381) goes well beyond Britain. When deploring his country's war with Napoleon he quotes against himself 'Brutus, thou sleepest' (Journal, 18 Feb. 1814; LJ, II, 384; *Julius Caesar,* II, i, 46). Ought he not to act, not only for Britain, but for all Europe? Anxiously he followed the fortunes of Napoleon, whom both he and Hobhouse (Journal, 18 Feb. 1814; LJ, II, 383) admired. Napoleon was Byron's Fortinbras, always on his horizon as the man of action shaming the more finely-tuned introvert of ineffectual profundities. He could see, and in his poetry diagnosed (*Childe Harold,* III, 36–45; *Ode to Napoleon Buonaparte,* 1814), the faults, but at least Napoleon stood for action against moribund dynasties (LBCV, III, 153–160). At his abdication Byron was in distress. 'Napoleon Buonaparte has abdicated the throne of the world. "Excellent well" . . .' Hamlet's phrase here carries a bitter irony. Though himself an 'insect' compared with Napoleon, Byron believes, thinking of suicide, that even he could have struck a nobler gesture than this miserable retreat, concluding with Hamlet's 'Something too much of this' (Journal, 9 April 1814; LJ, II, 409–10; *Hamlet,* II, ii, 174; III, ii, 79). His next entry registers despair. His faith in man is in shreds. *Hamlet* is scarcely adequate. The conclusion, that 'the Bourbons are restored', is accompanied by violent quotations from *Macbeth* and *King Lear* (Journal, 19 April 1814; LJ, II, 411–12; p. 3 above).

He did, however, establish contact with social normality in two ways, one romantic and the other artistic. Among his many loves heterosexual, homosexual and familial, one alone blended social normality with ideal fervour: this was his youthful love for Mary Anne Chaworth, who rejected him, as Ophelia rejected Hamlet. Henceforth she remained to Byron a symbol of what might have been. In his *Epistle to a Friend,* in 1811, Byron prophesied that Mary's rejection might make him end up as one of 'the worst anarchs of the age'; her love was as his life-line, now broken. So too in *Hamlet* the Queen had hoped that Ophelia might prove Hamlet's saviour (III, i, 40–2; V, i, 266).

Mary's subsequent lot was as unhappy as Ophelia's, and Byron's poem *The Dream,* written in 1816, describes it. First we have the youthful love, followed by the parting in an 'antique Oratory' recalling Ophelia's 'orizons' in Hamlet's scene with Ophelia (III, i, 89). The boy's actions, the controlled anguish, are Hamlet's:

> He rose, and with a cold and gentle grasp
> He took her hand; a moment o'er his face
> A tablet of unutterable thoughts
> Was trac'd, and then it faded, as it came;
> He dropp'd the hand he held, and with slow steps
> Retir'd . . .
>
> (III)

Byron may be remembering a performance of *Hamlet*. The lines recall both Ophelia's description of Hamlet's visit to her in distraction and his behaviour at their subsequent meeting. Byron's fateful marriage is described, his thoughts still on 'the Starlight of his Boyhood' (VI); and then comes Mary's unhappy life and subsequent insanity. The vein is pure *Hamlet:*

> Oh! she was chang'd
> As by the sickness of the soul; her mind
> Had wander'd from its dwelling, and her eyes
> They had not their own lustre, but the look
> Which is not of the earth; she was become
> The Queen of a fantastic realm; her thoughts
> Were combinations of disjointed things;
> And forms, impalpable and unperceiv'd
> Of others' sight, familiar were to hers.
> And this the world calls frenzy . . .
>
> (VII)

Compare from *Hamlet* these words on Ophelia:

> . . . speaks things in doubt
> That carry but half sense: her speech is nothing,
> Yet the unshaped use of it doth move

The hearers to collection; they aim at it,
And botch the words up fit to their own thoughts.

(IV, v, 6)

'The wise', Byron's poem tells us, endure 'a far deeper madness',
being 'melancholy' through too close a view of 'truth' stripping the
veil of 'fantasies' from 'cold reality' (VII). Such was the madness of
Hamlet and Byron in contrast to Ophelia's and Mary's. How deep
and enduring Byron's love of Mary was may be questioned, but he
for long, as in his poem *The Duel* (1818; P, IV, 542-4; see LBM,
123-4), liked to regard it so, with as much or as little sincerity as
Hamlet's

> I lov'd Ophelia. Forty thousand brothers
> Could not, with all their quantity of love,
> Make up my sum.

(v, i, 291)

Byron was generally as ready as Hamlet to cap such extravagances of
'rant' (v, i, 306) with a disclaimer; but he may have felt deeply about
Mary's insanity. Hamlet was, of course, himself responsible for
Ophelia's. Byron, without such responsibility, nevertheless deplored
the extraordinary ill fortune that appeared to overtake anyone he
loved (Hoppner, 2 July 1819; LJ, IV, 325; and see LBM, 127);
his 'embrace', like Manfred's, was 'fatal' (*Manfred*, II, i, 87; II, ii,
118-19).

Despite their anti-social propensities, Hamlet and Byron had the
potentiality of social grace. In Hamlet Ophelia (III, i, 159-70) saw,
as we can see in Byron, 'the courtier's, soldier's, scholar's, eye, tongue,
sword', all cast in a mould of visible perfection; Moore used her
phrase 'sweet bells jangled out of tune' as an apt description of Byron
(*Hamlet*, III, i, 167; Moore I, 186 or VIII, 88); and Byron himself in
his *Monody on the death of Sheridan* (1816) wrote bitterly of

> Men who exult when minds of heavenly tone
> Jar in the music which was born their own.

In a conversation with Lady Blessington on this poem Byron's
reported words, 'Poor Sherry! what a noble mind was in him overthrown by poverty!' (Blessington, IX, 217), refer back to Ophelia's

speech. Byron was for a while fashion's darling, one who, in his wife's clever lines,

makes all the envious Dandys despair
By the cut of his shirt and the curl of his hair.
(LJ, III, 291)

True, he once said that he was but 'a miserable beau at the best of times'; but Hamlet might have said the same, and years later his recollection was more favourable (Lady Melbourne, 21 Sept. 1813; C, I, 182; *Detached Thoughts*, 1821; 29; LJ, V, 423). Women—in the style of Ophelia's 'O what a noble mind is here o'erthrown'— would murmur of Byron 'What a pity it is!' (quoting Countess Albrizzi, LJ, IV: App. ii, 443; *Hamlet*, III, i, 159).

Whatever their own failures to maintain grace and poise, both Byron and Hamlet sustain themselves by images of a more than human excellence such as Byron recognized in the loved chorister Edleston as 'a dream of Heaven' and the boys in Greece as 'sylphs'; in freedom's banner coloured like a 'seraph's eyes'; and in the 'unseen seraph' of *Childe Harold*, luring and tormenting man with its unrealizable beauty (*If Sometimes in the Haunts of Men;* Hobhouse, 23 Aug. 1810; C, I, 14; *On the Star of The Legion of Honour*, P, III, 437; *Childe Harold*, IV, 121). These touch Hamlet's intermittent intuitions of man angelic in action, god-like in apprehension, and Mercurial in grace (*Hamlet*, II, ii, 325–7; III, iv, 58; and see my *The Wheel of Fire*, enlarged, second appendix, on Shakespeare's angels).

Since such seraphic insights are evanescent and hard to possess, one is forced back on art. Byron found a reasonable equivalent in sculpture, especially the Apollo Belvedere (*Childe Harold,* IV, 161–3; *The Prophecy of Dante*, IV, 25–33; pp. 48–50); and in the sylph-like, almost bisexually conceived, person of his Juan, praised for his dancing and grace of manner (*Don Juan*, XIV, 38–40; XV, 12–15). But both Hamlet and Byron found their most practical equivalent *in the art of acting*. Hamlet's gloom is dispelled by the arrival of the Players; they arouse him to action; and some of his best thought is in his speech to them counselling a balance of passion and temperance generally unattainable in life, though basic to acting. This, at least, is something to believe in, and hold on to. So, too, was it with Byron.

He won honour for declamation and gesture at Harrow. In his *Detached Thoughts* (1821; 88) he writes:

My qualities were much more oratorical and martial than poetical; and Dr. D., my grand patron (our head-master) had a great notion that I should turn out an Orator, from my fluency, my turbulence, my voice, my copiousness of declamation, and my action.

(LJ, v, 453)

Dr. Drury's own recollections bear out Byron's statement (LJ, I, 28–9, note). Byron was also a good amateur actor, engaging in some performances at Southwell in 1806, in which he won a considerable success: 'Byron, who was the star of the company, repeatedly brought down the house by his acting' (LJ, I, 118, note, and see *Detached Thoughts*, 71; LJ, v, 445). During preparations for a performance of *Othello* in Italy wherein he was to play Iago, Byron showed his histrionic powers: 'His voice had a flexibility, a variety in its tones, a power and pathos beyond any I ever heard; and his countenance was capable of expressing the tenderest as well as the strongest emotions' (Medwin, 160–1). Hamlet's declamation and 'action' were praised by Polonius (II, ii, 497–8).

Acting was Byron's favourite among the arts and his comments on the first actors of his day, Kemble, Kean and Cooke, in letters and reported conversations, are keen and pointed. In *Detached Thoughts* (56) he wrote: 'Of actors, Cooke was the most natural, Kemble the most supernatural, Kean a medium between the two, but Mrs. Siddons worth them all put together' (LJ, v, 437). He found Kemble's Coriolanus 'glorious' (Harness, 15 Dec. 1811; LJ, II, 90). His admiration for Kean was strong. Of his Iago he wrote:

Was not Iago perfection? particularly the last look. I was *close* to him (in the orchestra), and never saw an English countenance half so expressive.

I am acquainted with no *im*material sensuality so delightful as good acting; and, as it is fitting there should be good plays, now and then, besides Shakespeare's, I wish you or Campbell would write one:—the rest of 'us youth' have not heart enough.

(Moore, May 1814; LJ, III, 81; *1 Henry IV*, II, ii, 93)

Byron's many comments on Kean (e.g., LJ, II, 385-7; III, 45; C, I, 281) have flash and point.

The acting scenes in *Hamlet* are remembered when he refers in a poetic discussion to Polonius' comment on the Players' lines, 'That's good'; and he is said to have expressed his reluctance to sully his devotion to Kean by seeing the newly famous actress Miss O'Neil, with a *Hamlet* pun: 'No—I am resolved to continue *un*-Oneiled' (Hobhouse, 5 March 1818; C, II, 69; LJ, II, 386, note, quoting Moore; *Hamlet,* II, ii, 535; I, v, 77). Byron's dissatisfaction with the famous boy-player Betty reminds us of the 'little eyases' in *Hamlet* (Lord Holland, 10 Sept. 1812; LJ, II, 142; *Hamlet,* II, ii, 362). Here is a pregnant passage on society, loneliness, and art:

> Here I am alone, instead of dining at Lord H's, where I was asked—but not inclined to go any where. Hobhouse says I am growing a *loup garou*—a solitary hobgoblin. True—'I am myself alone.' The last week has been passed in reading—seeing plays —now and then visitors—sometimes yawning and sometimes sighing, but no writing—save of letters. If I could always read, I should never feel the want of society. Do I regret it?—um!— 'Man delights not me', and only one woman—at a time.
>
> (Journal, 27 Feb. 1814; LJ, II, 388; *3 Henry VI,* v, vi, 83; *Hamlet,* II, ii, 329)

The *Hamlet* phrase has here a stage relevance, since Shakespeare used it to underline Hamlet's inability to delight in man except under stage artistry (II, ii, 329-51).

That to Byron stage art was from the start a matter of high importance is clear in *English Bards and Scotch Reviewers* (1809); *Hints from Horace* (composed 1811) is one long demand for a drama worthy of Shakespeare; and similar thoughts recur in his *Monody* on Sheridan's death and his *Address* for the opening of Drury Lane with its *Hamlet*-like (III, ii, 29-33) plea for a judicious audience and condemnation of 'misplaced applause'. In composing this 'address', as never elsewhere in matters of poetry except in regard to his own plays, Byron was for once *nervy* (letters to Lord Holland, 10 Sept.—14 Oct. 1812; LJ, II, 141-73). Only fear of failure appears to have prevented him from attempting dramas himself sooner than he did

(LJ, III, 233–4, note; and see Journal, 20 Feb. 1814; LJ, II, 387; Moore, May 1814; LJ, III, 81–2). On the living drama he felt strongly, poignantly, intimately. He once had a kind of fit watching Kean in Sir Giles Overreach and again during a performance of Alfieri's *Mirra* (Murray, 12 Aug. 1819; LJ, IV, 339–40 and note; LJ, II, 386, note). Byron's comment on the satiric genius of Foote with its wide and fearless range of attack unequalled since is 'Alas, poor Yorick' (*Hints from Horace*, 335; *Hamlet*, V, i, 201). But he is mainly interested in heavy drama. When in 1814 he became a member of the Drury Lane committee (see LJ, III, 191, note), he took his duties seriously, reading through scripts and searching vainly for good plays; praising Coleridge's *Remorse* and urging him to do another as good; always assiduous in search for talent (*Detached Thoughts*, 1821; 67–70; Coleridge, 31 March 1815; LJ, V, 442–4 and III, 191; and see variously III, 195–233).

He was now married, and at this third act of his life's drama we find three forces exerting on him their pressures: (i) the troubles of his married life; (ii) his Drury Lane interests and anxieties; and (iii) his distress at the final defeat of Napoleon, after his temporary return to power, at Waterloo. They are all part of a single complex.

He was as unsuited for marriage as Hamlet. Once, thinking of it and dismissing a candidate that might be Ophelia as young and beautiful but foolish, he concludes with a near-quotation from *Hamlet*: 'So "I'll none on't," but e'en remain single and solitary' (Journal, 16 Jan. 1814; LJ, II, 380–1; *Hamlet*, III. i, 155–8). Hobhouse was in France during the 'hundred days', but marriage precluded Byron from revolutionary activities and left him only the drama. His committee work at Drury Lane had social if not revolutionary implications, since his will towards great drama was one with his wider interests, as may be seen from his own plays, composed after he left England; and together with his earlier attack on the Regent it may be allowed to correspond to Hamlet's 'Mousetrap'; and indeed Hamlet's play before the King had already been imitated and expanded in the central scene of Coleridge's *Remorse,* which Byron so intensely admired and is sometimes thought to have helped towards production in 1813 (LJ, III, 190, note). There was yet a third outlet. Now, when a Bourbon was being restored to the French throne, Byron published anonymous, yet easily recognized, verses for the revolutionary cause in the British press. More, he seems to have thought of going abroad, perhaps for direct action. 'The Paris Scheme', wrote his wife, 'was *very near* executed in the Summer' (LJ, III, 'The Separation', 302; and see Byron's letter to Leigh Hunt, May or June 1815; LJ, III, 200; also Augusta Leigh to Lady Byron 22 and 27 Jan. 1816; Elwin, 369, 382, the first occurring beside Byron's claim to be a greater than Napoleon; see p. 102). The activities seemingly referred to I have discussed in *Lord Byron's Marriage* (263–7). Here it is enough to observe that Byron, whose potential of power was considerable, was striking fear into the ruling interests of his country. It is likely that these interests deliberately aroused and used the marriage-scandal to get him removed (Teresa, Int., 23 and note; 1869, 39–40 and note; LBM, 267, 274).

Byron unburdened his tormented soul to his wife much as Hamlet unburdened his to his mother, and both women were terrified. When Lady Byron says that 'it is in the nature of such malady to reverse the affections, and to make those who would naturally be dearest the greatest objects of aversion, the most exposed to acts of violence, and the least capable of alleviating the malady' (LJ, III, 'The Separation', 316), it might be the Queen talking of Hamlet. His wife thought Byron mad, as Hamlet was thought mad by the Queen (LJ, III, 'The Separation', 296, 300, 310, 315–16; *Hamlet*, IV, i, 7, 25; V, i, 306). He had for long been willing to regard his Calvinistic 'hypochondria' as 'a disease of the mind' in the manner of Hamlet's 'my wit's diseased' (Gifford, 18 June 1813; LJ, II, 222; *Hamlet*, III, ii, 340); and if he was guilty of some sexual abnormality such as sodomy, we can, having regard to its unnatural and death-pointed implications, group it with Hamlet's challenge of regal state in Claudius by reminders of corruption and death (*Hamlet*, IV, iii, 17–34). Inevitably, the forces of healthy normality close their ranks against the intruder. Lady Byron thought that Byron was motivated by some kind of 'revenge' and accused him of 'a boundless and impious pride' (LJ, III, 'The Separation', 297, 300, 311, 313). At the climax Augusta Leigh, writing to Lady Byron on 22 January 1816, reported as part of Byron's distracted behaviour his statement that he 'considered himself *the greatest man existing*'. When his cousin

George Byron said laughing 'Except Buonaparte', his answer was, 'God! I don't know that I do except even him!' 'I was struck previously', writes Augusta, 'with a wildness in his eye(s).' She repeats the thought: 'There was wildness *and incoherency* to the greatest degree in all he said last night: G. B. was *astonished*, never having seen him so bad' (The Lovelace Papers).[1] Here Byron speaks in the vein of Hamlet's

> The time is out of joint. O cursed spite,
> That ever I was born to set it right!
>
> (I, v, 188)

The first words of that he was to quote later in *Don Juan* (IX, 41). Meanwhile he suffered from knowing himself a threat, an anarch, a messiah; and he knew, like Hamlet, that he, and not the smooth society that he was aiming to blast from within, was right. He, like Hamlet, in the scene with his mother, was still ghost-ridden. Of this period in London he told William Parry at Missolonghi: 'and then the old house was a mere ghost-house; I dreamed of ghosts, and thought of them waking' (Parry, IX, 219). Byron, like Hamlet, is simultaneously a ghost-begotten life-threatener and a superman of supreme insight and majestic vision. Can such a man rightly claim to be an 'enlightener of nations' (*Manfred*, III, i, 107)? For society, as for Claudius, there appears, whatever their own deep-seated guilt, to be only one sane conclusion: 'His liberty is full of threats to all' (*Hamlet*, IV, i, 14). Byron and Hamlet must be expelled.

III

We know little of Hamlet's mental experiences on his travels. Byron's life helps to explain them. Hamlet left with the words:

> O! from this time forth,
> My thoughts be bloody, or be nothing worth!
>
> (*Hamlet*, IV, iv, 65)

1. I have used the versions of the letter given by Sir John Fox, *The Byron Mystery*, 106; E. C. Mayne, *Life and Letters of Lady Byron*, 207; and Malcolm Elwin, *Lord Byron's Wife*, 369. The incident is discussed at LBM, 270-1.

'Bloody' means 'virile'. Byron fulfils Hamlet's vow: his 'thoughts' in anger, in imprecations of vengeance, in literary creation, all show an access of energy.

His mood is this:

> I am a lover of Nature and an admirer of Beauty. I can bear fatigue and welcome privation, and have seen some of the noblest views in the world. But in all this—the recollections of bitterness, and more especially of recent and more home desolation, which must accompany me through life, have preyed upon me here; and neither the music of the Shepherd, the crashing of the Avalanche, nor the torrent, the mountain, the Glacier, the Forest, nor the Cloud, have for one moment lightened the weight upon my heart, nor enabled me to lose my own wretched identity in the majesty, and the power, and the Glory, around, above, and beneath me.
> I am past reproaches; and there is a time for all things. I am past the wish of vengeance, and I know of none like for what I have suffered; but the hour will come, when what I feel must be felt, and the—but enough.
>
> (Journal, 29 Sept. 1816; LJ, III, 364)

That, coming after the severance, is a more energic variation on Hamlet's words in the earlier period of paralysis:

> I have of late—but wherefore I know not—lost all my mirth, forgone all custom of exercises; and indeed it goes so heavily with my disposition that this goodly frame, the earth, seems to me a sterile promontory; this most excellent canopy, the air, look you, this brave o'erhanging firmament, this majestical roof fretted with golden fire, why, it appears no other thing to me but a foul and pestilent congregation of vapours.
>
> (*Hamlet*, II, ii, 313)

We may suppose, in fact we know, that Hamlet's own paralysis was lifted after leaving Denmark.

In his thoughts on vengeance Byron, like Hamlet when he calls himself Heaven's 'minister' (III, iv, 175), feels himself in contact with supernal powers. Thinking that unfair means had been used to blacken his name and remove him from England, he invokes 'Nemesis' on his wrongers:

Thou, who did'st call the Furies from the abyss,
And round Orestes bade them howl and hiss . . .
(*Childe Harold*, IV, 132)

In his *Lines on Hearing that Lady Byron was Ill* (1816) his wife is 'the moral Clytemnestra of her lord'. On the suicide of Sir Samuel Romilly, whom Byron regarded as one of his betrayers, he wrote letters grimly remembering his invocation of Nemesis and carrying vengeful hate beyond death in the dark manner that so disturbs us in Hamlet's speech over the praying Claudius (Lady Byron, 18 Nov. 1818; Murray, 7 June 1819; Hobhouse, 23 Nov., 12 Dec., 1818; LJ, IV, 268, 316; C, II, 92, 96; *Hamlet,* III, iii, 73–96). He thought of challenging another enemy, Henry Brougham, to a duel (Kinnaird and Hobhouse, 16 and 21 Nov. 1819; Hobhouse, 21 Sept. 1820; C, II, 127, 131, 153). On wider issues he expected revolution at home and thought of returning to assist (LBM; 143–7; see pp. 155, 200 below). He attacked the throne in *The Irish Avatar* (1821) and *The Vision of Judgment* (1822). He was on the war-path.

Nevertheless, it did not come easily. When he once assured Lady Melbourne that despite his calm he could be 'as savage and revengeful as anybody' (March 1814; C, I, 247), the remark was as true and as false as Hamlet's 'I am very proud, revengeful, ambitious . . .' (*Hamlet*, III, i, 128). Byron once remarked with what might have been a Hamlet's self-diagnosis that though he could be violent 'on an impulse', he would be sorry to put his hatred of the Austrian tyranny into action (Journal, 12 Jan. 1821; LJ, V, 172). Honour and codes of duelling are regarded as 'mere stuff', masks for natural impulse; and there is one man he hopes will not come to Italy lest his own 'vindictive' nature might take advantage, by-passing the codes, of the Italian habit for assassination. Byron's remark here about 'trampling' on him as on any other 'venomous animal' corresponds to Hamlet's similarly unpleasant moments, as at the death of Polonius, or when recounting his turning of the tables on Rosencrantz and Guildernstern (Hobhouse, 30 July 1819; C, II, 118–9). In his '*Blackwood's Defence*' we hear that he resides abroad to avoid temptations of

vengeance consequent on the Scots fire inherited from his mother
(LJ, IV, App. ix, 480). That on the one side; on the other are his
darker statements, where he seems to be unnaturally whipping himself up to a vengeful state, almost as a duty, as does Hamlet in his
soliloquies. He deliberately tries to 'harden' his heart, but 'the fact is',
he wrote, 'I cannot *keep* my *resentments,* though violent enough in
their onset' (Moore; 14 June 1814; 6 March 1822; LJ, III, 92; VI,
35). Such ambivalences are equally true of Hamlet; like Hamlet's,
Byron's natural tendency was to 'speak daggers' but 'use none'
(*Hamlet,* III, ii, 421). The agonies he endured after leaving England,
oscillating between vengefulness and reluctance, may be supposed to
have been endured, at the corresponding period, by Hamlet too.

Both seem to have been gradually drawn to accept their own
madness. After his return Hamlet frankly admits his to Laertes (V,
ii, 240–58). Byron had feared eventual madness as early as the year
1811, noting 'a want of method in arranging my thoughts' (Hodgson,
13 Oct. 1811; LJ, II, 54). After leaving England in 1816 he often
referred to it. He was 'half mad' during the composition of the third
Childe Harold; 'If I don't write to empty my mind, I go mad'
(Moore, 28 Jan. 1817; 2 Jan. 1821; LJ, IV, 49; V, 215). He
wondered if he would end up mad, like Swift (Hobhouse, 23 Aug.
1819; Journal, 6 Jan., 2 Feb. 1821; C, II, 123; LJ, V, 156, 199).
Hamlet, wrote Robert Bridges in *The Testament of Beauty* (I, 579),
was set by Shakespeare 'gingerly' on the border-line between sanity
and madness; and Byron was thinking of himself when he observed
that poets 'rarely go mad' though they are often 'near' it, their art
saving them (Miss Milbanke, 10 Nov. 1813; LJ, III, App. iii, 405).
Stendhal thought Byron 'labouring under an access of folly, often
approaching to madness' (LJ, III, App. viii, 440). Byron saw his
own mental gymnastics as Hamlet-like characteristics. His melan-
cholia was a 'temperamental illness' that sometimes made him 'fear
the approach of madness' (Teresa, 29 Sept. 1820; Origo, V, 222).
When critics objected to the sharp alternations of 'fun and gravity'
in *Don Juan,* he replied:

You might as well make Hamlet (or Diggory) 'act mad' in a
straight waistcoat as trammel my buffoonery, if I am to be a
buffoon . . . (Murray, 12 Aug. 1819; LJ, IV, 342)

Like Hamlet, he confesses to madness:

> I wish that I had been in better spirits, but I am out of sorts, out of nerves; and now and then (I begin to fear) out of my senses. All this Italy has done for me, and not England: I defy all of you, and your climate to boot, to make me mad. But if ever I do really become a Bedlamite, and wear a strait waistcoat, let me be brought back among you; your people will then be proper compagny.
>
> (Murray, 24 Aug. 1819; LJ, IV, 348)

'Make me mad': the phrase and mood are Hamlet's, 'Go to, I'll no more on't; it hath made me mad.' The conclusion is another *Hamlet* reminiscence, from the Gravedigger's comment on England, "Twill not be seen in him there: there the men are as mad as he' (III, i, 155; V, i, 168). The truth is, Hamlet and Byron are enduring that 'deeper madness', born of insight, which we have noted in *The Dream*. Once the acute intelligence of Lady Byron recognized that what might appear aberration was perhaps an 'absorption in deep thought' (LJ, III, 'The Separation', 297).

Hamlet returns from his travels with a new serenity and poise. How it was won may be best understood by watching Byron gradually mastering his mental universe. The process involves: (i) death; (ii) humour; (iii) humility and (iv) action.

Byron, after a long reluctance, finding it a way to the *control* of his tormented universe, turned, as did Hamlet in 'The Murder of Gonzago' (II, ii, 570–5), to dramatic composition. If it be objected that Byron's historical plays are built on neo-classic principles and an intellectualized critique of society diverging from Shakespeare, we may observe that Hamlet's dramatic theories are themselves, in regard to both acting and play-writing, classical, and nearer Jonson than Shakespeare. Acting was to be temperate, plays didactic, and only the approval of the cultured to be valued (III, ii, 1–40). When Byron turned to drama, he was determined to avoid *rant*, which was as distasteful to him as to the Hamlet of

> Nay, an thou'lt mouth
> I'll rant as well as thou.
>
> (*Hamlet*, V, i, 305)

This was Byron's natural approach, at least in his manhood, to all high sounding adventures and values. Once, wanting 'a passage in a ship of war', he wrote: 'They had better let me go; if I cannot, patriotism is the word—"nay, an they'll mouth, I'll rant as well as they"' (Moore, 13 July 1813; LJ, II, 231). That referred to actual heroics. It was the same with his dramatic theories:

What I seek to show in *The Foscaris* is the *suppressed* passion, rather than the rant of the present day. For that matter—
Nay, if thou'lt mouth,
I'll rant as well as thou—
would not be difficult, as I think I have shown in my younger productions . . .
(Moore, 20 Sept. 1812; LJ, V, 372)

Byron rejected Shakespeare as a dramatic model for strong personal, and very Hamlet-like, reasons. He admired and envied the poetry of Pope for the same reason that caused Hamlet to admire and envy Horatio, and to look to him for support:

Give me that man
That is not passion's slave, and I will wear him
In my heart's core, ay in my heart of heart,
As I do thee.
(*Hamlet*, III, ii, 76)

Hobhouse, Byron's Horatio, loved Pope too. But Shakespeare was disturbing. *Macbeth, King Lear* and *Timon of Athens* give rein to extravagant passions which Byron-as-Hamlet was trying to control.

He had more experiences of ghosts. In the palazzo at Pisa his servant Fletcher was disturbed by ghosts and Byron 'bothered' about it; Medwin, referring to the matter, calls them both 'superstitious' (Murray, 4 Dec. 1821; LJ, V, 486–7 and note). According to Lady Blessington Byron believed that the ghost of Shelley had been seen (Blessington, II, 36–7).

Though as a young man he had kept skulls in his study, he could not imagine people he had known so reduced 'without a hideous sensation' (Dallas, 12 Aug. 1811; LJ, I, 327). After leaving England his interest in bones and skulls was written into *Manfred* (II, ii, 79–83); he collected bones from a battlefield (note to *Childe*

Harold, III, 63). Writing to Murray about the deaths of a dentist and a hairdresser, he ruminates on the present state of their teeth and hair, remarking, after Hamlet, 'My jaws ache to think on't' (18 Nov. 1820; LJ, v, 119; *Hamlet,* v, i, 99). Our most interesting correspondence to the Graveyard scene comes in his visit to a graveyard at Bologna. The Sexton reminded him of 'the Gravedigger in *Hamlet*', drawing from his collection of skulls one of a Capuchin monk and recording, just like the Gravedigger on Yorick, that he 'was the merriest, cleverest, fellow', who wherever he went 'brought joy', cheering the melancholy with his jokes. This Sexton had 'the greatest attachment' to 'his dead people'; the epitaphs 'Implora pace' and 'Implora eterna quiete', together with the flowers placed on the graves, Byron found deeply moving. Contrasting the Sexton's beautiful daughter with the skulls the man has collected of ladies once clothed by a similar beauty, Byron is troubled after the manner of Hamlet's 'Now get you to my lady's chamber, and tell her, let her paint an inch thick, to this favour she must come' (Murray, 7 June, 24 Aug. 1819; LJ, IV, 313–14, 317, 349; *Hamlet,* v, i, 211). These descriptions, in all their delicate balance of irony and serenity, are pitched on a note of acceptance matching the lyric prose of Hamlet's graveyard meditations.

In satiric thrust Byron could be fierce as Hamlet, but both learn to replace anger by humour. Apart from *The Age of Bronze* and *The Irish Avatar* Byron's major satires are now dominated by humour. *The Vision of Judgment* contains a mixture of disrespect to royalty and irreverence to religion that faintly recalls Hamlet's answer to the King regarding Polonius' whereabouts:

> In Heaven. Send thither to see. If your messenger find him not there, seek him i' the other place yourself.
>
> (IV, iii, 36)

There is, however, a sting in that absent from Byron's poem, except where Southey is concerned, and the poem's mood demands that George III should get to Heaven after all:

> And when the tumult dwindled to a calm,
> I left him practising the hundredth psalm.
>
> (106)

The humour is good-natured. It sets, moreover, the tone for the whole of *Don Juan*, which exists as an extensive record of Byron's self-conquest. Apart from its anti-militarist satire and the attacks on Wellington and Castlereagh, the prevailing tone is that of humour; good nature abounds, ranging from deep pathos to admirable fooling. And what of Hamlet? This new manner matches the tone of Hamlet's banter with Osric. Criticisms may be sharp, but they are carried lightly, without bitterness, and in a spirit of personal unconcern.

The new mode to which Byron is attuning himself is already clear in his attitude to the Prince Regent. In *Don Juan* Byron takes pleasure in recalling the Prince's splendid promise in youth:

> There, too, he saw (whate'er he may be now)
> A Prince, the prince of Princes at the time,
> With fascination in his very bow,
> And full of promise, as the spring of prime.
> Though royalty was written on his brow,
> He had *then* the grace, too, rare in every clime,
> Of being, without alloy of fop or beau,
> A finish'd gentleman from top to toe.
>
> (XII, 84)

The poetic gesture is an act of some significance. Nor was it only a question of the Prince's youth. Once in what is surely the most gracious address from subject to sovereign that our literature affords, Byron honoured the Prince Regent, soon to become George IV, with his noble sonnet *On the Repeal of Lord Edward Fitzgerald's Forfeiture* (1819: see Murray, 12 Aug. 1819; LJ, IV, 345):

> To be the father of the fatherless,
>   To stretch the hand from the throne's height, and raise
>   *His* offspring, who expir'd in other days
> To make thy Sire's sway by a kingdom less—
> *This* is to be a monarch, and repress
>   Envy into unutterable praise.
>   Dismiss thy guard, and trust thee to such traits,
> For who would lift a hand, except to bless?

109

Were it not easy, Sir, and is't not sweet
To make thyself belovéd? and to be
Omnipotent by mercy's means? for thus
Thy sovereignty would grow but more complete:
A despot thou, and yet thy people free,
And by the heart, not hand, enslaving us.

Can we imagine Hamlet thinking kindly of Claudius' promise as a young man, or responding to some gracious action from the throne? Perhaps not; and yet Hamlet too at the close shows a new respect to the King and the Queen, evident in such phrases as 'his majesty', 'your grace' and 'good madam' (v, ii, 181, 275, 304). There may be a difference in degree, but the change is of similar kind. Hamlet, like Byron, has learned a measure of social self-adjustment. The stage tradition whereby Hamlet and Laertes salute the throne with their rapiers before the duel is in attunement with this prevailing mood.

Both Hamlet and Byron are now set for action. Central in both has always been a craving for some line of action that corresponds to 'that within', some action which is spiritually adequate. Each has a strong, almost Hotspur-like, manly side to him, distrusting sentiment. Byron repudiated the romantic Childe Harold and thought Hamlet less of a man than Richard III (Dallas, 31 Oct. 1811; Journal, 19 Feb. 1814; LJ, II, 66 and 386). After watching Fortinbras' army and leaving Denmark, Hamlet determines to assert himself in action and does so, twice; by undermining the trickery of Rosencrantz and Guildernstern and sending them to their deaths, and again during the fight with the Pirates. So too Byron during these years settles with Southey in *The Vision of Judgment* and elsewhere (LJ, VI, App. i), and also with the 'political parasite' and 'sycophant' (note to *Don Juan;* Dedication, 6), Wordsworth. Thinking of a duel, Byron observes that Southey would be 'too much of a poet' to risk his 'blood'; afterwards he sent a challenge, which was not however delivered by his agent (Murray, 24 Nov. 1818; LJ, IV, 272; VI, App. i, 392). In assisting the Italian rising, Byron had a cause, and acted for what was, however ineffectual, a blow aimed against tyranny; and he sometimes thought of returning to England to join in the revolution he expected at home (pp. 155, 200). Both Hamlet and Byron may be felt as working *up* to their final achievement. For

Hamlet, this will be the duel and the killing of the King; his habit of fencing practice, for he has 'been in continual practice' while away—like Byron with his shooting, riding and swimming—has a significance contrasting with his earlier *neglect* of 'all custom of exercises' (*Hamlet*, v, ii, 221; II, ii, 315). Byron's more fully documented story helps us to fill out and interpret the less detailed account of Hamlet's transition.

A good way of pointing their similarity as men-of-action is to compare their epistolary styles where action is the subject. Here is Hamlet's letter to Horatio:

> Finding ourselves too slow of speed we put on a compelled valour. In the grapple, I boarded them: on the instant they got clear of our ship, so I alone became their prisoner. They have dealt with me like thieves of mercy, but they knew what they did; I am to do a good turn for them.
>
> (IV, vi, 17)

If we compare with this any of Byron's accounts of action—a good example is his account of his and Shelley's escape from drowning in Switzerland (Murray, 15 May, 1819; LJ, IV, 296–7; see p. 264 below)—we find the same terse objectivity. Hamlet's accents, the realism of 'compelled valour', the pregnancy of phrase in 'thieves of mercy', and the following deflation; all are Byronic. Here is Byron:

> Gamba and the Bombard (there is a strong reason to believe) are carried into Patras by a Turkish frigate, which we saw chase them at dawn on the 31st: we had been close under the stern in the night, believing her a Greek till within pistol shot . . .
>
> (Muir, 2 Jan. 1824; LJ, VI, 298)

Such passages abound whenever action or movement is the theme (e.g., on ships again, pp. 263–8 below). Byron's letters from Greece are those of a man happy in action.

He knew that he was approaching the climax and justification of his life. Like Hamlet, who has grown to thirty in the graveyard scene (v, i, 152–176), he was swiftly aging (Journal, 2 Feb. 1821; LJ, v, 199), and the Greek campaign was undertaken in the spirit of Hamlet's 'it will be short; the interim is mine' (*Hamlet*, v, ii, 73). From the *Conversations* with Lady Blessington it appears that he sensed the approach of death (Blessington, xiv, 353, and see Moore, 1 Oct. 1821; LJ, v, 384). So did Hamlet:

Hamlet: . . . But thou would'st not think how ill all's here about my heart; but it is no matter.
Horatio: Nay, good my lord—
Hamlet: It is but foolery; but it is such a kind of gain-giving as would perhaps trouble a woman.
Horatio: If your mind dislike anything, obey it; I will forestall their repair hither, and say you are not fit.
Hamlet: Not a whit; we defy augury. There's a special providence in the fall of a sparrow. If it be now, 'tis not to come; if it be not to come, it will be now; if it be not now, yet it will come; the readiness is all. Since no man has aught of what he leaves, what is't to leave betimes? Let be.
(V, ii, 222)

The accent is exactly Byronic. 'It is no matter', 'Let be': Byron's own writings contain many such little disclaimers, following what might appear egotism or sentiment. After referring to his own troubles, he breaks off with Hamlet's 'it is no matter' and 'but no matter' (Rogers, 23 Jan.; Hunt, 8 Feb.; 1816; Lady Melbourne, 10 Oct. 1813; LJ, III, 258, 261; C, I, 194). Hamlet's 'Something too much of this' comes in as a characteristic Byronic mannerism (*Childe Harold*, III, 8; Journal, also Moore, 9 April 1814; LJ, II, 410; III, 65; *Hamlet*, III, ii, 79).

On leaving Italy for Greece Byron's ship was forced to return by a storm. They had embarked on a Friday, but despite his well-known superstitions Byron preserved a calm. He was now beyond superstition. Moore comments: 'In truth, notwithstanding his encouraging speech to Count Gamba, the forewarning he now felt of his approaching doom seems to have been far too deep and serious to need the aid of any such accessory' (Moore, II, 668 or LI, 592). The correspondence in mood with that of Hamlet's remarks to Horatio is close.

As for Hamlet's belief in an over-ruling 'providence', that too was Byron's. His religious feelings are clear from his conversations with James Kennedy, reported so excellently in Kennedy's valuable book, at Cephalonia. Byron was blamed for waiting there so long, but dramatically these conversations were in place. It is as though Byron were deliberately *preparing himself* for the final sacrifice; as though Cephalonia was his Gethsemane. From Missolonghi he later wrote to Kennedy, who was anxious regarding his health:

> Should I become, or be deemed, useless or superfluous, I am ready to retire; but in the interim I am not to consider personal consequences; the rest is in the hands of Providence, as indeed are all things.
>
> (Kennedy, 4 March 1824; LJ, VI, 339)

Byron knew that his life was obeying a pattern. Again and again in his conversations with William Parry at Missolonghi the religious mood is evident (pp. 322–4 below).

At Missolonghi he was at last, through the London committee, collaborating with his own compatriots in a cause enlisting his total belief; and in conversation he expressed a personal faith in the British constitution (Parry, VIII, 173–4). He now both accepted, and was being accepted by, his country. He was making terms with life, even insisting that the liberation journal *The Greek Chronicle* should not be allowed to antagonize the hated Austrians (LJ, VI, 355, note; p. 325 below). Genius, and perhaps more than that, Byron had for long possessed; now he was learning statesmanship. And he was now a soldier.

In his verses *On this Day I complete my Thirty-Sixth Year* Byron wrote:

> But 'tis not *thus*—and 'tis not *here*—
> Such thoughts should shake my soul, nor *now*
> Where glory decks the hero's bier,
> Or binds his brow.
>
> The sword, the banner, and the field,
> Glory and Greece, around me see!
> The Spartan, borne upon his shield,
> Was not more free.
>
> Awake! (not Greece—she *is* awake!)
> Awake, my spirit! Think through *whom*
> Thy life-blood tracks its parent lake,
> And then strike home!

'Strike home': the thought is of a single blow, like Hamlet's at the King, seeing the Greek campaign as a thrust in freedom's cause, to reverberate throughout Europe. Byron concludes by thought of dying on the 'field' in 'the land of honourable death'; and of deliberately *seeking out* 'a soldier's grave'.

Both statesman and soldier. And yet, as his almost superhuman attempts to alleviate the sufferings of foe as well as friend witness, no ordinary example of either. In drawing level, as man of action, with Napoleon, Byron inevitably and at once surpasses him. Whether he, who so consistently aimed to blend the Sermon on the Mount with the warrior, Renaissance, virtues, and who even refused to take the life of animals, could have shed human blood, we cannot know; though he would, as always, have been fearless for himself. True to his twin if paradoxical alignments, Byron died on active service without, by the grace of Providence, being forced to engage in the bloodshed which he loathed. But war exerts its heroic radiations, its glory. Despite our own contemporary and Byronic repudiations of militarism, we can, as a community, still find no greater honour for a sovereign or great leader, such as Churchill, than to bear his body to rest on a gun-carriage. For this symbolizes those high, perhaps supreme, values of action and heroism in face of death such as Hamlet so admired in Fortinbras,

> Whose spirit with divine ambition puff'd
> Makes mouths at the invisible event,
> Exposing what is mortal and unsure
> To all that fortune, death and danger dare . . .
> (IV, iv, 49)

It is not so much the killing, nor even the victory, that constitutes the glory: it is rather the daring, the trust, the surpassing of 'mortal' uncertainties in action.

It is accordingly right that our Hamlets and Byrons, personifying a synthesis as yet perhaps inconceivable in other than personal and dramatic terms, should be accorded military honours:

> Let four captains
> Bear Hamlet, like a soldier, to the stage;
> For he was likely, had he been put on,

To have prov'd most royally: and, for his passage,
The soldiers' music and the rites of war
Speak loudly for him.

(v, ii, 409)

There is a dead march and 'a peal of ordnance is shot off'. Byron lay in state, in a church; and then the guns spoke, also, for him. In his *Narrative of Lord Byron's Last Journey to Greece* Pietro Gamba writes:

At sunrise, on the morning after his death, seven-and-thirty minute guns were fired from the principal battery of the fortress; and one of the batteries of the corps under his orders also fired one gun every half hour for the succeeding four-and-twenty hours.

(VI, 272)

For both this cannon thunder makes the same, indefinable, statement.

IV

Tolstoy complained that Shakespeare's Hamlet had no recognizable 'character'. The same was said of Byron by Lady Blessington and others. And yet in both we sense a mysterious unity. Hamlet scorns those who would 'pluck out the heart' of his 'mystery' (*Hamlet*, III, ii, 389). Byron, with less scorn, also knew that his personality was mysterious. His early journal indulges in mystification and in the *Detached Thoughts* we read: 'I must not go on with these reflections, or I shall be letting out some secret or other to paralyze posterity' (*Detached Thoughts*, 1821; 76; LJ, v, 447). When in his parting lines in 1816 to his wife *Fare Thee Well* he writes:

All my faults perchance thou knowest—
All my madness—none can know . . .

(P, III, 539)

he implies the presence of that 'something unearthly' in him of which he speaks in *Childe Harold* (IV, 137), corresponding to that 'incomprehensible phantasma' which Galt sensed hovering about his personality (Galt, VIII, 63). Manfred is a man, or superman, above normal categories (II, i, 38; II, ii, 123; II, iv, 51; III, i, 138); and the

Doge in *Marino Faliero* offers as his defence the line 'The secret were too mighty for your souls' (v, i, 285). Byron expected to prove an enigma to biographers, hoping to 'do something or other—the times and fortune permitting—that, "like the cosmogony, or creation of the world, will puzzle the philosophers of all ages"' (Moore, 28 Feb. 1817; LJ, IV, 62). The mystery in him was like the 'creation'; it was a new creation, the creation of a new man, a new state of being, an answer to Hamlet's poser, 'To be or not to be'.

Naturally, both Hamlet and Byron feared misrepresentation. Hamlet wanted Horatio to save his 'wounded name' (v, ii, 358) by explaining what was dark, thinking perhaps of the Ghost; and Byron left his memoirs expecting his friends Moore and Hobhouse to preserve his name (Hobhouse, 23 Nov. 1821; C, II, 205), a task which they set about not wisely but too well, with the result that the mystery remains today in all its virgin purity, or impurity. Meanwhile our observation of these correspondences with Hamlet contributes to a mutual elucidation, while doing honour to both. To act Hamlet on the stage is not easy; to live Hamlet on the stage of Europe may be regarded a yet greater achievement. And the comparison honours Shakespeare too; for, even when we have granted that, for one writing from 'the prophetic soul of the wide world dreaming on things to come' (Sonnet 107), it may have fallen well within the scope of Shakespeare's genius to envisage his great successor, it yet remains remarkable that he should, by so excellent a use of selection and emphasis, have succeeded in condensing so much of the Byronic story into a single drama.

IV

FALSTAFF AND COMEDY

I

WE HAVE NOTICED Byron's tendency, resembling Hamlet's, to engage in comic behaviour. His contemporaries were baffled by one who struck them variously as a kind of avenging fiend and a high-spirited buffoon. Roughly, we can say that he had two selves, the poetic and the prose selves, and that the latter covers a wide range from good sense and caustic cynicism to Bacchanalian exuberance and Puckish fun; though this last can often be expressed in nonsense rhyme too; and everything is covered by *Don Juan*.

Byron's humour and wit shows many correspondences with Shakespearian comedy. In his *Memories of the Affairs of Greece etc.* (XII, 116) Julius Millingen wrote of Byron:

Among his works, that which may perhaps be more particularly regarded as exhibiting the mirror of his conversation, and the spirit which animated it, is *Don Juan*. The following lines, too, from Shakespeare seem as if prophetically written for him:

> Biron, they call him; but a merrier man,
> Within the limit[1] of becoming mirth,
> I never spent an hour's talk withal.
> His eye begets occasion for his wit;
> For every object that the one doth catch
> The other turns to a mirth-moving jest,
> Which his fair tongue, conceit's expositor,
> Delivers in such apt and gracious words,
> That aged ears play truant at his tales,

1 Millingen's text reads: limits.

117

And younger hearings are quite ravished;
So sweet and voluble is his discourse.

The quotation is from *Love's Labour's Lost*, II, i, 66. 'Biron' is a variant of 'Berowne', the spelling of the original Shakespearian texts, and the name cognate with 'Byron'. People were regularly surprised to find one whom they expected to be at the worst sullen and misanthropic and at the best sublime, to be instead just courteous, affable and vivacious (Teresa, XIX, 352-3; Blessington, I, 4; Kennedy, 3-5; Moore, quoting W. E. West, II, 602; or XLIX, 562). Kennedy regards his merry talk, his puns—which he enjoyed as much as Shakespeare—and repartee among the young officers at Cephalonia as unworthy of his powers (Kennedy, 300-2).

Byron shares with Mercutio a mercurial wit and a dashing cavalier and honour-barbed impetuosity, together with a loathing of braggadocio and a manly approach; in some of these qualities touching Hotspur. He can also enjoy sheer fooling. His characteristics cover the whole range of Shakespearian humour from Puck to Falstaff. He quotes, as we have seen (p. 90), from Jaques in *As You Like It*; *Twelfth Night* (II, iii, 157-9) gives him the phrase 'exquisite reasons' (Lady Melbourne, 22 Nov. 1813; Kinnaird, 30 May 1817; Hobhouse, 17 Oct. 1820; C, I, 216; II, 55, 159); and he is especially fond of *Much Ado About Nothing*.

In his *A Life of Shakespeare* Hesketh Pearson contended that Shakespeare's comedy contains a strong autobiographical element:

Whether Shakespeare played Benedick in his third money-maker for the Globe, *Much Ado About Nothing*, we do not know, but the character is closely related to Berowne, and both of them are portraits of the man as he believed the world saw him, not as he saw himself. Benedick suits himself to his company, 'a lord to a lord, a man to a man' (I, i, 57). He has 'every month a new sworn brother', who 'will hang upon him like a disease'. He is 'sooner caught than the pestilence, and the taker runs presently mad' (I, i, 73; 87-9). This faithfully describes Shakespeare as a social magnet, one whose wit and charm made him exceedingly attractive to young men, who found him irresistible until, tired of their society, he showed them a different side of himself, 'for what his heart thinks his tongue speaks' (III, ii, 13).

Beatrice calls Benedick 'the prince's jester', and Benedick reflects
'It may be I go under that title because I am merry' (II, i, 144,
214;). Shakespeare was naturally merry in company and he
must often have resented the imputation that because he talked
a lot of nonsense he was shallow and scatter-brained. They 'only
are reputed wise for saying nothing' (*Merchant of Venice*, I, i, 96)
is Gratiano's criticism of long-faced silent folk, whom Shakespeare distrusted so much that he makes his villain Don John
a man of few words.

> (83–4; the reference numerals are my own insertions)

The biographical deduction may be hazardous, but there is clearly
a common element, varying from merriment to critical attack, in
Berowne, Mercutio, Benedick, Feste, and Touchstone; though first
based on fantasy it draws towards prose, leading to the caustic comments of Iago, Enobarbus and Menenius; and this common element
may be supposed part of the Shakespeare his friends knew. It is
certainly part of the Byron whom *his* friends knew.

For a while Byron was a typical bachelor, as averse from marriage
as Benedick, though like him eventually manœuvred into it: he
fittingly applies a phrase from Don Pedro's 'She were an excellent
wife for Benedick' to his own marriage (Moore, 8 March 1822; LJ,
VI, 38; *Much Ado about Nothing*, II, i, 368). Writing of the reception
of his youthful poems, he will not be afraid of these 'paper bullets of
the brain'; and he modifies Benedick's 'if a man will be beaten with
brains, a' shall wear nothing handsome about him' to 'an a man will
be beaten with brains, he shall never keep a clean doublet' (Becher,
28 March 1808; Hodgson, 8 Dec. 1811; LJ, I, 186; II, 83; *Much
Ado about Nothing*, II, iii, 260–1; V, iv, 104). Dogberry in particular
was a fertile source, apt for an author in taunting vein to his publisher: 'I hear that you go about talking of yourself, like Dogberry,
"as a fellow that hath had losses"'; and he repeats it. Hearing of Lady
Caroline Lamb's dishonest attempt to get possession of a picture, he
comments 'This is "flat burglary"'; and believing his last Grecian
adventure a 'fool's errand' he will, 'like Dogberry, "spare no wisdom"' (Murray, 23 Sept., 9 Dec. 1822; 8 Jan. 1813; Napier,
9 Sept. 1823; LJ, VI, 117, 147; II, 186; VI, 257; *Much Ado about
Nothing*, IV, ii, 90; IV, ii, 54; III, v, 66).

Such Shakespearian borrowings regularly draw pregnancy from their source. In these quotations Dogberry's whole personality is present, making points that speak volumes. Byron liked, while seeing the absurdities of, simple people. His faithful servant Fletcher, whom Mr. Peter Quennell once neatly described as playing the part in Byron's story of one of Shakespeare's clowns, was a continual support to his sense of fun: 'Fletcher is fat and facetious'; he is 'the learned Fletcher' (Hobhouse, 16 Nov. 1811; Murray, 4 Dec. 1821; C, I, 60; LJ, v, 487). In the Levant his 'boundless credulity' afforded Byron 'an ever-ready fund of amusement' (Millingen, XII, 116). Byron composed an amusing letter as from Fletcher on his own supposed death (Hobhouse, June 1818; LJ, IV, 234).

Byron could identify himself with all sorts of comedy: with the simplicity of a Dogberry or Fletcher as well as with the sparkling convivality of Scrope Davies. At the heart of his humour was a boyish or Puckish sense of fun closely resembling that so continually noted by his acquaintances in T. E. Lawrence. He told Lady Blessington that it was the child in a poet's temperament that prevented his soaring from earth and that he himself had always had 'a strong love of mischief' in his nature; society she saw as his 'playground', which he approached with a 'boyish glee' (Blessington, XII, 294; VIII, 179). Moore says that he mixed up 'humour and fun' with everything, and W. E. West quoted by Moore noted his 'reckless levity of manners' (Diary, 11 June 1828, quoted LJ, II, 98, note; Moore, II, 604 or XLIX, 562). When he laughed, writes Teresa, 'the very air surrounding him appeared to laugh' (Teresa, XXIII, 406). She quotes Stanhope's remarks that he was 'like a child for simplicity and joyousness' and 'natural and playful as a boy' (Teresa, XIX, 352; XXIII, 409), and Moore's

It was like the bursting gaiety of a boy let loose from school, and seemed as if there was no extent of fun or tricks of which he was not capable.

(Teresa, quoting Moore, XXIII, 406)

His sense of fun was strong even at the time of the separation. Lord Russell (Bertrand Russell) recorded in a letter to me of 31 January 1957, that his grandfather Lord John Russell wrote to his father on

15 September 1869: 'She (i.e. Lady Byron) told Lord Holland her husband was mad, but her eye had power over him! He was always half-mad, mischievous as a monkey, wild as a tiger, but with many good feelings' (see *The Amberley Papers*, ed. Bertrand and Patricia Russell, 1937; II, 284).

On the lowest level he engaged in practical jokes. 'No boy cornet', wrote Trelawny, 'enjoyed a practical joke more than Byron' (XVIII, 177). Some must have been extremely annoying, as when on the ship to his Greek expedition he dived, if indeed we are to believe Trelawny,[1] into the sea in the Captain's decorated waistcoat (Trelawny, XVIII, 178). At Missolonghi, wrote Gamba, 'he not infrequently diverted himself in the evening by playing off some pleasantry on some one of those about him'; these included the rolling of cannon-balls to stage an imitation earthquake to frighten William Parry (Gamba, V, 204–5). Of similar quality was his lampoon, which so infuriated its object, on Hobhouse's political activities in the verses 'My boy Hobbie-O' (Murray, 25 March 1820; LJ, IV, 423; and see App. xi, 498–500). Behind his squib on the Prince Regent (p. 91) the same Puckish impulse was at work. In Byron we cannot draw any firm line between pranks and politics.

There was, in fact, generally a serious, at least semi-satiric, purpose. He took pleasure in 'mortifying conceited people', enjoying it the more for the difficulty of the task, and even, according to Lady Blessington, liked to think of certain of his lampoons on his friends being published after his death (Blessington, XIV, 334, 359). His light conversation was in part satiric:

> His delight with intimates was to bring out strongly their defects, as well as their qualities and merits, by dint of jests, clever innuendo, and charming sallies of humour. The promptitude with which he discovered the slightest weakness, the faintest symptom of exaggeration or affectation, can hardly be credited. It might almost be said that the persons on whom he bestowed affection became *transparent* for him . . . (Teresa, XXIII, 407)

How 'charming' such penetrations were to the recipients may be questioned, but Teresa insists that his laughter 'was ever devoid of

1. Trelawny also reports (XVIII, 177) an indulgence in pistol practice on live poultry which sounds most un-Byronic.

malice' (XXIII, 406). Perhaps the best summing up is a phrase of Lady Blessington's: 'It is as though one were struck down by summer lightning while admiring its brilliant play' (Blessington, V, 110). Through it all ran an impish fun, the key being Puck's 'Lord, what fools these mortals be!' (*A Midsummer Night's Dream*, III, ii, 115).

II

Byron's critique of society was not limited to writing and conversation; in this, as in other matters, he was an actor. We have fortunately a neatly documented account of his behaviour as comic and satiric agent in the letters he wrote concerning his association with Lady Frances, wife of J. Wedderburn Webster whose pretensions Byron, while staying with the Websters, found annoying. The letters from which I shall quote were written to Lady Melbourne.

The visit occurred in the year 1813 at a time when Byron had the reputation of being, though in actuality he was not, a seducer of the type delineated in Etheredge's Dorimant; and our little drama is to be of Restoration quality. At first, hearing that a famous dandy is to join them and knowing Webster, Byron expects merely to 'have some comic Iagoism with our little Othello' (21 Sept. 1813; C, I, 181). But Lord Petersham does not come, and Byron, finding it apparently expected of him by the lady and prompted further by a self-imposed duty to reduce Webster's absurd pretentions, slips himself into the role of seducer. Webster is a character easily jealous and apt for comic treatment; and Byron notes that the study of such problems and personalities enthrals him. The man boasts simultaneously of his wife's virtue and his own licentiousness. He records their conversation:

'I think any woman fair game, because I can *depend* upon Ly F.'s principles—she can't go wrong and therefore I may.'
'Then, why are you jealous of her?'
'Because—because—zounds! I am not jealous. Why the devil do you suppose I am?'

(1 Oct. 1813; C, I, 188)

Webster's comic jealousy, for he *is* jealous, recalls Ford's in *The Merry Wives of Windsor* or Kitely's in Jonson's *Every Man in his Humour*, while his simultaneous licentiousness adds a dimension of *hubris* at which Byron was genuinely shocked. Webster continues his absurdities, says Byron, 'in a tone which, as I never use it myself, I am not particularly disposed to tolerate in others', boasting of 'what *he* may do with impunity, it seems, but not suffer' (8 Oct., 1813; C, I, 190). Webster arouses in him a kind of dramatic moralism. References to the theatre are continual, including Cumberland's *The West Indian* and *Othello*, Webster being 'the Moor' (8 Oct. 1813; C, I, 192). Surreptitious encounters between Byron and Lady Frances have begun, with messages, and the moment-by-moment account of them has all the dramatic immediacy of Richardson's *Pamela*:

> My billet prospered, it did more, it even (I am this moment interrupted by the *Marito*, and write this before him, he has brought me a political pamphlet in MS. to decypher and applaud, I shall content myself with the last; oh, he is gone again), my billet produced an *answer*, a very unequivocal one too, but a little too much about virtue . . .
>
> (8 Oct. 1813; C, I, 191)

Dramatic comedy is rich, but there is a serious aspect too:

> I need not say that the folly and petulance of Webster has tended to all this. If a man is not contented with a pretty woman, and not only runs after any little country girl he meets with, but absolutely boasts of it; he must not be surprised if others admire that which he knows not how to value. Besides, he literally provoked and goaded me into it, by something not unlike bullying, *indirect* to be sure, but tolerably obvious: 'he *would* do this, and he would do that', 'if any man' etc. etc., and *he* thought that every 'woman' was *his* lawful prize, nevertheless. Oons! who is this strange monopolist? It is odd enough, but on other subjects he is like other people, on this he seems infatuated. If he had been rational, and not prated of his pursuits, I should have gone on very well, as I did at Middleton. Even now, I shan't quarrel with him if I can help it; but one or two of his speeches have blackened the blood about my heart, and curdled the milk of

kindness. If put to the proof, I shall behave like other people, I presume.

(8 Oct. 1813; C, 1, 192)

'Milk of kindness' comes from *Macbeth* (1, v, 18), but the prevailing tone is that of a moralistic comedy, like *Volpone*, or the Falstaff of *2 Henry IV*, Byron functioning as minister of comic retribution. Once when Webster, while being sure of his own wife's virtue, proposes a bet to the assembled company that he would win any woman against any rival, Byron, now well engaged with Lady Frances, comments, 'Is not this, at the moment, a perfect comedy?' (8 Oct. 1813; C, 1, 193).

The intrigue's rapid growth leaves him, he says, as astonished as Lord Ogilby in *The Clandestine Marriage* (by George Colman the Elder). Lady Frances is rapidly disproving Webster's assurance of her passionless temperament, and Byron is himself astonished, if not shocked, noting, with perhaps a reminder of Desdemona (*Othello*, IV, ii, 22), that 'she is a thorough devotee, and takes prayers, morning and evening, besides being measured for a new Bible once a quarter' (10 Oct. 1813; C, 1, 195). As we have seen, he observes too that Webster is perfectly reasonable on all other matters. Moreover, while all this is going on Byron is simultaneously negotiating a loan of £1,000 to Webster and helping him in various ways; and yet, despite all provocation, Byron also knows himself in the wrong, and if it comes to a duel he will not return the other's fire (13 Oct. 1813; C, 1, 200). What we are watching is the paradoxical discontinuity between sexual instincts and all the normal affairs of life, together with the double code in which the society of his day had worked out its dubious compromises. No literary comedy ever composed offers a more compact presentation of these subtle discontinuities than this of Byron's. Though himself both author and leading actor Byron is nevertheless at a loss, finding himself utterly 'astonished how, and why, all this has happened' (13 Oct. 1813; C, 1, 200).

They all go to Newstead. Byron, angered by Webster's boasting, drinks too much. He and Lady Frances are alone, at night; she offers herself to him, admitting that she will regret it after; he refuses, for her sake, to take advantage of the opportunity (17 Oct. 1813; C, 1, 203).

Afterwards, they corresponded. Emotions remained strong on both sides. Byron continued to wonder both at the lady and at his own behaviour. Was she, or was he, sincere? Should he not, according to the prevalent code of gallantry, have gone ahead regardless? Were his motives deeply good that last night, or was some self-deception at work? Surely it was a matter of genuine 'ethics'? (21 and 23 Oct. 1813; C, I, 209, 211). As for the lady, what really, quoting *Twelfth Night* (II, iii, 157), were her 'exquisite reasons'? She seems now to write of 'deceiving *un marito*' as though it were a merit. Good and evil are tangled. As in Restoration comedy, we remain simultaneously baffled and instructed:

Is not all this a comedy? . . . It has enlivened my ethical studies on the human mind beyond 50 volumes. How admirably we accommodate our reasons to our wishes!

(22 Nov. 1813: C, I, 216)

However, we are really less in the comparatively simplified world of Etheredge than with the Jacobeans or Wycherley, meeting continual references to Othello while Byron as protagonist plays the roles simultaneously of sinner, moralist and plot-controller, for it is all a consciously activated drama run by one person, like *Volpone*, or Wycherley's *The Country Wife*. There is no cynicism: we are aware rather of a profoundly sympathetic, humorous and moral sensibility, complicated by a sense of the compulsion on a man to respond to a lady's advances, itself a kind of ethic, an ethic of courage and gallantry, sex-prompted, a duel being felt as the right *dramatic* conclusion (25 Nov. 1813; C, I, 217–18).

As so often elsewhere, Byron found himself the centre of a vortex. But he was simultaneously inside the drama and above it; these letters show less levity of heart than the non-attachment of the artist. He was living in the artistic dimension, analyzing everyone including himself, probing into self-deceptions and deceptive conventions, ready to bear guilt, helping others, thinking altruistically, yet an agent of moral judgment. He is here more than a satiric voice; he is a satiric embodiment, like Falstaff analyzing and fooling Justice Shallow; or like Volpone, and Horner. To Byron it was all, as was an earlier adventure to which he applies the word (Lady Melbourne,

12 Aug.; 13 Sept.; 1812; SP, I, 140; C, I, 75), a 'drama'; a drama on the mysteries and complexities of sexual behaviour.

When Byron is infuriated by Webster's braggadocio, seeing it as, with references to Jonson's *Every Man in his Humour* and to *Othello*, a 'Bobadil jealousy', all 'horribly stuffed' with 'epithets of war' (Lady Melbourne, 14 Oct. 1813; C, I, 202; *Othello*, I, i, 14), we are reminded of Falstaff's words on Justice Shallow:

> As I return, I will fetch off these justices: I do see the bottom of Justice Shallow. Lord, Lord! how subject we old men are to this vice of lying. This same starved justice hath done nothing but prate to me of the wildness of his youth . . . I do remember him at Clement's Inn like a man made after supper of a cheese paring . . . And now is this Vice's dagger become a squire, and talks as familiarly of John a Gaunt as if he had been sworn brother to him. . . . Well, I will be acquainted with him, if I return; and it shall go hard but I will make him a philosopher's two stones to me. If the young dace be a bait for the old pike, I see no reason in the law of nature but I may snap at him. . . .
>
> (*2 Henry IV*, III, ii, 327)

There are, of course, differences. Byron had more on his hands than playing Falstaff; he was Timon too, and so whereas Falstaff borrowed £1,000 of Shallow it is Byron who lends £1,000 to Webster. Byron, always fully *conscious* of such implications as we are analyzing, sees himself as Falstaff and Webster as Shallow; and accordingly comments, changing Shakespeare's 'owe you' to 'owes me', 'I must write tomorrow to "Master Shallow, who owes me a thousand pounds"' (Journal, 17 Nov. 1813; LJ, II, 328; *2 Henry IV* V, v, 77).

The peculiar blend of satire and comedy covered by Falstaff is deep in Byron. Here he is on William Sotheby:

> He may be an amiable man, a moral man, a good father, a good husband, a respectable and devout individual. I have nothing to say against all this; but I have something to say to Mr. S's literary foibles, and to the wretched affectations and systematized Sophistry of many men, women, and Children, now extant and absurd in and about London and elsewhere;— which and whom, in their false pretensions and nauseous

attempts to make learning a nuisance and society a Bore, I consider as fair game—to be brought down on all fair occasions,
and I doubt not, by the blessing of God on my honest purpose,
and the former example of Mr. Gifford and others, my betters,
before my eyes, to extirpate, extinguish and eradicate such as
come within the compass of my intention.

(Murray, 23 April 1818; LJ, IV, 230)

'Fair game': just as in any fine comedy, it is both social service and
good sport.

III

There is much of Falstaff in Byron. It may be objected that Byron's
ethereal and angelic beauty and ascetic habits show little resemblance
to Shakespeare's 'huge hill of flesh' (1 *Henry IV*, II, iv, 273). But
throughout his life Byron was fighting corpulence. He was *naturally*
fat. Trelawny writes of his 'broad beam' and 'round limbs' all 'built
for floating'; 'he was of that soft lymphatic temperament which it is
almost impossible to keep within a moderate compass' (Trelawny,
VI, 40, 43). Byron records in 1807 how by violent exercise, fasting,
playing cricket in seven waistcoats and a great coat, limiting himself
to one small meal a day and taking hot baths, he has reduced his
weight and become 'very thin' (Hanson, 2 April; Pigot, April;
1807; LJ, I, 126–7). On returning from his travels in 1811 he was
'in tolerable leanness' (Augusta, 9 Sept. 1811; LJ, II, 31), but
towards the end of 1812 he was beginning to grow fatter and in 1813
deliberately 'eating and drinking' to grow 'fat' and disguise his
wretchedness (Lady Melbourne, 11 and 18 Nov. 1812; 20 Aug.
1813; C, I, 106, 110, 173). He was thin during his stay with the
Websters and starving himself in November 1813 (Kinnaird, 1 Dec.
1822; Journal, 17 Nov. 1813; C, II, 235; LJ, II, 328), but in 1814
we find him succumbing to an 'enormous dinner' and fearing con-
gratulation on the 'fatness' which he abhors (Lady Melbourne,
8 April, 1814; C, I, 249). He was thin enough during the separation at the age of twenty-eight (Webster, 2 July 1819; LJ, IV, 323),
but after leaving England tells Augusta that he has 'got large, ruddy

and robustious' (10 May 1817; *Astarte*, XI, 283). He was thin on arriving at Venice (Hoppner, 27 Feb. 1823; LJ, VI, 169), but in 1818 he was reported by Newton Hanson as 'very fat' and his face 'pale, bloated and sallow,' the knuckles of his hands 'lost in fat' (LJ, 267, note). He had in Peter Quennell's words become 'the very image of a superannuated man of pleasure' (*Byron*, Selections, 1959; Biographical Introduction, 53).

At this period he reminds us of Oscar Wilde. Moore notes that his features in 1819 had lost their former 'refined' and spiritualized look and, though less suited to a 'high romantic character', were now better fitted for 'that arch, waggish wisdom, that Epicurean play of humour, which he had shown to be equally inherent in his various and prodigally gifted nature' (Moore, II, 248 or XXXV, 410). He next took 'drastic if intermittent steps to grow thin again', but when Leigh Hunt saw him in 1822 'he had swelled again to almost unrecognizable proportions' (Nicolson, I, 8). Later in 1822, after a period of illness, he had become 'thinner even than in 1813' and reports himself in 1823 'as thin as a Skeleton' (Kinnaird, 1 Dec 1822; Hoppner, 27 Feb. 1823; C, II, 235; LJ, VI, 169). On 1 April 1823 Lady Blessington found him so 'extremely thin', that 'his figure has almost a boyish air' (Blessington, I, 2).

Byron's physical and moral qualities were interdependent. He starved himself variously to avoid corpulence, indigestion and evil passions. Even a fish dinner, he says, 'kills me with heaviness, stupor and horrible dreams' and continues:

> I wish I were in the country, to take exercise—instead of being obliged to *cool* by abstinence, in lieu of it. I should not so much mind a little accession of flesh—my bones can well bear it. But the worst is, the devil always came with it—till I starved him out—and I will *not* be the slave of *any* appetite.
>
> (Journal, 17 Nov. 1813; LJ, II, 328)

'I swallowed the Devil', he writes to Lady Melbourne, 'in the shape of a collar of brawn' (8 April 1814; C, I, 249). Moore recounts how the poet Rogers was embarrassed to find Byron, whom he had invited to dinner, unwilling to eat anything but potatoes and vinegar, though he would have preferred biscuits and soda-water. Byron appeared 'to have conceived a notion that animal food has some peculiar influence on character'; once he asked, 'Moore, don't you find eating beef-steak makes you ferocious?' (Moore, I, 314, 324 or XIII, 145, 150). Abstinence did not come easily. Dallas, who knew him after his return from Greece in 1811, tells us that his daily diet was two thin biscuits and a cup of tea, and regards his abstemiousness as 'hardly credible' (Dallas, VIII, 198). Trelawny, reporting his 'terror of getting fat', said that he was so constituted that it was almost impossible to keep his body 'within a moderate compass'; whenever his vigilance was relaxed, 'he swelled apace'. He exercised amazing restraint to 'the point of absolute starvation', and after existing 'on biscuits and soda-water for days together', would devour a mash of fish, vegetables and vinegar 'like a famished dog' (Trelawny, VI, 43–4). 'When I *do* dine', he once wrote, 'I gorge like an Arab or a Boa snake, on fish and vegetables, but no meat' (Journal, 30 Nov. 1813; LJ, II, 353).

He was not a consistent abstainer. He was sometimes aware of a 'monstrous appetite' (Hobhouse, 31 March 1817; C, II, 40), and on occasion satisfied it. Sometimes he even indulged in beef (Moore, quoting a letter by Henry Joy, II, 142 or XXXI, 365; Journal 24 Jan. 1821; LJ, V, 184). He liked returning 'to a beef-steak at Bellamy's' to get away from Parliamentary debates (Hobhouse, 17 Oct. 1820; C, II, 158). His naturally convivial temperament enjoyed dining out with friends and Moore reports the exuberance of these occasions (Moore, II, 250 or XXXV, 411).

His dining could include drink. From Cambridge he wrote to Elizabeth Pigot that his life had been 'one continual routine of dissipation' and that he had been 'drunk every day' (5 July 1807; LJ, I, 133, 135); though both Teresa (XVI, 309) and Trelawny (VI, 40) say that he overstated the extent of his youthful drinking. He had a good cellar at Newstead and describes it later with some pride, though now an abstainer (Lady Melbourne, 10 Oct. 1813; C, I, 194). Wine had lost its 'power' over him in 1811; he does not 'quaff as formerly', and claims to have left it all 'entirely' (Hobhouse, 22 Oct.; 17 Nov.; 1811; C, I, 51, 61). The claim was short-lived. A dinner of fish and wine leaves him in a state of 'heaviness, stupor and horrible dreams' (Journal, 17 Nov. 1813; LJ, II, 327;

the editor gives notes of Byron's dinner bills at this period). Again:

> I have been eating and drinking; which I always do when wretched; for then I grow fat and don't show it; and now that I am in very good plight and spirits I can't leave off the custom. . . .
>
> (Lady Melbourne, 20 Aug. 1813; C, I, 173)

At the period of the Separation Byron's drinking with Kinnaird, Colman and Sheridan assumes a central importance in his life-story (LBM, 167–8, 206–7; Mayne, *Life and Letters of Lady Byron*, XIII, 194–5; Elwin, *Lord Byron's Wife*, XI, 327). Lord Lovelace tells us that Kinnaird's brandy 'brought him to the verge of madness' (Lovelace, II, 38). These parties worried Lady Byron, who seems to have associated them with other dangers (LBM, 206–7).

Drink was not normally an excess. Byron could suffer from thirst, drinking 'fifteen bottles of soda-water in one night' (Journal, 2 Feb. 1821; LJ, V, 198), but he did not succumb to intoxicants. 'In general', he says, he was 'temperate', taking only 'a pint of light clary wines' at his '*one* meal' (Hobhouse, 9 March 1822; C, II, 218). However, he certainly liked the *idea of drinking*, the Falstaff-state, as it were, that drinking suggested, as in his remark on Sir Walter Scott: 'Wonderful man! I long to get drunk with him' (Journal, 5 Jan. 1821; LJ, V, 151). Naturally Falstaff is in this connexion remembered as when, after confessing to Lady Melbourne that he has been goaded into drinking too much by Webster's braggadocio, he adds, 'Company, villainous company, hath been the spoil of me'; though normally he 'detests' it (Lady Melbourne, 17 Oct. 1813; C, I, 203; *1 Henry IV*, III, iii, 10). What in Falstaff is ironic is transferred by Byron to a more direct assertion: he did *not* like drinking but he *did* like the conviviality that conditioned it. Thinking of his early travels with Hobhouse, Byron remarks: 'As Justice Shallow says, "Oh the merry days that we have seen"' (Hobhouse, 21 Sept. 1820; C, II, 155; *2 Henry IV*, III, ii, 236); and of remembered parties, he quotes Falstaff to Moore: 'Ah, Master Shallow, we have heard the chimes at midnight' (Moore, 10 July 1817; LJ, IV, 148; *2 Henry IV*, III, ii, 231).

Drink naturally made Byron think of Falstaff. In Greece, when getting some gin for his servant Tita at Ithaca, he remarked:

Now, gentlemen, 'Drink deep, or taste not the Pierian spring'; it is the true poetic source. 'I'm a rogue if I have drunk today'.
(Edgcumbe, 55–6)[1]

The first quotation is from Pope and the other from Falstaff (*Essay on Criticism*, 216; 1 *Henry IV*, II, iv, 171). Byron was perhaps thinking of Falstaff's speech on sherris-sack as a source of mental illumination:

A good sherris-sack hath a two-fold operation in it. It ascends me into the brain; dries me there all the foolish and dull and crudy vapours which environ it; makes it apprehensive, quick, forgetive, full of nimble, fiery, and delectable shapes; which, deliver'd o'er to the voice, the tongue, which is the birth, becomes excellent wit. The second property of your excellent sherris is the warming of the blood . . .
(2 *Henry IV*, IV, iii, 103)

Byron found drink a help to composition. Stendhal reports:

He often sat up all night, in the ardour of composition, and drank a sort of grog made of hollands and water—a beverage in which he indulged rather copiously when his muse was coy. But, generally speaking, he was not addicted to excessive drinking, though he has accused himself of that vice.
(LJ, III; App. viii, 443)

Falstaff sees sherris-sack as a Mercutio-like inspiration for delicate, volatile, wit. To Byron champagne was an equivalent; it was the only drink suitable for a lady (Lady Melbourne, 25 Sept., 1812; C, I, 84). *Don Juan* is on the Mercutio wavelength:

And the small ripple spilt upon the beach
    Scarcely o'erpass'd the cream of your champagne,
When o'er the brim the sparkling bumpers reach,
    That spring-dew of the spirit! the heart's rain!
Few things surpass old wine; and they may preach
    Who please—the more because they preach in vain—

1. Quoted from an anonymous narrator who is the 'Mr. S— —' of Charles Mackay's *Medora Leigh*: see Nicolson, VI, 126.

131

Let us have wine and woman,[1] mirth and laughter,
Sermons and soda-water the day after.

Man, being reasonable, must get drunk;
The best of life is but intoxication:
Glory, the grape, love, gold, in these are sunk
The hopes of all men and of every nation;
Without their sap, how branchless were the trunk
Of life's strange tree, so fruitful on occasion!

(*Don Juan*, II, 178)

So the advice is, 'get very drunk' and afterwards—hock and soda-water. Falstaff's speech on sherris-sack comes in handy for a comment on Napoleon's marriage to an Austrian: 'I never knew any good come of your young wife, and legal espousals, to any but your "sober-blooded boy" who "eats fish" and drinketh "no sack"' (Journal, 17 Nov. 1813; LJ, II, 324; 2 *Henry IV*, IV, iii, 93–9).

Falstaff found a deep response in Byron. One of his favourite quotations is from Falstaff's 'us youth' (*1 Henry IV*, II, ii, 93), sometimes applied to the new generation of writers (Gifford, 12 Nov. 1813; Journal, 15 March 1814; Moore, May 1814, 2 Feb. 1818; Hobhouse, 27 April 1816, 4 Aug. 1819; *Detached Thoughts*, 1821, 70; LJ, II, 278, 400; III, 82; IV, 196; C, II, 3, 120; LJ, V, 444). Of the convivial and to that extent Falstaffian Scrope Davies he neatly remarks: 'We could have better spared not only a "better man", but the "best of men"' (Hobhouse 3 March 1820; C, II, 135; *1 Henry IV*, V, iv, 104). He likes quoting Falstaff's 'Company, villainous company hath been the spoil of me', once grouping it with Falstaff's 'I have drunk medicines' (Hobhouse, 29 July 1810; Lady Melbourne, 17 Oct. 1813; Murray, 6 May 1819; Journal, 14 Nov. 1813; C, I, 11, 203; LJ, IV, 294; II, 319; *1 Henry IV*, III, iii, 10; II, ii 22). If Kean does not triumph over everyone, then 'merit hath no purchase in "these costermonger days"'; or the implications of Falstaff's phrase may be political (Journal, 20 Feb. 1814; Hunt, 7 Oct. 1815; LJ, II, 387, III, 225; 2 *Henry IV*, I, ii, 193; for 'no purchase', *1 Henry IV*, III, iii, 45). If he himself has cause for bitterness, a Falstaffian reference may soften and enrich, as when, hearing that

1. All the early editions read: woman. See P, VI, 132, note.

the *Edinburgh Review* has attacked him, he comments: 'Et Tu, Jeffrey?—there is nothing but rogery in villanous man' (Moore, 28 Feb. 1817; LJ, IV, 62; *Julius Caesar*, III, i, 77; *1 Henry IV*, II, iv, 140). The range is wide, and may be simply poetical: 'This part of the night, the "sweet of it" (as Falstaff says) in London, is the drowsiest here' (Lady Melbourne, 6 Feb. 1815; C, I, 302; *2 Henry IV*, V, iii, 51; but the words were spoken by Silence). From early in Byron's life Falstaff references are ready. From Malta he wrote:

I must egotize a little. I am in bad health and worse spirits, being afflicted in body with what Hostess Quickly in *Henry V* calls a villainous 'Quotidian Tertian'; it killed Falstaff and may me. (Hobhouse, 15 May 1811; C, I, 32; *Henry V*, II, i, 124)

He feels himself and Falstaff as akin, almost as one.

There are various Falstaffs: the convivial rogue of the first *Henry IV* and the anti-social satirist of the second; and the Falstaff who fools the jealous Ford and is in turn fooled in *The Merry Wives of Windsor*. There is the Falstaff of vice and the Falstaff of mercurial, or Mercutio-like, wit. Byron is all of them.

Falstaff is an unmoral, Rabelaisian figure asserting, in the manner of all great comedy as discussed by John Cowper Powys in the concluding chapters of his *Rabelais* (1948), the rights of the physical against spiritualities and conventional taboos. In drama, the extent of vice or obscene reference allowed is naturally limited, and we have to allow Falstaff to cover by implication more than is said or shown. The primary emphasis is on eating and drinking, but he cohabits with Doll Tearsheet, a prostitute, his addiction to low life is obvious, and his wit may be supposed to be bolder off-stage than it is when we overhear him.

Byron liked retreating from society to low life. He enjoyed mixing with the boxing world at Tom Crib's tavern (p. 146 below). On another level he found release from his tensions in the sophisticated brilliances of Sheridan and Colman (*Detached Thoughts*, 107; LJ, V, 461; LBM, 168; and see Blessington, IX, 215–16). Since Colman was the leading spirit, we may deduce that indecencies sparkled. Byron's sojourn in Italy had much to do with his inability to remain contented with a puritanical climate. Both in temperature and moral code Italy suited him; and he rioted gladly in its masques and carnivals. From Venice he writes to Kinnaird of the carnival and his staying up all night, for ten days, though, in the vein of Falstaff's religious counterings, 'Lent will bring me round again, with early hours and temperance' (Kinnaird, 3 and 24 Feb. 1817; 22 Feb. 1819; C, II, 34–6, 104). The Carnival could leave him in a state of violent emotion: 'I write in a passion and a Sirocco, and I was up till six this morning at the Carnival' (Murray, 25 Jan. 1819; LJ, IV, 278). We have Byron's studied description of it, printed in Appendix viii of *Letters and Journals*, VI:

The concluding festivals of the Carnival, that universal Harlequinade in Catholic countries, but more especially in Italy, were now in their final orgasm of Buffoonery, intrigue, and universal amusement. As their term approached, their joy, or at least their hilarity, was redoubled. All was Mime, and Masque, and 'Christian fools with varnished faces'. Beneath these same 'varnished faces', chiefly confined to the females, there were many beautiful, and a *quantum sufficit* of some which acquired their beauty from the mystery of their vizor. But grave and gay, old and young, handsome and those who might be called so by courtesy, were all abroad, laughing, flirting, tormenting, pleasant and sometimes pleasing . . .

A masque is merely a dress, or a disguise, but not an attempt at farce or comedy. Their parts are not studied. On the contrary . . . it may be observed that a woman, at least a Continental woman, is never less a Masque than when a Masque, unless, perhaps, to her husband, or some truculent relation.

It is at this periodical Saturnalia . . . that all ranks are jostled, and mingled, and delighted, and all this without fear, observance, or offence. A Masque is privileged to a certain point, and that is decency, and there are, the multitude considered, few who transgress the rule.

There is—to a foreigner—a mixture of mystery and hilarity, in this general burst from every day cares, that renders a Carnival peculiarly attractive . . . Curiosity is always excited, sometimes Passion, and occasionally Pleasure. If you do not always recognize, you are generally recognized (the men, that is, who rarely masque)—and the jest, or the hint, or the present of a flower with

134

which you are greeted, have a novelty even from a former acquaintance. Life becomes for the moment a drama without the fiction.

Perhaps the Italians would but ill exchange their Carnival for a Parliament; but they long for the latter, and if England would barter with them, there might be no great loss to either; it would be Masquerade for Masquerade—with the people represented by themselves.

(LJ, VI, 440; *The Merchant of Venice*, II, v, 33)

Perhaps the most Byronically revealing comment of all comes in a letter to Murray from Ravenna dated 21 February 1820:

The Conventual education, the Cavalier Servitude, the habits of thought and living are so entirely different, and the difference becomes so much more striking the more you live intimately with them, that I know not how to make you comprehend a people, who are at once temperate and profligate, serious in their character and buffoons in their amusements, capable of impressions and passions, which are at once *sudden* and *durable* (what you find in no other nation), and who actually have *no society* (what we would call so), as you may see by their Comedies: they have no real comedy, not even in Goldoni; and that is because they have no Society to draw it from . . . . . . Their best things are the Carnival balls and masquerades, when everybody runs mad for six weeks. After their dinners and suppers, they make extempore verses and buffoon one another; but it is a humour which you would not enter into, ye of the North.

(LJ, IV, 408)

Clearly, this is as much a self-description as a guide to the Italian temperament.

It may seem strange that Byron should be capable of writing *Childe Harold, Manfred* and *Cain* with as much ease as *Beppo* and *Don Juan*, of switching from agonies of spiritual guilt to wild buffoonery with no sense of discrepancy. T. E. Lawrence showed a similar co-presence of misery and fun. Powys gave us studies of Dostoievsky and Rabelais within a couple of years and with equal enthusiasm. Such apparent anomalies await an integration in some future order of man at present hard to conceive.

135

Byron found it possible to live a more complete life in Italy than he could in England. He could, among other things, be more phalli-cally conscious; he could live, as it were, the implications of great humour, leading to a more than ordinary indulgence. Just as Aristophanes and Rabelais shock us by their references to ordure, so Byron at Venice indulges in sexual and perhaps homosexual practices presumably involving sodomy. This he had experienced, as I have shown in *Essays in Criticism* (p. 351 below), in Greece on his first travels; and perhaps on other occasions. In Italy he appears to have indulged with the abandon described by Shelley to Peacock on 22 December 1818:

The fact is, that first, the Italian women with whom he associates are perhaps the most contemptible of all who exist under the moon—the most ignorant, the most disgusting, the most bigoted; Countesses smell so strongly of garlic, that an ordinary Englishman cannot approach them. Well, L.B. is familiar with the lowest sort of these women, the people his gondolieri pick up in the streets. He associates with wretches who seem almost to have lost the gait and physiognomy of man, and who do not scruple to avow practices, which are not only not named, but I believe seldom even conceived in England. He says he disapproves, but he endures. He is heartily and deeply discontented with himself; and contemplating in the distorted mirror of his own thoughts the nature and the habits of man, what can he behold but objects of contempt and despair? But that he is a great poet, I think the address to Ocean proves. And he has a certain degree of candour while you talk to him, but unfortunately it does not outlast your departure. No, I do not doubt, and for his sake, I ought to hope, that his present career must end soon in some violent circumstance.

(LJ, IV, 260, note)

He 'disapproves', but 'endures'. Such descents are of the kind described by Shakespeare in Sonnet 118 where 'sick' of 'welfare' he descends to sickness as a cure (*The Mutual Flame*, 125; p. 62 above); and by Nietzsche, when he describes his Zarathustra as so rich in solitary self-attainment that his very virtue makes hunger for 'wicked-ness', for some sort of *taking* instead of the everlasting giving of creative genius, in order to 'touch' the 'souls' of others (*Thus Spake Zarathustra*, 31, 'The Night-Song'; see also above pp. 62–3). The passages are discussed in the epilogue to the 1962 issue of *The Christian Renaissance* (Epilogue, 286), where I group them with a study of Oscar Wilde, who experienced a similar urge to mix with the underworld of society in the underworld of vice. Such adventures are covered by Byron's line in *Manfred*, 'I plung'd amidst Mankind' (II, ii, 145). A similar instinct drove T. E. Lawrence from his heroic pedestal to the world described in *The Mint*.

That said, we can admit that Byron suffered revulsions. According to Moore he 'defyingly' 'abandoned himself' to the 'headlong career of licence', used to go out in his gondola to get away from it, and afterwards hated Venice (II, 180–2 or XXXII, 381–83). Venice was the 'Sea-Sodom' (Webster, 8 Sept. 1818; Hoppner, 31 Dec. 1819; LJ, IV, 255, 393). In *Marino Faliero* (V, iii, 99) it is apostraphized as 'Gehenna of the waters! thou Sea-Sodom!'

Nevertheless Moore observes that at this period Byron's mind was more 'actively in the full possession of all its energies' than at any other period of his life (II, 181 or XXXII, 382). Life is made of antithetical stuffs and literary genius exists in large part from recognition that it is so made. Of Burns' letters Byron wrote:

. . . They are full of oaths and obscene songs. What an antithetical mind!—tenderness, roughness—delicacy, coarseness—sentiment, sensuality—soaring and grovelling, dirt and deity—all mixed up in that one compound of inspired clay!

It seems strange; a true voluptuary will never abandon his mind to the grossness of reality. It is by exalting the earthly, the material, the *physique* of our pleasures, by veiling these ideas, by forgetting them altogether, or, at least, never naming them hardly to one's self, that we can alone prevent them from disgusting.

(Journal, 13 Dec. 1813; LJ, II, 376)

It is as though Byron were attempting, at this, Venetian, period of his life, to *live* the implications of these words; and as though this newly comprehensive freedom, this living from his whole, good-and-bad self, actually empowered—as for most men it could not have done—his writing. He once told Lady Blessington that Italian vices were as 'weeds' luxuriant in growth under the 'sun'. 'Nature', he said, 'is all-powerful in Italy, and who is it that would not prefer the sins of her exuberance to the crimes of art?' (Blessington, VII, 167). Byron knew what he was doing. It is likely that he never really lost control, any more than Wilde; it was all, as Bradley said of Macbeth, undertaken as an 'appalling duty'. One of our neatest comments comes from Lord Lovelace writing of Kinnaird's brandy parties in *Astarte*, a passage in which Byron is shown, like Shakespeare's Hal, as part and yet not part of the riotous company with which he mixes:

He adapted himself too conspicuously to the tone of company of the meanest kind. His tumultuous spirits at Kinnaird's brandy parties (presided over by a left-handed Mrs. Kinnaird) were overacted. Those ignoble boon companions deceived themselves when they thought Byron most gay and unconcerned. When he took a part in the low comedy of bad company, his immutable self, unknown to such bystanders, was watching in tragic contemplation of the ribald nightmare, judging and condemning the transient self with the surrounding crew.

(Lovelace, I, 12)

It could not have been put better. These sentences shine like diamonds from the mess and muddle of Lord Lovelace's dishonest book.

Byron's adventures in the underworld of society and morals, whether in London or abroad, may be compared with those of Hal and Falstaff, one a prince and the other an aristocrat, in Eastcheap. Such men, and Wilde too, as he himself has described it, descend for a purpose, preferring for a while this human sub-soil to the falsities of society.

IV

Though a knight Falstaff is a living challenge to royalty and its attendant values, including soldiership and law. He mocks the King and Prince in a charade (*1 Henry IV*, II, iv, 426–535). He makes fun of Owen Glendower, and the famous Douglas becomes

that sprightly Scot of Scots, Douglas, that runs
o' horseback up a hill perpendicular.

(*1 Henry IV*, II, iv, 382)

He fools 'that hot termagant Scot' (*1 Henry IV*, v, iv, 114), Douglas, by pretending to be killed on the field of battle. He makes a butt of all respectability. He is himself a law-breaker and thief. His shameless lack of valour at the Gadshill robbery and his pretended death at Shrewsbury, where he captains a ludicrously ragamuffin army, the result of his corrupt misuse of the 'King's press' (*1 Henry IV*, iv, ii, 13), constitute living and comic repudiations of the heroic. His instinct is to turn war to farce; he carries a bottle in his pistol holster. Told that he owes God a death he ruminates:

'Tis not due yet: I would be loth to pay him before his day. What need I be so forward with him that calls not on me? Well, 'tis no matter; honour pricks me on. Yea, but how if honour prick me off when I come on? how then? Can honour set to a leg? No, or an arm? No. Or take away the grief of a wound? No. Honour hath no skill in surgery then? No. What is honour? A word. What is the word honour? Air. A trim reckoning! Who hath it? He that died o' Wednesday. Doth he feel it? No. Doth he hear it? No. It is insensible then? Yea, to the dead. But will it not live with the living? No. Why? Detraction will not suffer it. Therefore I'll none of it: honour is a mere scutcheon; and so ends my catechism.

(*1 Henry IV*, v, i, 128)

As his story develops Falstaff's challenge grows more keen. Comedy in Part 1 is replaced by the more seriously anarchical thrust of Part 2, the opposition of Falstaff and the Lord Chief Justice assuming a primary importance. Falstaff touches Hamlet as an anarchic threat.

Much of this is in Byron. The conclusion to *Don Juan*, wherein a ghostly presence turns out to be a plump and amatory duchess closely corresponds to the metaphysical humour of Falstaff's lumbering body rising from the field of battle where we thought that he had died. In both, numinous or tragic emotions are first stimulated and then reversed by a this-worldly, physical, shock. Byron's drama *Sardanapalus* (1821) has for hero a pleasure-loving and enlightened monarch for whom, as in Falstaff's speech on sherris-sack, wine 'opens a new world' (I, ii, 191). Sardanapalus is a pacifist repudiating bloodshed. Of the conquest of India by his imperial ancestress Semiramis he asks:

> And how many
> Left she behind in India to the vultures?
>
> (I, ii, 131)

Sardanapalus is throughout sharply criticized for his considered repudiation of the heroic values. His pacifism is the central theme of a drama which might be called an expanded working out, in deadly earnest, of the thoughts in Falstaff's speech on honour. Thoughts in Shakespeare given to a humorous figure are in Byron developed and expanded in deadly, rational earnest.

Here is a lighter touch, barbed nevertheless by genuine feeling:

> Mem.—I have forgotten to pay Pitt's taxes, and suppose I shall be surcharged. 'An I do not turn rebel when thou art king'— Oons! I believe my very biscuit is leavened with that impostor's imports.
>
> (Journal, 6 Dec. 1813: LJ, II, 367)

Byron is thinking of Falstaff's 'By the Lord, I'll be a traitor then, when thou art king' (1 Henry IV, I, ii, 163). There may be a reference to the Prince Regent. Pitt's taxes, we remember, would have been supporting the war against Napoleon. Byron was, as revolutionary, in earnest, but there is a Falstaffian humour too, as again when he writes that if Napoleon 'don't drub the Allies, there is "no purchase in money"' (Moore, 27 March 1815; LJ, III, 188; 1 Henry IV, III, iii, 45). As we have shown (p. 91), he deliberately attacked the throne; and state ceremonial was merely the 'romantic melodrama' of a 'royal Roscius' (Lady Melbourne, 26 Nov. 1812; C, I, 110). Byron, like Falstaff, existed as an ironic challenge to the ruling powers.

On fights of any kind Falstaff and his followers are ready to hand. Pistol is remembered and quoted (Moore, 10 Jan. 1815; 6 Nov. 1816; LJ, III, 169, 381; 2 Henry IV, V, iii, 129; The Merry Wives of Windsor, I, iii, 30), and when annoyed with Hobhouse for getting entangled with an absurd challenge from the radical Major Cartwright, then in his eighty-ninth year, Byron punningly and pithily referring simultaneously to age and bravado—punning on the dual meanings of 'antient'—designates the latter 'Antient Pistol' (Hobhouse, 26 June 1819; C, II, 115). But Byron's favourite quotation is from the comically philosophic Nym. Nym has quarrelled with Pistol, and says:

> I dare not fight; but I will wink and hold out mine iron. It is a simple one; but what though? it will toast cheese, and it will endure cold as another man's sword will: and there's an end.
>
> (*Henry V*, II, i, 7)

'Wink' means 'close the eyes'. In this burlesque of human wrangling the wizened—for so I see him—Nym's philosophic and honest attitude appealed to Byron, who uses the phrase 'wink and hold out my iron' again and again. Thinking that a letter of his to Lady Frances may have fallen into her husband's hands, he observes 'If so—and this silence looks suspicious—I must clap on my "musty morion" and "hold out my iron"' (Journal, 17 Nov. 1813; LJ, II, 323). His secret political foes are like Falstaff's 'men in buckram' (*1 Henry IV*, II, iv, 217) and if he discovers them, then, 'like the redoubtable Nym, "I can wink and hold out my cold iron" as well as another'; or the phrase can be applied to his antagonist (Lady Melbourne, 14 Dec. 1812; Moore, 26 Feb. 1814; C, I, 116; LJ, III, 50). He uses the phrase for his prospective support of the Italian rising (Hobhouse, 22 April 1820; C, II, 144). When the Pope's gendarmerie object to the liveries of Byron's servants, he plans resistance:

> However, I can 'wink and hold out mine iron'. It makes me think (the whole thing does) of *Romeo and Juliet*—'now Gregory, remember thy *swashing* blow'.
>
> (Moore, 9 June 1820; LJ, V, 43)

The quotation from *Romeo and Juliet* (I, i, 68) exactly underlines Byron's comoedic approach to such matters. Similar comic overtones accompany expectance of civil war at home:

> I should like to stay out another year or more, if I could; but I presume we must all come back, and put our 'musty morrions on' (as Beaumont and Fletcher have it), so 'now Gregory, remember thy swashing blow'.
>
> (Kinnaird, 24 Feb. 1817; C, II, 37)

The truth is, Byron, while knowing the necessity of war, cannot take it quite seriously. Of his projected venture in Greece he told Lady Blessington that such 'ludicrous images' kept arising in his mind that

> the whole subject, which, seen through the veil of passion, looked fit for a sublime epic, and I one of its heroes, examined now through reason's glass, appears fit only for a travesty.
>
> (XII, 289)

'The laughing devils,' said Byron, 'will return', and there is, 'as Napoleon said, but one step between the sublime and the ridiculous' (Blessington, XII, 289).

Falstaff's own fighting, of which the burlesque attitudes of Pistol and Nym are shadows, is remembered to excellent effect. Byron thinks that he may fall in love with a lady—probably his future wife—'if it came "a warm June" (as Falstaff observes)', though the words 'a hot June' were in fact Prince Hal's in conversation with Falstaff on the coming civil war. Murray in England has been cudgelled by 'misbegotten knaves, "in Kendal Green"'; and Italian thieves come on 'in bodies of thirty ("in buckram and Kendal Green") at a time' (Lady Melbourne, 29 April 1814; Moore, 12 June 1815; Murray, 15 Oct. 1816; C, I, 253–4; LJ, III, 204, 375–6; 1 Henry IV, II, iv, 401, 250, 217). Byron recalls Falstaff's words on his miserable soldiers:

> I have led my ragamuffins where they are peppered: there's not three of my hundred and fifty left alive, and they are for the town's end, to beg during life.
>
> (1 Henry IV, V, iii, 36)

This he uses with exact sense of the leader's responsibility, applying it first to Canning's disbanding of his party (Moore, 25 July 1813; LJ, II, 237) and later to Murray when in trouble from the publication of Byron's Cain:

> But now (as you really seem in a damned scrape), they may do what they like with me, so that I can get you out of it; but, cheer up: though I have 'led my ragamuffins when they are well peppered', I will stick by them as long as they will keep the field.
>
> (8 Feb. 1822; LJ, VI, 18; 1 Henry IV, V, iii, 36–7)

The use of 'ragamuffins' in this context is a happy touch, as again when used for Leigh Hunt's followers ('The Bowles Controversy', LJ, v, App. iii, 589). In more serious vein Byron applies the passage to General Normann's loss of a pro-Hellenic party, cut down by the Turks (Bowring, 21 May, 1823; LJ, VI, 215). Here it marks an attempt to veil in bluff style his own distress. Probably the neatest reference of all to Falstaff's soldiers comes in a comment on literary animosities:

They seem to be an irritable set, and I wish myself well out of it. 'I'll not march through Coventry with them, that's flat'. What the devil had I to do with scribbling?
(Journal, 17 March 1814; LJ, II, 402; 1 Henry IV, IV, ii, 42)

The stage appearance of Falstaff's army remembered, the implied critique of literary squabbles and squabblers has a comic eternality.

The varieties played on such quotations are remarkable. Byron often makes so apt and multi-directional a use of them, that they not only illumine his wide meanings in compact brevity, but themselves live henceforth enriched in our minds by Byron's handling. Falstaff's comic claim to have fought Hotspur for 'a long hour by Shrewsbury clock' (1 Henry IV, v, iv, 151), used earlier by Byron in a letter (Lady Melbourne, 6 Nov. 1812; C, I, 101), comes in pointedly during Byron's conversations in Cephalonia reported by James Kennedy. Byron had been out bathing by night with a gentleman given to exaggerate, who had said: 'We were two hours in the water last night'. 'Yes,' said Lord Byron emphatically, 'by Shrewsbury clock' (Kennedy, 297).

However he might mock at warring, Byron knew its necessity, though it was a necessity as unwelcome as to Falstaff. Writing of the Convention of Cintra, the young Byron quoted Falstaff to voice his fears:

We have heard wonders of these Portuguese lately, and their gallantry—pray heaven it continue; yet, 'would it were bed-time, Hal, and all were well!' They must fight a great many hours by 'Shrewsbury clock' before the number of their slain equals that of our countrymen . . .
(Dallas, VII, 182; 1 Henry IV, v, i, 125; v, iv, 151)

143

Having been invited in 1813 to join the forces on the Continent, 'to wink and hold out mine iron', he observes that a fit of ill-humour or vanity might lead him where 'Honour comes unlooked for' (Lady Melbourne, 23 Oct. 1813; C, I, 211). Falstaff's words were: 'Give me life; which if I can save, so; if not, honour comes unlook'd for, and there's an end' (*1 Henry IV*, v, iii, 63). They admirably sum up Byron's general thoughts on duelling and war. When in *Don Juan* he doubts if an honourable record in a 'bulletin' can make up for a 'bullet in' one's body, noting that the thought is Shakespeare's, he is thinking of Falstaff on honour (*Don Juan*, VII, 21). He undertook the support of the Italian cause in this mood. On 5 November 1820 he wrote to Moore from Ravenna:

There will be the devil to pay, and there is no saying who will or who will not be set down in his bill. If 'honour should come unlooked for' to any of your acquaintance, make a Melody of it, that his ghost, like poor Yorick's, may have the satisfaction of being plaintively pitied—or still more nobly commemorated, like 'Oh breathe not his name'. In case you should not think him worth it, here is a Chant for you instead—

When a man hath no freedom to fight for at home,
   Let him combat for that of his neighbours;
Let him think of the glories of Greece and of Rome,
   And get knock'd on the head for his labours.
               (LJ, v, 111; *1 Henry IV*, v, iii, 64)

On 2 January he wrote: 'I shall remain here till May or June, and, unless "honour comes unlooked for", we may perhaps meet in France or England, within the year' (Moore, 2 Jan. 1821; LJ, v, 215). The philosophic quality of Falstaff's thoughts on death is recaptured when, questioning in meditation the final validity of life, he comes up against a 'but' leading to—'What?' 'I do not know', he says, 'and who does? "He that died o' Wednesday"' (*Detached Thoughts*, 1821; 60; LJ, v, 439; *1 Henry IV*, v, i, 138). He turns next to the horror of a forthcoming execution: 'It is detestable to *take* life in that way, unless it be to preserve two lives' (LJ, v, 439).

That a common area exists within the thought-realms of Hamlet and Falstaff was demonstrated by Sir Herbert Beerbohm Tree's favourite experiment of speaking Hamlet's and Falstaff's soliloquies on death in each other's voices.

V

The qualities we are studying are mainly prose qualities, such as those of Shakespeare's prose from low comedy to sophisticated cynicism, from Dogberry to Iago. Or manliness. Byron's prose is pre-eminently manly. The two parts of *Henry IV* cover a great deal of this range; and indeed, our present study can use Byron to show how there is a unity running through *Henry IV* from Falstaff to Hotspur. They are all conceived as physical types; one may be a fat glutton, the other a brawny soldier; the one is, on principle, a coward, the other almost comically brave; they hold diametrically opposite views of honour. But they belong to the same prose, forthright, world.

Byron responded to the anti-militaristic common-sense of Falstaff, but he was nevertheless forced to play Hotspur. In the Bowles Controversy he quotes Hotspur, noting that Pope was adored by a 'cankered Bolingbroke' and that 'villainous saltpetre' was used by Satan's artillery in *Paradise Lost*; and aptly transposes to a literary battle the King's reference to Hotspur in 'Why, *yet* he doth *deny* his prisoners' (The Bowles Controversy, LJ, v, App. iii, 571, 555, 540; *1 Henry IV*, I, iii, 176, 60, 77). Prince Hal's

> The Douglas and the Hotspur both together
> Are confident against the world in arms
> > (*1 Henry IV*, v, i, 116)

becomes 'the Jeffrey and the Moore together are confident against the world in ink' (Moore, 28 Oct. 1815; LJ, III, 232). The quotation is used again, of himself and Moore (Moore, 10 July 1817; LJ, IV, 148). Byron scorned what he regarded as extravagances in the mood of Hotspur, whose phrase 'skimble-skamble stuff' (*1 Henry IV*, III, i, 153), applied to Glendower's superstitions, Byron uses for Hunt's views on poetry (Moore, 1 June 1818; LJ, IV, 238), as well as for Webster's irritating talk: 'He talked a deal of skimble-skamble stuff and is gone to Florence' (Kinnaird, 1 Dec. 1822; C, II, 235).

Byron's views on poetry were at any time likely to correspond to Hotspur's

> I had rather be a kitten and cry mew
> Than one of these same metre ballad-mongers;
> I had rather hear a brazen canstick turn'd,
> Or a dry wheel grate on the axle-tree;
> And that would set my teeth nothing on edge,
> Nothing so much as mincing poetry:
> 'Tis like the forc'd gait of a shuffling nag.
>
> > (1 *Henry IV*, III, i, 128)

He appended the first two of these lines to his *English Bards and Scotch Reviewers*. Numerous passages from his prose attest that he could feel like Hotspur, not only about poetry he disliked, but about all poetry, even all literature. In this mood he was, like Hotspur, a man of action. The ill-fated Carbonari rising, in which he had taken part, was 'as pretty a plot as Hotspur's'; he is thinking of Hotspur's 'our plot is a good plot as ever was laid' (Kinnaird, 1 Oct. 1820; C, II, 156; 1 *Henry IV*, II, iii, 19). Once, hearing that the Austrians are to march, he calls Hotspur to his support: 'Let them —"They come like sacrifices in their trim", the hounds of hell!' (Journal, 9 Jan. 1821; LJ, V, 163; 1 *Henry IV*, IV, i, 113). *Macbeth* is also helpful: 'The cry is still, they come' (Journal, 23 Jan. 1821; LJ, V, 183; *Macbeth*, V, v, 2).

That this strain of manly courage in Byron was an extension of his Falstaffian affinities may be seen from his liking for low yet virile associates. High society never for long satisfied him. He refers often in his letters to his servants and he gravitated towards the lower social strata very naturally, like Prince Hal. The boxing world especially appealed to him, countering the world of *Macbeth* nightmare with its tough, unsophisticated, manliness:

> I must not dream again;—it spoils even reality. I will go out of doors, and see what the fog will do for me. Jackson has been here: the boxing world much as usual;—but the club increases. I shall dine at Crib's tomorrow. I like energy—even animal energy—of all kinds; and I have need of both mental and corporeal. I have not dined out, nor, indeed, *at all*, lately: have

heard no music—have seen nobody. Now for a *plunge*—high
life and low life. *Amant* alterna *Camoenae!*

(Journal, 23 Nov. 1813; LJ, II, 336)

After this he notes that he has returned from the dinner, after meeting
some famous pugilists, among them Tom Crib, at the tavern he
controlled:

Tom has been a sailor—a coal-heaver and some other genteel
profession, before he took to the cestus. Tom has been in action
at sea, and is now only three-and-thirty. A great man! has a
wife and a mistress, and conversations well—bating some sad
omissions and misapplications of the aspirate. Tom is an old
friend of mine; I have seen some of his best battles in my nonage.
He is now a publican, and, I fear, a sinner . . .

(Journal, 24 Nov. 1813; LJ, II, 345)

Byron was abused for his association with Tom Crib (Blessington,
XIV, 338).

These quotations form an apt prelude to our concluding theme:
Byron's association with William Parry, who had been sent out to
take charge of the artillery at Missolonghi. Here, when all other
interests were losing authority before the stark need for manliness and
courage, the burly Parry, a naval 'fire-master' of non-commissioned
status and low social caste, became Byron's chief stand-by and con-
fidant. He alone, with the rough bandit-like retainer Tita (see the
picture of him facing LJ, IV, 404) and the boy Loukas, remained
in Byron's favour when the rest were under his displeasure (Nicolson
X, 240). The association is carefully documented in Parry's wise and
excellent book *The Last Days of Lord Byron*.

Harold Nicolson calls Parry 'shrewd', 'vigorous', 'burly' and
'sodden' (Nicolson, IX, 211–12); phrases which serve to define his
function as a union of Hotspur and Falstaff. Being a composite of
both he existed as an external symbol of the same composite in
Byron. Pietro Gamba called him 'an excellent rough Englishman'
and 'an immoderate drinker', who made Byron drink more than was
wise (Origo, IX, 377). Trelawny writes:

The fire-master was a rough burly fellow, never quite sober, but
he was no fool, and had a fund of pothouse stories which he

told in appropriately slang language; he was a mimic and amused Byron by burlesquing Jeremy Bentham and other members of the Greek Committee. . . . All he did was to talk and drink.

(Trelawny, XXI, 208; LJ, VI, 272, note, gives 246)

This is scarcely fair. Parry appears to have been a good mechanic (LJ, VII, 272, note); and he had a good mind. Trelawny and Nicolson are probably correct in saying that Parry's natural remedy for any illness was the Falstaffian: 'Brandy, my lord, nothing but brandy will save you' (Trelawny, XXI, 208; Nicolson, X, 222). Falstaff was in the air. Julius Millingen writes that Parry was an 'excellent mimic' and had 'a fund of quaint expressions':

He could tell, in his coarse language, a good story, could perform the clown's or Falstaff's part very naturally, rant Richard the Third's or Hamlet's soliloquies in a mock-tragic manner, unrivalled by any of the players of Bartholomew fair, and could always engender laughter enough to beguile the length of our rainy evenings.

(Millingen, XII, 117)

Parry's extempore buffooning recalls Falstaff's burlesquing of Prince Hal and the King in the Boar's Head Tavern (1 Henry IV, II, iv). He, like Falstaff, existed as a living critique of any over-pretentious, poetic or other, refinements and romanticisms. As an embodiment of anti-romantic realism he had affinities with both Falstaff and Hotspur. He belonged to the world of Henry IV. He records that Byron compared the mixed corps at Missolonghi of women, camp-followers and helpers of various nations to Falstaff's army (Parry, VII, 156).

Parry's book is, as Mrs. Langley Moore has rightly maintained, a good one. What Byron's associates, some of whom objected on social grounds to Parry's rapid advancement under Byron, did not realize was that it was precisely the Falstaff, or Falstaff-Hotspur, qualities in Parry that made him at this final period so valuable a support. Byron responded easily to people of the lower social order; more, in part of his multifarious personality he was himself one of them. Parry observes that 'of the different languages and terms used by soldiers, sailors, tradesmen, and other classes of men, or of what is called *slang*, he was quite a master'. He knew as many as did Parry in his own profession and many more drawn from other ways of life of which Parry 'knew nothing'. He regularly carried on his conversations with Parry in nautical phrases (Parry, IX, 220–1).

Byron's letters witness his semi-humorous regard. On Parry's arrival he wrote of him as 'a fine rough subject', 'a fine fellow, extremely active, and of strong, sound, practical talent'; as physically 'very strong'. He is not to be interfered with, and is 'doing all that can be done'; he is 'a sort of hardworking Hercules' and a general military factotum doing '*all* that is done here' (Hancock, 7 and 8 Feb.; Osborne, 15 Feb.; Stanhope, 19 March; Kinnaird, 30 March; 1824; LJ, VI, 317, 319, 324, 352–3, 363–4). Byron angered his officers by promoting Parry, who drilled his men 'in an apron, with a hammer in his hand', major of the artillery brigade (LJ, VI, 272–3, note). Byron's relation to Parry is summed in the comment: 'Parry is here, and he and I agree very well' (Kinnaird, 21 Feb. 1824; LJ, VI, 329).

This on the one side; on the other, we have Parry's drinking, his mimicry recalling Falstaff's charades, and Byron's view of him as comic, in part for his very burliness and the fiery aura of his professional title. He is surprised to find Parry, whose claim to be ready to prepare the expedition with all the latest in artillery techniques had been set out with so incisive and detailed a confidence (LJ, VI, 272, note), complaining of the cold:

> I should as soon have expected to hear a volcano sneeze, as a firemaster (who is to burn a whole fleet) exclaim against the atmosphere. I fully expected that his very approach would have scorched up the town like the burning-glasses of Archimedes.
>   (Hancock, 7 Feb. 1824; LJ, VI, 318)

As so often, Byron's light touch holds a profound suggestion. His thoughts on Parry touch the macabre, pointing to the scientific extensions of our own time, and their fearful, earth-shaking, potentialities. We may remember Hotspur's aspersions on the lord who deplored the digging of 'this villainous saltpetre' from the 'harmless earth' to do 'many a good tall fellow' to death (*1 Henry IV*, I, iii, 60–2). Parry was both Hotspur and Falstaff. There was a kind of poetic or cosmic justice behind Byron's staging of a mock earthquake

149

to frighten the burly fire-master by rolling cannon-balls in the room above, so reducing this Hercules, who could not stand earthquakes, to terror, and forcing him by Puckish trickery from his Hotspur explosives into the position of Falstaff at Gadshill.

When Byron was dying Parry was sent for to persuade him to take a certain medicine. Moore observes:

> From this circumstance, as well as from the terms in which he is mentioned by Lord Byron, it is plain that this person had, by his blunt, practical good sense, acquired far more influence over his Lordship's mind than was possessed by any of the other persons about him.
>
> (Moore, II, 770 or LVI, 638; note)

' "It was to Parry", Count Gamba writes, "to whom Lord Byron tried to express his last wishes" ' (Parry, V, 114; and see Gamba, V, 261).

Parry realized his position and power. Byron, he says, being dissatisfied with the pretentiousness of frivolous minds, was 'glad to meet with a plain, practical man'; Byron told him, 'I should never talk nonsense if I always found plain men to talk to'; 'with me', says Parry, he was 'sedate and serious', his 'whims and pranks' being left for others (Parry, II, 39, note; IX, 220; X, 258). Parry, as his book so abundantly witnesses, had a gravity of his own, and a wealth of good sense, and he deplored Byron's wasting so much of his time with others in light and trivial talk; and even though his personality had itself for Byron a comic side, that only made it easier for Byron, in this grim context, to be serious with him, since war was to Byron nearer to macabre comedy than to sentimental tragedy. Later, after his return to England, Augusta could write of Parry as 'a most *vulgar, rough, bearish* person' (to Lady Byron, 2 March 1825; Doris Langley Moore, *The Late Lord Byron*, V, 169); and so no doubt he would have appeared in London society. Nevertheless his is among the best of our Byronic source-books, crammed with convincing records of Byron's talk on a wide field. At Missolonghi the seraphic dream, personified in the boy Loukas, though its power remained, had become a torment (pp. 35–6). In sending Parry to his side, Providence had sent exactly the man best able to support Byron during these last, heroic, weeks.

V

RICHARD III AND MACBETH

I

There is some soul of goodness in things evil
Would men observingly distil it out.
(*Henry V*, IV, i, 4)

THE ANTI-SOCIAL IMPULSE which we noted in *Hamlet*
is isolated and given fiercer impetus in the more forceful
heroes of *Richard III* and *Macbeth*. In each of these three
plays ghosts appear.

Byron knew that he was a Hamlet type while deploring its
limitations. The dreaming Childe Harold, he claimed, was only a
part of him and he 'would not be such a fellow as I have made my
hero for all the world' (Dallas, 31 Oct. 1811; LJ, II, 66). In his
Preface to *The Corsair* he half admits an identification with his
darker, criminal, heroes, while being less ready to see himself as that
'very repulsive personage', Childe Harold. Byron would rather be a
Richard III or Macbeth than a Hamlet. This was not all self-
deception: he knew in himself the power-instincts and inward
agonies so brilliantly diagnosed in his stanzas on Napoleon in *Childe
Harold* (III, 36–45). Certainly he feared the softer compulsions that
embarrass action; and the logical extreme of all independent action
is, as Wordsworth's Oswald in *The Borderers* argues, crime (*The
Borderers*, III, 1470–1586; IV, 1684–1844; *The Golden Labyrinth*, 214).
Wordsworth's early drama, written in a poetic mood to be distinguished firmly from his later orthodoxies, attempts a bold and
even shocking, Iago-like—though Iago never went so far in justification—rationalization of certain truths, or half-truths, more cautiously
handled by Shakespeare, Byron and Nietzsche.

151

Richard III made a peculiarly strong impression on Byron:

Just returned from seeing Kean in Richard. By Jove, he is a soul! Life—nature—truth without exaggeration or diminution. Kemble's Hamlet is perfect;—but Hamlet is not Nature. Richard is a man; and Kean is Richard.

(Journal, 19 Feb. 1814; LJ, II, 385–6)

Byron liked Richard. He was attracted by his extraordinarily effective use of 'vein' in his rebuff to Buckingham 'I am not in the giving vein today' and 'Thou troublest me. I am not in the vein' (*Richard III*, IV, ii, 115, 117). After noting the power of Kean's Richard, his Journal continues with reminders of it. We have first:

Hobhouse says I am growing a *loup garou*—a solitary hobgoblin. True—'I am myself alone'.

The words were spoken by Richard when he was Duke of Gloucester (*3 Henry VI*, v, vi, 83). Next Byron notes that he can easily be made to laugh 'when I am "i' the vein"' (Journal, 27 Feb. 1814; LJ, II, 389–90). The phrase is twice applied to his mood for composition in letters to Murray (25 and 26 April 1814; LJ, III, 74–5). Richard was a solace; there was a kind of fellow-feeling as for one criminal outcast for another: we find Byron writing to Murray for Sir George Buc's life of Richard III on 5 October 1816 and again, impatiently, on 25 May 1819 (LJ, III, 371; IV, 306).

There was a central reason for this obsession. Richard was deformed, and Byron's lameness, slight though it was (the contradictory evidence regarding it is surveyed at LJ, I, 11, note) caused him continual embarrassment, or worse; the sense of it appearing to 'haunt' him 'like a curse' (Moore, I, 94 or IV, 45; Blessington, I, 3). Once when a beggar woman mimicked his movements we are told that he was intensely moved (LJ, II, 122, note).

The anguish dated from his childhood when his own mother is said to have mimicked him and insulted him as a 'lame brat' during a fit of rage (Galt, III, 24); and Byron himself seems to have told Lord Sligo that she once 'uttered an imprecation upon me, praying that I might prove as ill-formed in mind as I am in body' (Moore, I, 242 or X, 113). We are reminded of Queen Margaret's curses against Richard (*Richard III*, I, iii, 216–33). This remembrance seems to have become part of a complex related to Byron's life-long horror of tyranny. As a boy he felt his Mother's control as a tyranny, writing to Augusta on 11 November 1804, 'Am I to be eternally subjected to her caprice? I hope not;—indeed a few short years will emancipate me from the Shackles I now wear' (LJ, I, 47). The 'complex' became a sense of himself as a pariah, willing self-assertion in return. As with Richard III the deformity goaded his ambition, as he himself recognized, referring to Pope (Hunt, Nov. 1815; LJ, III, 247; Moore, II, 2 or XXVI, 306. See pp. 156-7 below).

It became a nightmare horror. It seems that after her death his Mother's passions still disturbed his sleep:

I awoke from a dream!—well! and have not others dreamed?—Such a dream!—but she did not overtake me. I wish the dead would rest, however. Ugh! how my blood chilled,—and I could not wake—and—and—heigho!

> Shadows tonight
> Have struck more terror to the soul of Richard
> Than could the substance of ten thousand . . .
> Arm'd all in proof, and led by shallow . . .

I do not like this dream—I hate its 'foregone conclusion'. And am I to be shaken by shadows? Ay, when they remind us of—no matter—but, if I dream thus again, I will try whether *all* sleep has the like visions.

(Journal, 23 Nov. 1813; LJ, II, 334)

The reference may not be to his Mother, but the similarity to Sardanapalus' dream of his ghostly ancestress Semiramis (*Sardanapalus*, IV, i, 24–165) suggests it. In Byron's quotation from *Richard III* (V, iii, 217–20; used for a more direct ghost experience at *Don Juan* XV, 96) the words 'soldiers' and 'Richmond' are apparently omitted. 'Foregone conclusion' is from *Othello* (III, iii, 429). Byron's sleep-agonies were real enough; he damaged his teeth by gnashing them in sleep (Journal, 19 Feb. 1814; LJ, II, 387). After this outburst he plans to visit Tom Crib's tavern, moving from nightmare to burly physical life: 'I like energy—even animal energy—of all kinds' (Journal, 23 Nov. 1813; LJ, II, 336; p. 146 above). On 30 November 1813 he tells Moore, quoting Colley Cibber's version of

Richard III, that 'Richard's himself again' (LJ, II, 293 and note). Both the nightmare and the burly energy, action functioning as an outlet, as a relief from pressure, were in Richard, whose address to his troops has a burly vigour missing from Richmond's.

Like Richard, he was, or believed himself, no lady's man. Writing to Lady Melbourne on 11 November 1812 he referred to his 'manifold imperfections' adding

> which, I may say with Richard the Third, incapacitate 'me from skipping in a lady's chamber'.
>
> (C, I, 106)

Shakespeare's lines, from Richard's opening soliloquy, are:

> He capers nimbly in a lady's chamber
> To the lascivious pleasing of a lute.
> But I, that am not shap'd for sportive tricks . . .
>
> (I, i, 12)

The soliloquy is present again when on 1 May 1814 Byron writes to Lady Melbourne of his sins, 'As for me, brought up as I was, and sent into the world as I was, both physically and morally, nothing better could be expected' (C, I, 257). This comes from Richard's

> Deform'd, unfinish'd, sent before my time
> Into this breathing world, scarce half made up . . .
>
> (I, i, 20)

However, both are successful in love, and Richard's phrases are again apt:

> 'Since I have crept in favour with myself, I must maintain it';
> but I never 'mistook my person', though I think others have.
> (Journal, 10 March 1814; LJ, II, 399; *Richard III*, I, ii, 260, 254)

Both endured a sense of inferiority coupled to knowledge of unusual powers. Despised, or believing themselves despised, they reacted anarchically, so arousing a greater hatred. During the turmoil aroused by his lines on the Prince Regent (p. 91) Byron wrote:

> I see all the papers in a sad commotion with those eight lines; and the *Morning Post*, in particular, has found out that I am a

sort of Rd. III—deformed in mind and *body*. The *last* piece of information is not very new to a man who passed five years at a public school.

(Murray, 7 Feb. 1814; LJ, III, 27)

But again, as with Richard, open conflict brings the stronger accent of his letter to Moore of 28 January 1817:

I think of being in England in the spring. If there is a row, by the sceptre of King Ludd, but I'll be one; and if there is none, and only a continuance of 'this meek, piping time of peace',

—then he will still come and write so as to terrify the times and *Times* (LJ, IV, 48; the quotation repeated at Journal, 5 Feb. 1821; LJ, V, 200; *Richard III*, I, i, 24; Shakespeare's word is 'weak' not 'meek').

Byron's 'Richard' complex was finally expanded into his un-finished drama *The Deformed Transformed* composed in 1822. Its hero Arnold is a hunchback dwarf who endures a mother's scorn. Descriptions of Arnold recall Byron's favourite, Pope, whose de-formity must have played a part in Byron's sympathy. The phrase-ology also recalls Shakespeare's Richard III and Caliban. The ugly words 'incubus', 'nightmare', 'abortion', 'monstrous sport of nature', 'Devil' (I, i, 1–20, 40) remind us of terms applied to Richard, such as 'indigest deformed lump' (*3 Henry VI*, V, vi, 51), 'elvish-mark'd, abortive, rooting hog', 'hell-hound', and 'cacodemon' (*Richard III*, I, iii, 228; IV, iv, 48; I, iii, 144); and also to that 'freckled whelp hag-born, not honour'd with a human shape', Caliban; called by Prospero a 'devil' whose mind 'cankers' as his body grows 'uglier', a 'mis-shapen knave' and 'demi-devil' (*The Tempest*, I, ii, 283; IV, i, 188–92; V, i, 268–72). When Arnold, looking in a spring, says

> Hideous wretch
> That I am! The very waters mock me with
> My horrid shadow—like a demon plac'd
> Deep in the fountain to scare back the cattle
> From drinking therein

(I, i, 49)

we remember Richard seeing his own 'shadow'; and the dogs that 'bark at me as I halt by them' (I, i, 26; 23).

In his bitterness Arnold wonders why, if he has the Devil's form,

155

he should not also have his 'power' (I, i, 42). When his attempt at suicide is interrupted by the appearance of the 'Stranger', a kind of Mephistopheles who offers to change his shape, Arnold, though refusing to 'compromise' his 'soul', which though ill-lodged is an 'aspiring one' (I, i, 144–6), accepts; and he is given a choice. Figures are raised: Julius Caesar, symbolizing the Napoleonic values, who fails to satisfy Arnold's 'quest for beauty', though 'laurels' imperially cover his baldness; Alcibiades, for glamour (*Detached Thoughts*, 1821; 108; LJ, V, 461); Socrates, for wisdom; Antony, the great lover; Demetrius Poliorcetes, described as a god-man of beauty and power, sun-flashing and immortal; and last Achilles. The figures rise from the spring or fountain, pass and disappear, like the Apparitions and show of Kings in *Macbeth*. Arnold, to his credit, chooses Achilles.

The choice corresponds to Byron's final aim and direction, rejecting pleasures and ambitions for a greater good. Achilles is shown as a self-reflection of Byron's best; presented as beautiful, gentle, lover of Polixena 'with sanctioned and with soften'd love, before the altar', and with 'remorse for Hector slain'. His vulnerable heel is remembered. He symbolizes the state of mind and soul in which Byron, after a deeply true and semi-marital relationship with Teresa Guiccioli, undertook, without ambition, his Greek campaign. Achilles is said to symbolize the 'best' in Greece (I, i, 267–83).

'Greatest deformity' and 'the extremest beauty' are shown interacting, for in mortals 'extremes meet' (I, i, 285–8). Byron physically incarnated the metaphysical truth, of which the many dark but fascinating heroes of drama such as Richard III and Macbeth are symptomatic, that extreme evil and extreme good have an element in common. That the physical is here a symbol of the metaphysical is clear when Arnold expects to assume Achilles' size as well as his shape, and the Stranger replies that were Arnold too far removed from men 'all would rise' against him as some 'new-found mammoth' (I, i, 296–311). Arnold's acceptance of the limitation again corresponds to the *new humility* of Byron's final period. Valour he has already:

> I ask not
> For Valour, since Deformity is daring.

It is its essence to o'ertake mankind
By heart and soul, and make itself the equal—
Ay, the superior of the rest. There is
A spur in its halt movements, to become
All that the others cannot, in such things
As still are free to both, to compensate
For stepdame Nature's avarice at first.
They woo with fearless deeds the smiles of fortune,
And oft, like Timour, the lame Tartar, win them.

(I, i, 313)

The diagnosis fits many: not only Timour and Byron, but Richard III, and Alexander Pope; and Napoleon, whose short stature may be remembered.

In a lengthy speech heavy with Byronic autobiography Arnold describes his story, including the despair caused by 'this vile crooked clog which makes me lonely', cutting him off, like Richard, from amatory and social pleasures. However, courage and perseverance have saved him as in the past they have saved, and made, heroes out of similar stuff. His recent attempt at suicide showed him 'master of his life'; and whoever is that is 'the master of whatever dreads to die' (I, i, 328–356).

Arnold's emphasis on love, which was also clear in his address to Antony, is vivid after the change:

I love and I shall be belov'd! Oh, life!
At last I feel thee!

(I, i, 421)

We remember Richard's opening soliloquy and his subsequent and cynical wooing of Anne, and his comments thereon.

But the Stranger now takes Arnold's old shape, saying:

In a few moments
I will be as you were, and you shall see
Yourself for ever by you, as your shadow.

(I, i, 447)

Though horrified, he must not 'shrink' from seeing what he *had* been; and he is henceforth accompanied by his 'shadow' (I, i, 449); his anti-self. There is here a clear correspondence to Byron's life-long sense of Ishmael outlawry and Calvinist sense of sin. There is an even clearer correspondence to Shakespeare's Prospero who admits that Caliban is *his* anti-self: 'This thing of darkness I acknowledge mine' (*The Tempest* V, i, 275). Lucio's slandering of the disguised Duke to his face in *Measure for Measure* may be supposed to contain a similar implication. He is hinting a psychological truth, and that is why he proves so maddeningly provocative: 'Nay, friar, I am a kind of burr; I shall stick' (IV, iii, 193). These Shakespearian themes are in the usual fashion being expanded and clarified by Byron.

Our drama becomes complex. Arnold, like Goethe's Faust with Mephistopheles, enters the world of action, embracing the Napoleonic and Fortinbras values to which Byron half aspired, though they serve here the peculiarly questionable action of the Bourbon's attack on Rome.[1] Arnold has become an honourable soldier, but the poetry in normal Byronic style insists on the wickedness of the enterprise. Rome, in fine passages, is regarded as a sacred, eternal, city.

The Stranger calls himself 'Caesar'; he is a burlesque deformed, hunch-back Caesar, corresponding to what may be called 'Caesarism'; to the devil of political ambition that had been to Byron simultaneously vocation and anathema. His function is to burlesque the action. His scathing wit deflates the mighty Bourbon exactly as Shakespeare's Thersites deflates the Greek commanders in *Troilus and Cressida*. Like Thersites, he jeers at war's brainless folly:

> Keep thought aloof from hosts!
> If the knaves take to thinking, you will have
> To crack those walls alone.
>
> (I, ii, 296)

His comments are scathing:

> He comes
> Hand in hand with the mild twins—Gore and glory.
>
> (II, ii, 11)

To him the slaughter of Catholic priests by Lutheran soldiers is an exquisitely amusing comment on Christianity.

It is the Devil—or some Mephistophelean equivalent—who makes these criticisms; and this devil, as hunchback, is right. Arnold

---

1. For Charles de Bourbon who attacked Rome in 1527, see P, v, 498–9, note.

has bought looks, respectability, honour and—remembering the *goodness* of Achilles—virtue, at the cost of sharing the guilt of civilization. Beside him is the hunchback devil, asking all the awkward questions.

As always in Byron, good and evil intertwine distractingly; as the Stranger reminds us, 'the deeper sinner, better saint' (I, i, 522). Our grim action is based on age-old horrors. The ghosts of past heroes 'flit along the eternal city's rampart', raising their 'death-like hands' against the aggressor; and yet Rome itself rose from a brother's blood, when Romulus killed Remus (I, ii, 189–200; II, i, 37–8, 84). History itself is ghostly and ghastly. The action is soaked in past and present evil; it is 'red Bellona's banquet' (II, ii, 44; compare *Macbeth*, I, ii, 18, 55).

The *Deformed Transformed* is a disturbing fragment. But it serves as a brilliant clarification of the Byronic complex, at once a disentangling and a new complexity; its inter-knotted meanings relate precisely to those which are constituent to such Satanic works as *Richard III* and *Macbeth*, together with the dramatic fascination they arouse in us all; and beyond all literary surfaces, to the instinct and love of bloodshed which seems to be rooted, from age to age, in the human psyche.

II

Byron's affinities with Richard III may be discussed in psychological terms, but to go deeper we must turn to *Macbeth*. The two plays study the same problem on different levels. Byron recognized the resemblancies. After relating his nightmares, as we have seen (p. 153), to Richard's, he naturally moves on to the *Macbeth* phraseology of:

No dreams last night of the dead, nor the living; so—I am 'firm as the marble, founded as the rock', till the next earthquake.
(Journal, 24 Nov. 1813; LJ, II, 341; *Macbeth*, III, iv, 22)

Again, writing to Lady Melbourne on 12 January 1814:

By-the-bye, don't you pity poor Napoleon? and are these your heroes? Commend me to the Romans, or Macbeth, or Richard III. This man's spirit seems broken . . . A thorough mind would either rise from the rebound, or at least go out 'with harness on its back'.

(C, I, 231; *Macbeth*, v, v, 52)

In *Don Juan* the Ghost is given first a *Macbeth* reminiscence in 'He moved as shadowy as the sisters weird' (XVI, 21) and subsequently one from *Richard III*:

> How odd, a single hobgoblin's nonentity
> Should cause more fear than a whole host's identity!
>
> (XVI, 120)

Compare:

> By the apostle Paul, shadows tonight
> Have struck more terror to the soul of Richard
> Than can the substance of ten thousand soldiers
> Armed in proof and led by shallow Richmond.
>
> (*Richard III*, v, iii, 217)

'Shallow' suggests a depth in Richard outspacing ethic while Richard, on his side, recognizes mysteries incommensurable with physical strength. This depth and these mysteries *Macbeth* was written to explore.

Byron's Calvinistic up-bringing and various sexual adventures and divagations made him vividly aware of man's fallen state:

> Our life is a false nature: 'tis not in
> The harmony of things—this hard decree,
> This uneradicable taint of Sin,
> This boundless Upas, this all-blasting tree,
> Whose root is earth, whose leaves and branches be
> The skies which rain their plagues on men like dew—
> Disease, death, bondage—all the woes we see,
> And worse, the woes we see not—which throb through
> The immedicable soul, with heart-aches ever new.
>
> (*Childe Harold*, IV, 126)

Such is the philosophical core, or root, of the many darkly worded confessions and veiled mysteries of Byron's letters and journals. He leaves the autobiographical elements in his stories half admitted and half denied. Writing to Lady Melbourne on 16 January 1814 he hints at a dark secret: 'You do not know what a devil any bad passion makes me', adding: 'I have more reasons than you are aware of, for mistrusting myself on this point' (C, I, 237–8). Lady Byron records that of *Lara* he told her 'with a shudder' that there was 'more in that than any of them' (Lady Byron's notes, March 1817; Lovelace, I, 20–1). Byron developed a satanic aura and reputation with an extraordinary ease. Stendhal suspected a crime 'similar to that which wrecked Othello's fame', and Goethe seemed to think he might have committed a murder (LJ, III, App. viii, 440; v, App. ii, 506). He once took pains to make a lady acquaintance think so (*Memoirs, Journal and Correspondence of Thomas Moore*, entry for 10 Nov. 1827; v, 233; LBM, 41). Our thesis would be empowered could Byron be credited with some appalling crime, but we must remain content with supposing that he may have lived through the *Macbeth* guilt in some lesser, probably sexual, terms; as indeed may Shakespeare himself, for *The Rape of Lucrece* and *Macbeth* are closely similar in tone (*The Imperial Theme*, 133, 333).

Possibly the girl whom he saved from death in Athens after she had been convicted of associating with a stranger, and who died soon after, might, if Byron himself was that stranger, though this is far from certain and indeed improbable, have been a cause for disquiet, perhaps remorse; certainly Byron drew on the incident for his narratives (LBM, I, 13–14). In these narratives he expresses in outward and fictional terms essences which he had experienced inwardly. He put the issue to Lady Melbourne on 25 November 1813:

> When I speak of this *tale* and the *author*, I merely mean *feelings;* the characters, and the costume, and the tale itself (at least one very like it, I heard) are Mussulman. This no one but *you* can tell.
>
> (C, I, 219).[1]

He is referring to *The Bride of Abydos*. He admitted a personal element in *The Giaour* (Lady Melbourne, 28 Sept. 1813; C, I, 183). On the identification of himself with Conrad in *The Corsair*, he supports his comments with a peculiarly useful quotation from *Macbeth*:

People sometimes hit near the truth; but never the whole truth.

1. The text reads: are very like it. My emendation appears necessary.

H. don't know what I was about the year after he left the Levant nor does any one—nor—nor—nor—however, it is a lie—but, 'I doubt the equivocation of the fiend that lies like truth!'
  (Journal, 10 March 1814; LJ, II, 398; *Macbeth*, V, v, 43)

Or he can be yet vaguer. He could, he says, explain the causes of the 'melancholy' for which he has become so famous, but will not; he refers vaguely to the experiences of his early life; but he must not let out secrets to 'paralyse posterity' (*Detached Thoughts*, 1821; 74–6; LJ, V, 446–7).

For a great part of his life Byron's favourite *imaginative* territory was that of *Richard III* and *Macbeth*. They, and all that they stood for, fascinated him. On a remark of his reported to have been made during his early travels in 1810. Moore comments:

One circumstance related to me, as having occurred in the course of the passage, is not a little striking. Perceiving, as he walked the deck, a small yataghan, or Turkish dagger, on one of the benches, he took it up, unsheathed it, and, having stood for a few moments contemplating the blade, was heard to say, in an under voice, 'I should like to know how a person feels, after committing a murder!' In this startling speech we may detect, I think, the germ of his future Giaours and Laras. This intense *wish* to explore the dark workings of the passions was what, with the aid of imagination, at length generated the *power;* and that faculty which entitled him afterwards to be so truly styled 'the searcher of dark bosoms', may be traced to, perhaps, its earliest stirrings in the sort of feeling that produced these words.
  (Moore, I, 235 or X, 110)

This is near the mood in which *Macbeth* commits the crime he fears despite, and almost because of, his horror of it. In *Don Juan* Byron ruminates on the fascination of the mysteries beyond life. He observes profoundly that 'there's a courage which grows out of fear' ready to 'dare the worst to *know* it', as men are tempted to leap from a precipice. Even though we 'shudder' we have a 'lurking bias' to 'the unknown', and of this, he says, the fascination which ghosts have for us is a proof (*Don Juan*, XIV, 5, 6). This is as good a commentary as one could wish for on the conception, the human diagnosis and the subsequent popularity of *Macbeth*.

Byron was, to use the popular term, 'superstitious'. Galt records that it was correctly foretold at Cheltenham in 1801 that Byron would 'incur some great misfortune' in his twenty-seventh year; and that Byron regarded the prophecy 'with a sentiment of superstition' (Galt, III, 30). Numerous examples of Byron's addiction to super-stition are recorded: Lady Byron's notes on her marriage give some (Maurois, XXIII, 227). Moore records that Byron was deeply troubled by having by mistake trod upon Marino Faliero's tomb; for he was 'very superstitious' and would not begin any undertaking on a Friday (LJ, IV, App. viii, 472). He was fascinated by the Witch of Endor. Commenting to Murray on an anonymous letter on 15 July 1817, he says

So let him look to it: he had better have written to the Devil a criticism upon hell-fire. I will raise him such a Samuel for his *Saul* as will astonish him without the Witch of Endor.

(LJ, IV, 152)

Moore refers to Byron's 'frequently expressed admiration of "the ghost-scene", as he called it, in Samuel, and his comparison of this supernatural appearance with the Mephistopheles of Goethe' (Moore, II, 685 or LII, 600; and see Kennedy, 154, 233–4).

He regarded himself as an 'Ishmael' whose 'hand was against all men', and 'all men's' against his; because of this, his pride was originally defensive (Miss Milbanke, 26 Sept.; Journal, 22 Nov.; 1813; LJ, III, 402; II, 330). He was a 'fallen spirit' (Caroline Lamb, 1 May 1812; LJ, II, 121). He thought he must have belonged to the Devil before he was born; he was often in hell, 'one day in high health and the next on fire, or ice' (Lady Melbourne, 10 and 12 Jan. 1814; C, I, 226, 230).

Such was certainly the appearance he bore to many of his critics. An extended critique of *Don Juan* in *Blackwood's Edinburgh Magazine* of August 1819 regards it as a 'filthy and impious poem'; his lines therein on his wife are 'unhallowed strains of cold-blooded mockery'; they are 'brutally, fiendishly, unexpiably mean'; his is 'the wilful and determined spite of an unrepenting, unsoftened, smiling, sarcastic, joyous sinner'; for such diabolical wickedness there can exist 'neither pity nor pardon'; and all this, says the writer, from 'one of the most powerful intellects our island has ever produced'. He was 'no longer a human being, but a cool, unconcerned fiend' (LJ, IV, 385, note; C, II, editorial passage, 134). In answer Byron composed what I designate his *Blackwood's* Defence', to which he set as prefix 'Why, how now, Hecate? You look angrily' (LJ, IV, App. ix, 474; *Macbeth*, III, v, 1). Attacks on Byron as Satanist seem to have inspired reviewers to their best. Here is a good one, from *The Courier* of 26 October 1822:

With a brain from heaven and a heart from hell—with a pen that can write as angels speak, and yet that riots in thoughts which fiends might envy—with the power to charm, instruct, and elevate—but with the ruling passion to provoke our loathing and deserve our scorn—this compound of rottenness and beauty—this unsexed Circe, who gems the poisoned cup he offers us, and extorts our admiration of its rare and curious workmanship, while the soul sickens at the draught within— seems to have lived only that the world might learn from his example, how worthless and how pernicious a thing is genius when divorced from religion, from morals, and from humanity.

(LJ, VI, 122, note)

Strangers were surprised on meeting Byron to find that he was not a 'fiend incarnate' (Kennedy, 318).

He had every reason to feel at home with *Macbeth*, and quotations from it start early. On 10 August 1806 he tells Elizabeth Pigot that notice of his mother's approach has driven the 'natural ruby from my cheeks' and 'blanched' his countenance; however, 'they've tied me to the stake, I cannot fly', and so he will 'bear-like fight the course'; and, thinking of the domestic quarrels approaching, he concludes with 'Lay on Macduff, and damned be he who first cries, Hold, enough' (LJ, I, 103; *Macbeth*, III, iv, 115; V, vii, 1; 62). On 17 December 1808 he tells Hodgson that the strange content of a letter from B. H. Drury makes him think that his eyes 'are made the fools of the other senses, or else worth all the rest' (LJ, I, 207; *Macbeth*, II, i, 44). Since Byron's *Macbeth*-affinities were pre-eminently imaginative, his references relate mainly to literary matters, as when he gives Moore the advice to 'screw your courage to the sticking place' and accuses him of 'flaws and starts' unbecoming to such a writer which must be 'authorized by your grandam' (8 Dec. 1813; 3 Aug. 1814; LJ, II, 303; III, 120; *Macbeth*, I, vii, 60; III, iv, 63–6). While working on his Drury Lane address he tells Lord Holland that his poems 'come like shadows, so depart' and that for the moment 'I pull in resolution' (28 and 30 Sept. 1812; LJ, II, 160, 167; *Macbeth*, IV, i, 111; V, v, 42).

His own writings had a *Macbeth* tone: 'I have just', he tells Rogers, '"supped full of horrors" in two cantos of darkness and dismay' (27 June 1814; LJ, III, 101; *Macbeth*, V, v, 13). He wrote *The Bride of Abydos* to take refuge from reality by employing himself with 'imaginings' however 'horrible' (Moore, 30 Nov. 1813 LJ, II, 293; *Macbeth*, I, iii, 138). In an enigmatic letter we hear that 'the antithetical state' of his 'lucubrations' awakes him from 'stagnation' to a more 'alive' condition, a state where 'Macbeth can "sleep no more"'; the *Macbeth* nightmare being preferable to a 'drowsy' wakefulness (Moore, 6 Jan. 1814; LJ, III, 6; *Macbeth* II, ii, 44). He felt himself a literary Macbeth. On 21 August 1811, he wrote to Dallas of *Childe Harold*: 'As for me, "I have supped full of criticism", and I don't think that the "most dismal treatise" will stir and rouse my "fell of hair" till "Birnam wood do come to Dunsinane"' (LJ, I, 336; *Macbeth*, V, v, 11–13). The passage was yet more appropriate years later, when, writing to Kinnaird on the probable criticisms of *Don Juan*, he says again that he has supped full of horrors, and that it must now be a 'dismal treatise' indeed that can make his 'fell of hair' to 'stir and move'. There is to be no mutilation of his text: 'Rather than that, come critics into the list, and champion me to the uttermost' (6 March; 24 April; 1819; C, II, 105, 109; *Macbeth*, V, v, 11–13; III, i, 71–2).

He deeply experienced in himself the *Macbeth*-like themes of his poetry: 'I have certainly enough', he writes in his Journal on 18 February 1814, of 'that perilous stuff which weighs upon the heart'; and he hints darkly at 'the real cause'; (LJ, II, 383; *Macbeth*, V, iii, 44). When odium oppresses him he envies Moore the 'honour —love—obedience—troops of friends' he has won (Moore, 8 March

1816; LJ, III, 272; *Macbeth*, V, iii, 25). Then, in a lighter vein, again to Moore:

My 'way of life' (or 'May of life', which is it, according to the Commentators?)—my 'way of life' is fallen into great regularity . . .

(24 Dec. 1816; LJ, IV, 25; *Macbeth*, V, iii, 22)

His servant Fletcher is still 'a prosperous gentleman' (Hobhouse, 19 Dec. 1816; C, II, 28; *Macbeth*, I, iii, 73). More usually the tone is sombre. At the tragic deaths of 1811 Byron has 'almost forgot the taste of grief' and 'supped full of horrors'; and the last phrase recurs in connection with Lady Melbourne's death (Dallas, 11 Oct. 1811; Murray, 23 April 1818; LJ, II, 52; IV, 228; *Macbeth*, V, v, 9, 13). *Macbeth* is used poignantly on Allegra's death: 'Would that I "could answer this comfort with the like"' (Scott, 4 May, 1822; LJ, VI, 55-6; *Macbeth*, IV, iii, 192). Or on his own death, and Pope's: 'I shall be where "nothing can touch him farther"'; 'Pope himself "sleeps well"—nothing can touch him further"' (Lady Byron, 3 April 1820; LJ, V, 2; The Bowles Controversy; LJ, V, App. iii, 568; *Macbeth*, III, ii, 22-6).

As early as 1814 Byron was writing 'I 'gin to be a-weary of the sun' (Journal, 27 Feb. 1814; LJ, II, 390; *Macbeth*, V, v, 49); but his life's central torment was the marriage separation and its attendant accusations. The human symbol of this complex of apparent evil and certain agony was, as it was for Macbeth, a woman. Wives are accordingly to be associated with *Macbeth*. Before the marriage Byron's future wife is 'invested with "golden opinions of all sorts of men", and full of "most blest conditions" as Desdemona herself' (Moore, 20 Sept. 1814; LJ, III, 139; *Macbeth*, I, vii, 33; *Othello*, II, i, 256). Earlier he had expected that whoever he married, 'even-handed justice' would reward him with cuckoldom (Hobhouse, 27 Nov. 1812; C, I, 112; *Macbeth*, I, vii, 10), and after the Separation, hearing of Romilly's suicide at the death of *his* wife, Byron quotes in full from *Macbeth* (I, vii, 10):

This even-handed justice
Commends the ingredients of our poison'd chalice
To our own lips.

Byron regarded Romilly as a main agent in the destroying of his own marriage and at the letter's conclusion observes that 'it was not in vain that I invoked Nemesis in the midnight of Rome from the awfullest of her ruins' (Lady Byron, 18 Nov. 1818; LJ, IV, 268–9; see *Childe Harold*, IV, 132–5). Once he relates Lady Byron directly to Lady Macbeth:

Three o'clock—I must 'to bed, to bed, to bed', as mother Siddons, that tragical friend of the mathematical * * *, says.
(Moore, 16 March 1818; LJ, IV, 215; *Macbeth*, V, i, 72)

The three asterisks represent some derogatory name for Lady Byron, a student of mathematics. After the Separation Byron cannot go back, for 'returning were as tedious as go o'er' (Lady Blessington, 6 May 1823; LJ, VI, 204; *Macbeth*, III, iv, 138).

As 'that evil Genius of a woman' who 'was born for my desolation' Lady Byron corresponds, in a general sense, to Lady Macbeth; or she may be 'Vittoria Corombona—the White Devil'; or 'Lady Medea' (Murray 27 Jan. and 2 Feb. 1821; Hobhouse, 6 July 1820; LJ, V, 232, 236; C, II, 152). Webster's Vittoria was in part responsible for her husband's murder and Medea murdered her husband's new lover and his and her own children to avenge herself. But Byron's favourite analogy comes from that near-equivalent to *Macbeth*, the *Agamemnon* of Aeschylus: each has both a fearful protagonist-woman and dark female powers, the Weird Sisters and the Furies; and Clytemnestra deliberately murders her lord. In *Lines on Hearing that Lady Byron was Ill* Byron designates his wife 'the moral Clytemnestra of her lord'. Henceforth that was his regular name for her. In a letter to Lord Blessington Byron refers to Dr. Parr:

. . . a great friend of the other branch of the House of Atreus, and the Greek teacher (I believe) of my *moral* Clytemnestra—I say *moral*, because it is true, and is so useful to the virtuous, that it enables them to do anything without the aid of an Aegistheus.
(6 April 1823; LJ, VI, 190)

For his personal life this shift to the *Agamemnon* was apt; but in other respects *Richard III* and *Macbeth* suited best the darker strains in Byron's life.

Socially he was regarded, and could regard himself, as an anarchic threat. In his *Epistle to a Friend* (1811) he wrote:

But if, in some succeeding year,
When Britain's 'May is in the sere',
Thou hear'st of one, whose deepening crimes
Suit with the sablest of the times,
Of one, whom love nor pity sways,
Nor hope of fame, nor good men's praise;
One, who in stern Ambition's pride,
Perchance not blood shall turn aside;
One rank'd in some recording page
With the worst anarchs of the age,
Him wilt thou *know*—and *knowing* pause,
Nor with the *effect* forget the cause.

'Sere' is from *Macbeth* (v, iii, 23). Byron is thinking of his rejection by Mary Anne Chaworth and all the evils into which, in his view, it had plunged him. We see how his unrestful sexual self activates his anarchic challenge, just as Shakespeare's *The Rape of Lucrece* is imaginatively one with *Macbeth*.

Normally Byron's revolutionary actions had what we today can regard as a full moral backing. But there is no easy distinction: as the Doge in *Marino Faliero* points out (III, i, 67–80), the revolutionary's repute depends mainly on his success or failure. Macbeth's cause may be felt either on the side of revolution or the reverse. In 'There is no good in so much prating, since "certain issues strokes should arbitrate"' (Murray, 24 July 1814; LJ, III, 112; *Macbeth*, v, iv, 21) —Byron is referring to Parliamentary speeches—the quoted lines were spoken against Macbeth; and in 'I should have thought that the word "invariable" might have stuck in Southey's throat like Macbeth's "Amen"!' (The Bowles Controversy, LJ, v, App. iii, 558; *Macbeth*, II, ii, 33), Macbeth is being aligned with the loathed reactionary. But again, he may feel himself as Macbeth, as when, hearing of the forces opposing the Italian rising, he notes that 'the cry is still, They come'; and he advises those raising the Greek loan to 'make assurance doubly sure' (Journal, 23 Jan. 1821; Bowring, 10 Dec. 1823; LJ, v, 183; VI, 283; *Macbeth*, v, v, 2; IV, i, 83).

None of these recent comparisons hold deep significances. But where Napoleon is concerned we have an exact and profitable, because ethically ambivalent, equation. One example we have already (pp. 159–60) noted. Here is another:

What! 'kiss the ground before young Malcolm's feet' and then 'be baited by the rabble's curse!' I cannot bear such a crouching catastrophe. I must stick to Sylla, for my modern favourites don't do. . . .
(Moore, 9 April 1814; LJ, III, 66; *Macbeth*, v, vii, 57–8)

He had previously, as noted in his Journal, tried to preserve his devotion even though 'all his admirers have, "like the thanes, fallen from him".' But soon he is in despair, life is henceforth meaningless; he quotes

And all our *yesterdays* have lighted fools
The way to dusty death.

So he will make no more entries concerning 'that same hesternal torchlight' (Journal, 9 and 19 April 1814; LJ, II, 410–12; *Macbeth*, v, iii, 49; v, v, 22).

As we have seen (pp. 93–4), Byron had great though unformulated ambitions. He attacked the Regent, he would be 'aut Caesar aut nihil', feeling himself a potential Brutus and hearing a voice murmur 'Brutus thou sleep'st' (Journal, 23 Nov. 1813; 18 Feb. 1814; LJ, II, 339, 384; *Julius Caesar*, II, i, 46). At the time of the Separation he may have had some great design of which no clear record exists (p. 101) above). To this extent he knew, in his own life as well as in his art, a genuine correspondence to Macbeth on a national scale. He felt himself, variously, to be a fallen angel, an Ishmael, an anarch, a liberator, a saviour.

His early life had attuned him to *Macbeth*. Galt (II, 20) discusses his childhood at Aberdeen. Though, he says, Byron's dark temperament must have descended from the 'silent rages' of his childhood in Scotland, this 'dark colouring' was 'plainly imbibed in a mountainous region, from sombre heaths, and in the midst of rudeness and grandeur'; and the two experiences, internal and external, were henceforth associated. The longest of Byron's juvenile poems 'is an imitation of the manner of the Homer of Morven'. His Scottish mother moreover would have recounted traditions of the land and her own royal ancestry, for Mrs. Byron claimed descent from 'the fated line of the Scottish kings'. To such traditions Galt ascribes the 'dark and guilty beings' of Byron's subsequent imaginings (Galt, II, 20–1).

Beyond these, we may suppose that Byron's more ghostly apprehensions, of the kind we have in Celtic legend and Scottish history, in *Macbeth*, and in William Collins' *Ode on the Popular Superstitions of the Highlands*, were born in this period. The wild and ghostly Scottish scenery is poetically recorded in the early lyrics *Lachin Y Gair*, *When I Rov'd a young Highlander*, and *The Adieu*. It meant much to him, lived in his imagination and coloured his poetic temperament, as he records, near the end of his life, in *The Island* (p. 269 below).

In *Lachin Y Gair* he senses the 'shades of the dead', and their voices. He remembered his own Gordon descent. Fearing the temptation to avenge his wrongs, he had gone abroad, 'for I am not quite sure that I could resist it, having derived from my mother something of the *perfervidum ingenium Scotorum*' (*Blackwood's* Defence; LJ, IV, App. ix; 480). Again: 'All the bad blood in my own composition I derive from those bastards of Banquo' (Lady Melbourne, 7 April 1813; C, I, 147). However, he could strike a happier note:

> As 'Auld Lang Syne' brings Scotland, one and all,
>   Scotch plaids, Scotch snoods, the blue hills, and
>   clear streams,
> The Dee—the Don—Balgounie's brig's *black wall*—
> All my boy feelings, all my gentler dreams
> Of what I *then dreamt*, cloth'd in their own pall—
>   Like Banquo's offspring—floating past me seems
> My childhood, in this childishness of mine:—
> I care not—'tis a glimpse of 'Auld Lang Syne'.
>   (*Don Juan*, X, 18)

That suggests a happy childhood. But Galt's description of Byron in young manhood at Gibraltar inhaling poetical sympathy 'from the gloomy rock', as—quoting from *Macbeth*—'a man forbid' (*Macbeth*, I, iii, 21), dwelling psychologically in 'the murk and the mist' (Galt, VIII, 62–3; see p. 231 below), holds another truth.

III

Much of Byron's poetry is devoted to unravelling the paradox of literary evil. On this paradox, he says, great writing regularly turns; he quotes Aristotle's 'pity and terror', and claims that a tragic poem should both handle guilt and arouse sympathy for the guilty:

> I must also ask you, is *Achilles* a *good* character? or is even Aeneas anything but a successful runaway? It is for Turnus men feel and not for the Trojan. Who is the hero of *Paradise Lost*? Why Satan—and Macbeth, and Richard, and Othello, Pierre, and Lothario, and Zanga?
>
> (Hodgson, 12 May 1821; LJ, v, 284)

Byron was consciously—he is a peculiarly *conscious* writer—involved in this central problem.

The Giaour (1813) is a study in guilt accompanied by remorse without repentance. The distraught hero lives, rather like Byron at Newstead, in a monastery, a cowled figure of burning eye, dark countenance and scornful lips:

> If ever evil angel bore
> The form of mortal, such he wore . . .
>
> (912)

He does not commit suicide:

> Nor sought the self-afforded grave
> Of ancient fool and modern knave.
>
> (1006)

There is a reminder of Macbeth's refusal to 'play the Roman fool' and die on his own sword (*Macbeth*, v, vii, 30). Religious consolation, repentance, thoughts of an after-life are repudiated. All that the hero wants is rest.

The Corsair (1814) gives us a more comprehensive portrait. Conrad, as pirate, is a social pariah, but he is also, like Milton's Satan, a fine leader: Byron's Napoleonic instincts are written into him. Like Napoleon, he dominates by 'the power of Thought—the magic of the Mind' (1, 8); but also, like Shakespeare's power-burdened kings, he knows 'the weight of splendid chains' (1, 8).

One was aware of a 'laughing devil' (i, 9) in him. He is a man of mysteries and terror, and yet, whatever the evil, we cannot know the *whole* truth:

> Behold—but who hath seen, or e'er shall see,
> Man as himself—the secret spirit free?
>
> (i, 10)

This 'spirit' must be felt as an *objective entity*, such as is often supposed to be freed at death; it is that in Macbeth which is 'tempest-toss'd' but not 'lost' (*Macbeth*, i, iii, 24). We recognize it active in Lady Macbeth's sleep-walking, speaking from a consciousness outside waking life (*Shakespearian Production*, 1964; 281–2). Byron, always strongly aware of such categories, is here handling a supreme spiritualistic truth.

Conrad has many good qualities. He seems to have become what he is by a too-uncompromising wisdom, and is accordingly said to be 'doom'd by his very virtues for a dupe' (i, 11). There is in him a certain softness, and his worse suffering recalls *Macbeth* when he is horrified at the blood on the woman Gulnare, whose crime was perpetrated for his sake (iii, 10). Indeed we may wonder what exactly *was* the cause of his 'impenitent remorse' (ii, 10). But it is the soul-state, not the cause, that interests Byron:

> The spirit burning but unbent
> May writhe—rebel—the weak alone repent!
>
> (ii, 10)

There may be a reference to Byron's amatory experiences in the Levant:

> Things light or lovely in their acted time,
> But now to stern reflection each a crime;
> The withering sense of evil unreveal'd,
> Not cankering less because the more conceal'd.
>
> (ii, 10)

We have recently found Byron relating *The Corsair* to what appears to be his own experiences (pp. 161–2; and see LBM, 203–4).

Byron felt himself both an outcast of unorthodox sexual instincts and a potential revolutionary who admired Napoleon in part perhaps because the Napoleonic Code did not regard the expression of such instincts as a crime. *Lara* (1814), more obviously autobiographical than *The Corsair*, makes contact with both Byron's Newstead life and his revolutionary interests.

Lara, like Byron, had left his European home, gone east and returned, like Othello, from 'deserts vast' (I, 6; 'antres vast and desarts idle', *Othello*, I, iii, 140) with Kaled, a foreign page who turns out to be a girl in disguise, so forming a composite of Nicolo Giraud and the Greek servants whom Byron brought back to England. Some crime, of which Kaled alone shares the knowledge (I, 14), is on his conscience; and after he has killed a man in an honourable duel, suspicions concerning this other deed are aroused. He becomes the leader of a revolutionary movement. In *Lara* Byron knots his revolutionary interests to his own sexual psychology. Though 'contemptuous' of the great he is considerate to the humble (II, 8). The poor love him, disregarding his reputation. Like earlier heroes, he refuses religious consolation.

We have already (p. 77) reviewed Lara's ghostly experience in his Newstead-like hall. Like Macbeth facing his air-drawn dagger and Banquo's ghost he shows his old courage under this new and greater test. Though rendered senseless with 'more than Nature's fear' before what was presumably an accusing presence,

> Yet he was firm, or had been firm till now,
> And still defiance knit his gather'd brow;
> Some half-form'd threat in utterance there had died,
> Some imprecation of despairing pride.
>
> (I, 13)

The words suit Macbeth in whom courage is simultaneously baffled yet firm before the supernatural horrors which he banishes.

Lara in youth had been an idealist and a student, but when grown-up

> He stood a stranger in this breathing world,
> An erring Spirit from another hurl'd.
>
> (I, 18)

'Breathing world' is from *Richard III* (I, i, 21; see p. 154 above). He 'confounded good and ill', regarding his choice as fated, but

173

even so he was ever ready to 'resign his own for others' good', not from ethic but simply being 'too high for common selfishness', a 'strange perversity of thought' and 'secret pride' urging him to do what was unusual, with impulses as ready for crime as for virtue:

> So much he soar'd beyond, or sunk beneath,
> The men with whom he felt condemn'd to breathe.
>
> (I, 18)

Separated from 'all who shared his mortal state', his mind lived in 'regions of her own' (I, 18). Lara represents a super-type beyond moral categories, but 'in his own heart secure' (I, 24), who exerts, like Conrad, a fascination which is neither 'love' nor 'hate'; he 'haunts' people (I, 19). As for his life abroad, that remains ambiguous. He dies 'all unknown his glory or his guilt' (II, 23).

In *Lara* Byron is unravelling his own sense of kinship to Richard III while rationalizing his conviction that such heroes are in essence superior to their companions. But there is a difference. Lara, like Conrad but unlike Richard, has a peculiar gentleness, a softness; and somehow this very gentleness—it is to happen to Cain later—is *part of the crime*. Somehow, like Othello or Timon, he has been forced 'to hate for having loved too well' (I, 17; *Othello*, V, ii, 343). This is why

> the stern
> Have deeper thoughts than your dull eyes discern.
>
> (II, 22)

Much the same will be said by Marino Faliero (p. 350). Deep love, thwarted by society, may assume an iron exterior.

The relation of these studies to Byron's own inward experiences is the clearer for their resemblance to the more explicit self-portrait in *Childe Harold* (e.g. III, 12). Probably both *The Corsair* and *Lara* may be referred to Byron's homosexual engagements in Greece. *The Bride of Abydos* and *Parisina* may be with due caution referred to Byron's affections for Augusta Leigh. *Manfred* may be referred to both, though neither is explicit. This amazingly compact work is simultaneously comprehensive and non-committal. Much of it we shall discuss later. Here we may note that the drama aims to fuse an undefined sense of sexual sin with bloodshed, making for a composite of *The Rape of Lucrece* and *Macbeth*. Manfred's blood-guilt is peculiarly enigmatic:

> I have shed
> Blood, but not hers—and yet her blood was shed.
>
> (II, ii, 119)

The statement corresponds to Byron's sense of a *Macbeth*-guilt in relation to love and without having committed a murder.

Manfred (1817) is in the Faust tradition. It is also Gothic, starting 'in a Gothic gallery' (I, i). Manfred, recognizing that 'the Tree of Knowledge is not that of Life' (I, i, 12), is baffled; but he knows that he has in him a 'Mind', 'Spirit' and 'Promethean spark', called the 'lightning' of his 'being' (I, i, 154-5), and in this conviction *commands* (II, ii, 159) the lower spirits as slaves to his will and mind, as do, in their different ways, both Macbeth, in the Cauldron scene, and Prospero. He has Macbeth's courage:

> But I can act even what I most abhor,
> And champion human fears.
>
> (II, ii, 203)

The strange use of 'champion' recalls Macbeth's 'champion me to the utterance' (*Macbeth*, III, i, 72). He determines to raise the dead, thinking of the Witch of Endor and the ghost of Samuel (II, ii, 181).

Manfred communes with various spirits, with the Witch of the Alps, with Nemesis and Arimanes, in an ascending process; but all are inferior to him, as a man. The three 'sister' Destinies meet and recount their grim doings like Shakespeare's Weird Sisters; and to them comes Nemesis, their superior, said to have been engaged on 'some great work' (II, iii, 58), corresponding to Shakespeare's Hecate and her

> Great business must be wrought ere noon:
> Upon the corner of the moon . . .
>
> (*Macbeth*, III, v, 22)

Nathaniel Lee in his *Sophonisba* had already copied Shakespeare's Cauldron scene in reference not to crime but to war in such a way as to give it a more general relevance to us all (*The Golden Labyrinth*, 159–60). Byron expands yet wider. Nemesis and the Destinies are powers of nature and society as we know them, associated with tyranny, shipwreck and plague, and the deity Arimanes is a deity less of any ethical evil than of life itself 'with all its infinite of agonies' (II, iv, 15). These dark powers correspond simply to created existence as man inevitably knows it; and it is against all this that Manfred claims superiority. He refuses to kneel to Arimanes (II, iv, 34–49), believing in an 'over-ruling Infinite', a 'Maker' of Arimanes, and in 'powers deeper still beyond'; and for these he searches (II, iv, 47, 76). Shakespeare's Weird Sisters recognized in the Apparitions they called up their 'masters' (*Macbeth*, IV, i, 63). Shelley in his *Prometheus Unbound* followed Byron's scheme, using Jupiter and Prometheus to correspond respectively to Arimanes and Manfred.

Manfred, like Conrad and Lara, was a leader who had aimed to be 'the enlightener of nations', but could not collaborate with his inferiors, degrading himself to their level. Rather he pressed beyond, aiming to rise 'I knew not whither' (III, i, 104–23).

Though like Faustus he rejects religious assistance, simple good is recognized. To Manfred the simple, kindly and pious Chamois Hunter has the appeal that simple work-people held for Shakespeare's burdened kings (*3 Henry VI,* II, v, 21–54; *Henry IV,* III, i, 4–31; *Henry V,* IV, i, 288–304); like them the Hunter works healthily and sleeps soundly (II, i, 63–73). When Manfred says 'I am not of thine order', the Hunter's answer 'I would not be of thine for the free fame of William Tell' (II, i, 38–40) recalls Lady Macbeth's sleepwalking scene with the Gentlewoman's 'I would not have such a heart in my bosom for the dignity of the whole body' (*Macbeth*, V, i, 60). Manfred is superior without being, as it were, *better* than other men. When Astarte, called up like the Apparitions in *Macbeth*, rises, she is, like the ghosts in *Richard III* and *Macbeth*, an accusing figure. Manfred's will to some supreme good is accompanied by guilt and his effect on others has been like 'the red-hot breath of the most lone Simoom' (III, i, 128).

The Abbot, corresponding to the Old Man in Marlowe's *Doctor Faustus*, is shocked by Manfred's having held forbidden converse with spirits who 'walk the valley of the Shade of Death' (III, i, 38). Manfred respects him, but must go his own way. He suffers 'Remorse without the fear of Hell'; 'no future pang' could deal that 'justice' on 'his own soul' which he, 'self-condemned', inflicts on himself (III, i, 71–8). The fiends who come for him he dismisses with 'The hand of Death is on me, but not yours' (III, iv, 141). The Abbott does not claim to know where he has gone, any more than we know the final fate of Macbeth.

Manfred has throughout shown himself, as indeed, after his own fashion does Macbeth, superior to the powers of darkness; and his occult researches have been scientifically justified (p. 298). But he endures unrest. *Macbeth* threats of blood such as 'Will it then never, never, sink in the earth?' (II, i, 22) are present, but left undefined. He suffers from 'some half-maddening sin (II, i, 31). The net result is an expanded study in that peculiar vein of 'impenitent remorse' (*The Corsair*, II, 10) which *Macbeth* so exactly forecasts. What *Manfred* does is to rationalize our approval of Richard III and Macbeth, and our demand, as theatregoers, that they *should not repent*. Manfred's soul-star, called a 'bright deformity' (I, i, 122), is a metaphysical analogy to Richard as a theatrical success. Richard may get off, in Shakespeare, comparatively easily—he for the most part enjoys him-self—but both Macbeth and Manfred endure agonies. The soul's 'bark', though not 'lost', is certainly 'tempest-toss'd' (*Macbeth*, I, iii, 24). Manfred is, like Macbeth, his own 'proper Hell'; the 'immortal' mind punishes itself in its own 'place' and 'time' (*Manfred*, III, iv, 129–32). The course is fearful.

Manfred not only helps to explain our immoral delight in dark heroes. It even hints that within that delight there lies recognition of a supreme good. In our 'star condemned' (*Manfred*, I, i, 44) with all its horrors of nature and society, the great soul must and should be an outlaw, an Ishmael, perhaps even, as Wordsworth's *Borderers* suggests (p. 151), though this may be to drive logic too far, a criminal: imaginatively at least there may be little difference. Man-fred is of 'no common order' (II, iv, 52); he is an embryo superman; and Macbeth was a step to his making. Somewhere within, or beyond, lies 'the golden secret', the 'sought "Kalon"'[1] (*Manfred*, III, i, 13), the justification.

Cain (1821) takes us further. In it the *Macbeth*-evil is both (i)

1. The Greek '*kalon*', meaning 'beautiful', was used also to designate virtue of high worth indefinable in moral terms.

traced to its source in Western tradition by studying the first murder in the Bible and (ii) related to the two great quests of post-Renaissance thought, scientific and occult. The one shows 'an aerial universe of endless expansion' at which the soul 'aches to think', 'intoxicated with eternity' (II, i, 107); the other, the world beyond sense-perception, where forms long dead exist in another dimension. Futurity is also considered: the infinitude of the 'innumerable yet unborn myriads of unconscious atoms' to be 'animated' (II, ii, 41) leaves us stunned.

Lucifer is, as his name implies, a 'light-bearer', a star-spirit, and the poem has wondrous lights of pearly star, 'empurpled night', and blue-bright Elysium (pp. 307–8 below). Lucifer is the inquiring, Renaissance mind; and through and in him the supposedly bad is shown as good. We are invited to ask why the Trees of Knowledge and of Life have been forbidden? Must we submit to such tyrannous and illogical commands? Remembering Manfred and Hades in *Cain* we may put the question like this: why have occult sciences and sexual impulses been saturated in guilt? What lies behind the Faust and Don Juan archetypes, or myths? Cain is wife to his twin sister Adah. When Lucifer, asked if Adah's love for Cain is a sin, replies that it is not but one day will be, Adah insists that the quality of a sin should not depend on social circumstances (I, i, 364–83). There are lengthy arguments, some turning on the question whether creation, as we see it, is or is not good. What of its never-ending conflicts? Are there '*two* Principles' (II, ii, 404)? Lucifer's final advice is that good and evil are essences rather than moral laws, and that he must 'endure', 'form an inner world' and live by that, so drawing nearer to 'the spiritual nature' (II, ii, 463); as did Manfred, when refusing damnation while admitting his *inward* torment.

In *Cain* the Byronic hero reaches its most lucid definition, *Manfred* being the most complex. The use of a well-known myth naturally helps. Like his predecessors Cain, loving and gentle, has many virtues of Christian tone. As in *Manfred* we are aware that nature is itself cruel; if man is evil, so is nature; and if nature is, so is God—that is how the thought runs. Like Manfred before Arimanes, Cain will not kneel to God, though he is willing to offer fruits:

Abel, more religiously humble, offers a blood-sacrifice. Values are criss-crossed: Abel accepts the blood-law of nature and of God, whereas Cain, rejecting it, is impious. He aims at a good *beyond nature*. Paradoxically his very sensibility leads to his quarrel with Abel and to Abel's murder. He is plunged into the *Macbeth* world. He gazes distraught, like Macbeth (II, ii, 60), on his blood-stained hand (III, i, 321, 344-5) and is to endure a similar agony:

> May his dreams be of his victim!
> His waking a continual dread of Death!
> May the clean rivers turn to blood as he
> Stoops down to stain them with his raging lip!
> (III, i, 430)

Cursed by his mother, branded by the Angel, Cain goes forth 'a vagabond on earth'. Like Manfred he endures guilt and remorse, but his integrity remains: 'That which I am, I am', he says, following Shakespeare's Sonnets, Richard Duke of Gloucester and Parolles (Sonnet 121; *3 Henry VI*, v, vi, 83; *All's Well that Ends Well*, IV, iii, 373).

Like Conrad, Cain is 'doomed for his very virtues for a dupe'. The balances are justly held: Jehovah is not definitely evil, like Arimanes or Shelley's Jupiter, and the prayers of Adam and Abel are convincing. No better comment could be found than those enigmatic words from *Macbeth* (I, i, 11), 'Fair is foul and foul is fair', in which Byron's satanic works reveal a new precision. In them that which fascinates us in *Macbeth* and *Richard III* is given a positive interpretation. What, Byron asks, is the new virtue of which those, and we may add all the Faust and Don Juan plays too, all 'Gothic' heroes, and Milton's Satan—and Heathcliff in *Wuthering Heights*— are negative symptoms?

Our last dark drama is *Werner*, composed and published in 1822 though an earlier draft had been made in 1815 (see Byron's Preface; also Hobhouse, 16 Oct. 1821; C, II, 201). The story had for long fascinated Byron. The result nevertheless stands outside the 'transvaluation of values', to use Nietzsche's phrase, for which our other dramas labour, the relation between goodness and crime being more normally handled.

The drama is in the 'Gothic' tradition. Werner is a nobleman living in poverty and exile under a father's curse (IV, i, 429) caused by his own 'faults and follies' (I, i, 98). To him comes the opportunity of slaying his chief persecutor and the rival for his inheritance, Siegendorf. He resists, but takes a little money. He confesses to his son, defending the deed. The rival is subsequently murdered and Werner gains his inheritance. He is however tortured by guilt for the theft and subsequently discovers that it was his son, in part led astray by his father's example, who committed the murder.

We face the inrush of evil attending the smallest slip, the swift descent in crime from father to son corresponding to Macbeth's rapid fall. 'Twenty thousand' years may not suffice to expiate 'the madness and dishonour of an instant' (IV, i, 316). The dishonour may be no more than a 'venial' (II, ii, 148) slip, but its deadly effect matures. This is morality at an extreme as unnerving as the opposite extreme of the Iago-gospel put forward in Wordsworth's *The Borderers* (p. 151). But the two are almost the same, since *Werner* comes near to suggesting that we are all potentially, or perhaps inevitably, responsible, directly or indirectly, for crime; it touches us more closely than does *Macbeth*, while helping to explain the relevance of *Macbeth* to ourselves.

We start with a tempestuous night in a decayed edifice in northern Silesia set in 'a lone spot of wintry desolation' and the home of 'ghosts' and 'rats'. (I, i, 171, 182). In this 'Gothic labyrinth of unknown windings' (III, i, 94) with its 'cursed pattering feet and whirling wings' of rats and bats (III, iii, 15–17), we have an objective equivalent to the tortuous twistings of man's soul. The key to both the theft and the murder is a secret passage.

King Lear (III, iv, 28–36) is recalled by thought of the sufferings of poor people in this terrible night (I, i, 25–33), and again in

> Had he been a wolf, I could not
> Have in such circumstances thrust him forth.
> (III, iv, 92)

We are reminded of *King Lear* (IV, vii, 36–8; for 'thrust', III, vii, 93). Werner's son, young Ulric, fine and fierce as the royal boys in *Cymbeline* (IV, ii, 173–6), is 'strong and beautiful as a young tiger'

(IV, i, 24). His youth, strength and beauty are 'almost superhuman', but they are accompanied by 'the assassin's eye' (V, i, 267).

A typical *Macbeth*-like excitement is generated. Werner leaves by a secret passage with a knife for the chamber where that 'cool, calculating fiend' (I, i, 617), his rival, is lying, and on his return is confronted—as was Macbeth—by his wife:

> Discover'd! then I'll stab—Ah, Josephine,
> Why art thou not at rest?

(I, i, 735)

He shows her the gold he has taken. The tense scene closes:

> Josephine: Yet one question—
> What hast thou *done?*
> Werner: Left one thing *undone,* which
> Had made all well: let me not think of it!
> Away!

(I, i, 747)

Werner, though tempted, had not committed the murder.

Confessing the theft to Ulric Werner defends himself in a speech crammed with *Macbeth* associations. The young man may be himself one day in such a position:

> Should that day e'er arrive—
> Should you see then the Serpent, who hath coil'd
> Himself around all that is dear and noble
> Of you and yours, lie slumbering in your path,
> With but *his* folds between your steps and happiness,
> When *he,* who lives but to tear from you name,
> Lands, life itself, lies at your mercy, with
> Chance your conductor—midnight for your mantle—
> The bare knife in your hand, and earth asleep,
> Even to your deadliest foe; and he as 'twere
> Inviting death, by looking like it, while
> His death alone can save you:—Thank your God!
> If then, like me, content with petty plunder,
> You turn aside—I did so.

(II, ii, 110)

Crimes may be made 'venial by the occasion' (II, ii, 148). Macbeth's crime was caused largely by Werner's 'chance' as 'conductor'. For him as for Werner 'time' and 'place', as Lady Macbeth puts it, had 'made themselves'; and in *Macbeth* sleep is, just as in Werner's thought, 'death's counterfeit' (*Macbeth*, I, vii, 51–3; II, iii, 83). Phrase similarities recall *Macbeth*, 'You have harp'd the very string next to my heart' (II, ii, 411) balancing 'Thou hast harp'd my fear aright' (*Macbeth*, IV, i, 74). Guilt leaves one, as in *Macbeth*, with 'nightmare upon his heart o' nights' (III, i, 38).

The theft raises an outcry. Werner has to assist the escape of a suspected man. He is distraught by guilt and danger:

> In what
> A maze hath my dim destiny involv'd me!
> And one base sin hath done me less ill than
> The leaving undone one far greater. Down,
> Thou busy devil, rising in my heart!
> Thou art too late! I'll nought to do with blood.
>
> (III, i, 145)

His son, however, now becomes a Lady Macbeth hinting that such 'petty fear' must be scorned (III, i, 158). Strong enemies need strong measures:

Werner: Show me *how?*
Ulric: Can you not guess?
Werner: I cannot.
Ulric: That is strange.
        Came the thought ne'er into your mind *last night?*
Werner: I understand you not.
Ulric: Then we shall never
        More understand each other.

                                (III, i, 164)

The interchanges of nervous dialogue continually remind us of *Macbeth*. From now on Ulric despises his father for his weakness. Werner, thinking of restitution, is startled: 'Hark, what noise is that?' (III, iv, 26) recalls Macbeth's 'Did'st thou not hear a noise?' in the murder scene (*Macbeth*, II, ii, 16). Ulric enters. Question and answer, broken lines and thought of an 'assassin' (III, iv, 31), follow rapidly. Siegendorf has been murdered. Ulric, unknown to his father, is the murderer.

Werner is installed in his patrimony, Siegendorf. The theft now coalesces in his mind with the mysterious murder. After a series of gripping complications Ulric's crime is revealed. He calmly reminds his father how *he* formerly justified his own fault:

> If *you* condemn me, yet,
> Remember *who* hath taught me once too often
> To listen to him! *Who* proclaim'd to me
> That *there were crimes* made venial by the occasion?
> That passion was our nature? that the goods
> Of Heaven waited on the goods of fortune?
>
> (v, i, 439)

Again and again we are reminded of Macbeth's dialogues with his wife. This is pure Lady Macbeth:

> The man who is
> At once both warm and weak invites to deeds
> He longs to do, but dare not. Is it strange
> That I should *act* what you could *think?* We have
>   done
> With right and wrong; and now must only ponder
> Upon effects, not causes.
>
> (v, i, 450)

'Fortune' recalls the part played by chance in *Macbeth*. We remember Lady Macbeth's 'that which rather thou dost fear to do than wishest should be undone' and 'letting "I dare not" wait upon "I would" ' (*Macbeth*, I, v, 25; vii, 44). Ulric, like Lady Macbeth, rejects anxiety regarding 'things which cannot be undone' (v, i, 470; blending *Macbeth*, III, ii, 11 and v, i, 74). Werner finds his son a 'demon' (v, ii, 57) and his own father's curse fulfilled.

Ulric's 'we have done with right and wrong' might be read as an ironic critique on Byron's usual dramatic valuations. Here our ethical standards are normal, and fixed; we are invited to feel everything from Werner's standpoint, Ulric as an intruder from the other more dangerous order being given little enough approval. *Werner* reflects that in *Macbeth* which is, or seems, directed by the obvious moral valuations; Byron's other dark dramas reflect that in *Macbeth* which leaves us with the sense that these valuations do not cover the problem. Now because Byron is using the ordinary valuations instead of engaging in a thought-adventure, he can employ a normal stage technique. The criminal psychology, the stabs of irony, the tense atmosphere and gripping dialogues, the mysteries and the thrills, all are from the hand of a master. If Byron's other plays, including the historical dramas, appear to lack obvious drama, that is from no lack in Byron's genius of dramatic instinct or power, but derives simply from the dangerous nature of the Nietzschean advance being made, with the concomitant necessities of classic control and lucid definition.

And yet *Werner* too has its place in this advance. In so firmly driving home the extreme of its moral lesson that the most venial slip may, by example and influence, be responsible for some great crime, it tends to make criminals of us all in such a way that moral values are undermined as surely as in Wordsworth's *Borderers*. Extremes meet. Macbeth's sensitivity had much to do with his criminal course. In the field of Renaissance thought-adventure it seems that sensitivity of conscience cohabits naturally with satanism; and it is those, like Byron and Nietzsche, who have such a sensitivity who most clearly see how far moral distinctions may be from covering the human problem.

IV

We may conclude with Galt's description of the young Byron on the boat off Gibraltar; aloof, 'inhaling, as it were, poetical sympathy from the gloomy rock, then dark and stern in the twilight' (I, 61). Quoting *Macbeth* (I, iii, 21) he sees him as 'a man forbid':

If my remembrance is not treacherous, he only spent one evening in the cabin with us—the evening before we came to anchor at Cagliari; for, when the lights were placed, he made himself a man forbid, took his station on the railing between the pegs on which the sheets are belayed and the shrouds, and there, for hours, sat in silence, enamoured, it may be, of the moon. All these peculiarities, with his caprices, and something inexplicable in the cast of his metaphysics, while they served to awaken interest, contributed little to conciliate esteem. He was often strangely rapt—it may have been from his genius; and, had its grandeur and darkness been then divulged, susceptible of explanation; but, at the time, it threw, as it were, around him the sackcloth of penitence. Sitting amidst the shrouds and rattlings, in the tranquillity of the moonlight, churming an inarticulate melody, he seemed almost apparitional, suggesting dim reminiscences of him who shot the albatross. He was as a mystery in a winding-sheet, crowned with a halo.

The influence of the incomprehensible phantasma which hovered about Lord Byron, has been more or less felt by all who ever approached him. That he sometimes came out of the cloud, and was familiar and earthly, is true; *but his dwelling was amidst the murk and the mist, and the home of his spirit in the abysm of the storm, and the hiding places of guilt.* He was, at the time of which I am speaking, scarcely two and twenty, and could claim no higher praise than having written a clever worldly-minded satire; and yet it was impossible, even then, to reflect on the bias of his mind, as it was revealed by the casualites of conversation, without experiencing a presentiment, that he was destined to execute some singular and ominous purpose.

(Galt, VIII, 62–3)

I have italicized the key-phrases bringing to mind 'the fog and filthy air' and 'murky' Hell of *Macbeth* (I, i, 12; V, i, 39). Remembering Galt's relation of Byron's temperament to the mists and mountains of Aberdeenshire (p. 169), we may suggest that it needed a Scotsman such as Galt to receive the full impact of his dark personality; and we can see why Shakespeare, in his mature probing of evil, chose Scotland for his stage.

That Byron did, in certain moods, plumb so darkly the depths, may be felt from a sensitive reading, enriched by our own fears of atomic destruction, of his poem *Darkness* (1816); which may be also read as an expansion of Macbeth's or Timon's more nihilistic thoughts (e.g. *Macbeth*, III, ii, 16; IV, i, 52–61; V, v, 49–50; *Timon of Athens*, V, i, 227–8).

Beside Galt's grim passage we may place Thomas Mulock's observations, set down in 1819, on Byron. Though written from a Christian standpoint, they are not unsympathetic. Though 'some sin' torments him, God's agency is at work. In 'the religion of

Christ', he says, 'all the grandeur' of Byron's 'most unearthly aspirations' would find rest in adoration. Mulock's insight was keen:

He seems to himself to be a fated voyager upon an ocean untracked by any other keel.

But, 'though man may not, and perhaps cannot, sound the depths of his mental distress', there is a 'mercyseat' to be approached through 'an everlasting Mediator', where his woes will be 'intelligible'. The Scriptures unsealed 'by the Spirit of the living God' will reveal what 'introspection' cannot, the cause and cure of these ills. 'Sin' is *within*; salvation *without*. The thought is exact. Byron is given his due:

Lord Byron, whose awful state of mind enables him to view, with supernatural strength of vision, the fallacy of carnal life, without discerning the *fulness of him who filleth all in all*—has wrought into a single stanza more solid truth than can be detected in the philosophy and theology of all ages.

(LJ, IV, App. x, 496–7)

But poetry—Byron himself once said as much (Murray, 3 Nov. 1821; LJ, V, 470)—has in itself no effective action on man: 'This', says Thomas Mulock, 'is the prerogative-royal of sovereign grace.'

There is a clear divergence, not easily healed. What is most important in the relation of the Byronic imagination to *Macbeth* is the sense we have in both of the necessity that the hero should be (i) impenitent in the orthodox sense and yet (ii) self-condemned. Of this paradox in *Macbeth* I have often written (e.g. *The Sovereign Flower*, 249). We feel nevertheless that somehow condemnation would be *our* wrong reaction. In Byron external crime flowers from a central good. In *Manfred* and *Cain* what our dramatic response suggests in *Macbeth* becomes explicit and assertive. That is the usual process: in Byron, as in other dramatists of the period, the Shakespearian poetry attains a newly explicit, and rational, consciousness; though there is nothing in Byron so extreme as the fearful rationalization and defence of evil in Wordsworth's *The Borderers*. This is all part of the 'ocean untracked'—though not uncharted (pp. 22–3 above)—to which Mulock refers; and the voyage points ahead to Ibsen and Nietzsche. To risk loss of academic dignity by a cant phrase, the demand seems to be that man should not rely on

186

grace but rather 'lift himself by his own bootstraps'. Whether that is possible is another matter. A solution might come from realizing that, as Ibsen assumed (*Ibsen*, Conclusion, 111), there is already deep embedded in man an instinct and a power and a will sufficient for the task; and it is towards the awakening of that power, Pope's 'God within the mind' (*Essay on Man*, II, 204) and Byron's 'Promethean spark' (p. 175), that our poet-prophets direct us.

VI

TIMON AND SHYLOCK

I

ESPITE HIS COMOEDIC and satanic extravagances we can in Shakespeare detect a central development running from the Sonnets through *Hamlet* to *King Lear, Timon of Athens* and *The Tempest,* which might, after all due reservations are admitted, be called a 'spiritual autobiography'. So, too, in Byron: despite all extravagances there was in him a depth of purpose never finally disturbed. As we have seen, both Sir Walter Scott and Lady Byron regarded 'melancholy' as his dominating characteristic (p. 74 above). We have discussed Byron's relation to Shakespeare's Sonnets and *Hamlet:* now we turn to *Timon of Athens.*

Timon of Athens shows us a man of superlative generosity plunged into disillusion, bitterness and death. The hero's friendships are male, and women, apart from two regarded as prostitutes and those who disguise themselves as Amazons in the masque, absent. Sex-nausea is strong. To this extent we are in the world of the Sonnets. We have already (p. 27) compared Byron's bitter lines on 'successful passion' to Shakespeare's sonnet on lust; he could even write tersely, 'You know I hate women' (Hobhouse, 3 Nov. 1811; C, I, 57); and certainly his most natural, and perhaps most genuine, human relationships were those with his male friends. He shows as many similarities to Shakespeare's Timon as to Hamlet.

Timon is generous to friends, a patron of artists and a father to his servants. He has wealth and an aristocratic lustre. He could be called a Renaissance saint in descent from medieval feudalism; a saint, that is, in terms not of religion but of worldly position and humanistic feeling. Byron was that too. His Timon-like generosities I have already reviewed in my *Lord Byron: Christian Virtues* (II). His assiduous and selfless will to assisting the literary careers of Coleridge, Moore and Hunt is striking; and his attitude to any young aspirant was regularly avuncular, if not paternal. To all servants and especially to the old retainer, Joe Murray, his valet Fletcher, the boy Robert Rushton, and the charwoman Mrs. Mule, he was deeply considerate. Joe Murray was often on his mind: 'While I live he shall never be abandoned in his old age'; he is 'the head of my household' and 'I should be a great Brute, if I had not provided for him' (Augusta, 22 March 1804; 14 Dec. 1808; LJ, I, 22, 204). In 1811 the old man, though seventy-five, is, says Byron, 'still like a Rock', and in 1813 he is called 'honest and faithful, but fearfully superannuated' (Augusta, 21 Aug. 1811; Webster, 2 Sept. 1813; LJ, I, 333; II, 259). After the separation Byron was still concerned for his welfare (Hanson, 28 Aug. 1816; 25 March 1817; 31 May 1818; Lady Byron, 3 April 1820; LJ, III, 344; IV, 76, 232; V, 5). Though Murray is older than Shakespeare's Flavius and not dramatically concerned in our story, Byron's consideration is of the same tone as Timon's

> Prithee, be not sad.
> Thou art true and honest; ingenuously I speak,
> No blame belongs to thee.
>
> (II, ii, 230)

Again, when Timon uses his wealth to help his young servant Lucilius to a happy marriage, the act is exactly Byronic. Byron felt a semi-paternal, feudalistic, responsibility for his retainers, including their morals (e.g. Mrs. Byron, 28 June 1810; LJ, I, 283). In his letters he refers continually to his servants, Fletcher especially.

In both Timon and Byron selflessness and generosity are instinctive and extreme. Byron really *wants* the good fortune of Moore, even in rivalry to himself (LBCV, 54–5). He is not content with helping Coleridge towards publication but proceeds to arrange for a good review too (LBCV, 59) on the lines of Timon's help to Ventidius:

> 'Tis not enough to help the feeble up,
> But to support him after.
>
> (I, i, 108)

Byron's benevolences continued throughout his life; they were often anonymous. Of his later years Hoppner, Gamba and Teresa speak with one voice on the matter. All this I have discussed before (LBCV, 87–92). The record is superlative: in instinctive generosity Byron *was* Timon.

He had Timon's failings. Hoppner says that he could be 'culpably lenient' to those who traded on his goodness (LJ, IV, 388, note; LBCV, 87). As a young man at Cambridge he spent freely if not rashly, but generosity was part of it. His mother writes: 'Lord Byron has given £31. 10. 0. to Pitt's statue. He has also bought a Carriage, which he says was intended for me, which I *refused* to accept of, being in hopes it would stop his having one' (LJ, I, 95, note: other relevant examples are given). Byron admitted that he was 'naturally extravagant' (Mrs. Byron, 26 Feb. 1806; LJ, I, 95), but as he grew older he certainly did his best to shoulder his financial responsibilities, which were complex, involving the burden of Newstead and his Lancashire mines. 'I always was,' he wrote, 'and always shall be, an embarrassed man, and I must e'en fight my way through between the files of ruined nobles and broken shopkeepers which increase daily' (Hobhouse, 3 Nov. 1811; C, I, 57). This transition from nobles to shopkeepers is as relevant to Byron as to Timon, since the two stories express similar tensions of social change. Byron passed from an aristocratic attitude to money, refusing royalties as unworthy of a lord, to an acute sense of literary business and a realization of money as power. The crash of 1816 was the turning point.

Byron's finances are hard to follow. He loved Newstead, but its sale was forced, though not actually effected until 1817 (Mrs. Byron, 6 March 1809; Bankes, 28 Sept. 1812; LJ, I, 216; II, 162, and note). After his marriage in 1815 Byron found himself in severe straits, his financial anxieties being 'such as to drive him half-mad' (J. C. Hobhouse, Lord Broughton, *Recollections of a Long Life,* II; XV, 201). Creditors, expecting returns from his marriage settlement, descended in force. Bailiffs were in the house. His aristocratic pretensions, carrying as they did a certain superiority to money, were, just like Timon's, being rendered ridiculous by the facts. Much of Byron's distraction at this period may be referred to these disasters. His wife

wrote to Augusta about Byron's 'inexorable pride' and the shame
which he endured from the presence of a bailiff:

> I wish George B. or some man friend of common-sense were in
> the way to laugh B. out of his excessive horrors on this subject,
> which he seems to regard as if no mortal had ever experienced
> anything so shocking.
>
> (Mayne, *Life and Letters of Lady Byron*, 195)

Byron's books were seized, and had to be sold. He reports on the
seizure to Murray:

> This is about the tenth execution in as many months; so I am
> pretty well hardened; but it is fit I should pay the forfeit of my
> forefathers' extravagances and my own; and, whatever my faults
> may be, I suppose they will be pretty well expiated in time—or
> eternity.
>
> (6 March 1816; LJ, III, 271)

Beside this confession we must place Byron's record of manifold
benevolences, personal and public; we must not forget his speeches,
in the cause of the oppressed, in the Lords; nor his poetry, that had
given pleasure to his native land and electrified Europe.

He had every reason to feel, though he could not logically claim,
that society had responded with ingratitude. He knew himself to be,
as was Timon, one like Conrad 'doom'd by his very virtues for a
dupe' (*The Corsair*, I, 11); who, though 'a hater of his kind', had
been compelled—in a phrase fusing *Othello* (v, ii, 343) and *Timon of
Athens*—'to hate for having lov'd too well' (*Lara*, I, 17): one

> With more capacity for love than earth
> Bestows on most of mortal mould and birth.
>
> (*Lara*, I, 18)

He was well aware of the nature of ingratitude, though he rarely
referred to it. Here is a neat comment:

> I understand *Coleridge* went about repeating Southey's lie with
> pleasure. I can believe it, for I had done him what is called a
> favour. I can understand Coleridge's abusing me, but how or
> why *Southey* . . .
>
> (Murray, 24 Nov. 1818; LJ, IV, 272)

Byron means this, and there is in it a certain truth. On 20 January 1816—at the height of his financial anxieties—he asked Rogers to arrange for a gift of copyrights to Godwin, who was in distress, adding, 'Only don't let him be plagued, nor think himself obliged and all that, which makes people hate one another' (LJ, III, 256). It was partly, no doubt, for this very reason that so many of Byron's benevolences were anonymous (LBCV, 88–9).

II

At the collapse of his household Byron endured a reversal similar to Timon's:

> Such a house broke!
> So noble a master fall'n! All gone! and not
> One friend to take his fortune by the arm
> And go along with him!
>
> (IV, ii, 5)

The feeling here expressed might well have been that of Byron's servants. But more is involved than an individual's financial and domestic disaster. In Shakespeare's play we feel a feudalistic-Renaissance aristocracy being opposed by powers that forecast both the under-thrust of Swiftian satire and the social severance and return to nature of the Romantic Revival; and also the new order of money in the capitalist era to follow. Byron at the end of the process covers the whole movement as did Shakespeare at the start of it.

Even more is involved. *Timon of Athens* is Shakespeare's expression of that recurring Western drama, from the Prometheus myth down, in which some great personality passes from popularity to infamy, from honour to degradation, and from society to loneliness. Sophocles' two *Oedipus* plays show the pattern, and it recurs in the lives of Socrates and Christ. Since Byron's day we have seen it in the lives of Oscar Wilde and T. E. Lawrence. The spiritual levels may vary, but the rhythm does not, except superficially. In such persons one feels that the surface causes of the break are secondary; that there was from the start a discrepancy awaiting the opportunity to assert itself; both Wilde and Lawrence appear to force the break. Such patterns are revelatory of genius, widely understood; and it is no chance that *Timon of Athens* has of all Shakespeare's works excited the greatest influence on our dramatic tradition and been a peculiar favourite of poets.[1]

For these reasons we shall not be surprised to find Byron concentrating on Timon long before the actual climax. In his early *Love's Last Adieu* Timon's presence is felt:

> Oh! who is yon Misanthrope, shunning mankind?
> From cities to caves of the forest he flew:
> There, raving, he howls his complaint to the wind;
> The mountains reverberate Love's last adieu!
>
> Now Hate rules a heart which in Love's easy chains,
> Once Passion's tumultuous blandishments knew;
> Despair now inflames the dark tide of his veins;
> He ponders in frenzy on Love's last adieu!

From youth on Byron thought of himself as a Timon. At the age of sixteen he told Augusta that he was 'an absolute Hermit' living in 'solitude' (2 April 1804; LJ, I, 26). A few years later he wrote to her:

> I live here much in my own manner, that is, *alone*, for I could not bear the company of my best friend, above a month; there is such a sameness in mankind upon the whole, and they grow so much more disgusting every day, that, were it not for a portion of Ambition, and a conviction that in times like the present we ought to perform our respective duties, I should live here all my life, in unvaried Solitude. I have been visited by all our Nobility and Gentry; but I return no visits.
>
> (14 Dec. 1808; LJ, I, 204)

In 1811, after his return from the east, we hear: 'I am quite alone and never see strangers without being sick, but I am nevertheless on good terms with my neighbours' (Augusta, 9 Sept. 1811; LJ, II, 30). In

---

1. The substance of this paragraph is more fully set out in my article '*Timon of Athens* and its Dramatic Descendants', *A Review of English Literature*, II, 4; Oct. 1961; reprinted in *Stratford Papers on Shakespeare 1963*, ed. Berners W. Jackson, Toronto 1964; and to be included in my forthcoming collection *Shakespeare and Religion*.

such letters we are reminded of Timon's: 'His semblable, yea, himself, Timon disdains' (IV, iii, 22).

Byron early recognized the kinship, as a rejected couplet of his *Childish Recollections* indicates:

> Weary of love, of life, devour'd with spleen,
> I rest a perfect Timon, not nineteen.
>
> (P, I, 84, note)

His 1813 preface to *Childe Harold* I and II concludes:

> Had I proceeded with the poem, this character would have deepened as he drew to the close; for the outline which I once meant to fill up for him was, with some exceptions, the sketch of a modern Timon, perhaps a poetical Zeluco.

After the break with society in 1816, the association became obvious. People visiting him expected to find a 'haughty misanthrope' (Moore, quoting W. E. West, II, 602 or XLIX, 562). In *Detached Thoughts* Byron notes Timon as one of the famous figures to whom he has been compared, and when he talks of a young American 'approaching me in my cavern', Timon is being assumed (1821; Int., and 25; LJ, V, 408, 421). Later Trelawny reports him as saying, 'Now, confess, you expected to find me a "Timon of Athens" or a "Timur the Tartar"' (Trelawny, V, 23). As his story develops Byron masters his bitterness, and his closing years and writings show comparatively little; but before that, the Timon rhythm is clear. That in the autumn of 1816, the year of Byron's break with his native land, Edmund Kean should have appeared in *Timon of Athens* at Drury Lane was exactly appropriate.

His loneliness and seeming misanthropy were, like Timon's, the obverse of a craving for affection. This Moore regards as the key to his life:

> A disposition, on his own side, to form strong attachments, and a yearning desire after affection in return, were the feeling and the want that formed the dream and torment of his existence.
>
> (Moore, I, 177 or VIII, 84)

As early as the time of his leaving England in 1809 he suffered, in

194

full dramatic style, the very experience of Timon. Moore's diagnosis (which Byron himself corroborates; Blessington, VII, 149–54; XII, 282–3) might be used as a Shakespearian commentary:

Baffled, as he had been, in his own ardent pursuit of affection and friendship, his sole revenge and consolation lay in doubting that any such feelings really existed. The various crosses he had met with, in themselves sufficiently irritating and wounding— were rendered still more so by the high, impatient, temper with which he encountered them. What others would have bowed to, as misfortunes, his proud spirit rose against, as wrongs; and the vehemence of this reaction produced, at once, a revolution throughout his whole character, in which, as in revolutions of the political world, all that was bad and irregular in his nature burst forth with all that was most energetic and grand. The very virtues and excellences of his disposition ministered to the violence of this change. The same ardour that had burned through his friendships and loves now fed the fierce explosions of his indignation and scorn. His natural vivacity and humour but lent a fresher flow to his bitterness, till he, at last, revelled in it as an indulgence; and that hatred of hypocrisy, which had hitherto only showed itself in a too shadowy colouring of his own youthful frailties, now hurried him, from his horror of all false pretensions to virtue, into the still more dangerous boast and ostentation of vice.

(Moore, I, 186 or VIII, 88)

Thenceforward he gained and maintained the reputation of 'a stern, haughty, misanthrope, self-banished from the fellowship of men', other attributes regarded as subsidiary (Moore, II, 649 or LI, 583).

Though both Byron and Timon are, to a profound understanding, less rejected than 'self-exiled' (*Childe Harold*, III, 16), yet both regard their community as guilty of some gigantic crime, to be avenged by 'Jove' in Shakespeare (p. 201) and by 'Nemesis' in Byron:

And thou, who never yet of human wrong
Left the unbalanc'd scale, great Nemesis!
Here, where the ancient paid thee homage long—
Thou who didst call the Furies from the abyss,

And round Orestes bade them howl and hiss
For that unnatural retribution—just,
Had it but been from hands less near—in this
Thy former realm, I call thee from the dust!
Dost thou not hear my heart?—Awake! thou shalt, and
    must.

                    (*Childe Harold*, IV, 132)

So the future will 'pile on human heads the mountain of my curse';
and even though that curse is to be 'forgiveness', the identity of
charity with scorn of 'the reptile crew' only makes the indictment the
more terrible (IV, 134–6). They are forgiven *as* reptiles. We are
reminded of the icy reserve of Angiolina's address to the pathetically
repentant Steno in *Marino Faliero:*

> Nothing of good can come from such a source,
> Nor would we aught with him, nor now, nor ever:
> We leave him to himself, that lowest depth
> Of human baseness. Pardon is for men,
> And not for reptiles—we have none for Steno,
> And no resentment: things like him must sting,
> And higher beings suffer: 'tis the charter
> Of Life. The man who dies by the adder's fang
> May have the crawler crush'd, but feels no anger:
> 'Twas the worm's nature; and some men are worms
> In soul, more than the living things of tombs.

                    (V, i, 455)

Byron's uncompromising attitude resembles Timon's. Asked to
suppress his *Childe Harold* stanzas he replied that Nemesis was his
'particular belief and acquaintance'; again, 'I can't give up Nemesis
—my great favourite—I can't, can't.' (Hobhouse, 5 March 1818; also
note on proofs; see C, II, 69 and 70, note). Anger burned in him:

> I could have forgiven the dagger or the bowl—any thing, but
> the deliberate desolation piled upon me, when I stood alone
> upon my hearth, with my household gods shivered around me
> ... Do you suppose I have forgotten it? It has comparatively
> swallowed up in me every other feeling, and I am only a specta-
> tor upon earth, till a tenfold opportunity offers.

             (Moore, 19 Sept. 1818; LJ, IV, 262)

The 'dagger or the bowl': both Timon and Byron exist in a value-world wherein the subtler vices are rated worse than open conflict, however terrible.

Byron refused, as his '*Blackwood's* Defence' records (LJ, IV, App. ix, 480; pp. 104–5, 170, above), to take vengeance, leaving the outcome to the higher powers: 'However, time and Nemesis will do that, which I would not, even were it in my power remote or immediate' (Lady Byron, 5 March 1817; LJ, IV, 68); and, as his grim letter on Sir Samuel Romilly's suicide (Murray, 7 June 1819; LJ, IV, 316) records, his trust was justified. Timon likewise called down supernal wrath on his countrymen, as in his references to Jove as minister of retribution and the 'prosperous gods' as 'keepers', or prison-warders, of a wicked society (IV, iii, 104, 109–11; V, i, 188), while himself remaining physically inactive. Both suffer a fierce amalgam of love and hatred. We often feel Byron trying, in his own natural despite, to, as he himself puts it, 'harden my heart', though he did not find it easy to maintain his 'resentments' (Moore, 14 June 1814; 6 March 1822; LJ, III, 92; VI, 35; LBCV, 97). So too we can feel Timon trying to 'harden his heart' when Flavius visits him:

Had I a steward
So true, so just, and now so comfortable?
It almost turns my dangerous nature mild . . .
How fain would I have hated all mankind,
And thou redeem'st thyself. But all save thee
I fell with curses.

(IV, iii, 499)

Byron was perhaps more instinctively tuned to forgiveness than the later Timon. He could say of England 'I hate your country' (Kinnaird, 11 May 1817; C, II, 52), but he knew that

There is no passion
More spectral or fantastical than Hate;
Not even its opposite, Love, so peoples air
With phantoms, as this madness of the heart.
(*The Two Foscari*, IV, i, 334)

'Anger's my meat', says Shakespeare's Volumnia, 'I sup upon myself, and so shall starve with feeding' (*Coriolanus,* IV, ii, 50): but, though he knew the dangers of hatred, Byron certainly left London in the mood of Coriolanus leaving Rome, or Dante Florence. Shakespeare's Timon is as an archetype of all towering persons whose stature forces a severance from their community.

Byron's refuge was his writing, which corresponds in satire to Timon's curses and in cosmic extensions to Timon's communings with nature. But, in attunement with Timon's scorn of Poet and Painter, flatterers like Rosencrantz and Guildernstern in *Hamlet* or Wordsworth and Southey in Byron's story, Byron, though himself a writer, could loathe the insincerities of the literary world. He wanted no reviews: 'The fact is, that they irritate and take off one's attention, which may be better employed than in listening to either libels or flattery. . . . Let them chatter or scribble, so that I neither hear, nor see them' (Hobhouse, 16 Oct. 1821; C, II, 202). If he ever returns he will write a poem to which *English Bards and Scotch Reviewers* will be nothing: 'Your present literary world of mountebanks stands in need of such an Avatar' (Murray, 12 Sept. 1821; LJ, v, 362). As for Murray's *Quarterly* circle, 'backed by all the corruption, and infamy, and patronage of their master rogues and slave renegadoes', they had better not rouse him (Murray, 28 Oct, 1821; LJ, v, 399; and see 24 Sept., 373–6).

He was not independent of others' criticisms, which he could feel acutely, and most of all with respect to those dramas which were becoming his favourite medium. His agony when *Marino Faliero* was put on at Drury Lane against his will was extreme. Acted drama is a more direct challenge to one's contemporaries than literature, existing publicly in the order of action; and Byron feared the result. The play had not been composed for production: 'They might as well act the Prometheus of Aeschylus'; 'I want neither the impertinence of their hisses, nor the insolence of their applause'; he stands to lose either way, because 'the kick of an Ass or the sting of a Wasp may be painful to those who would find nothing agreeable in the Braying of the one or in the Buzzing of the other' (Moore, 20 and 22 Jan.; as composed for the press, on 22 Jan., Murray, 2 March; 1821; LJ, v, 229–31, 256–7). Byron's suffering was acute. For four days he had reason to believe the play 'damned': 'Ten years ago I should have gone crazy; at present I have lived on as usual'

(Hobhouse, 20 May 1821; C, II, 174–5; and see LJ, V, 294, note).

Marino Faliero, despite its firm objectivity, was written from Byron's most personal experiences. It is simultaneously a social satire and a drama of political action. We have already quoted Angiolina's words to Steno, and the play concludes with the Doge's denunciation of society which, though exactly related to and toned for Venice, nevertheless *also* expresses Byron's own social revulsions:

> Vice without splendour, Sin without relief
> Even from the gloss of Love to smooth it o'er,
> But in its stead, coarse lusts of habitude,
> Prurient yet passionless, cold studied lewdness,
> Depraving Nature's frailty to an art . . .
>
> (v, iii, 85)

We remember old mad King Lear's aspersions on 'yon simpering dame' of false purity (*King Lear*, IV, vi, 121–6) and Timon's inclusive sexual curses.

We cannot clearly demark Byron's personal from his political revulsions; and, as I have often, following Teresa, suspected (p. 101 above), Byron's enforced break with England may have been engineered by those in power for political reasons, the more scandalous matters being used for the purpose.

In *Timon of Athens* likewise there are two main challenges: that of Timon as personal, prophetic, and spiritual; and that of Alcibiades as political, involving the direct action which Timon ('I myself would have no power'; I, ii, 36) avoids. In Alcibiades' scene with the Senate we are aware of virile manhood and soldierly values, like those covered by the warrior Doge in *Marino Foliero*, aligned in true Byronic style with a plea for clemency, against the smugness, ease, usurious ways, and legalism—in his letter on Romilly's suicide (p. 197 above; 202 below) Byron referred bitterly to his having been sacrificed on Romilly's 'legal altar'—of the governing class. Both Byron and Alcibiades are up against not a single tyrant but a governing clique. Byron's political enemies are what he regarded as the utterly irresponsible nobility of England, the Hanoverian kings being non-entities (p. 93 above); and of this ruling class we have neat historical correlatives in the oligarchies of *Marino Faliero* and *The Two Foscari*. Alcibiades, successor to Fortinbras in *Hamlet*, corresponds in Byron's thought to Napoleon as an active revolutionary to be contrasted with the more spiritually conditioned protagonist. For Italy and Greece Byron was himself involved in military action, but not against his own country, nor was he ever in fact called upon to engage in the bloodshed which he loathed.

He expected revolution in England and sometimes thought of returning to assist (LBCV, 143–6). The possibility of his return caused considerable fear at home, exactly like the fear instilled into Athens by Alcibiades' threat. Throughout his life, and especially after his semi-exile, Byron existed as a Sword of Damocles above social injustice in England.[1]

It is nevertheless unlikely that Byron would ever actually have played the Coriolanus against his land. In 1819 he wrote that, though he felt no 'love' for England, he did not 'hate it enough to wish to take a part in its calamities'; 'revolutions are not to be made with rose-water'; and his 'taste for revolution' was 'abated' with his 'other passions' (Hobhouse, 3 Oct. 1819; LJ, IV, 358). His attitude is exactly that of Timon who counters his refusal to help Athens with the reservation:

> But yet I love my country, and am not
> One that rejoices in the common wrack,
> As common bruit doth put it.
>
> (v, i, 196)

The truth is, both Timon and Byron endure simultaneously a revolutionary instinct and a loathing of bloodshed. Their attitude is defined in Timon's dialogue with Alcibiades:

Timon: Warr'st thou 'gainst Athens?
Alcibiades: Ay, Timon, and have cause.

1. For the possibility of Byron's return and the fear it aroused, see David V. Erdman, 'Byron and Revolt in England' or 'Byron's Threatened Invasion of England', a paper read before the Modern Language Association of America, New York, December 1944 and published in *Science and Society*, XI, 3; Summer 1947. For Byron's revolutionary activities in general see also Erdman in *PMLA*, LVI and LVII, December 1941 and March 1942; also *Keats–Shelley Journal*, XI; Winter 1962.

Timon: The gods confound them all in thy conquest;
          And thee after when thou hast conquer'd!
Alcibiades: Why me, Timon?
Timon: That, by killing of villains, thou wast born
          to conquer my country.

                              (IV, iii, 102)

There is a weary disgust at the whole miserable business of social wickedness and bloody retribution. Timon can see Alcibiades as an instrument of justice, or, as Byron would say, of 'Nemesis':

    Be as a planetary plague, when Jove
    Will o'er some high-vic'd city hang his poison
    In the sick air . . .

                              (IV, iii, 109)

But in his following lines pity burns *within* his wrath:

    Put armour on thine ears and on thine eyes,
    Whose proof nor yells of mothers, maids, nor babes,
    Nor sight of priests in holy vestments bleeding
    Shall pierce a jot.

                              (IV, iii, 124)

The 'armour' most needed is armour against not weapons but pity; the pity and religious reverence that beats poetically in these lines. As in Byron, the very curses are curses impelled by love. It happens again, when the Senators at the conclusion visit Timon imploring his aid against Alcibiades. Timon maintains his course, and will not personally align himself with either side:

          But if he sack fair Athens,
    And take our goodly aged men by the beards,
    Giving our holy virgins to the stain
    Of contumelious, beastly, mad-brain'd war;
    Then let him know, and tell him Timon speaks it,
    In pity of our aged and our youth
    I cannot choose but tell him, that I care not,
    And let him take't at worst . . .

                              (V, i, 176)

It is as though that pity and reverence for all the sanctities that the phrases so clearly witness are themselves forcing Timon to pursue his undeviating course. His very pity renders him pitiless. It is exactly this underlying softness that we feel so often within Byron's most terrible passages, as in his letter to Murray on Romilly's suicide (7 June 1819; LJ, IV, 316); he is, as it were, often *forcing* himself, in his own despite, to be bitter; and on such occasions, the surface, ever so slightly, gives him away; the writing is keyed-up, artificially; he is cursing, as it were, through tears.[1]

As for Timon's 'contumelious, beastly, mad-brain'd war', the Byronic correspondences are too manifold, in *Don Juan, Sardanapalus* and elsewhere, to need elaboration. Byron could view Wellington as the inferior 'in rational greatness' to a good dentist or hairdresser; and so is any ' "bloody blustering booby" who gains a name by breaking heads' (Murray, 18 Nov. 1820; LJ, V, 119). And yet he knew also that vicious rule might force opposition. Napoleon had for him just as much, and just as little, justification as Alcibiades had for Timon. When Byron himself took to arms in Italy, he was ironically aware of all the issues (p. 144); and in Greece he countered generalship with an all but inhuman, and most unwarlike, clemency (LBCV, 197–200).

His political thinking was uncompromising in its opposition to social injustice; but again, as in questions of war and pacifism, his pursuance of a *middle course* remained firm. He could not tolerate the radicals. Himself an aristocrat, he believed, despite his affection for all humble persons as persons, that government was safer with men of birth and breeding. The paradox is crisply stated:

> If we must have a tyrant, let him at least be a gentleman who has been bred to the business, and let us fall by the axe and not by the butcher's cleaver.
>
> (Murray, 21 Feb. 1830; LJ, IV, 410)

He believed still in the British Constitution and its aristocracy despite their abysmal failures (LBCV, 145–7, 232; and see in general LBCV, Index A, Politics; 'Failure of Aristocracy' and 'Belief in British Institutions and Aristocracy'). Writing of 'Bristol' Hunt and

---

1. See my discussion of the Romilly letter in *Byron's Dramatic Prose*, Byron Foundation Lecture, 1953; University of Nottingham Press, 1954; to be included soon in a new volume (p. ix above). For a similar reading of the *Lines on Hearing that Lady Byron was Ill*, see W. W. Robson, *Byron as Poet*, Chatterton Lecture, 1957.

Cobbett, he says that 'the man who would overthrow all laws' should not 'have the benefit of any'; 'our classical education alone should teach us to trample on such unredeemed dirt as the *dis*-honest bluntness, the ignorant brutality, the unblushing baseness of those two miscreants . . .' (Hobhouse, 22 April 1820; C, II, 143).

And what now of Timon? His *middle course* is precisely Byron's. Apemantus has throughout personified the extreme of social criticism, and after his philosophy has been proved true, we might have supposed that, when he visits Timon in the wilds, Timon would welcome him. But Timon refuses to recognize an affinity:

Apemantus: Thou should'st desire to die, being miserable.
Timon:　　Not by his breath that is more miserable.
　　　　　Thou art a slave, whom fortune's tender arm
　　　　　With favour never clasp'd, but bred a dog . . .
　　　　　　　　　　　　　　　　　　(IV, iii, 249)

The contrast is developed at some length in purely social, almost irrational, terms, exactly as by Byron. Byron's belief in a benevolent aristocracy that should *raise* the masses, whose interests he never forgot (LBCV, 232),[1] corresponds to Timon's early behaviour as *a personification of aristocratic benevolence and example;* wherein we see a new, symbolical, depth-level in his first apparent foolishness, as a man. But although idealism has failed, neither Timon nor Byron believe that anything will be gained by a dragging down. The Radicals, whom Byron saw rather as Shakespeare saw the rebellion of Jack Cade in *2 Henry VI,*—and we may remember the crowds in *Julius Caesar* and *Coriolanus*—were to him merely levellers, negative and destructive. So is Apemantus:

Timon:　　What would'st thou do with the world, Apemantus,
　　　　　if it lay in thy power?
Apemantus: Give it the beasts, to be rid of the men.
Timon　　 Would'st thou have thyself fall in the confusion of
　　　　　men, and remain a beast with the beasts?
Apemantus: Ay, Timon.
Timon:　　A beastly ambition, which the gods grant thee to attain
　　　　　to.
　　　　　　　　　　　　　　　　　　(IV, iii, 321)

1. The reference given, (Parry, IX, 211–14), should have been, (Parry, IX, 204–14).

In an extended passage Timon argues that any levelling to the beasts, each preying on the other, would merely lead to a worse slavery:

> What beast could'st thou be, that were not subject to a beast? and what a beast art thou already, that seest not thy loss in transformation!
>
> (IV, iii, 348)

That is Byron's view, precisely.

The differences between Byron's Radicals and Shakespeare's Apemantus are as obvious as those between Napoleon and Alcibiades, or indeed Byron himself and Timon; but these differences are external only. What is certain is this: that the *relation* of Byron to Napoleon and the Radicals corresponds to the *relation* of Timon to Alcibiades and Apemantus. The differences are of their period, and ephemeral; the relation deep and enduring.

Another subtlety may be observed. In such matters as we are discussing consistency need not be maintained. For his purpose a satirist may be allowed both to repudiate the low and also to compare it favourably with the falsities of the supposedly high. So the Bandits who visit Timon are given credit at least for honesty:

> Yet thanks I must you con
> That you are thieves profess'd, that you work not
> In holier shapes; for there is boundless theft
> In limited professions . . .
>
> (IV, iii, 431)

Byron similarly could regard a pirate as more honest than those in high places:

> Let not his mode of raising cash seem strange,
>   Although he fleec'd the flags of every nation,
> For into a prime minister but change
>   His title, and 'tis nothing but taxation;
> But he, more modest, took a humbler range
>   Of life, and in an honester vocation
> Pursued o'er the high seas his watery journey
> And merely practis'd as a sea-attorney.
>
> (*Don Juan*, III, 14)

Byron's strongest indictment of economic slavery, whereby the rich are safeguarded and rents kept up 'for fear that plenty should attain the poor' occurs in *The Age of Bronze* (1823), which levels an attack on usurious international bankers (XIV–XV; for the economic situation see P, V, 539–40). We remember Alcibiades' taunting reference to 'usury that makes the Senate ugly' (III, V, 101). In general, Timon's words to the Bandits, 'The laws, your curb and whip, in their rough power have uncheck'd theft' and 'nothing can you steal but thieves do lose it' (IV, iii, 449, 453) are just forecasts of Byron's thought.

III

In the wilds Timon finds gold; and this gold makes him still a man of power; he is sought after; he still gives; dramatically it preserves his status. The glitter of his early scenes changes to the dull glint of his new and *weightier* nuggets or ingots.[1] What we watch is a transition from (i) gold as an easy currency of give and take in an ordered and amiable society to (ii) gold as a more widely operative power, functioning sometimes symbolically and sometimes as an active agent in a disrupted society. The gold of (i) had vanished, become irrelevant, with the passing of the old order. The gold of (ii) has both positive and negative pointings. Positively it helps to maintain Timon's innate, spiritual aristocracy and as symbolism may be regarded as a visual externalization of the soul-state behind his poetic denunciations and aspirations; and to these symbolic properties we shall return. On the lower plane of direct action it enables Timon to empower Alcibiades' revolutionary campaign: 'There's gold to pay thy soldiers' (IV, iii, 127). But it may be regarded also as the potential nourisher of wickedness, a 'yellow slave' that yet overrules religions (IV, iii, 33–4).

Byron, like Shakespeare, was deeply concerned with the paradox of wealth. After the break he, like Timon, became wealthy. Newstead was at last sold; he gained financially from the death of Lady Noel, his mother-in-law; his writings made more and more money; and living in Italy was comparatively cheap. He grew very interested in money.

1. For the stage use of these rather than coins see my *Shakespearian Production*, 1964; 180.

He could write of 'ambrosial cash' (*Don Juan*, XIII, 100) with light though incisive recognition of its dangerously entrancing quality. The claim of love to rule human affairs is false:

> But if Love don't, *Cash* does, and Cash alone:
> Cash rules the grove, and fells it too besides;
> Without cash, camps were thin, and courts were none;
> Without cash, Malthus tells you—'take no brides.'—
> So Cash rules Love the ruler, on his own
> High ground, as virgin Cynthia sways the tides . . .
>
> (*Don Juan*, XII, 14)

Note that the reference to Cynthia lends money a certain imaginative status. Byron had for long respected money, as his wife's 1815 couplet indicated:

> Then there's Byron, asham'd to appear like a Poet,
> He talks of Finances, for fear he should show it . . .
>
> (LJ, III, 291)

He knew that, whatever we say, 'riches are power, and poverty is slavery all over the earth' (Journal, 16 Jan. 1814; LJ, II, 381). This thought grew in conviction after the Separation: 'They say that "Knowledge is Power":—I used to think so; but now I know that they meant "*money*"', for '*Cash is Virtue*' (Kinnaird, 6 Feb. 1822; LJ, VI, 11). Byron freely admitted his love of money. 'The noble feeling of cupidity' he wrote, 'grows upon us with our years'; his passions gone, 'I *loves lucre*' (Kinnaird, 23 Feb. 1822 and 18 Jan. 1823; C, II, 217; LJ, VI, 163). The ironic self-mockery of the phraseology accompanies a genuine respect. Emotions are involved: the love of money succeeds early passions; just as in Timon's drama the new gold succeeds his ardent friendships.

Byron was criticized for meanness by Leigh Hunt and Mary Shelley (Origo, 329). He was so careful of his household accounts (Moore, II, 267–8 or XXXVI, 420) that his under-servants—like Launcelot Gobbo—went short.[1] Byron, says Moore, had been 'rudely

---

1. See the Note on the hand-list by Mrs. Fletcher (née Aspasia Zambelli, wife of William Fletcher, son of Byron's valet) in 'The Zambelli Papers', British Museum. This note (Add. MS 46878 fol. 22) shows some of Byron's directions as to his servants' food, with exact weights, made out for Lega Zambelli, his house steward.

schooled into the advantage of *possessing* money, when he had hitherto thought but of the generous pleasure of *dispensing* it' (Moore, II, 391 or XL, 469). He had become a composite of Timon and Shylock.

In *The Age of Bronze* Byron's attack on international Jewry corresponds to Alcibiades' reference to 'usury that makes the Senate ugly' (III, v, 101). Byron saw banks beginning to rule the world. But his Jewish sympathies were strong. In 1814 he told Isaac Nathan,[1] who had persuaded him to write the *Hebrew Melodies,* that if the occasion presented itself he was prepared to join in action for the liberation of the Holy Lands. The poems themselves, made for Hebrew tunes, have been welcomed by the chronicler of Zionism, Nahum Sokolov, as authentic Zionist songs: 'There is in his work an intensity of grief and yearning . . . a tenderness which make him comparable only to the sweet Hebrew muse of Jehuda Halevi. Zionist poetry owes more to Byron than to any other Gentile poet.' Byron had an instinctive sympathy for 'the captive Jews by Babel's waters, still remembering Sion' (*Don Juan,* II, 16). He made his Dante, into whom he poured so much of himself, say:

> What the great Seers of Israel wore within,
> That spirit was on them, and is on me.
>
> (*The Prophecy of Dante,* II)

The Old Testament was throughout his life Byron's treasured reading, though his response to the New was, superficially at least, less evident, its place being taken for him so far as *reading* was concerned —for the New Testament clearly influenced his life—by the poetry of Pope.[2] Both *Cain* and *Heaven and Earth* witness Byron's Biblical response, and so does his favourite thought of himself as an 'Ishmael' (Miss Milbanke, 26 Sept.; Journal, 22 Nov.; 1813; LJ, III, 402; II,

1. I draw my material here and in my reference to Nahum Sokolov from a letter to me from Robert G. Wilkinson, author of *Lord Byron: an Examination of a Rebellious Outsider,* a thesis at the Graduate School of The Claremont Colleges, California, 1957. Mr. Wilkinson refers us to Joseph Slater, 'Byron's *Hebrew Melodies*', *Studies in Philology,* January 1952; 75–94. (Slater's citations are from Nathan's *Fugitive Pieces and Reminiscences of Lord Byron,* 1829; and Sokolov's [Sokolow's] *History of Zionism,* 1919.)

2. See the essay on Byron's love of Pope, 'The Book of Life', in my *Laureate of Peace,* reissued (1965) as *The Poetry of Pope: see p. viii above.

330). Byron's sympathies with the Jew-as-Outsider were instinctive, and he accordingly found *The Merchant of Venice* a congenial drama. This and *Timon of Athens* are Shakespeare's only two plays to concentrate on riches. In both, wealth and gold have various pointings: they may function (i) as the false wealth of avarice and selfish gain, and (ii) as power for good, as in Portia's riches, and the gold given to Alcibiades; and (iii) as symbolism, suggesting the soulworth or magic that gold-imagery in every age suggests, as in the importance to Shylock of his loved wealth as soul-treasure, as that on which his lonely soul-self relies in an alien and hostile community, and the semi-spiritual status given Portia dramatically by her possession of what I have called 'an infinite bank-balance' (*Shakespearian Production*, 1964; 127–8). Timon's new gold has similar properties.

Now what the Jews turned to when forced to live a pariah existence in alien communities as their one means of self-making and self-defence, Byron too turns to in his banishment: money. Aptly, he had retired to Venice and *The Merchant of Venice* was often in his mind. Marianna's husband was a 'merchant of Venice' (Murray, 25 Nov. 1816; LJ, IV, 16). He liked Venice because of its associations with the immortal presences of 'Shylock and the Moor' (*Childe Harold*, IV, 4). He visits the Rialto 'for the sake of Shylock' (Murray, 2 April 1817; LJ, IV, 92). *The Vision of Judgment* was introduced by words drawn from *The Merchant of Venice* (IV, ii, 223, 342):

A Daniel come to judgment! yea, a Daniel!
I thank thee, Jew, for teaching me that word.

He was pleased with this motto, telling Moore of it (1 Oct. 1821; LJ, V, 385). Any business transaction might bring Shylock to his mind. To his banker Kinnaird he writes: 'Now to business—"Shylock! I must have moneys"' (23 April 1818; C, II, 80). Writing to Murray about the posthumous publication of his Memoirs, he notes: 'So your Cent per Cent Shylock calculation will not be in so much peril, as the "Argosie" will sink before that time, and "the pound of flesh" be withered previously to your being so long out of a return' (Murray, 28 Sept. 1821; LJ, V, 379). The 'Argosie' is his own life. Byron bitterly attacked Jewish bankers in *The Age of Bronze* (xv) with Shakespearian references—'Jewish gaberdine' (*The Merchant of*

Venice, I, iii, 113), 'Shylock', 'pound of flesh'—but he could also recognize a personal affinity in other contexts. His own interest in money was, like Shylock's, the interest of a lonely individual fighting society by its aid. He once identified himself with Shylock in an impassioned statement to Murray, on 6 April 1819:

> I know the precise worth of popular applause, for few Scribblers have had more of it; and if I chose to swerve into their paths, I could retain it, or resume it, or increase it. But I neither love ye, nor fear ye; and though I buy with ye and sell with ye, and talk with ye, I will neither eat with ye, drink with ye, nor pray with ye. They made me, without my search, a species of popular Idol; they, without reason or judgment, beyond the caprice of their good pleasure, threw down the Image from its pedestal; it was not broken with the fall, and they would, it seems, again replace it—but they shall not.
>
> (LJ, IV, 285)

Shylock's words were:

> I will buy with you, sell with you, talk with you, walk with you, and so following; but I will not eat with you, drink with you, nor pray with you.
>
> (*The Merchant of Venice*, I, iii, 36)

In Byron's letter they are beautifully engrafted. Observe too how exactly applicable is Byron's conclusion to Timon's rejection of the Senators when they come to implore his return. Shylock, Timon, Byron are all close, and Coriolanus not far off, since in this same letter Byron refuses to flatter the 'sweet voices' (*Coriolanus*, II, iii, 119) of his public.

So he became a keen and astute man of business, like Shakespeare and Ibsen. He drove a vigorous bargain with Murray for *Manfred* and threatened to take the Fourth Canto of *Childe Harold* elsewhere (Murray, 17 June 1817; LJ, IV, 138). Again, to Murray on 1 July, 1817:

> I mean to be as mercenary as possible, an example . . . which I should have followed in my youth, and I might still have been a prosperous gentleman.
>
> (LJ, IV, 142; for 'prosperous gentlemen', *Macbeth*, I, iii, 73)

What the public think of his work does not concern him: 'The profit is the point.' He cares 'for little but the copyright'. The loss of the copyright of *Don Juan* would 'break my heart' (Hobhouse, 19 May 1818; Kinnaird, 19 Jan. and 22 Feb. 1819; C, II, 81, 97, 104). He means it:

If you suppose I don't mind the money you are mistaken; I do mind it most damnably, it is the only thing I ever saw worth minding—for, as *Dervish* told me, it comprehends all the rest.
(Hobhouse, 25 Jan. 1819; C, II, 101)

That, as Bernard Shaw would have agreed, holds a truth.

Byron had many of the instincts of a man of action, and action in the modern world involves money. He regularly rated politics, history, and religion above poetry; and now money too. And yet the money is bought by his poetry; poetry as commerce enters the arena of direct action; and Byron could feel poetically about money. Thus, on 13 September 1821, urging Kinnaird to get money from Murray for *Cain* and *The Two Foscari,* Byron wrote:

. . . You must really pursue him

As when a Gryphon in the wilderness
Follows an Arimaspian . . .

Follow the Arimaspian Murray, who seems as reluctant to part with 'gold' as the rest of his nation.
(C, II, 197)

The quotation is from *Paradise Lost* (II, 943). The Arimaspians were a one-eyed people who adorned their hair with gold; gold-mines were guarded by Gryphons (C, II, 197, note). Byron repeated the thought with reference to *Sardanapalus* (Moore, 28 Oct. 1821; LJ, V, 398). Money had for Byron a poetic aura.

His money-love was, of course, not independent of his other purposes. He refused, as his Shylock-letter itself shows, to write for the public's taste. He 'would not change a word to regain their favour' (Kinnaird, 6 March 1816; C, II, 105). His generosity was, as we have seen (p. 190), maintained; more, it was expanded. He was generous to Leigh Hunt, out of gratitude and on principle, and while planning to help him wrote:

I am determined to have all the monies I can, whether by my own funds, or succession, or lawsuit, or wife, or MSS. or any lawful means whatsoever.

(Kinnaird, 23 Feb. 1822; C, II, 217)

He needed money to fight the 'haughty shopkeepers' (*Don Juan*, X, 65) of the new society in England. It was not, he said, for himself, but rather to leave sums to his relatives and 'to be able to do good to others to a greater extent' (Kinnaird, 18 Jan. 1823; LJ, VI, 163-4; for his generosity, see Moore, II, 268 or XXXVI, 420). When the time for it came, he used his money freely—it was just *that* sort of cause for which he had been instinctively preparing—in the cause of Greece. The copyright sale of *Werner* was to be used for Greece (Kinnaird, 23 Dec. 1823; LJ, VI, 287); it was, appropriately enough, a drama with money as its central theme. From Cephalonia he wrote to Hobhouse on 27 September, 1823:

Of all things, to do anything amongst these fellows, *money* is the most essential; and I have no wish to spare mine, though I will not allow a sixpence to be expended except to a public purpose, and under my own eye.

(C, II, 278)

How well he used it I have elsewhere (LBCV, 185-6) recorded. He would have his credit stretched 'to the uttermost', writing 'Never mind *me*, so that the *cause goes on*,' and he was soon almost maintaining 'the whole machine' at his own cost (Hobhouse, 27 Dec. 1823; Kinnaird, 21 Feb. 1824; C, II, 286, 289).

Timon's financing of Alcibiades' army may seem to be directed into a less obviously idealistic purpose, but in both there is the general purpose of infusing life-blood into a revolutionary cause against what both regard as tyranny.

Byron, leaving far behind his old aristocratic refusal to accept money for writing, makes terms with his age, fighting it *with its own weapons*. His story helps us to understand the gold-symbolism in the later scenes of *Timon of Athens* as a forecast of the new age, darkly foreseen.

IV

There is more in Timon's new-found gold than can be defined in historical and social terms. It is, far more potently than Portia's fairy-tale wealth, a magical power, of supreme excellence and extreme danger:

> O thou sweet king-killer, and dear divorce
> 'Twixt natural son and sire! Thou bright defiler
> Of Hymen's purest bed! Thou valiant Mars!
> Thou ever young, fresh, lov'd, and delicate wooer,
> Whose blush doth thaw the consecrated snow
> That lies on Dian's lap! Thou visible god,
> That solder'st close impossibilities
> And mak'st them kiss! that speak'st with every tongue
> To every purpose! O thou touch of hearts!
> Think thy slave man rebels, and by thy virtue
> Set them into confounding odds, that beasts
> May have the world in empire.
>
> (IV, iii, 384)

On the stage the gleaming gold will exert strong radiations, the more active for Timon's phrases. It is simultaneously honoured and de-nounced; above all it has 'virtue', meaning 'power', or perhaps 'good power'. The magical potency indicated is made yet more explicit by Byron when he redeveloped the lines in *Werner,* in an address to a jewel:

> O thou sweet sparkler!
> Thou more than stone of the philosopher!
> Thou touchstone of Philosophy herself!
> Thou bright eye of the Mine! Thou lodestar of
> The soul!—the true magnetic Pole to which
> All hearts point duly north, like trembling needles!
> Thou flaming Spirit of the Earth!
>
> (III, i, 328)

A spiritual dignity is asserted; a magic.[1]

Byron was, at times, obsessed with this magic. He kept a box of gold coins and 'his great delight' was to open it and 'contemplate his

---

1. On jewels, as mystical powers, see *The Christian Renaissance,* 1962, 288–9.

store' (Moore, quoting Alexander Scott, LJ, IV, App. viii, 472; and see Moore, II, 268 or XXXVI, 420). He told Kinnaird of it: 'I have imbibed such a love for money, that I keep some sequins in a drawer, to count and cry over them once a week' (27 Jan. 1819; C, II, 103). To Lady Blessington Byron described how, now that he was descending 'into the vale of years' (Othello, III, iii, 266), the 'golden dreams' of his youth had been replaced by the 'golden realities' of wealth; but he feared that his expedition to Greece would 'create wings for my golden darlings, that may waft them away from me for ever' (Blessington, XII, 287–8). Such an obsession cannot be easily rationalized.[1] Of course gold, from Greek mythology to medieval alchemy, has always been, in its own right, a power. Within our present context we can suggest that the lustre formerly housed in warrior-ship, feudalism, and royalty, exists no longer in them. Timon had been an eminent soldier (IV, iii, 94–5), and afterwards a lord and patron, almost a prince. All that has passed. Nevertheless, the old lustre was, and is, *an objective reality in the spiritual order;* it takes different forms but cannot be dispelled; and in the new age its forms are various. Money, with all its maddening ethical ambiguities, is one of them. Personal wealth means personal freedom, responsibility and power, for good or ill; it is, in our society, freedom's essence and man's individual royalty. The crown of our constitutional monarchy attempts to preserve and place the needed virtue in our political system.

Gold, gems, and royalty are all close and there is no final distinction between their material and spiritual properties. Our lines to the jewel in *Werner* continued, after 'flaming Spirit of the Earth', as follows:

> which, sitting
> High on the Monarch's Diadem, attractest
> More worship than the majesty who sweats
> Beneath the crown which makes his head ache, like
> Millions of hearts which bleed to lend it lustre!
> Shalt thou be mine? I am, methinks, already
> A little king, a lucky alchymist!—

1. For some interesting dramatic correspondences, see *The Golden Labyrinth,* 249–50.

A wise magician, who has bound the devil
Without the forfeit of his soul.

(III, i, 334)

Psychologically, poet after poet uses gold or jewels to signify some
high, some royal, state of being: this is the 'golden secret' and 'Kalon'
(i.e. goodness which is also beauty) of *Manfred* (III, i, 13), to be
developed later in the gold-symbolism of Nietzsche's *Thus Spake
Zarathustra* (*Christ and Nietzsche*, v, 193–5).[1]

Timon's new gold corresponds to his total poetic, satiric and
romantic, stature. Timon's poetic self is to be distinguished from the
writings of self-seeking poetasters, such as the flattering poet who
visits him, using their technique for cheap and dishonest ends:

And for thy fiction,
Why, thy verse swells with stuff so fine and smooth
That thou art even natural in thine art.

(V, i, 88)

To get the point, we must suppose that this is the *good poetry* of a
writer who nevertheless aims first to please and avoid offence, so
assuring his own advance; as most poets do, in every age, being
cautious not to offend overmuch. This is how Byron saw Wordsworth and Southey; but Byron's own life and writings correspond
to a Timon's, or a Nietzsche's, uncompromising course. Timon's
curses sound nihilistic enough; his satiric thrusts seem too violent for
safety; and Byron's poetry regularly incurred charges of wickedness
and satanism. And yet as Timon hurls gold with his curses, he is,
like all great attacking writers who *inject their literature into life,* such as
Swift, Tolstoy, Ibsen and Nietzsche, despite all superficial appearance, labouring for man's highest good, the hard-won 'golden secret'.
That is why, when Timon greets the Bandits with (i) a far-flung
cosmic poetry of sun, moon, earth and sea and (ii) advice to thieve
and destroy to their hearts' content and (iii) quantities of his new
gold—he has, in fact, *reformed them:* 'He has almost charmed me
from my profession by persuading me to it,' says one; and another,
'I'll believe him as an enemy, and give over my trade' (IV, iii, 457–62).

1. Compare C. G. Jung's work on the psychological attributes of alchemy in
The Integration of the Personality (trans. S. M. Dell, 1940), 205–80.

That is the way greatest men, so regularly regarded as emissaries of the Devil, as was Christ, are in effect gracious and saving. Somehow Swift's most nauseating and man-blasting satire acts for sweetness and light.

Both Timon and Byron at their most dangerous radiate power and love, even in their own despite; it is their state of being, they cannot help it. When Timon says to Flavius

> Here, take; the gods out of my misery
> Have sent thee treasure
>
> (IV, iii, 533)

he speaks for all whose own suffering has crushed from them the wine of a universal good. In *The Winter's Tale* the treasure found by the old shepherd is called 'fairy gold' (III, iii, 127); Timon's we may call 'tragic gold'. During his exile Byron's greatest poetry in satire, tragedy and humour was composed; as a man he became a legend, a healing power, a beacon. In him Shakespeare's poetry became incarnate in a man; and the symbol for that marvel is gold.

Apart from all surface details *Timon of Athens* dramatizes a move from (i) social glitter to (ii) elemental grandeur. The imaginative areas correspond to Nietzsche's two principles in *The Birth of Tragedy*, Apollonian and Dionysian. They also correspond to the balance of classical humanism and romantic revolt in Europe's literary history. Timon in the wilds communes with nature, addresses sun and earth, listens to the ocean surf, comments on the animal creation and the cosmic scheme. These scenes are composed from a 'romantic' rather than an 'Elizabethan' standpoint. In staging the 'woods' mentioned in the text (IV, i, 35; IV, iii, 224) will be probably less helpful than a background of low rocks, the sea (IV, iii, 381; V, i, 219–23; V, iv, 78) to be imagined as beyond; though one vast tree-trunk might be used, in the foreground (see p. 220 below, note).

After leaving England Byron assuaged his tormented soul by contemplation of vast nature in Switzerland. The hero of the early *Childe Harold*, uneasy amidst 'the crowd, the hum, the shock of men', preferred 'the life of godly eremite' on Mount Athos whose attention turns from 'blue' seas 'to hate a world he had almost forgot'

(II, 26–7). Lara was such another, one apart from 'the men with whom he felt condemn'd to breathe' and aiming to separate himself 'by good or ill' from all 'who shared his mortal state', his own mind set 'far from the world, in regions of her own' (*Lara*, I, 18). Such too was Timon's dismissal of mortal humanity: 'His semblable, yea himself, Timon disdains' (IV, iii, 22). In 1816 this strain in Byron assumed terrific force, finding its objective correlatives in the mountains of Switzerland. The Byron-Harold of Canto III is 'the most unfit of men to herd with Man', one like Timon

> Proud though in desolation; which could find
> A life within itself, to breathe without mankind.
>
> (III, 12)

The very rhyme recalls Timon's

> Timon will to the woods, where he shall find
> The unkindest beast more kinder than mankind.
>
> (IV, i, 35)

'High mountains' are now Byron's companions and 'the hum of human cities torture' (III, 72). Byron's prose bears simultaneous witness to the effect on him of this terrific scenery (p. 270). It was so strong that he composed in *Manfred* a metaphysical drama of what might be called 'mountain mysticism'. Timon retired to 'the woods' (IV, i, 35), and great trees are potent in his, and Apemantus', poetry. For Byron too, trees were mighty powers:

> Passed *whole woods of withered pines, all withered*; trunks stripped and barkless, branches lifeless; done by a single winter,—their appearance reminded me of me and my family.
>
> (Journal, 23 Sept. 1816; LJ, III, 360)

The thought is expanded in *Manfred*:

> To be thus—
> Grey-hair'd with anguish, like these blasted pines,
> Wrecks of a single winter, barkless, branchless,
> A blighted trunk upon a cursèd root,
> Which but supplies a feeling to decay—

And to be thus, eternally but thus,
Having been otherwise!

(I, ii, 65)

Timon compares himself to a great tree, denuded in—again—a
single winter. Those who formerly clustered round him,

That numberless upon me stuck as leaves
Do on the oak, have with one winter's brush,
Fell from their boughs, and left me open, bare,
For every storm that blows.

(IV, iii, 264)

Despite the tragic feeling, the tree-image itself suggests strength, as
we shall see.

We shall not respond to Shakespeare's drama unless we can see
Timon as a near-superman, a dramatic Prometheus; that is anyway
its dramatic direction and effect. As so often, what is in Shakespeare
embedded becomes in Byron *explicit*. Manfred is 'of no common order';
such normality he would 'rise above'; and there is 'an order of
mortals on the earth' that can so rise (II, ii, 123; II, iv, 52; III, i, 138;
and see II, i, 38). He is as a higher being, the height symbolized by
mountains, by trees, and by the eagle:

Thou wingéd and cloud-cleaving minister,
Whose happy flight is highest into heaven,
Well may'st thou swoop so near me—I should be
Thy prey, and gorge thine eaglets; thou art gone
Where the eye cannot follow thee; but thine
Yet pierces downward, onward, or above,
With a pervading vision.

(I, ii, 30)

The eagle is similarly in *Timon of Athens* a symbol of visionary pur-
pose. The Poet's lines acting as a prologue to the whole play—the
Poet *at this point* incurring no such satire as later—we are told that
Shakespeare's mighty parable

flies an eagle's flight, bold and forth on,
Leaving no tract behind.

(I, i, 50)

'Forth on' matches neatly Byron's 'onward': the thoughts correspond. Apemantus has an eagle too:

> Will these moss'd trees,
> That have outliv'd the eagle, page thy heels,
> And skip when thou point'st out?
>
> (IV, iii, 224)

The eagle is a bird of mountains and vision; it occurs strongly in Shakespeare's one mountain-adventure, the Timon-like Welsh scenes of the much wronged Belarius and the royal boys, severed from society, in *Cymbeline;* and in the vision Jupiter descends on an eagle (III, iii, 21, 27–8; V, iv, 92; direction). The eagle is a sun-gazing creature: so are Timon and Manfred. Timon's last scenes open with 'O blessed breeding sun', and he returns to it (IV, iii, 1, 69, 442–4; V, i, 136, 228). Belarius and the virile, pagan and magnificent, *innately* royal, boys in *Cymbeline* had their ritual of sun-worship (III, iii, 7), recalled by Manfred's extended address relating the sun to just such primitively splendid manhood:

> Glorious Orb! the idol
> Of early nature, and the vigorous race
> Of undiseas'd mankind, the giant sons
> Of the embrace of Angels . . .
>
> (III, ii, 3)

Its worship throughout early ages is remembered; it is the one 'material God' and symbol of the great 'Unknown' (III, ii, 14–15). Byron here and in the two great sun speeches on 'the burning oracle of all that lives' in *Sardanapalus* (II, i, 1–36; V, i, 1–22), and elsewhere, is our greatest sun poet, following the intuitions of sun-as-power in *Timon of Athens* and *Cymbeline*.

In *Timon of Athens* and *Cymbeline* the falsities of society and the court are rejected for the simple grandeurs of nature and true manhood. The satire in Timon or Byron is the obverse of this golden virtue. Manfred has from youth felt himself outside society, and attuned only to the elements. Though he wears the 'form' he has had 'no sympathy with breathing flesh', his 'joy' being 'in the wilderness', with high mountains where no life stirs, and ocean, and moon, stars and lightning:

> For if the beings of whom I was one—
> Hating to be so—cross'd me in my path,
> I felt myself degraded back to them
> And was all clay again.
>
> (II, ii, 50–79)

This is again Timon's 'His semblable, yea, himself, Timon disdains' (IV, iii, 22). Timon too, addressing the Bandits, enjoys extravagant companionship with sun, moon, ocean and earth (IV, iii, 442–8).

From these heights molten satire streams scalding, and what it most scalds are the subtler vices of flattery and intrigue:

> Who dares, who dares,
> In purity of manhood stand upright,
> And say, 'This man's a flatterer'? If one be,
> So are they all; for every grize of fortune
> Is smooth'd by that below: the learned pate
> Ducks to the golden fool: all is oblique;
> There's nothing level in our cursed natures
> But direct villainy. Therefore, be abhorr'd
> All feasts, societies, and throngs of men.
>
> (IV, iii, 13)

The soul-state from which this is said is the soul-state of *Childe Harold* and *Manfred*. Here is *Childe Harold:*

> I have not loved the world, nor the world me;
> I have not flatter'd its rank breath, nor bow'd
> To its idolatries a patient knee,
> Nor coin'd my cheek to smiles, nor cried aloud
> In worship of an echo; in the crowd
> They could not deem me one of such; I stood
> Among them, but not of them . . .
>
> (III, 113)

And here Manfred:

> I could not tame my nature down; for he
> Must serve who fain would sway; and soothe, and sue,
> And watch all time, and pry into all place,
> And be a living Lie, who would become

A mighty thing amongst the mean—and such
The mass are; I disdain'd to mingle with
A herd, though to be leader—and of wolves.
The lion is alone, and so am I.

(III, i, 116)

This titanic strength is in *Childe Harold* given a tree-image, which
helps us to read a new depth, corresponding to Keats's 'green-rob'd
senators of mighty woods' (*Hyperion*, I, 73), in Shakespeare's 'moss'd
trees that have out-liv'd the eagle' (*Timon of Athens*, IV, iii, 224):

                    . . . yet springs the trunk, and mocks
The howling tempest, till its height and frame
Are worthy of the mountains from whose blocks
Of bleak, gray granite into life it came,
And grew a giant tree;—the mind may grow the same.

(IV, 20)

'The mind': all our symbols, sun, mountains, sea, eagle, lion, gold
are pointers towards some new and greater spiritual, transcendental,
stature; symbols and companions, to be addressed as equals by the
mind approaching self-realization.[1]

'Companions': and yet the elements can never quite be that; but
animals, the eagle and lion, can; and others too, perhaps. Timon
recognizes the kinship:

Timon will to the woods, where he shall find
The unkindest beast more kinder than mankind.

(IV, i, 35)

The thought is deeply Byronic. In his 1808 *Inscription on the Monu-
ment of a Newfoundland Dog* Byron contrasts man's false pride and
lying pretensions with his dog Boatswain's faithfulness, continuing:

Oh Man! thou feeble tenant of an hour,
Debas'd by slavery, or corrupt by power,
Who knows thee well must quit thee with disgust,
Degraded mass of animated dust!

1. Byron's poetry makes me doubt whether I have done justice to its tree-poetry
in my various presentations of *Timon of Athens* (see *Shakespearian Production*, 1964;
178–9). A single, vast, tree-trunk might be used in the wing foreground.

Thy love is lust, thy friendship all a cheat,
Thy smiles hypocrisy, thy words deceit!
By nature vile, ennobled but by name,
Each kindred brute might bid thee blush for shame.
Ye! who perchance behold this simple urn,
Pass on—it honours none you wish to mourn:
To mark a Friend's remains these stones arise;
I never knew but one,—and here he lies.

It was the same years later at Missolonghi where Byron used to talk to his dog Lyon, saying, according to Parry, 'Thou art more faithful than men, Lyon; I trust thee more'; with Lyon alone, says Parry, he seemed at peace and 'perfectly happy' (Parry, IV, 75).

Timon is not shown as finding actual companionship with any animals; and on the stage he hardly could be. But there are many references, some derogatory. They, and nature in general, both here and in *King Lear,* are used ambivalently: they can often show up man in comparison, and yet it is no use man becoming a beast. It is Apemantus, as we have seen, who would have man return to the beast-state. But the merits of animals in comparison with man are at least *seriously* considered by Timon in an extended passage, before he concludes that this is no solution (IV, iii, 329–51). In both *King Lear* and *Timon* animal references cluster as part of the return to nature being dramatized; and here we may recall the part animals play in Byron's story.

For Byron lived it all; what is 'poetry' in others, is for him part of life itself. He could, of course, use animal-references in a denigratory way, seeing Napoleon's dynastic rivals as wolves in comparison to Napoleon as lion (*Childe Harold,* III, 19); and there are other examples. But of his life-long devotion to animals—his poetry abounds in it—there is no question. I have already written at length on it (LBCV, 3–16). Here we need only recall the amazing menagerie he kept in Italy, which accompanied him as he moved from place to place. At Ravenna he kept, besides ten horses, 'eight enormous dogs, three monkeys, five cats, an eagle, a crow and a falcon'; also 'five peacocks, two guinea-hens, and an Egyptian crane'; all but the horses moving freely about the house (LJ, V, 339, note). The accompanying inconveniences, for both Byron and his friends, need not be denied; nor is it certain that the animals themselves were always at ease. What cannot be denied is this:—That Byron loved animals not only idealistically and symbolically, but as themselves. He loved their energies, their acrobatics, their nearness, probably their smells; like Gulliver at the end of his travels retiring to the stables to get away from the horrors of humanity; or the old man in O'Neill's *Desire under the Elms* (ii, ii) retiring to the cow-shed for peace. Byron was living old King Lear's preference 'to be a comrade with the wolf and owl' (ii, iv, 213) rather than associate with human depravity; and in this return to nature *King Lear* and *Timon of Athens* are at one.

But neither the beasts nor, finally, the elements meet Timon's demands, which go beyond the created universe. The intertangling of elements and heavenly bodies in mutual thievery and interaction (iv, iii, 441–8) cannot correspond to the one absolute to which only he is attuned. That absolute is death, here conceived as a kind of 'nothing', or Nirvana.

That Byron's thoughts could dwell on such positive nothingness is witnessed by his Hamlet-like obsession from youth with graves and skulls; and by his terrible 1816 poem *Darkness* beginning

> I had a dream, which was not all a dream.
> The bright sun was extinguish'd, and the stars
> Did wander darkling in the eternal space,
> Rayless, and pathless, and the icy earth
> Swung blind and blackening in the moonless
> air . . .

It continues with fearful description of animals and men in hideous torment till all is 'void' and a mere 'lump of death'. What should make Byron write it? It is an expansion of Timon's last farewell to manifestation, to 'Maya', to the illusion of created existence:

> My long sickness
> Of health and living now begins to mend,
> And nothing brings me all things.

(v, i, 191)

He is beyond all politics and revolutions. As for the Senators of Athens:

> Be Alcibiades your plague, you his,
> And last so long enough!
>
> (v, i, 194)

If they wish an end to mortal sufferings, he tells them that there is one obvious and only way: death. Timon goes to his death as to some vast universal, beyond creation: 'Sun, hide thy beams; Timon hath done his reign' (v, i, 228).

'Nirvana' is not a mere negative.[1] Timon, knowing himself on the edge of 'all things', is at the stage reached by Manfred who all but feels

> The golden secret, the sought 'Kalon', found,
> And seated in my soul.
>
> (III, i, 13)

Nirvana can only be expressed symbolically, and in *Timon of Athens* our symbols are (i) gold and (ii) the sea. The sea is, in all its various moods, Shakespeare's most comprehensive symbol. In Macbeth (I, vii, 6) 'time' is as a 'bank and shoal', a little island, in the ocean of being. So Timon dies by, and into, the sea, passing from earth, woods and beasts to this vast sea-Nirvana. His greater, numinous, self addresses the mortal Timon:

> Then, Timon, presently prepare thy grave.
> Lie where the light foam of the sea may beat
> Thy grave-stone daily.
>
> (IV, iii, 380)

Again:

> Come not to me again; but say to Athens,
> Timon hath made his everlasting mansion
> Upon the beachéd verge of the salt flood;

---

1. A good way to gain insight as to how 'nothing' can be 'all things' is to study the more philosophical passages in C. B. Purdom's study of Meher Baba, *The God-Man* (1964); e.g. 66; 195, 'in the infinity of God . . . nothing means Everything'; 241; 328–9, on Nirvana. Compare also Bergson's equation of 'nothing' with 'the all' (*Creative Evolution*, trans. A. Mitchell, 1928; IV, 'The Idea of Nothing', especially 'everything', 312).

Who once a day with his embosséd froth
The turbulent surge shall cover: thither come,
And let my grave-stone be your oracle.

(v, i, 219)

Truly a 'rich conceit', as Alcibiades puts it,

Taught thee to make vast Neptune weep for aye
On thy low grave, on faults forgiven. Dead
Is noble Timon . . .

(v, iv, 77)

The sea's symbolic effect here is of (i) expanse and (ii) of sound, for the surf must be heard; it suggests the vast illimitable, the mystery. Height is obviously negated; on the stage it would be an error to have the rock-line too high, as then the sea-expanse beyond would lose authority (see the picture in my *Shakespearian Production*, 1964; 179). These impressions are deeply Shakespearian. Shakespeare has few heights and *The Tempest*, strong though its mystic fabric may be, remains 'horizontal' (*The Crown of Life*, 251).

In Byron, the transition from the third to the fourth cantos of *Childe Harold* is one from forested mountains to sea, corresponding to Timon's woods and sea and Byron's move through Switzerland to Venice. Though he responds far more than Shakespeare—it is a matter of period imagination—to mountains, the sea remains Byron's, as it is Shakespeare's, favourite elemental power: throughout the early Tales, in *Childe Harold, Don Juan, The Two Foscari,* and *The Island,* in the sea-Hades of Cain and the Flood in *Heaven and earth.* It is a symbol of uttermost immensity called in the invocation concluding *Childe Harold* 'sublime', the 'image of eternity' and 'throne of the Invisible' (IV, 183). Though the words 'sublime' and 'throne' stick out awkwardly, suggesting height where we expect expanse, this very awkwardness is organic: expanse assumes the prerogative of height. Despite his ability to engage himself with mountains, Byron's final emphasis follows Shakespeare in remaining horizontal; that is, humanistic.

Byron himself followed Timon in retiring to the sea. In his 'Blackwood's Defence' he records how, pursued by slander, he crossed Europe and the Alps to settle finally 'by the waves of the Adriatic,

1. *Newstead Abbey during the residence of Lord Byron; by C. Fellows (engraved by E. Finden)*

2. *Lord Byron with Robert Rushton; by G. Sanders (engraved by W. Finden)*

like the stag at bay, who betakes him to the waters' (LJ, IV, 479). Like Timon, he plans a sea-grave, telling Murray that he wanted a grave 'in the foreigners' burying-ground at the Lido, within the fortress by the Adriatic' (Murray, 7 June 1819; LJ, IV, 314–15). This 'rich conceit' meant as much to him as to Timon. Hoppner describes his daily rides with Byron and continues:

> At the foot of this stone, Lord Byron repeatedly told me that I should cause him to be interred, if he should die in Venice, or its neighbourhood, during my residence there; and he appeared to think, as he was not a Catholic, that, on the part of the Government, there could be no obstacle to his interment in an unhallowed spot of ground by the sea-side. At all events, I was to overcome whatever difficulties might be raised on this account. I was, by no means, he repeatedly told me, to allow his body to be removed to England, nor permit any of his family to interfere with his funeral.
>
> (Moore, II, 161 or XXXI, 373)

Byron did not die at Venice, but his death did come by the sea, at Missolonghi.

V

Naturally he could not live all Timon's story to the end; there were the other claims, of Hamlet, Falstaff, and Antony, all demanding expression. The main Timon-bitterness concludes at Venice, and thenceforward, with Teresa as an influence, a happier mood pervades, though *Timon* reminders recur.

Sardanapalus (1821) is a blend of *Timon of Athens* and *Antony and Cleopatra*. The hero is a resplendent prince, or emperor, of generosity, feasting and revel. Sardanapalus, like Timon, rejects the advice of worldly wisdom until he finds that he has been deceived in taking 'the breath of friends' for 'truth'. Like Timon he endures base ingratitude from those whom he has 'gorged with plenty' (IV, I, 519; 313). As an imperial pacifist suffering for his beliefs he is in the direct line of Timon's 'contumelious, beastly, mad-brain'd war' (p. 201 above). Nothing could so well point the relevance of *Antony and Cleopatra* to *Timon of Athens* as a close study of *Sardanapalus*.

As we have seen, Byron could not maintain his resentments at full pitch. We can accordingly view his undertaking of the Greek campaign in close accord with the English committee in London as an acceptance, albeit in a libertarian cause, of what we today call the 'establishment'. Like Hamlet before Claudius in his fifth act, he shows a new respect for established authority at home; his letters on the last adventure witness it; the cause to which he was devoting himself demanded a more statesmanlike manner and caution (see pp. 324–9 below). Despite a difference in political direction, he was behaving almost as a Timon who at the last accepts the Senators' plea, and puts his virtues to the—or at least to a—public cause.

A good summing up of Byron's Timon-like affinities is given by these lines from his poem *Prometheus* (1816):

Thy Godlike crime was to be kind,
To render with thy precepts less
The sum of human wretchedness,
And strengthen Man with his own mind . . .

'Mind'. Prometheus was a giant. As we have seen (p. 220), Byron compared the potential of man's 'mind' to a vast tree. We are pointed on to Prospero and *The Tempest*.

VII

ANTONY AND CLEOPATRAS; OTHELLO

I

Our next discussion may be introduced by some lines from Byron's *Stanzas to the Po* (1819), probably addressed to Teresa Guiccioli:

A stranger loves the lady of the land,
Born far beyond the mountains, but his blood
Is all meridian, as if never fann'd
By the black wind that chills the polar flood.

My blood is all meridian; were it not,
I had not left my clime, nor should I be,
In spite of tortures ne'er to be forgot,
A slave again of love—at least of thee.

In that there is much of Byron, and of Shakespeare's Antony too, who left the mountains of Italy to be a 'slave' to Cleopatra, Queen of Egypt.

The sexual glamour of Shakespeare's *Antony and Cleopatra* might seem to contrast with the more spiritualized sequence within which it occurs. But its glamour is deeply conceived; sexual instinct is felt linking man to the cosmos, even the divine. As I observed in *The Imperial Theme* (IX), it may be regarded as the opposite, positive against negative, of *Macbeth*. Sickening nightmare is replaced by entanglements less dangerous which, though un-moral or even im-moral, are yet backed by life. Both handle unruly instincts, but whereas those of *Macbeth* are nihilistic those of *Antony and Cleopatra* are creative.

227

Sexual instincts have never in the West been finally placed. Christian marriage has not been able to impose on them an unconditional surrender, and there remains some fiery centre or vital essence unplaced and perhaps unplaceable in our moral schemes. The lonely progress recorded from *Hamlet,* through *King Lear* and *Timon of Athens,* to *The Tempest* might seem to have needed no supreme sexual apocalypse; but *Antony and Cleopatra* comes at the hinge from tragedy to beyond-tragedy, fertilizing the whole as with a strength unknown to spiritualities.

So was it in Byron's story. His own social status and the manners of the period made it possible for his strong, if ambivalent, moral idealism and Calvinistic sense of guilt to cohabit with a high degree of sexual freedom. But the libertinism was no easy course. A liaison with a married woman might lead to a duel in which the offender might, as did Byron, feel in honour bound not to return the other's shot (p. 124 below). There was a double compulsion. The gentleman's code allowed and on occasion demanded a sexual boldness which both Church and society condemned. There may be a wisdom in such apparent confusions. Women probably understand these matters better than men with their tidy systems. From a woman's standpoint *Antony and Cleopatra* might logically be rated as worth the whole sequence of Shakespeare's more solemn, Nietzschean, dramas. However that may be, the heterosexual amours of Byron's Italian temperament still draw women to his feet for whom Wordsworth holds no magnetism.

Despite his homosexual and seraphic compulsions, women were for Byron a necessity: 'I cannot exist', he wrote to Lady Melbourne, 'without some object of love' (9 Nov. 1812; and see 13 Oct. 1813; C, I, 104, 198). That 'object' was normally a woman. To Byron, quite apart from passion, there was something 'very softening in the presence of a woman' which he could not account for since he had 'no very high opinion of the sex' (Journal, 27 Feb. 1814; LJ, II, 389). Despite their transience, his amatory affairs were a succession of passionate sincerities: 'I could never live for but one human being at a time' (Murray, 24 Aug. 1819; LJ, IV, 349). In 1821 he recalled that his 'early passions, though violent in the extreme, were concentrated', and he could—remembering Dryden's *'All for Love or The*

World Well Lost—'have left or lost the world with or for that which I loved'; and though his temperament was 'naturally burning' he could not share in 'the common place libertinism' of his Cambridge associates (*Detached Thoughts, 72*; LJ, V, 445–6). In 1813 he had noted that he would '*not* be the slave of *any* appetite'; 'if I do err, it shall be my heart, at least, that heralds the way' (Journal, 17 Nov. 1813; LJ, II, 328). Normal sex-love, even when illicit, could act as a moral force; it could vanquish his 'demon' by 'transferring' his affections to 'another' (Lady Melbourne, 28 Sept. 1813; C, I, 183). The prevailing code, moreover, could exert its own, semi-moral, compulsions: 'It would have been want of gallantry, though the acme of virtue, if I had played the Scipio on this occasion' (Lady Melbourne, 13 Sept. 1812; C, I, 75). He was once ashamed of acting 'weakly' by refusing to consummate an illicit affair, and expected the lady—Lady Frances—to despise him (Lady Melbourne, 13 Jan. 1814; C, I, 233). Not that such encounters were cool and deliberate. Byron could write of them calmly, but they were in themselves fiery adventures and fierce enjoyments bought at the risk of death by duel. They had each a modicum of the *Antony and Cleopatra* fire, a play once remembered by Byron in a relevant context when, after asking if Scrope Davies was still 'full of fierce embraces' and hoping that he might marry and have children, he added: 'I do not know anyone who will leave such "a gap in Nature"' (Kinnaird, 3 Feb. 1817; C. II, 35; *Antony and Cleopatra,* II, ii, 226).

Perhaps sexual love, *as* sexual love, must contain an element that is un-moral. Byron admitted that it must include selfishness and jealousy; it is 'a sort of hostile transaction' (Lady —— ; 10 Nov. 1822; LJ, VI, 137). Passions exist in a dimension beyond mental categories: 'While you are under the influence of passions, you only feel, but cannot describe them' (Journal, 20 Feb. 1814; LJ, II, 388). Byron felt it a duty to live life to the full and as he grew older says that despite all attempts he could not repent anything done so much as what had been 'left undone'; that is 'not having seized every available instant of our pleasurable years'.[1] It was a kind of duty. Passion is a world, or dimension, to enter and *emerge* from, again

1. I cannot now trace this reference, which has been unfortunately mislaid.

and again, freely. Itself un-logical, it cannot submit to the logic of compacts and promises. If a lady is unreasonably exacting, the answer, quoting from *Romeo and Juliet*, is:

> But I cannot be sure, or answerable, for all I have said or unsaid, since 'Jove' himself . . . has forgotten to 'laugh at our perjuries'. I am certain that I tremble for the trunkful of my contradictions . . .
> (Lady Melbourne, 18 Sept. 1812; C, I, 81;
> *Romeo and Juliet*, II, ii, 92–3)

Again, 'How could anything of this kind be carried without 10,000 perfidies?' (Lady Melbourne, 21 Sept. 1812; C, I, 82). 'Of this kind': a mystery is admitted without more definition, as part of life's inscrutable composition. Yet though moral systems fail, 'honour' may in certain circumstances fill its place. If a lady be of equal rank a man is 'in honour bound to support her through' (Murray, 8 Nov. 1819; LJ, IV, 377): there was a code, running apart from but parallel to morality.

The ladies usually approached Byron, not he them, and gallantry demanded a response. Besides, like 'our courteous Antony whom ne'er the word of "No" woman heard speak' (*Antony and Cleopatra;* II, iii, 230), Byron found refusals hard. In certain moods he could regard himself as a martyr:

> Your Blackwood accuses me of treating women harshly: it may be so, but I have been their martyr. My whole life has been sacrificed *to* them and *by* them.
> (Murray, 10 Dec. 1819; LJ, IV, 386)

This is just how Shakespeare's Antony too, at certain moments, felt about Cleopatra.

Antony and Cleopatra is made of just such morally indecisive compulsions as we have been discussing. To the critical eye the story is woven of deceptions and faithlessnesses, though from a more emotional and poetic insight it reveals splendours. Were the passion not shown as existing outside the moral pale, its essential quality could not have been dramatically defined. But it carries with it a self-abnegation too, as well in Cleopatra's engrossing love as in Antony's sacrifice of worldly place and fortunes. Both in effect, whatever their failings—failings even towards love and mutual loyalty—die because of, and so for, their love, or passion. Cleopatra, like the ladies in Byron's story, is the compelling force, while Byron is often found saying like Antony 'I must from this enchanting queen break off' (*Antony and Cleopatra*, I, ii, 137).

Women held for Byron the enchantment so exquisitely expressed in his lyric (1816):

> There be none of Beauty's daughters
> With a magic like thee;
> And like music on the waters
> Is thy sweet voice to me . . .

A 'midnight moon' girdles the ocean with a 'bright chain'. Other lyrics, 'She walks in beauty, like the night' (1815) and 'So we'll go no more a-roving' (1817) with its emphasis on night and moon, make similar associations. Both Byron and *Antony and Cleopatra* labour to turn this moon-magic towards the sun.

II

Shakespeare's play dramatizes a clash of moral respectability and sensuous abandon. The opposition is also an opposition of male West and female East, Cleopatra's Egypt toning with the exotic mystery of female allure. In *Othello* Shakespeare gave us oriental glamour in a hero to show us a passionate upsurge breaking through male soldiership, western culture, and a western marriage. Central to *Othello* is the magic handkerchief woven by a sibyl and given to Othello's parent by an Egyptian. Egypt and Morocco together suggest warmth, mystery and passion of oriental and female quality—for, as Byron tells us, 'all passions in excess are female' (*Sardanapalus*, III, i, 381)—against male ethic and western convention.

Byron was by temperament drawn to reject the Scotland of his youth as a 'barren soil' rendering the 'mind'—or soul—'sterile' in resistance to every warm and 'genial influence'; it was 'a land of meanness, sophistry, and mist' (*The Curse of Minerva*; 1811; 138). At Cambridge he thought of a continental tour; next, of the Hebrides or Iceland; then Persia, or India, to study 'India and Asiatic policy and manners' (Mrs. Byron, 26 Feb. 1806; Elizabeth Pigot,

11 Aug. 1807; Mrs. Byron, 7 Oct. and 2 Nov. 1808; Hanson, 18 Nov. 1808; LJ, I, 96, 143, 193–5, 199). At the start of his Mediterranean tour in 1809 his letters from Portugal and Spain witness a new joy and freedom. Cadiz entranced him with 'the loveliness of its inhabitants', the women in his opinion being as superior in beauty as the men inferior in other respects to those of England (Hodgson, 6 Aug. 1809; LJ, I, 234). The Spanish belles, he told his Mother, have 'large black eyes and very fine forms,' though when one of them offered her favours his 'virtue' made him decline. His excitement was intense:

Long black hair, dark languishing eyes, *clear* olive complexions, and forms more graceful in motion than can be conceived by an Englishman used to the drowsy, listless air of his country-women, added to the most becoming dress, and, at the same time, the most decent in the world, render a Spanish beauty irresistible.

(11 Aug. 1809; LJ, I, 239)

The implied contrast with more static types recalls that of Shake-speare's Cleopatra with Octavia (pp. 240–2 below). Byron had a passing love affair at Malta and was attracted by girls in Athens; and there was the strange event there of his rescue of a girl condemned, according to Turkish custom, for associating with a European, though exactly what lay behind the incident we do not know (p. 161 above). Byron's writings witness an intense pre-occupation—of which his portrait in Albanian dress (included among our pictures) is a symbol—with the histories and cultures of the lands he visited. He has seen Actium where 'Antony lost the world'; he made extensive plans for further travel, perhaps to Egypt, or Persia (Mrs. Byron, 12 Nov. 1809; 19 March 1810; LJ, I, 251, 256, 258). Though he went no farther east than Turkey he was, if not oriental-ized, yet certainly Mediterraneanized, by the time he left, half regret-fully, for England.

His Levantine memories burned in him. They could accompany thoughts of soldiering that momentarily show Byron as an Othello or Antony in this sense also. He thought of joining the army in Portugal when on his outward travels in 1809 (Mrs. Byron, 11 Aug. 1809; LJ, I, 241; and see LBCV, 153); and after his return wrote to

Hodgson on 29 June, 1811 that he would soon be off again 'either to campaign in Spain or back again to the East' (LJ, I, 316); and later, with a rather different intention, that if he could not get a passage in a warship, 'patriotism is the word' (Moore, 13 July 1813; LJ, II, 231). He continually thought of returning to the east. He would make himself an oriental scholar, settle in the east and travel. He would go 'Levanting' again with Hobhouse; or with Lord Sligo, pressing on to Baghdad, or Teheran (Hodgson, 16 Feb. 1812; Lady Melbourne, 21 Dec. 1812 and 18 March 1813; LJ, II, 100; C, I, 118, 135, 142).

Life in the east was, he wrote to Miss Milbanke, 'more fiery'; it was 'a mixture of languid habits and stormy passions'. This appealed to him: 'I can't', he wrote, 'empty my head of the East', and that was why he composed oriental poems (Miss Milbanke, 29 Nov. 1813; LJ, III, 406–7). 'With those countries', he told Moore, 'all my really poetical feelings begin and end'; he could make nothing of any other subject (8 March 1816; LJ, III, 274).

Stifled in England, Byron gained relief by the publication of *Childe Harold,* which had been written during his travels, and then by composing oriental narratives of racial colour and fiery passions. He once deliberately rated poetic technique below what he called his 'costume', meaning topographical and cultural truth (Murray, 14 Nov.; Clarke, 15 Dec.; 1813; LJ, II, 283, 308–9); in *The Corsair* he remembers Cleopatra's 'timid tear' that caused a 'hero' to fly (II, 15), but he is more deeply involved in what he calls 'the wild passions of the East' (Clarke, 15 Dec. 1813; LJ, II, 309); in such violent Cleopatra-like passions as those of the couplet

> Her eye shot forth with all the living fire
> That haunts the tigress in her whelpless ire . . .
>
> (*Lara*, II, 25)

The Giaour was written as from a dimension of passion unknown to the north:

> The cold in clime are cold in blood,
>   Their love can scarce deserve the name;
> But mine was like the lava flood
>   That boils in Aetna's breast of flame.

I cannot prate in puling strain
Of Ladye-love and Beauty's chain:
If changing cheek, and scorching vein,
Lips taught to writhe, but not complain,
If bursting heart, and maddening brain,
And daring deed, and vengeful steel,
And all that I have felt, and feel,
Betoken love—that love was mine,
And shown by many a bitter sign.
'Tis true, I could not whine nor sigh,
I knew but to obtain or die.
I die—but first I have possess'd,
And come what may, I *have been* bless'd.

(1099)

Despite all moral systems, the thing in itself is authentic. More, it is divine, and more strongly so than any religious 'devotion':

Yes, Love indeed is light from Heaven;
A spark of that immortal fire
With angels shared, by Alla given,
To lift from earth our low desire.
Devotion wafts the mind above,
But Heaven itself descends in Love;
A feeling from the Godhead caught,
To wean from self each sordid thought;
A Ray of Him who form'd the whole;
A Glory circling round the soul!

(1131)

The lines could be used as a commentary on *Antony and Cleopatra.* That the experience was 'imperfect' is granted; that 'mortals' may find 'guilt' in it, is allowed; but it was yet authentic, revelatory, and divine. So, too, the love of Shakespeare's Antony and Cleopatra was simultaneously repudiated by ethic and yet somehow from 'heaven':

Eternity was in our lips and eyes,
Bliss in our brows bent. None our parts so poor
But was a race of heaven.
(*Antony and Cleopatra*, I, iii, 35)

The paradox is the same in Shakespeare as in Byron.

234

Our Byron quotations serve as admirable commentaries on the passionate worlds of *Othello* and *Antony and Cleopatra*. Stendhal suspected Byron of having himself committed a passion-impelled murder like Othello's (p. 161 above). Byron's Tales are of places 'replete with the *brightest* and *darkest,* but always most *lively* colours of my memory' (Journal, 5 Dec. 1813; LJ, II, 361–2), 'where the soul glows beneath a brighter star' (*Lara,* I, 25). Byron is our greatest poet of the Sun (p. 218), intermittently so powerful in *Antony and Cleopatra* (p. 254 below). It was in part for the 'cloudless skies' that Byron wished to return east, for he quickly grew 'sick' of England's climate (Mrs. Byron, 28 Feb.; Hodgson, 29 June; Augusta, 21 Aug.; 1811; LJ, I, 310–11, 316, 332). 'Give me a *sun,* I care not how hot', he wrote, 'and sherbet, I care not how cool, and *my* Heaven is as easily made as your Persian's' (Moore, 22 Aug. 1813; LJ, II, 250). He could not continue *Childe Harold* in England because it needed 'a warm sun, a blue sky' (Dallas, 7 Sept. 1811; LJ, II, 27).

Byron's foreign experiences are directly comparable with those of Shakespeare's Antony. Quite apart from Cleopatra the whole Egyptian adventure makes Antony a hero among his Roman friends who, in the scene on Pompey's galley, eagerly question him about this strangely wonderful Egypt. Byron had returned from the Levant like Antony, like Othello telling of his marvellous travels, his mind brimfull of the scenes and passions written into *Childe Harold* and the Tales. Shakespeare's externals hold spiritual correspondences:

> What 'antres vast and deserts idle' then
> Would be discover'd in the human soul!
> (*Don Juan,* XIV, 102; *Othello,* I, iii, 140)

But both Antony and Byron have home responsibilities: Antony, the affairs of Rome; and Byron the 'estates out of repair, and contested coal pits' that he was so reluctant to be involved in, while longing for 'cloudless skies' (Hodgson, 29 June 1811; LJ, I, 316).

It was natural that a young man so constituted and so placed as was Byron should have tried to live again in England some of those hot passions he had known abroad. It must of course be remembered that his own best amatory experiences, in the Levant at least, were homosexual; and so, according to what evidence we have, were

Shakespeare's. But the Tales, except for the boy-girl Kaled in *Lara*, are necessarily, as were Shakespeare's dramas, confined to hetero-sexual, though sometimes—to help preserve a guilt—incestuous, or seemingly incestuous, love. Moreover, whatever the strength of Byron's homosexual instincts, there is no question but that hetero-sexual love often burned in his imagination as, at least for passion as opposed to idealism, the best. Women could attract him fierily. His actual experience with them may never have drawn level with that that he knew ideally with Edleston and physically with Nicolo Giraud; yet again, Mary Chaworth shone from his youth onwards as a star, and his love for Augusta, whatever its exact nature, was probably his most enduring emotion of all. What we can say is simply this: that after returning to England Byron wanted amatory success, and it had, in England, to be found in heterosexual and if possible exotic, Cleopatra-like, terms.

In this matter many of us are more or less in Byron's position, and for such instincts the theatre exists, in every age, as a release. Byron naturally loved the theatre. He saw Mrs. Fawcit as Cleopatra at Covent Garden in 1813:

It was admirably got up, and well acted—a salad of Shake-spreare and Dryden. Cleopatra strikes me as the epitome of her sex—fond, lively, sad, tender, teasing, humble, haughty, beauti-ful, the devil!—coquettish to the last, as well with the 'asp' as with Antony.

(Journal, 16 Nov. 1813; LJ, II, 319)

The comment does exact justice to Shakespeare's queen

Whom every thing becomes, to chide, to laugh,
To weep; whose every passion fully strives
To make itself, in thee, fair and admir'd.

(I, i, 49)

Again:

Age cannot wither her, nor custom stale
Her infinite variety . . .

(II, ii, 243)

236

Byron's words the 'epitome of her sex' suggest an inclusiveness hard to find in any one woman. What Byron wanted was a real Cleopatra of equivalent female richness to both Shakespeare's conception and his own so richly varied temperament. If she could not be found in one woman, then he would be driven to keep searching for another. The only possible equivalent to Shakespeare's Cleopatra in real life will be not one but a number of women; and that is why we find so many in Byron's story.

We now approach the first.

III

Byron's first Cleopatra was Lady Caroline Lamb. Passionate, impetuous, violent, threatening self-destruction, mad but devoted, there was in her a vivacious appeal that for a while entranced Byron. She had in her that same shameless disregard of all the proprieties which made Cleopatra 'hop forty paces through the public street' (*Antony and Cleopatra*, II, ii, 237). Byron wrote to her early in 1812:

> . . . You know I have always thought you the cleverest, most agreeable, absurd, amiable, perplexing, dangerous, fascinating little being that lives now, or ought to have lived 2000 years ago. I won't talk to you of beauty; I am no judge. But our beauties cease to be so when near you, and therefore you have either some, or something better.
>
> (LJ, II, 117)

'Two thousand years' points obviously to Cleopatra who, while claiming to be

> with Phoebus' amorous pinches black,
> And wrinkled deep in time,
> (*Antony and Cleopatra*, I, v, 28)

exerted similarly a fascination that was less 'beauty' than 'something better'. But we cannot really regard Shakespeare's Cleopatra as old; she enjoys a kind of eternal youthfulness. Once for fun she dressed in Antony's clothes and wore his sword (*Antony and Cleopatra*, II, iv, 22-3). Lady Caroline wooed Byron by dressing herself, like Kaled in *Lara*, as a boy. Cleopatra was ready to pretend death at Antony's leaving her:

> Cleopatra, catching but the least noise of this, dies instantly.
> I have seen her die twenty times upon far poorer moment . . .
> *(Antony and Cleopatra, I, ii, 149)*

When Byron wished to break the affair Caroline once actually stabbed herself.

For it was not long before Caroline's persistencies became a torment. She had been the initiator, and Byron had for a time responded. He was willing to play the part expected of him up to a point, but no more. 'When our drama', he wrote to Lady Melbourne, 'was "rising" in the 5th act, it was no time to hesitate'; 'honour, pity and a kind of affection' demanded it; but now, 'If I can *honourably* be off . . .' (Lady Melbourne, 13 Sept. 1812; C, I, 75). We again recall Antony's 'I must from this enchanting queen break off' (*Antony and Cleopatra*, I, ii, 137). Caroline, said Byron, was a mass of absurd contradictions; she would not remain a friend but insisted on being either 'loved' or 'detested' (Lady Melbourne, 10 Nov. 1812; C, I, 104–5); and Byron's first fascination was turned, as was Antony's passion in Shakespeare's fourth act, to revulsion. The extent and nature of Byron's emotional involvement throughout are not very clear. His farewell letter of August 1812 reflected a genuine feeling (LJ, II, 135–9), but Caroline's extravagances became extreme, and Byron's attitude, which included consideration for the lady's own family, was reasonable.

Caroline does not measure up to Shakespeare's Cleopatra, and no one woman could; but there are vivid similarities including if not quite Cleopatra's 'infinite variety' yet what someone has called an 'infinite vivacity' (the phrase is quoted by Maurois, XVI, 151, with no reference).

Byron's subsequent affair, though in practice it went no farther than flirtation, with Lady Frances Wedderburn Webster has elements of interest already (p. 122) discussed. She was no Cleopatra. Byron, noting that she was 'thin and pale', adds: 'If she were once my wife, or likely to be so, a warm climate should be the first resort, nevertheless, for her recovery' (Lady Melbourne, 17 Oct. 1813; C, I, 205).

Like Antony, Byron was tugged between his more exotic experiences and the demands of convention and normality. Both take now the same, surprising, step. Both surprise us by following the conventional line and slipping, without resistance, into a marriage of expediency. In both we observe a similar inconsequence; and for both, disaster was the outcome. This is what Byron thought of matrimony:

> Oh! in the East women are in their proper sphere, and one has —no conversation at all. My house here is a delightful matrimonial mansion. When I wed, my spouse and I will be so happy!—one in each wing.
>
> (Hodgson, 9 Sept. 1811; LJ, ii, 33)

The touch is light, but there is a truth in it. Byron did not naturally regard a woman as a companion. However, embarrassed, like Antony, by the complexities of his own nature and the turmoils and confusions they were arousing on every side, Byron accepted marriage as an escape, conceding that 'a wife would be my salvation' (Journal, 16 Jan. 1814; LJ, ii, 380).

The choice of Annabella Milbanke, caused partly by her own advances and partly by his genuine esteem, was unfortunate. She was highly gifted: a student of theology and of Greek, an able mathematician and a versifier of merit. She made Byron uneasy: 'I have no desire', he once wrote to Caroline Lamb, 'to be better acquainted with Miss Milbanke; she is too good for a fallen spirit to know, and I should like her more if she were less perfect' (1 May 1812; LJ, ii, 121). However he 'esteemed' her highly, and perhaps esteem was a better basis for marriage than romance (Lady Melbourne, 13 and 18 Sept. 1812; C, i, 75, 79). Byron listed her qualities in his Journal (30 Nov. 1813; LJ, ii, 357).

But meanwhile he was 'falling in love' with 'a new Juliet', an actress; with an Italian songstress; and a Welsh seamstress; and also with his agent's wife and daughter, and 'a picture of Buonaparte's Empress, who looks as fair and foolish as she is dark and diabolical' (Lady Melbourne, 21 Sept. 1812; C, i, 83). Byron's amatory instincts were unlimited. Here we have a composite assortment to make up a complete Cleopatra: stage; Italy, for Italy to Byron was like Egypt to Antony; manual worker—remembering Cleopatra's

'maid that milks and does the meanest chares' (*Antony and Cleopatra,*
IV, xiii, 74); and empress. Against these, and especially the Italian,
Miss Milbanke demanding of a lover 'all the cardinal virtues' was a
dubious rival. The Italian was already married and spoke no English:
'a great point' because 'the very sound of that language is music to
me, and she has black eyes, and *not* a very white skin, and reminds
me of many in the Archipelago I wished to forget . . .' (Lady
Melbourne, 25 Sept. 1812; C, I, 84). All the same, Byron eventually did marry the 'amiable *Mathematician*' whom he called 'my
Princess of Parallelograms' (Lady Melbourne, 18 Oct. 1812; C, I,
93–4).
    Despite her many gifts Annabella lacked colour and variety.
Once Byron condemned a friend of admitted goodness, honour,
looks and intellect and 'a vast variety of insipid virtues' for being a
'*dull* man', which he said 'undoes all the rest' (Hobhouse, 20 Sept.,
14 Oct.; 1811; C, I, 47, 50). So was it, at least superficially, with
Annabella. 'Who would imagine', he wrote of her to Caroline, 'so
much strength and variety of thought under that placid countenance?'
(1 May 1812; LJ, II, 121). The same apparent dulness characterized
Antony's bride, Octavia. When Cleopatra questions the messenger
from Rome regarding her, she is said to be low voiced, round faced
and of low forehead, the features exactly corresponding to Annabella's portrait by Charles Hayter (LJ, III, Frontispiece; LBM,
facing p. 80), and above all lacking in vitality:

> She creeps;
> Her motion and her station are as one;
> She shows a body rather than a life,
> A statue than a breather.
>
> (III, iii, 18)

The lines fit Annabella's settled and deliberated existence. She
was, or appeared, a—perhaps prematurely—integrated personality.
Whether the integration was genuine or superficial we cannot readily
say, but to Byron—in some moods—the result was likely to irritate.
When, hearing the messenger's description of Octavia, Cleopatra
murmurs 'He cannot like her long' and Charmian answers 'Like
her! O Isis! 'tis impossible' (III, iii, 15), the words could have been

*3. Lady Caroline Lamb in her page's costume; from a miniature in the
possession of Sir John Murray*

4. *Teresa Guiccioli in 1839; by Count D'Orsay*

applied to Byron. The contrast of Cleopatra with Octavia is driven home:

Mecaenas   Now Antony must leave her utterly.
Enobarbus: Never; he will not.
               Age cannot wither her, nor custom stale
               Her infinite variety; other women cloy
               The appetites they feed, but she makes hungry
               Where most she satisfies; for vilest things
               Become themselves in her, that the holy priests
               Bless her when she is riggish.
Mecaenas: If beauty, wisdom, modesty, can settle
               The heart of Antony, Octavia is
               A blessed lottery to him.

(II, ii, 241)

Mecaenas' last 'If' clause might have been spoken of Byron and Annabella. She was not, in any sense, 'riggish'; Byron, very often, was. Byron observes that Annabella, whom Moore had called 'too strait-laced' for him, was full, like Desdemona, of 'most blest conditions' (Moore, 20 Sept. 1814; LJ, III, 139; *Othello*, II, i, 257). Probably he would expect Moore to cap the quotation with Iago's reply: 'Bless'd fig's end! The wine she drinks is made of grapes' (*Othello*, II, i, 258). Octavia, too, was 'straight-laced':

Enobarbus: . . . Octavia is of a holy, cold, and still conversa-
             tion.
Menas: Who would not have his wife so?
Enobarbus: Not he that himself is not so; which is Mark
             Antony. He will to his Egyptian dish again.

(II, vi, 129)

'Still conversation'. When parting from her brother she is speechless: 'Her tongue will not obey her heart' (III, ii, 47). This same quality of silence Byron observed in Annabella just before the marriage:

Annabella's meeting and mine made a kind of scene; though there was no acting, nor even speaking, but the pantomime was very expressive. She seems to have more feeling than we imagined; but is the most *silent* woman I ever encountered; which perplexes me extremely. I like them to talk, because then they *think* less. Much cogitation will not be in my favour; besides, I can form my judgments better, since, unless the countenance is flexible, it is difficult to steer by mere looks. I am studying her, but can't boast of any progress in getting at her disposition; and if the conversation is to be all on one side I fear committing myself; and those who only listen, must have their thoughts so much about them as to seize any weak point at once. However, the die is cast; neither party can recede; the lawyers are here— mine and all—and I presume, the parchment once scribbled, I shall become Lord Annabella.

> (Lady Melbourne, 4 Nov. 1814; C, I, 287)

He goes on to say that he fears she will not 'govern' him; that her love for him is not deep and that his love can only arise in answer to another's; but that there are some signs that her 'affections' and 'passions' may be stronger than he supposed. In this there was some truth.

In both our stories the marriage soon crashed, Lady Byron being supported by her family as was Octavia by her brother. The two husbands endured disgrace.

Lady Byron's indictment was couched mainly in moral terms, accusing her husband of a '*total* dereliction of principle' in himself, while demanding of his wife also a 'total abandonment of every moral and religious principle' (Lady Byron to Lord Byron; and to Hodgson; 13 and 15 Feb. 1816; LJ, III, 310, 313). From then on she remained implacable. In a letter to his wife penned but not sent Byron admitted being 'violent' though not 'malignant', whereas she was 'colder and more concentrated'; she was, he said, in danger of mistaking 'the depth of a cold anger for dignity, and a worse feeling for duty' (17 Nov. 1821; LJ, v, 480). In his *Lines on Hearing that Lady Byron was Ill* (1816) he called her 'the moral Clytemnestra' of her 'lord':

> But of thy virtues did'st thou make a vice,
> Trafficking with them in a purpose cold . . .

Again, the key word is 'cold'.

IV

That Byron should return to the Mediterranean was as inevitable as Antony's return to his 'Egyptian dish'. He chose Venice which, he says, 'has always been (next to the East) the greenest island of my imagination' (Moore, 17 Nov. 1816; LJ, IV, 7). Venice is a 'fairy city' (*Childe Harold,* IV, 18) immortalized by Shakespeare and Otway:

> Ours is a trophy which shall not decay
> With the Rialto; Shylock and the Moor
> And Pierre, cannot be swept or worn away . . .
> (*Childe Harold,* IV, 4)

Italy was crammed with Shakespearian reminders. At Verona Byron saw Juliet's supposed tomb and was excited to find there a living and seemingly factual tradition regarding the story (Moore, 7 Nov.; Murray, 25 Nov.; 1816; LJ, III, 386–7; IV, 13).

He had a peculiar reason for being interested in *Romeo and Juliet,* since he felt that his youthful love for Mary Anne Chaworth had been thwarted by a family feud arising from the death of Mary's grand-uncle at the hand of Byron's in a duel:

> For many a bar, and many a feud,
> Though never told, well understood,
> Roll'd like a river wide between . . .

So Byron wrote in *The Duel* (1818; first printed P, IV, 542–4; and see J. J. Coulmann, 12 (?) July, 1823; LJ, VI, 233–4; LBM, 24, 27; 123–4). 'Our union', Byron wrote, 'would have healed feuds, in which blood had been shed by our fathers; it would have joined lands broad and rich . . .' (*Detached Thoughts,* 1821; 65; LJ, V, 441). Byron does not at this point—he probably does elsewhere, though I cannot recall it—compare his ill-fated youthful love with *Romeo and Juliet,* but in it he had certainly lived the play's central theme.

Othello comes into his story too, in various ways. With reference to Italy's freedom in sexual matters he quotes Othello: '"I know the country's disposition well"—in Venice "they do let Heaven see those tricks they dare not show", etc. etc.' (Moore, 28 Jan. 1817; LJ,

IV, 49–50; *Othello*, III, iii, 201–3). These 'children of the sun', he says, 'consult nothing but passion'; the 'ethics' of married women are so 'singular' that though they regard adultery as 'very wrong', 'love' if genuine not merely excuses it but 'makes it an *actual virtue*' (Moore, 25 March 1817; LJ, IV, 81). The statement covers the ambiguous ethics of sex-relations among certain classes in other places and periods, and large areas of European drama. It corresponds exactly to the ethical paradox of *Antony and Cleopatra*.

To the Nordic temperament heterosexual passion will be characterized by the alien and the mysterious, by 'magic' (p. 231). That is why its normal poetic accompaniment is the moon. In *Antony and Cleopatra* the sun is *indirectly* realized for us; it is, as it were, being laboured for, though the *action* is more at home with darkness and moon; not until the sheep-shearing festival in *The Winter's Tale* is the sun a present love-ally (*The Crown of Life*, 102). But to the southern temperament of what Byron calls 'the children of the sun', these passions are instinctive and easy. Byron wanted to be like them; he felt that he *was*, by nature, like them; and that is why he found Italy congenial.

He took as by instinct to the Venetian carnivals which, as he told Murray, 'ye of the North' would never understand (p. 135 above), and which we may allow to correspond to the orgiastic feasting and 'Egyptian bacchanals' of *Antony and Cleopatra* (II, vii, 104–12). In Italy many kinds of 'riggishness' (p. 241 above) were allowed to which more puritan societies were hostile.

After the marriage desertion Byron 'plunged amidst mankind' (*Manfred*, II, ii, 145). He quickly found an acceptable mistress in Venice, Marianna Segati, a mild Cleopatra of oriental affinities:

I have got some extremely good apartments in the house of a 'Merchant of Venice', who is a good deal occupied with business, and has a wife in her twenty-second year. Marianna (that is her name) is in her appearance altogether like an antelope. She has the large, black, oriental eyes, with that peculiar expression in them which is seen rarely among *Europeans*—even the Italians —and which many of the Turkish women give themselves by tinging the eyelid—an art not known out of that country, I believe. This expression she has *naturally*, and something more

than this. In short, I cannot describe the effect of this kind of
eye—at least upon me.
(Moore, 17 Nov. 1816; LJ, IV, 7; cp.
`Don Juan`, III, 75)

The description is amplified a few days later, for Murray:

. . . I beg leave to tell you, that my goddess is only the wife of a
'merchant of Venice'; but then she is pretty as an Antelope, is
but two-and-twenty years old, has the large, black, Oriental
eyes, with the Italian countenance, and dark glossy hair, of the
curl and colour of Lady Jersey's. Then she has the voice of a
lute, the song of a Seraph (though not quite so sacred), besides
a long postscript of graces, virtues, and accomplishments,
enough to furnish out a new chapter for Solomon's Song. But
her great merit is finding out mine—there is nothing so amiable
as discernment. Our little arrangement is completed; the usual
oaths having been taken, and everything fulfilled according to
the 'understood relations' of such liaisons.
(25 Nov. 1816; LJ, IV, 16; `Macbeth`, II, iv, 124)

Though the lady was married the liaison was, 'according to the
incontinent continental system' (Kinnaird, 27 Nov. 1816; C, II, 22),
freely allowed.

More dramatic was Byron's association with Margarita Cogni,
known as La Fornarina, whom he met in the summer of 1817
(Murray, 1 Aug. 1819; LJ, IV, 328). He describes her to Moore:

I wish you a good night, with a Venetian benediction, '`Bene-`
`detto te, e la terra che ti fara:`'—'May you be blessed, and the `earth`
which you will `make!`'—is it not pretty? You would think it still
prettier if you had heard it, as I did two hours ago, from the
lips of a Venetian girl, with large black eyes, a face like Faus-
tina's, and the figure of a Juno—tall and energetic as a Pythoness,
with eyes flashing, and her dark hair streaming in the moonlight—one of those women who may be made anything. I am
sure if I put a poniard into the hand of this one, she would
plunge it where I told her—and into `me`, if I offended her. I like
this kind of animal, and am sure that I should have preferred
Medea to any woman that ever breathed.
(Moore, 19 Sept. 1818; LJ, IV, 262)

As 'Pythoness' she recalls Cleopatra as the 'serpent of old Nile' (*Antony and Cleopatra*, I, v, 25). She personifies the fiercer aspects of Cleopatra as Marianna the gentler.

On 1 August 1819 Byron wrote to Murray an account of his first meeting with her. Her face was of a 'fine Venetian cast of the old Time'; she had a 'Pantaloon humour'; she was always at extremes, crying or laughing, and so fierce when angered that she was the terror of men, women and children, 'for she had the strength of an Amazon, with the temper of Medea'; in short, 'a fine animal, but quite untameable'. He calls her 'the Gipsy'; she is wild as a 'witch' (LJ, IV, 328–36; for 'gipsy' and 'witch', *Antony and Cleopatra*, I, i, 10; IV, x, 41, 60).

She ran away from her irate husband, a baker, and planted herself without his consent in Byron's house. Her love for Byron was on occasion consuming. Here she is when Byron had been at sea in a squall:

On our return, after a tight struggle, I found her on the open steps of the Mocenigo palace, on the Grand Canal, with her great black eyes flashing through her tears, and the long dark hair, which was streaming drenched with rain over her brows and breast. She was perfectly exposed to the storm; and the wind blowing her hair and dress about her tall thin figure, and the lightning flashing round her, with the waves rolling at her feet, made her look like Medea alighted from her chariot, or the Sibyl of the tempest that was rolling around her, the only living thing within hail at that moment except ourselves. On seeing me safe, she did not wait to greet me, as might be expected, but calling out to me—*Ah! can' della Madonna, xe esto il tempo per andar' al' Lido?* (Ah! Dog of the Virgin, is this a time to go to Lido?) ran into the house and solaced herself with scolding the boatmen for not foreseeing the *'temporale'*. I was told by the servants that she had only been prevented from coming in a boat to look after me, by the refusal of all the Gondoliers of the Canal to put out into the harbour in such a moment: and that then she sate down on the steps in all the thickest of the Squall, and would neither be removed nor comforted. Her joy at seeing me again was moderately mixed with ferocity, and gave me the idea of a tigress over her recovered Cubs.

(Murray, 1 Aug. 1819; LJ, IV, 333)

At Byron's safe return she might have quoted Cleopatra's

O infinite virtue, com'st thou smiling from
The world's great snare, uncaught?

(IV, viii, 17)

But those accents are not Margarita's: rather she corresponds to
Cleopatra as tigress, threatening the Messenger in her impassioned
wrath; to Cleopatra-as-Medea. This Cleopatra Byron understood
and even liked; Euripides' *Medea* was one of his favourite dramas
(Murray, 12 Oct. 1817; LJ, IV, 174; and see Drury, 17 June 1810;
LJ, I, 276–7; also 'Bowles Controversy', LJ, V, App. iii, 545).

When at last Byron insisted that she should return to her husband
she refused, threatening revenge and cutting Byron with a dinner-
knife. When he remained cool and inexorable she threw herself into
the canal. On her rescue, all present remained terrified, but Byron
refused to send for the police: 'I had been used to savage women, and
knew their ways.' He noted, with his habitual delight in such paradoxes, that despite her passions Margarita was very devout and used
to cross herself at prayer-time (Murray, 1 Aug. 1819; LJ, IV, 334–5).

There was another affair that did not develop far. The girl
suggested that Byron should divorce his wife or 'get rid of her'.
Asked 'You would not have me *poison her*?', she was silent; and yet
she was 'little, pretty, sweet-tempered'. It seemed that 'the Passions
of a Sunny Soil are paramount to all other considerations'. Such
human paradoxes always fascinated Byron: 'I never strike out a
thought of another's or of my own without trying to trace it to its
source' (Murray, 18 May 1819; LJ, IV, 302–3). Byron's passionate
engagements were one with his dispassionate studentship of the
passions. Like Antony, only far more so, his delights 'showed his
back above the element they lived in' (*Antony and Cleopatra*, V, ii,
89). Besides, the ladies were so often the dominating partners: 'I have
been more ravished myself than anybody since the Trojan war'
(Hoppner, 29 Oct. 1819; LJ, IV, 370).

Neither Marianna nor Margarita could serve as lasting Cleopatra
equivalents. Byron had a strain of puritanical principle and even
instinct. He deeply respected sexual purity, as is shown by his treatment of Angiolina in *Marina Faliero*. He had always at least *respected*

Annabella's virtues and principles, and the ethical paradoxes of Italy fascinated him precisely because they were so strangely paradoxical. He himself certainly needed a relationship nearer to a true marriage than these ephemeral Venetian liaisons, even though his temperament and destiny could probably never have submitted to marriage as such with any real success. Somehow, as in *Antony and Cleopatra*, the relationship needed must be free in a way a legal marriage could never be. A perfect, if shameless—and perhaps perfect because shameless—expression of the paradox occurs in Dryden's *Amphitryon* (II, ii):

> No, no; that very name of wife and marriage
> Is poison to the dearest sweets of love:
> To please my niceness, you must separate
> The lover from his mortal foe—the husband.
> Give to the yawning husband your cold virtue;
> But all your vigorous warmth, your melting sighs,
> Your amorous murmurs, be your lover's part.

Somewhere within this area lies the reason why our greatest love drama, *Antony and Cleopatra* must, if it is to *be* that, dramatize an illicit love. And yet it should include also something at least of the enduring service and selflessness that marriage involves; there should be a total, or near-total, commitment. Such a commitment we feel in Shakespeare's drama. Could anything of the sort be attained in Byron's passionate life? Could he have the best of both worlds?

In April 1819 Byron met Teresa Guiccioli, the young wife of the elderly Count Guiccioli. They were mutually attracted, and after her return with the Count to their home in Ravenna she insisted on Byron following her. She was ill, and Byron's presence, agreed to by the Count, comforted and helped her. Afterwards Byron and Teresa went alone, again with the husband's approval, to Venice. When the Count arrived some weeks afterwards, Teresa quarrelled with him; he was now hostile, and Byron prepared to retire; but Teresa remained insistent, and after her return to Ravenna told Byron that all was well, and that he might come too. He did, renting a floor of the Count's home, and taking an active part in the Carbonari revolt, of which the Count disapproved. In July 1820 the Pope ruled—for reasons that did not concern Byron—that Teresa should be separated from her husband, and thenceforward she lived with her relations near Ravenna, Byron staying on in the Count's house and visiting her regularly until her family were banished in 1821 for their revolutionary sympathies, when they and Byron went to Pisa and afterwards, in 1822, to Genoa.

This was a far more settled affair than anything Byron had hitherto experienced. The Italian custom of the 'Cavalier Servente' (Hobhouse, 3 Oct. 1819; LJ, IV, 357) tolerated and even expected a lover in attendance on a young wife married to an elderly husband. There was a set of conventions to which Byron dutifully conformed. It was, in effect, a kind of marriage. Byron despite his years was himself feeling old, like Antony (*Antony and Cleopatra*, IV, viii, 19–22). He was ripe at last for a mature and fairly lasting relationship. This, wrote Byron, was love 'in the better sense of the word. *This* will be my last adventure—I can hope no more to inspire attachment and I trust never again to feel it' (Hoppner, 2 July 1819; LJ, IV, 326).

This gradual disentanglement of deep love from violent passions corresponds to the general effect on us of *Antony and Cleopatra*. But that does not mean serenity; indeed, the deeper feeling only brings a new series of anxieties, antagonisms and jealousies, as in the violent alternations of the latter half of Shakespeare's play. Byron's love for Teresa was genuine, while she, as her book on him witnesses (LBCV, 40–7), understood him with depth and sympathy. She was as near as Byron could get to a sexual soul-mate. His Italian love-letters, printed in translation by the Countess Origo, show a flow and fervour, together with a total absence of flippancy and wit, unexampled elsewhere in his prose.

Teresa had looks and charm. On 24 April 1819 Byron wrote to Kinnaird that she was 'as fair as sunrise, and warm as noon':

> She is a sort of Italian Caroline Lamb, except that she is much prettier, and not so savage. But she has the same red-hot head, the same noble disdain of public opinion, with the superstructure of all that Italy can add to such natural dispositions . . . I am damnably in love. (C, II, 109)

Her hair was of a 'rich golden tint' and her countenance lively. It was wavy, with many curls; and her eyes blue and animated

(LJ, IV, 292–3, note). She sometimes wore a sky-blue riding habit (Origo, I, 12). She appealed to Byron's love of agile and vivacious youth; and yet she also drew from him a love not unlike his love for Augusta (Origo, I, 13). 'It is only', writes the Countess Origo after referring to Byron's Venetian mistresses, 'when the heart is involved, that the lover begins to seek not the alien and exciting, but the familiar and kind' (Origo, IV, 162). In Teresa Byron found a unique blend of the exotic and the familiar.

The standard for both was high, and suspicions correspondingly strong. From the start Teresa's insistencies and tears were demanding. During 1821 Byron told her brother Count Gamba, 'Teresa writes to me like a lunatic—as if I wished to give her up' (9 Aug. 1821; Origo, VI, 267). In 1823 he told Lady Hardy that she was 'seized with a furious fit of Italian jealousy and was as unreasonable and perverse as can well be imagined' (Origo, VIII, 341). Such emotional waywardness we are used to in Byron's associates from Lady Caroline onwards; but what is new is that Byron too, as never before, experienced agonies of distrust. That he should, Antony-like, consider suicide if Teresa died is not surprising (Murray, 29 June; Scott, 12 July 1819; LJ, IV, 321; Origo, II, 92). But that he should also follow Antony in his fourth-act jealousies—in both, jealousy comes late, the life stories showing similar curves—is more surprising. Here is an example, dated 11 June 1819:

> It is impossible for me to live long in this state of torment—I am writing to you in tears—and I am not a man who cries easily. When I cry my tears come from the heart, and are of blood.
>
> (Origo, II, 67)

We are now, as we are also in the fourth act of *Antony and Cleopatra*, reminded of *Othello*. Byron has been hurt, like Othello, by Teresa's having sent back 'my handkerchief,' which he regarded as a sentimental token (Origo, II, 67). 'Shakespeare was right', Byron was to tell Medwin in 1821, 'in making Othello's jealousy turn upon that circumstance', because 'the handkerchief is the strongest proof of love, not only among the Moors, but all Eastern nations' (Medwin, 161; Origo, II, 67, note). It happened again with a ring: 'So you have lost the *ring*—without saying a single word to me! This is a lack of trust which surprises and hurts me, who have never made any mysteries with *you*' (7 Aug. 1819; Origo, II, 101). Though in a performance at Pisa Byron was to play Iago (p. 98 above), he had himself been living the part of Othello. In 1819 he told Alexander Scott that Hoppner had made insinuations regarding Teresa's duplicity, saying, in the style of Othello (III, iii, 176–92), that his love would go at 'the least change or trick on her part when I know it'. What was Hoppner insinuating? 'Give me but a proof or a good *tight suspicious confirmation,*' and he will give her up. Such '*hinting* and *teazing*' from people who 'distil their little drop of venom'—he is obviously thinking of Iago—is unbearable (Alexander Scott, 12 July 1819; Origo, II, 90–3). The phrases are redolent of *Othello* (e.g., 'To be once in doubt is once to be resolv'd'; 'Make me to see 't, or at the least so prove it . . .'; 'I'll have some proof;' III, iii, 179; 365; 387). Like Othello, Byron felt lonely and at a loss among Italian temperaments and Italian ways. He saw himself as 'a foreigner far from the moral customs and ways of thought and behaviour of my fellow-countrymen'. He talks of 'perfidious Italy' (Origo, IV, 150, 161, 184). Compare:

Iago: I know our country disposition well.
        In Venice they do let Heaven see the pranks
        They dare not show their husbands; their best conscience
        Is not to leav't undone, but keep't unknown.
Othello: Dost thou say so?

                          (*Othello,* III, iii, 201)

Byron just cannot understand it. He accuses Teresa of a 'morality without principle—a love without faith—and a friendship without esteem or trust'; he has found it 'impossible to extract a word of truth from a person for whom I have given up everything'; how *can* she 'reconcile your love for me with the liberties you have permitted to another man in my presence'? (Teresa, 3 Jan. 1820; Origo, IV, 152). We are minded of Cleopatra's dallying with Thyreus, and Antony's 'Favours, by Jove that thunders!' (III, xi, 85). Byron's bafflement is on the wavelength of Antony's sense of betrayal by 'this false soul of Egypt', his 'chief end', for whom he has sacrificed everything, 'whose heart I thought I had, for she had mine' (IV, x, 38, 40;

IV, xii, 16). It even seems that Teresa may have deliberately aroused quarrels in order to keep him subservient, following Cleopatra's 'cunning' in tormenting Antony by continual crosses, so as not to 'lose him' (I, ii, 155; iii, 1–10). Teresa, says the Countess Origo, had enough intelligence 'to know that tedium was, in Byron, her greatest enemy' (Origo, IV, 164).

But, just as much of *Othello* is written into *Antony and Cleopatra* without finally disrupting its statement of mutual and victorious love, so all these tears, suspicions and recriminations were somehow contained within a harmony corresponding to the enclosing harmony of *Antony and Cleopatra*. In both it was, in essence, a marriage. At the last Cleopatra could say, with justice, 'Husband, I come' (v, ii, 289). The right is won not by vow and compact but by experience and suffering. So too was it in Byron's story. In 1820 he wrote to Teresa that he would be 'when circumstances permit', her 'husband'. On the letter Teresa scribbled in delight: 'Promesse!!!! d'etre mon Époux!!' The Countess Origo comments:

He felt old, flat and sad; he embarked upon this new, permanent relationship with few illusions. But for the first time, he called himself her *husband*. Teresa, at last, had won.

(Origo, IV, 185–6)

It was a kind of marriage won despite a number of difficulties, as in Shakespeare. What was gained had its cost: 'Love', Byron told Teresa, 'has its martyrs like religion' (14 June 1819; Origo, II, 70).

Teresa too suffered. Of her was demanded a supreme sacrifice: to let Byron go to Greece. Byron wrote to Moore on 19 September, 1821 in true *Antony and Cleopatra* vein:

It is awful work, this love, and prevents all a man's projects of good or glory. I wanted to go to Greece lately . . . But the tears of a woman who has left her husband for a man, and the weakness of one's own heart, are paramount to these projects, and I can hardly indulge them.

(LJ, v, 365)

As the demand on him grew stronger he writes more bitterly. Teresa wanted to accompany him, like Desdemona, or Cleopatra—so fatally—at Actium: 'She wants to go to Greece too! forsooth, a precious place to go at present! Of course the idea is ridiculous, as everything must there be sacrificed to seeing her out of harm's way.' He fears more Caroline Lamb scenes: 'There never was a man who gave up so much to women, and all I have gained by it has been the character of treating them harshly.' If he was leaving her for another woman there might be some excuse, 'but really when a man merely wishes to go on a great duty, for a good cause, this selfishness on the part of the "feminie" is really too much' (Kinnaird, 21 May 1823; C, II, 260-1). The letter, springing from the age-old conflict of martial honour and love, reflects the mood of Antony's soldierly impatience when he wishes to return to the arena of his Roman responsibilities: 'You'll heat my blood, no more' (I, iii, 80). Teresa's plight was pathetic, but she tried, and in part succeeded, to live up to Cleopatra's:

> But, sir, forgive me;
> Since my becomings kill me when they do not
> Eye well to you: your honour calls you hence;
> Therefore be deaf to my unpitied folly,
> And all the gods go with you! Upon your sword
> Sit laurel victory! and smooth success
> Be strew'd before your feet!
>
> (I, iii, 95)

Teresa was, finally, brave (Origo, VIII, 346).

Obviously Byron could not live Shakespeare's story to its conclusion: even he could not at every point be both Hamlet and Antony. Teresa perhaps did better. After Byron's death she idealized him as did Cleopatra in her dream-speech on the cosmic Antony (V, ii, 76-100). Like Cleopatra thinking of Antony awaiting her in the other life (IV, ii, 303-5), she claimed to be in contact with her lover in the beyond. The Countess Origo tells us that, after 'making the acquaintance of Daniel Home, the spiritualist, she took to automatic writing, and was, she said, in frequent communication with Byron's spirit' (Origo, X, 415).

V

Meanwhile Byron's poetry had been maintaining, among much else, its sexual interests. The mysterious passions of the early tales and *Manfred* gave way to a more carefree sexual approach. *Don Juan* is full of sexual engagements lightly handled. Juan's first love is a Cleopatra:

> The darkness of her Oriental eye
> Accorded with her Moorish origin . . .
>
> (I, 56)

Her cheek glowed 'as if her veins ran lightning' (I, 61). Byron's poetry was now moving towards a transcendence of sexual guilt. Adam's Tree of Knowledge has been plucked, and this 'ambrosial sin', related to Prometheus' filching of heavenly fire, stands supreme (I, 127). Love is the one good left by Eve after the Fall (II, 186–9; and see 193). There is here a cosmic justification most readily expressed through paradox or humour:

> 'Tis a sad thing, I cannot choose but say,
>   And all the fault of that indecent sun,
> Who cannot leave alone our helpless clay,
>   But will keep baking, broiling, burning on,
> That howsoever people fast and pray,
>   The flesh is frail and so the soul undone:
> What men call gallantry and gods adultery,
> Is much more common where the climate's sultry.
>
> (I, 63)

Summer is a 'dangerous season' and erotic instincts 'universal as the sun' (I, 102; II, 167). Despite our reservations (p. 244) regarding the indirect nature of its presence, we remember the sun, called 'golden Phoebus' (v, ii, 319), throughout *Antony and Cleopatra*: its impregnation of the Nile ooze, 'the fire that quickens Nilus' slime'; Cleopatra 'with Phoebus' amorous pinches black'; Antony's 'O sun, thy uprise shall I see no more'; Cleopatra's 'O sun, burn the great sphere thou movest in!' (I, iii, 68 and II, vii, 29–31; I, v, 28; IV, x, 31; IV, xiii, 9). The lovers, we may say, are aspiring sun-wards. *They* may endure impediments, but the poet himself aligns them with the sun.

Somehow the erotic powers must be faced and placed:

> 'Tis the perception of the beautiful,
>   A fine extension of the faculties,
> Platonic, universal, wonderful,
>   Drawn from the stars and filter'd through the skies,
> Without which life would be extremely dull;
>   In short, it is the use of our own eyes,
> With one or two small senses added, just
> To hint that flesh is form'd of fiery dust.
>
> (II, 212)

Such an understanding it is that makes the Juan and Haidée romance (Cantos II, III, IV), which stands perhaps alone in our literature in creation of a perfect, unmarried, sinless, sexual love in association with Christian tonings; and it is given a magical setting of sea and star and sunlight, till the human and the divine seem as one to make, as Shakespeare has it, 'a race of heaven' (*Antony and Cleopatra*, I, iii, 37).[1] The delicate aesthetic handling offers us, as we shall see (p. 287), plastic and sculptural impressions, marking a sanctification, an eternalizing, of the love-flame, corresponding to Cleopatra's 'eternity was in our lips and eyes' (I, iii, 35) and, more precisely, to her move from 'infinite variety' to the sculptural:

> Now from head to foot
> I am marble-constant, now the fleeting moon
> No planet is of mine.
>
> (V, ii, 238)

Just such a move is Byron's, from all his former energies to this new, more settled, sun-blest, statued, mode.

Byron is labouring to bring sex and goodness together, and his fusing media are variously humour, aesthetic fervour and keen thought. Since we cannot call love 'the devil' it must be 'the god of evil' (II, 205); or perhaps we want some quite new ratification and

---

1. See my essay on Byron's poetry 'The Two Eternities', in *The Burning Oracle*, This essay is to be soon reprinted (see p. ix above).

sanctification for 'Alma Venus Genetrix' (XVI, 109); that is, for sex as the creative principle. Byron turns over and over, facet by facet, the various claims and compulsions of Eros. The women in *Don Juan* are many: Haidée, the Sultana Gulbeyaz, the Empress Catherine, the society ladies in England, the robust Fitz-Fulke, the spiritualized Aurora. In the kaleidoscopic varieties of *Don Juan* Byron may be said to distil the essences of *Venus and Adonis, Romeo and Juliet, Troilus and Cressida* and *Antony and Cleopatra*; but not of *The Rape of Lucrece*—that has been left behind in *Manfred*. Sexual guilt has gone.

The same happens in *The Island* (1823), where an idyllic youthful love rises from a south-sea, Melvillian, island setting in an unfallen state called

> The goldless Age, where Gold disturbs no dreams.
> (I, 10)

It is a place of

> such happy days
> As only the yet infant world displays
> (IV, 15)

set in contrast to a battle and the dangers of Torquil's arrest by a British warship. Here the young sailor, Torquil, is mated to the 'nut-brown' Neuha, 'daughter of the southern seas' (II, 7), the two, 'maid and boy', fused by love into 'one absorbing soul' outspacing all worldly considerations:

> His heart was tam'd to that voluptuous state,
> At once Elysian and effeminate,
> Which leaves no laurels o'er the Hero's urn:—
> These wither when for aught save blood they burn;
> Yet when their ashes in their nook are laid,
> Doth not the myrtle leave as sweet a shade?
> Had Caesar known but Cleopatra's kiss,
> Rome had been free, the world had not been his.
> And what have Caesar's deeds and Caesar's fame
> Done for the earth?
> (II, 13)

5. *Lord Byron in Albanian dress; by Thomas Phillips*

6. *Lord Byron; by Théodore Géricault* (*see p. ix*)

The lines serve to relate the youthful idylls of *Don Juan* and this poem to the 'world well lost', in Dryden's phrase, of *Antony and Cleopatra*. As in *Don Juan*, the Sun, 'fiery, full, and fierce', is finely, elaborately, honoured (II, 15).

Don Juan as a whole shows the same varying, inter-shifting psychology, the unmoral sliding from one value to another, the sense of value in independence of sexual morality, that we find in *Antony and Cleopatra*. Both move easily from grave to gay, from keen satiric thrusts to good-natured raillery, from man-of-the-world toughness to the softest, most intimate, refined emotion. Shakespeare's play is no ordinary tragedy: it is inter-shot with thoughts of gaming and makes contacts with the comedies (*The Imperial Theme*, 253–4). It is as though to the male intelligence the feminine principle were as uncapturable as the wit of Rosalind in *As You Like It*; for Rosalind is in Cleopatra (*The Imperial Theme*, 290, 294). Humour, in one form or another, appears to be a necessary medium in sex-writing, whether high or low: sex and laughter are related and humour a way of touching without finally placing the fiery centres of life's rose, of hinting, without forcibly unfurling, the flower.

'Fiery': because, whatever the gaming and the fun, the centre is both fierce and uncapturable, eternal in authority though bafflingly evanescent in appearance:

> Love bears within its breast the very germ
> Of change; and how should this be otherwise?
> That violent things more quickly find a term
> Is shown through nature's whole analogies;
> And how should the most fierce of all be firm?
> Would you have endless lightning in the skies?
>
> (XIV, 94)

The thought follows the Friar's 'These violent delights have violent ends' in *Romeo and Juliet* (II, vi, 9–15; for nature's 'analogies', II, iii, 1–30; with 'lightning', II, ii, 118–20). The problem is, how may we express, in art or life, this fiery heart? How follow the Friar's counsel to 'love moderately' (II, vi, 14–15) For 'to be wise and love exceeds man's might' and is the prerogative of the gods (*Troilus and Cressida*, III, ii, 163–4). In art the solution comes by eternalizing, by showing Cleopatra in death if not in life 'marble constant' (V, ii.

239), and by the so exquisitely devised plastic impressionism of *Don Juan*; and the spiritualized, gem-like, *Aurora* (p. 287).

In Byron's life two worlds, light and dark, wrestle for mastery. The distinction is not moral: the nobly moral conceptions of *Marino Faliero* and *The Prophecy of Dante* are dark; the immoral and prophetic conceptions of *Don Juan* and *Sardanapalus* are light. Byron labours to turn the dark substances to the light, to heal a broken and wicked world of moonlit sex-mystery, wherein woman is an alien danger, a dark passion, for to Byron 'femininely' is a synonym for 'furiously', because 'all passions in excess are female' (*Sardanapalus*, III, i, 380–1)[1]; a world, more widely, of cruelty, of war and animal-slaughter; to heal this world by a more radiant, sun-facing and sun-blest, sexual, gospel. The conclusion of *Don Juan*, where a ghost turns out to be an amorous duchess (pp. 139, 287), is, in terms of comedy, a vivid example. But for a more exactly patterned working out, we must turn to *Sardanapalus*.

Sardanapalus is a Byronic re-working of *Antony and Cleopatra*. The hero's position as imperial master criticized for sexual laxity and irresponsible hedonism closely corresponds to Antony's. In both dramas the conventional warrior and governmental values are in opposition to sexual and related enticements. The embedded meanings of Shakespeare's drama are in Byron's rendered, in the general manner of Byronic and other Romantic dramas, explicit. Antony is shown as instinctively abandoning all worldly expedience for a lover's passion; Sardanapalus, as a declared pacifist, consciously rates love and pleasure above the conventional warrior and imperial values.

But Sardanapalus *is* inefficient, and loses his empire; Byron does not, as a man, subscribe completely to his life-way. As we have seen, his southern sympathies could in the Tales be grouped with love and action together, so corresponding to Shakespeare's whole dramas, *Othello* and *Antony and Cleopatra,* both of which—and for that matter *Romeo and Juliet* and *Troilus and Cressida* too—are peculiarly concerned with both honour—in the heroic sense—and love; and these are all plays of warm climates. The same association appears in *The*

1. Compare John Cowper Powys's assertion that his sadistic instincts are of *female* quality (*Autobiography*, IX, 426; *The Saturnian Quest*, 60–1).

Deformed Transformed (1822; p. 155 above) when Arnold, a Byronic self-reflection, is asked by the Mephistophelean 'Stranger' where his ambitions lie:

Arnold: Where the world
Is thickest, that I may behold it in
Its workings.
Stranger: That's to say, where there is War
And Woman in activity. Let's see!
Spain—Italy—the new Atlantic world—
Afric, with all its Moors.

(I, i, 494)

Arnold has the choice of various heroes with which to identify himself, among them Antony:

What's here? whose broad brow and whose curly beard
And manly aspect look like Hercules,
Save that his jocund eye hath more of Bacchus
Than the sad purger of the infernal world . . .

(I, i, 231)

This, says the Stranger, is 'the man who lost the ancient world for love'. Arnold cannot blame him, though he decides on *rejection,* and the Stranger dismisses the form, telling it that 'thy Cleopatra's waiting' (I, i, 246). The comparisons with Hercules and Bacchus repeat the Shakespearian associations (IV, iii, 16; II, vii, 111). Arnold's rejection of Antony is important. He turns down the various choices in a *rising* sequence, as follows: Caesar, standing for imperial ambition; Alcibiades, for social glamour; Socrates, for wisdom; Antony, for sexual love; Demetrius Poliorcetes, as civically honoured superman. The choice falls, last, on Achilles. He stands for both innocent love and Greece. He is presented

as he stood by Polixena,
With sanction'd and with soften'd love, before
The altar, gazing on his Trojan bride,
With some remorse within for Hector slain
And Priam weeping, mingled with deep passion
For the sweet downcast virgin, whose young hand
Trembled in *his* who slew her brother. So
He stood i' the temple! Look upon him as

259

Greece look'd her last upon her best, the instant
Ere Paris' arrow flew.

(I, i, 274)

This is not quite Homer's Achilles (of whose nature Byron was well
enough aware; see p. 171). He is nearer to Sardanapalus and his
Greek love, Myrrha. He is a composite of all Byron's ideals: gentleness, perfected love, and Greece at its 'best'. He stands for those
human essences which alone won Byron's total and permanent
allegiance; and for which he was to die. The conception is non-
egotistic: he identifies himself finally with neither the superman nor
the passionate, Antonian, lover.

Nevertheless we must remember that the rejected essences are all
contained in his story, and among them Antony ranks high. As
between Caesarism and sexual passion there is no doubt:

If Anthony be well remember'd yet,
'Tis not his conquests keep his name in fashion,
But Actium, lost for Cleopatra's eyes,
Outbalances all Caesar's victories.

(*Don Juan*, VI, 4)

Byron's total self contained, but was not subdued by, the qualities
and experiences of Hamlet, Macbeth and Antony. As good an
epitaph for him as any is Cleopatra's dream-speech on Antony:

His legs bestrid the ocean; his rear'd arm
Crested the world; his voice was propertied
As all the tuned spheres, and that to friends;
But when he meant to quail and shake the orb,
He was as rattling thunder. For his bounty,
There was no winter in't; an Antony 'twas
That grew the more by reaping; his delights
Were dolphin-like, they show'd his back above
The element they liv'd in; in his livery
Walk'd crowns and crownets; realms and islands were
As plates dropp'd from his pocket.

(v, ii, 82)

Here are Byron's love of the sea and widely-ranging cosmopolitan,
geographic interests and insights; his marvellous voice, noted by

Medwin (p. 98 above); his thunderous passions and ingrained *love* of nature's thunder and lightning (pp. 271–80 below); his generosity in life and fertility in both life and literature ('a Croesus in creation', *Manfred*, II, ii, 142); and his ability to rise above, and remain untainted by, the element of sensuous abandon.

VIII

TEMPESTS, LEAR, PROSPERO

I

IN *The Shakespearian Tempest* I showed that Shakespeare's comedies and tragedies are dominated by symbolic agencies of sea, storms, thunder and lightning. The patterns vary from comic to tragic, but the tempest or some tempest-equivalent is always, or nearly always, functioning. In contrast, we have calm, idyllic, sea, and music. The contrast is easy and obvious. It is the key to Shakespeare's world, though less strongly used in the historical plays, where the dominating symbol is the crown, sea and tempests being confined in the main to imagery. Shakespeare's work concludes with (i) *The Tempest* and (ii) *Henry VIII*: these condense and sum his dominant imaginative interests, tempestuous and royal.

The sea is likewise Byron's primary elemental interest: in *The Corsair* and *The Bride of Abydos*; in the ship description of the second Canto of *Childe Harold* (17–19), the ocean as a bounding freedom in the second stanza of Canto III, the great invocation to ocean as the divine principle at the conclusion of Canto IV; in the *Ode on Venice*; in the tempest and wreck of Don Juan, Canto II; in the Juan and Haidée romance of *Don Juan*; and throughout *The Island*.

Byron was a fine and courageous swimmer. He risked his life at Brighton in 1808 and showed his powers at Lisbon in 1809 (LBCV, 114); he swam the Hellespont in 1810, a feat of which he was deeply, and in part for imaginative reasons, proud; at Venice in 1818 he engaged in a long-distance competition with success; in 1822 he made himself ill by swimming for too long under a fierce sun (LBCV, 107–8; 114). His delight in swimming is reflected in a long speech of Jacopo in *The Two Foscari* (I, i, 94–121), and in the lovers of *The Island*, both (IV; 4, 6) 'born playmates of the deep' (III, 7), their swimming brilliantly pictured:

> Young Neuha plung'd into the deep, and he
> Follow'd: her track beneath her native sea
> Was as a native's of the element,
> So smoothly—bravely—brilliantly she went,
> Leaving a streak of light behind her heel,
> Which struck and flash'd like an amphibious steel.
>
> (IV, 6)

Byron regarded himself as 'almost amphibious', and said that he came out of the sea 'with a buoyancy of spirits I never feel on any other occasion', so much so that he wondered whether he was a merman in some previous existence (Medwin, 137–9).

He enjoyed braving the elements and liked storms. On setting out from Falmouth in 1809 he expected a rough passage and wrote some comic verses on the prospect (*Lines to Mr. Hodgson*). Storms on sea or land fascinated him. Here is a letter written to his Mother on 12 November 1809, with one of each:

> Two days ago I was nearly lost in a Turkish ship of war, owing to the ignorance of the captain and crew, though the storm was not violent. Fletcher yelled after his wife, the Greeks called on all the saints, the Mussulmans on Alla; the captain burst into tears and ran below deck, telling us to call on God; the sails were split, the main-yard shivered, the wind blowing fresh, the night setting in, and all our chance was to make Corfu, which is in possession of the French, or (as Fletcher pathetically termed it) 'a watery grave'. I did what I could to console Fletcher, but finding him incorrigible, wrapped myself up in my Albanian Capote (an immense cloak), and lay down on deck to wait the worst. I have learnt to philosophise in my travels; and if I had not, complaint was useless. (LJ, I, 253)

The description recalls the wreck in the first scene of Shakespeare's *The Tempest*. The details are corroborated by Hobhouse (C, I, 7). The letter continues, describing an experience in the Albanian mountains:

> Fletcher's next epistle will be full of marvels. We were one night lost for nine hours in the mountains in a thunder-storm, and

since nearly wrecked. In both cases Fletcher was sorely bewildered, from apprehensions of famine and banditti in the first, and drowning in the second instance. His eyes were a little hurt by the lightning, or crying (I don't know which), but are now recovered.

(LJ, I, 254)

Fletcher 'is not valiant and is afraid of robbers and tempests' (LJ, I, 256).

Again and again we find Byron experiencing rough passages on water. He even managed to have one in Switzerland when he and Shelley were boating on the Lake of Geneva. He describes it to Murray on 15 May 1819:

The story of Shelley's agitation is true. I can't tell what seized him, for he don't want courage. He was once with me in a gale of Wind, in a small boat, right under the rocks between Meillerie and St. Gingo. We were five in the boat—a servant, two boatmen, and ourselves. The sail was mismanaged, and the boat was filling fast. He can't swim. I stripped off my coat, made him strip off his and take hold of an oar, telling him that I thought (being myself an expert swimmer) I could save him, if he would not struggle when I took hold of him—unless we got smashed against the rocks, which were high and sharp, with an awkward surf on them at that minute. We were then about a hundred yards from shore, and the boat in peril. He answered me with the greatest coolness, that 'he had no notion of being saved, and that I would have enough to do to save myself, and begged not to trouble me.' Luckily, the boat righted, and, baling, we got round a point into St. Gingo, where the inhabitants came down and embraced the boatmen on their escape, the Wind having been high enough to tear up some huge trees from the Alps above us, as we saw next day.

(LJ, IV, 296)

On such events Byron writes with the ease and precision of an expert; as of one, in every sense, in his element.

In Venice he used to put to sea in defiance of storms in small craft, rowing out however rough the waters in order to visit a monastery and commune with the monks (as recorded by the

264

Countess Albrizzi; LJ, IV, App. ii, 442–3). There was the occasion
when Margarita Cogni feared for his life (p. 246). Byron had been
'overtaken by a heavy squall, and the gondola put in peril—hats
blown away, boat filling, oar lost, tumbling sea, thunder, rain in
torrents, night coming, and wind increasing' (Murray, 1 Aug. 1819;
LJ, IV, 333). On leaving for Greece his ship encountered a fearful
storm. Here is Gamba's account of it:

> Towards midnight a strong westerly wind arose; we made head
> against it for three or four hours, but in the end the captain was
> obliged to steer back to the port of Genoa. The horses, un-
> accustomed to the sea, and badly accommodated, caused us
> serious inconvenience. They broke down their divisions, and
> kicked each other. We re-entered the port at six in the morning.
> Lord Byron passed nearly the whole night on deck. Those of
> his suite who were not affected with seasickness assisted him in
> his endeavours to prevent greater mischief amongst the horses.
> He did not feel himself unwell till towards morning, when we
> entered the port. I was half dead with sickness the whole night.
> When able to rise, he said to me, 'You have lost one of the most
> magnificent sights I ever beheld. For a short time we were in
> serious danger; but the captain and his crew did wonders. I was
> the whole time on deck. The sight is not new to me, but I have
> always looked upon a storm as one of the sublimest spectacles in
> nature'. He appeared thoughtful, and remarked, that he con-
> sidered a bad beginning a favourable omen.
>
> (Gamba, I, 11–12)

'One of the sublimest spectacles in nature': this is typical. Byron
loved such a spectacle whatever the dangers; it was a 'favourable
omen'.

When they were approaching Missolonghi there was again
danger. Gamba writes:

> On the 4th of January, steering for Missolonghi, he was over-
> taken by a violent storm, which threw him among the rocks.
> The sailors leapt on them, and got the vessel off unhurt. A
> second gust of wind drove them on again with greater violence.
> The sailors then, losing all hope of saving the vessel, began to
> think of their own safety. But Lord Byron persuaded them to

remain; and by his firmness, and no small share of nautical skill, got them out of danger, and thus saved the vessel and several lives, with 25,000 dollars, the greater part in specie. He arrived late in the port of Missolonghi, and landed in the morning . . .

(Gamba, II, 86–7)

In a note Gamba adds:

He had not pulled off his clothes since leaving Cephalonia; had slept upon the deck, and had purposely exposed himself to privations, which he thought would harden his constitution, and enable him to bear the fatigues of a campaign. He swam for half an hour on the 1st of January.

Of this storm Byron has left us an account, written to Charles Hancock on 13 January 1824:

But blowing weather coming on, we were driven on the rocks *twice* in the passage of the Scrofes, and the dollars had another narrow escape. Two thirds of the crew got ashore over the bowsprit: the rocks were rugged enough, but water very deep close inshore, so that she was, after much swearing and some exertion, got off again, and away we went with a third of our crew, leaving the rest on a desolate island, where they might have been now, had not one of the gun-boats taken them off, for we were in no condition to take them off again.

He refers to 'a Greek boy[1] (the brother of the Greek girls in Argostoli)' whom he told that 'there was no danger for the passengers, whatever there might be for the vessel, and assuring him I could save both him and myself without difficulty', since the water 'though deep, was not very rough—the wind *not* blowing *right* on shore (it was a blunder of the Greeks who missed stays) . . .' (LJ, VI, 303–4). At Cephalonia and Missolonghi there were earthquakes, but these troubled Byron as little as the sea-tempests, and he even made them the subject of a practical joke (pp. 121, 149–50).

Byron's interest in tempests was no simple love of the elements, pantheistically viewed: he liked them either, in the manner of John Masefield, as contestants, as challenges to man to be fought with, or

1. Loukas Chalandritsanos. For the incident see LBM, 216–17.

in the Shakespearian manner as objective correlatives, or mirrors, to the human soul. They hold generally for him either some human or if not that some semi-divine relation.

In the extended description of storm and wreck in *Don Juan* the contest of man or ship against the elements is finely explicit:

> Then rose from sea to sky the wild farewell—
> Then shriek'd the timid, and stood still the brave—
> Then some leap'd overboard with dreadful yell,
>   As eager to anticipate their grave;
> And the sea yawn'd around her like a hell,
>   And down she suck'd with her the whirling wave,
> Like one who grapples with his enemy,
> And strives to strangle him before he die.
>
> And first one universal shriek there rush'd,
>   Louder than the loud ocean, like a crash
> Of echoing thunder; and then all was hush'd,
>   Save the wild wind and the remorseless dash
> Of billows; but at intervals there gush'd,
>   Accompanied with a convulsive splash,
> A solitary shriek, the bubbling cry
> Of some strong swimmer in his agony.
>
> (II, 52–3)

Byron took pride in the many nautical terms used earlier in the description (Murray, 20 May 1819; LJ, IV, 305); as we have seen (p. 149) his conversation amazed the naval fire-master Parry by its resource of nautical terms. The line 'Like one who grapples with his enemy' maintains a vivid sense, like that of Masefield's prose and poetry in our day, of the *challenge to human heroism* of man's fearful elemental setting. Byron is no simple nature-worshipper. In his controversy with Bowles on the nature of poetry he insists that a human reference is needed to make nature poetical; that a ship is needed to make a sea-tempest interesting. He continues:[1]

I look upon myself as entitled to talk of naval matters, at least to poets:—With the exception of Walter Scott, Moore and

---

1. In order to facilitate reading I have given this remarkable passage paragraph divisions which are not in the original text.

Southey, perhaps, who have been voyagers, I have *swum* more miles than all the rest of them together now living ever *sailed,* and have lived for months and months on shipboard; and, during the whole period of my life abroad, have scarcely ever passed a month out of sight of the Ocean; besides being brought up from two years till ten on the brink of it.

I recollect, when anchored off Cape Sigeum in 1810, in an English frigate, a violent squall coming on at sunset, so violent as to make us imagine that the ship would part cable, or drive from her anchorage. Mr. H. and myself, and some officers, had been up the Dardanelles to Abydos, and were just returned in time. The aspect of a storm in the Archipelago is as poetical as need be, the sea being particularly short, dashing and dangerous, and the navigation intricate and broken by the isles and currents. Cape Sigeum, the tumuli of the Troad, Lemnos, Tenedos, all added to the associations of the time. But what seemed the most *'poetical'* of all at the moment, were the numbers (about two hundred) of Greek and Turkish craft, which were obliged to 'cut and run' before the wind, from their unsafe anchorage, some for Tenedos, some for other isles, some for the Main, and some it might be for Eternity.

The sight of these little scudding vessels, darting over the foam in the twilight, now appearing and now disappearing between the waves in the cloud of night, with their peculiarly *white* sails (the Levant sails not being of *'coarse canvas',* but of white cotton), skimming along as quickly, but less safely than the sea-mew which hovered over them; their evident distress, their reduction to fluttering specks in the distance, their crowded succession, their *littleness,* as contending with the giant element, which made our stout 44's *teak* timbers (she was built in India) creak again; their aspect and their motion, all struck me as something far more 'poetical' than the mere broad, brawling, shipless sea, and the sullen winds, could possibly have been without them.

(LJ, v, App. iii, 544)

This passage, in all its ease of technological and imaginative reporting, might serve as an introduction to Byron's sea-faring. It is a materpiece of precision and clarity born of knowledge and experience.

Byron felt all natural convulsions as expressive of something tumultuous in himself. Even earthquakes, the fearful earth-shaking of *Macbeth* (II, iii, 66–7), Byron wrote of with a characteristic zest (Augusta, 12 Oct.; Duffie, 23 Oct.; 1823; LJ, VI, 263, 265); and he staged the mock-earthquake for fun, in order to frighten Parry. This description from *The Island* (1823) has an autobiographical note:

> And who is he? the blue-eyed northern child
> Of isles more known to man, but scarce less wild;
> The fair-hair'd offspring of the Hebrides,
> Where roars the Pentland with its whirling seas;
> Rock'd in his cradle by the roaring wind,
> The tempest-born in body and in mind,
> His young eyes opening in the ocean foam,
> Had from that moment deem'd the deep his home,
> The giant comrade of his pensive moods,
> The sharer of his craggy solitudes . . .
>
> (*The Island*, II, 8)

Byron himself was 'tempest-born'. In Shakespeare sea, tempests and navigation are literary and dramatic powers. Byron lives what Shakespeare imagines. He spends hours in the sea and can navigate a ship in storm.

Grand nature suggests the 'sublime', a term by derivation suggesting the vertical which Byron, in his invocation at the conclusion of *Childe Harold* (IV, 179–84), applies to the ocean, so according to what is by nature horizontal the prerogative of height (see p. 271). The more obvious symbols of sublimity are mountains. During his boyhood at Aberdeen mountains were powerful influences on Byron, as his early verses (e.g. *Lachin y Gair* or *Loch na Garr* and *When I Roved a young Highlander*) record. In *The Island* Byron describes how his early life in the Highlands of Scotland coloured his subsequent experiences of mountain scenery:

> The infant rapture still surviv'd the boy,
> And Loch-na-Garr with Ida looked o'er Troy.
>
> (II, 12)

The thought is expanded in a note: 'From this period I date my love of mountainous countries' (P, v, 609, note). Byron had experience of mountains in Albania, and again in Switzerland. In his Journal of 22 September, 1816, Byron wrote (LJ, III, 357–9):

Arrived at the foot of the Mountain (the Yung frau, i.e. the Maiden); Glaciers; torrents; one of these torrents *nine hundred feet* in height of visible descent. Lodge at the Curate's. Set out to see the Valley; heard an Avalanche fall, like thunder; saw Glacier—enormous. Storm came on, thunder, lightning, hail; all in perfection, and beautiful.

A torrent reminds him of the tail of the horse on which Death rides in the Apocalypse:

It is neither mist nor water, but a something between both; its immense height (nine hundred feet) gives it a wave, a curve, a spreading here, a condensation there, wonderful and indescribable.

On it the sun makes a rainbow, purple and gold. Religious associations are aroused:

Heard the Avalanches falling every five minutes nearly—as if God was pelting the Devil down from Heaven with snow balls.

There are precipices up which clouds curl like the foam of this 'Ocean of Hell', all 'white and sulphury'. He looks down upon 'a boiling sea of cloud (LJ, III, 359). Nature's grandeur suggests divinity, the characteristically light touch doing nothing to reduce the statement, which has its Shakespearian correspondence in such lines as Pericles':

Thou God of this great vast, rebuke these surges
Which wash both heaven and hell.

(*Pericles*, III, i, 1)

Shakespeare has few actual mountains, but his sea-tempests may be given strong vertical associations, their waves as 'mountains' casting water on 'the burning bear' (*Othello*, II, i, 8, 14), and the winds entangling them in the clouds with a 'clamour' which awakes 'death' (*2 Henry IV*, III, i, 24–5). In such poetry Shakespeare gives us dramatic and dynamic equivalents to the sublimity which mountains more statically—and yet how dynamic are Byron's own comments on the Alps—held for a later age. Shakespeare's tempest-poetry helps us to place Byron's at first sight strange use of 'sublime' in his great invocation in *Childe Harold*:

> Thou glorious mirror, where the Almighty's form
> Glasses itself in tempests; in all time—
> Calm or convuls'd—in breeze, or gale, or storm—
> Icing the Pole, or in the torrid clime
> Dark-heaving—boundless, endless, and sublime—
> The image of Eternity, the throne
> Of the Invisible; even from out thy slime
> The monsters of the deep are made; each zone
> Obeys thee; thou goest forth, dread, fathomless, alone.
>
> (IV, 183)

In 'storm' the sea is certainly at its grandest, and it is just because tempest forces it *up* into the higher dimension that it is then so humanly and dramatically relevant. Tragedy becomes an ascent. In Shakespeare tempest and tragedy are felt as positive powers, as purposive: in Byron's tempest poetry we shall find this sense of tragic purpose even more emphatic.

In *Troilus and Cressida* Nestor explicitly relates the steadfastness of a strong ship in tempest to human courage which under a 'splitting wind' answers rage with rage, the 'true proof of men' being only known under adversity (I, iii, 33–54). Man is forced by it to realize his greater self; he is forced *up*. Shakespeare's most powerful dramatic exemplar of such tempest-rivalling courage is obviously the old King Lear, shown as 'contending with the fretful elements' and striving in 'his little world of man' to 'out-scorn the to-and-fro conflicting wind and rain' (III, i, 4–11). *King Lear* provides an exact forecast of Byron's tempest-poetry. Lear will not 'weep' (II, iv, 286); instead he sets, for a short while before the strain becomes too great, his human powers against the cosmos. In Byron too endurance was one with an aspiration forcing imagery of height. In his *Lines written among the Euganean Hills* Shelley aptly called him a 'tempest-cleaving swan'. Childe Harold is one

> Droop'd as a wild-born falcon with clipt wing,
> To whom the boundless air alone were home.
>
> (III, 15)

Being one who 'surpasses' other men, he resembles the 'loftiest peaks' that are 'wrapt in clouds and snow':

> Though high above the sun of glory glow,
> And far beneath the earth and ocean spread,
> Round him are icy rocks, and loudly blow
> Contending tempests on his naked head.
>
> (III, 45)[1]

That last line with its *Lear*-words 'contending' and 'head' ('contending', III, i, 4, quoted above; 'a head so old and white as this', 'this thin helm'; III, ii, 23; IV, vii, 36) recalls Shakespeare. Are not 'the mountains, waves and skies', asks Byron, 'a part of me and of my soul, as I of them'? (III, 75). There is even a blend of tempest-fire and man's sweetest emotions. Of Rousseau we are told that

> His love was passion's essence:—as a tree
> On fire by lightning; with ethereal flame
> Kindled he was, and blasted.
>
> (III, 78)

The 'lightning' is spirit-lightning, a spirit-compulsion, a high good, sweet yet blasting. As love is lightning, so are thunder-storms lovely as a Cleopatra:

> The sky is chang'd!—and such a change! Oh, night,
> And storm, and darkness, ye are wondrous strong,
> Yet lovely in your strength, as is the light
> Of a dark eye in woman! Far along,
> From peak to peak, the rattling crags among
> Leaps the live thunder!
>
> (III, 92)

'The joyous Alps' echo it. When thunder-bolts flash and forked lightnings—'the most terrible and nimble stroke of quick cross-lightning' of *King Lear* (IV, vii, 34) and the 'nimble, sulphurous flashes' of *Pericles* (III, i, 6)—play over the Rhone valley, Byron sees his own life reflected as on a screen:

> Sky, mountains, river, winds, lakes, lightnings! ye!
> With night, and clouds, and thunder, and a Soul

1. I suppress Byron's italics which, though valuable as pointers for reading aloud, tend to disturb the critical eye.

To make these felt and feeling, well may be
Things that have made me watchful; the far roll
Of your departing voices, is the knoll
Of what in me is sleepless—if I rest.
But where of ye, O Tempests! is the goal?
Are ye like those within the human breast?
Or do ye find, at length, like eagles, some high nest?

Could I embody and unbosom now
That which is most within me—could I wreak
My thoughts upon expression, and thus throw
Soul, heart, mind, passions, feelings, strong or weak,
All that I would have sought, and all I seek,
Bear, know, feel—and yet breathe—into *one* word,
And that one word were Lightning, I would speak;
But as it is, I live and die unheard,
With a most voiceless thought, sheathing it as a sword.

(III, 96–7)

Here we are at the very heart of Byron. The 'soul' of man responds
to the elements and also gets inside their own non-human 'feeling',
their subjective selves. Their sound speaks to, perhaps summons up
('knoll'),[1] that in Byron which is 'sleepless' when he 'rests'; which
means either that he lies awake listening, or more likely that they
address his soul-self awake during bodily sleep; the low thunder
corresponding to poetry regarded as 'the dream of my sleeping
passions' and a kind of 'somnambulism' (Murray, 2 Jan. 1817; LJ,
IV, 43; p. 38 above). In asking whether nature's tempests are part
of some cosmic purpose or futile as human agonies, Byron has subtly
used natural sublimity to raise suggestion of *a possible purpose in
human tragedy too*, a resolution being hinted in terms of height.
Following on, we have a more explicit statement equating the spirit-
fire which is the essential man ('most within') with 'lightning', un-
translatable into word-sequences. The meaning is that of Shakes-
speare's continual use of 'swift' thought for uncapturable emotions
and intuitions (*The Wheel of Fire*, enlarged, App. B., 339–41; and

1. This is a dictionary meaning, but Hartley Coleridge reads 'knoll' as equivalent
to 'knell' (P, II, 275). Probably both meanings are contained to suggest 'summon or
wake up with a knell'; i.e. awake the tragic, beyond-death, self.

see General Index, Index B, vi, 'Miscellaneous'; *The Sovereign Flower*, 317). Love, in thought or act, may be called

> Brief as the lightning in the collied night,
> That, in a spleen, unfolds both heaven and earth,
> And ere a man hath power to say, 'Behold!'
> The jaws of darkness do devour it up.
> (*A Midsummer Night's Dream*, I, i, 145)

Or as Juliet has it:

> I have no joy of this contract tonight:
> It is too rash, too unadvis'd, too sudden;
> Too like the lightning, which doth cease to be
> Ere one can say 'It lightens'.
> (*Romeo and Juliet*, II, ii, 117)

Love is a matter of swift vibrations

> tun'd too sharp in sweetness
> For the capacity of my ruder powers.
> (*Troilus and Cressida*, III, ii, 23)

To be won and preserved it must somehow be matched with the equivalent swiftness of 'a mind that doth renew swifter than blood decays' (III, ii, 169). In Sonnets 44 and 45 swift love-thoughts are as little Ariels, related to air and fire (p. 55). Byron's stanza pursues a Shakespearian course, corresponding to the 'thought-executing fires' of *King Lear* (III, ii, 4).

Lightning, even at its most destructive, is for Byron more friend than foe. In *The Corsair* the manacled Conrad, awaiting death by torment, responds from his dungeon to the roaring of the sea as to his natural 'element', and when tempest 'flash'd the lightning by the lattic'd bar',

> He rais'd his iron hand to Heaven, and pray'd
> One pitying flash to mar the form it made.
> His steel and impious prayer attract alike—
> The storm roll'd onward, and disdain'd to strike;
> Its peal wax'd fainter—ceas'd—he felt alone,
> As if some faithless friend had spurn'd his groan.
> (III, 7)

Lightning is simultaneously illumination, creation ('made'), and, in destruction, 'friend', even though here it refuses to complete its metaphysical role. Through 'lightning' Byron attempts to penetrate the meaning of human destiny. When in *Childe Harold* bitter-sweet memories are said to arise 'striking the electric chain wherewith we are darkly bound', the reference is to spirit-compulsions enclosing man like an aura (IV, 23; compare 'circling', p. 234). Light and dark, in the manner of tragedy, are interdependent, almost identified:

> And how and why we know not, nor can trace
> Home to its cloud this lightning of the mind,
> But feel the shock renew'd, nor can efface
> The blight and blackening which it leaves behind.
>
> (IV, 24)

'Spectres' are called up from the dead: beyond-death intuitions and lightning are close (IV, 24). Many such variations are played on lightning. The lightning which 'rent from Ariosto's bust' its 'mimick'd leaves' serves, we are told, to emphasize a 'glory' independent of mortal chance. Besides,

> the lightning sanctifies below
> Whate'er it strikes;—yon head is doubly sacred now.
>
> (IV, 41)

'Below': lightning is from the higher reaches, the spirit-sphere, the divinity, as when Jupiter in *Cymbeline* descends to throw his thunderbolt, saying 'Whom best I love, I cross' (V, iv, 101).

Byron's tempests and lightnings are simultaneously tragic and purposeful. As we have just seen (p. 272) Rousseau's love was 'passion's essence' like 'a tree on fire by lightning', himself simultaneously 'kindled' with 'an ethereal flame' and 'blasted'—blasted by his own finest apprehensions. Lightning is a spiritual principle: in the lines on Ariosto it '*sanctifies*'. When the bronze statue of the Wolf suckling Romulus and Remus, which had been, like Ariosto's bust, scorched, is addressed as 'Thou, the thunder-stricken nurse of Rome' and called 'black with lightning' from Jove's 'ethereal dart', every word registers an honour (IV, 88).

Manfred's 'soul' was 'scorch'd'; but he had gazed on 'the dazzling lightnings till mine eyes grew dim' (*Manfred*, II, i, 73; II, ii, 72);

and the two statements are related. As Shelley tells us in *Julian and Maddalo* (51), Byron's 'eagle spirit' had been blinded 'by gazing on its own exceeding light'. The 'fire' which Prometheus 'stole from Heaven' is the very cause of what 'we'—men such as Byron or Manfred, and in different degrees all tragic humanity—'endure' (*Childe Harold,* IV, 163). The suffering may be fearful, leaving one 'lone as some volcanic isle' (*On This Day I complete my Thirty-Sixth Year*). The worst terror comes from a too-high good like Rousseau's love, before which social communities, as communities, tremble

> Lest their own judgments should become too bright,
> And their free thoughts be crimes, and earth have
> too much light.
>
> (IV, 93)

Freedom—true freedom—is as a 'banner, torn but flying' which 'streams like the thunder-storm *against* the wind' (IV, 98). To be that thunder, that lightning, may be tragic, but within the tragedy is what Dryden in *Absalom and Achitophel* called 'a spark too much of heavenly fire'; the fire of the Apollo Belvedere (p. 49) whose features

> flash their full lightnings by,
> Developing in that one glance the Deity.
>
> (*Childe Harold,* IV, 161)

Lightning, uncapturable, evanescent, unthinkable, is man's tragedy and torment; it is also his contact with divinity.

Shakespeare's Ariel is a personification of lightning when in *The Tempest* he describes how he 'flam'd amazement' over the tempest-racked ship:

> Sometime I'd divide
> And burn in many places; on the topmast,
> The yards and boresprit, would I flame distinctly,
> Then meet, and join. Jove's lightnings, the precursors
> O' the dreadful thunder-claps, more momentary
> And sight-outrunning were not. The fire and cracks
> Of sulphurous roaring the most mighty Neptune
> Seem to besiege and make his bold waves tremble,
> Yea, his dread trident shake.
>
> (I, ii, 198)

The Tempest sums up symbolically Shakespeare's tragic world; that world, as I have often argued, is to a profound reading less pessimistic than invigorating; and accordingly Ariel's tempest is shown as in effect not destructive. No one is hurt, and the ship finally as 'trim' as when it first put to sea (I, ii, 217–19; V, i, 222–5, 236–7). *Byron's life and writings help to bridge the gap between the apparent disasters of Shakespearian tragedy and his symbolic interpretation of them in his last plays.*

I say 'symbolic': and yet there are truths we fail to recognize. John Davidson once remarked that 'all convincing imagery is scientific truth' (*The Triumph of Mammon*, 1907; 160). Now Ariel is a spirit, and spirits exist. More, they are described again and again by mediums and spirit-communications in terms of 'swift vibrations'. The 'etheric' plane and 'etheric body' are the usual terms. John Cowper Powys's spiritualistic thinking once forces him into thought of an 'atmospheric' or 'electronic body' (*Obstinate Cymric*, 1947; 157) as a spirit-equivalent. Today encephalographic experiments are claiming that thoughts and emotions may be detected electrically, even to the extent of deciding whether a man is lying.[1] In Byron the concepts of mind, thought, emotion, fire and electricity are co-extensive. Examples are everywhere, as in this from *Lara*:

> And the wild sparkle of his eye seem'd caught
> From high, and lighten'd with electric thought.
>
> (*Lara*, I, 26)

Men of genius 'bear hearts electric—charg'd with fire from Heaven' (*Monody on the Death of Sheridan*). We have already (p. 275) observed the 'electric chain' and 'lightning of the mind' in *Childe Harold* (IV, 23–4). 'Mind' is a 'fiery particle' in *Don Juan* (XI, 60).

---

1. But there also appear to be powers in the mind beyond the 'electro-magnetic'. See L. L. Vasiliev (of the University of Leningrad), *Experiments in Mental Suggestion*, authorized translation, Institute for the Study of Mental Images, Church Crookham, England; 1963; especially ch. X. An important letter by Mrs. Anne Dooley, *T.L.S.*, 18 February 1965 (132), written in answer to a review of J. Gaither Pratt's *Parapsychology: an Insider's View of ESP* in *T.L.S.*, 28 January 1965 (71), sums up Vasiliev's findings neatly.

Our comprehensive statement comes in some words of Manfred to the spirits he has invoked:

> Slaves, scoff not at my will!
> The Mind—the Spirit—the Promethean spark,
> The lightning of my being, is as bright,
> Pervading, and far-darting as your own.[1]
>
> (*Manfred*, I, i, 153)

As so often, what for others is 'imagery' only is for Byron more; it is part of his being, and not that by metaphor only. Lightning here is Powys's 'electronic body', the etheric or astral body of Spiritualism; or the 'spiritual body' of St. Paul (1 Corinthians, XV, 44–5). When he said in *Childe Harold* (III, 97) that his whole self could be defined *as* lightning, he was not merely writing great imaginative literature. He meant it.

By one who knew him Byron could be regarded as naturally akin to the sea in calm or storm. I quote from the Countess Albrizzi a passage reminiscent of Cleopatra's description of Antony (p. 260) and Belarius' of the 'gentle' princes in *Cymbeline*, whose 'royal blood' could nevertheless be moved to pass suddenly as with a change from 'zephyrs' to 'the rudest wind' (IV, ii, 171–6):

> His face appeared tranquil like the ocean on a fine spring morning; but, like it, in an instant became changed into the tempestuous and terrible, if a passion (a passion did I say?) a thought, a word, occurred to disturb his mind. His eyes then lost all their sweetness, and sparkled so that it became difficult to look on them. So rapid a change would not have been thought possible; but it was impossible to avoid acknowledging that the natural state of his mind was the tempestuous.
>
> (LJ, IV, App. ii, 442)

With that conclusion Galt, who found 'the home of his spirit' in 'the abysm of the storm' (VIII, 63; p. 185 above), would have agreed. The Countess Albrizzi's elemental comparisons are well chosen. But the kinship went beyond analogy: Byron's being was *intimately*

---

1. I follow Byron's original as printed by Hartley Coleridge, which is here superior to the Oxford text which reduces the capitals and puts commas for dashes. A deleted manuscript variant reads: 'The Mind which is my Spirit—the high Soul'. See P, IV, 90, note.

responsive to nature's electricity. 'I write to you', he tells Murray, 'with thunder, lightning, etc., and all the winds of heaven whistling through my hair' (9 Aug. 1819; LJ, III, 338). The words witness a pleasure, perhaps a pride, in the intimacy suggested. But this intimacy, or kinship, had its troubles too. From Cephalonia, writing on 12 October 1823 of a ride to Argostoli, he told Augusta:

> and then I had one of my *thunder* headaches (*you* know my head aches like a barometer when there is electricity in the air) and I could not resume till the morning.
>
> (LJ, VI, 260–1)

Thunder recurs strangely in a tantalizing phrase of Lady Byron during the troubles leading to the Separation. Writing to Augusta on 25 January 1816 she says:

> 'The thunder' to which you allude would not be so terrible. If it be disease any strong shock will for a time restore reason, though in the end it can make no difference, and as far as a boundless and impious pride may be combined with it, reverses and humiliations would be mercies, indulgence and success more impious than anything.
>
> (LJ, III, 300)

The 'thunder' is related somehow to the 'terrible', to the 'boundless', to 'impiety' and to 'pride'; the terms of our challenging poetic passages are present, though viewed with distaste. Probably Byron could exert fearful *radiations*, like Antony, who

> when he meant to quail and shake the orb
> He was as rattling thunder.
> (*Antony and Cleopatra*, v, ii, 85)

We may relate Lady Byron's phrase to Byron's reported claim at this period to be the greatest man living, together with his own distress at this appalling self-recognition (pp. 101–2, 342). It must all have been deeply disturbing. Byron *was* the 'thunder and lightning' of Shakespeare's stage-directions in living actuality, and his death had, appropriately enough, its own cosmic accompaniment. The burly, prosaic Parry writes:

At the very time Lord Byron died, there was one of the most

awful thunder storms I ever witnessed. The lightning was teriffic. The Greeks, who are very superstitious, and generally believe that such an event occurs whenever a much superior, or as they say, a supreme man dies, immediately exclaimed, 'The great man is gone!' On the present occasion it was too true; and the storm was so violent, as to strengthen their superstitious belief.

(Parry, v, 128, note)

This was rather remarkable, and we shall have to search far for an analogy.

II

The central imaginative prepossession of Shakespeare's dramas is accordingly Byron's also. Byron goes far beyond Shakespeare, whose storms are all very much alike, in exactitude of realism and variety of example; besides, as always, being himself an active exemplar. But if he has more to offer regarding tempests, he has at first sight less to correspond with Shakespeare's opposing principle of music, which, as I have shown in *The Shakespearian Tempest*, is used throughout at occasions of accomplished love, social harmony or transcendental vision: in the early romances, for feast scenes, at the Lear and Cordelia reunion, and at the miraculous events of the last plays; at one point, in *Pericles* (v, i, 231), called 'the music of the spheres'. Naturally the descriptive writer is at an advantage with the one and the dramatic poet with the other. There is 'soft music' at the opening of *Sardanapalus* (i, i, 27; direction), but the use of ominous thunder *during* the feast (iii, i; direction) marks a variation on Shakespeare's symbolic practice. Sardanapalus is shown, like Shakespeare's Cassius, to whom Byron here corresponds, as unmoved by thunder (iii, i, 32–6). The Shakespearian contrast of tempests and music tends in Byron to be softened, since however fierce they may be tempests are, as we have seen, acceptable to him:

> Then let the winds howl on! their harmony
> Shall henceforth be my music . . .
> (*Childe Harold*, iv, 106)

Shakespeare's tempests too are part of his dramatic harmonies; artistically they are to be as much enjoyed as any actual music (*The Shakespearian Tempest*, 291–2). What in Shakespeare is artistry becomes in Byron, as so often elsewhere, explicit. He interprets the positive grandeur of Shakespearian tragedy. He enjoys his own tempests, and accepts, and even, poetically at least, *likes* his tragic destiny.

Byron responded keenly to music, which was among his natural diversions (Journal, 23 Nov. 1813; LJ, II, 337). During the troubled days at Ravenna he listened to music; 'Music', he wrote, 'is a strange thing' (Journal, 9 Jan., 2 Feb.; 1821; LJ, V, 163, 199).

The aural properties of poetry are powerfully present in the *Thyrza* lyrics and *Childe Harold*, and Byron enjoyed an infinite resource in rhyme. Like Shakespeare, he wrote songs. His *Hebrew Melodies* were advertised by Murray as composed—though some may have been only selected—for Hebrew tunes (P, III, 375). Singing he appreciated: 'Moore has a peculiarity of talent, or rather talents— poetry, music, voice, all his own; and an expression in each which never was, nor will be, possessed by another' (Journal, 22 Nov. 1813; LJ, II, 333). In Italy he attended the opera and was interested as to what Rossini's *Otello* would 'make of Shakespeare in music' (Murray, 20 Feb. 1818; LJ, IV, 204). Stendhal, who knew him in Italy, wrote:

> On his return from the theatre in the evening, still under the charm of the music to which he had listened, he would take up his papers, and reduce his hundred verses to five-and-twenty or thirty . . . His extreme sensibility to the charms of music may partly be attributed to the chagrin occasioned by his domestic misfortunes. Music caused his tears to flow in abundance, and thus softened the asperity of his suffering. His feelings, however, on this subject, were those of a *debutante*. When he had heard a new opera for upwards of a twelve-month, he was often enraptured with a composition which had previously afforded him little pleasure, or which he had even severely criticized.
>
> (LJ, III, App. viii, 443–4)

Music touched the more sentimental, nostalgic, melting quality in him, corresponding to Jessica's 'I am never merry when I hear sweet music' in *The Merchant of Venice* (V, i, 69). But it certainly affected him strongly: 'When he is listening to music', wrote Stendhal, his 'countenance' was 'worthy of the *beau-ideal* of the Greeks' (LJ, IV, App. iv, 450).

Music to Byron held a spiritual reference: 'He reminds me', he once wrote of an acquaintance, 'of Hunt, but handsomer, and more musical in soul, perhaps' (Moore, 25 July 1813; LJ, II, 234). Love's voice was 'like music on the waters' (p. 231 above). The key to what music meant to Byron will be found in his reiterated use of the word 'tone'. In *To Thyrza* he remembers the singing of the loved Edleston, thinking of its blessed 'tone' in

> The song, celestial from thy voice,
> But sweet to me from none but thine.

So in *Away, away, ye Notes of Woe* the well-known music, heard from another, strikes pain. 'All that once was harmony' becomes 'discord', or merest silence, while the true 'tone' awakes:

> 'Tis silent all!—but on my ear
> The well remember'd echoes thrill;
> I hear a voice I would not hear,
> A voice that now might well be still.
> Yet oft my doubting soul 'twill shake;
> Even slumber owns its gentle tone,
> Till consciousness will vainly wake
> To listen, though the dream be flown.

Byron's 'soul' responds to the 'tone' as *still living*; and it visits him *in sleep*. Sleep may be to Byron the medium of supernal insight or in-feeling (pp. 38, 273). These are all intuitions of some great truth or wisdom. When 'Wisdom' in men of genius fails, then

> minds of heavenly tone
> Jar in the music which was born their own.

'Wisdom', 'tone', music, all are identified (*Monody on the Death of Sheridan*).

The *Thyrza* poems, with the word 'tone'—the word comes in again for the similarly *self-reflecting* love of *Manfred* (II, ii, 106)—as a key, may assist our deeper understanding of certain stanzas in *Childe*

Harold of direct spiritualistic significance. Music may be identified, in Shakespearian wise, with an infinitude beyond death:

Then stirs the feeling infinite, so felt
In solitude, where we are *least* alone;
A truth, which through our being then doth melt,
And purifies from self: it is a tone,
The soul and source of Music, which makes known
Eternal harmony, and sheds a charm
Like to the fabled Cytherea's zone,
Binding all things with beauty;—'twould disarm
The spectre Death, had he substantial power to harm.
(*Childe Harold*, III, 90)

'Tone'. So too 'a tone of music' is listed among those prompters of scorching intuition that strike the spirit-self's 'electric chain' and raise 'spectres' of the dead (p. 275; *Childe Harold*, IV, 23-4). By the tomb of an unknown lady, Byron experiences—the technical term for it is 'psychometry'—her long-forgotten life, and feels near to visualizing, clairvoyantly, the dead:

I know not why—but standing thus by thee
It seems as if I had thine inmate known,
Thou Tomb! and other days come back on me
With recollected music, though the tone
Is chang'd and solemn, like the cloudy groan
Of dying thunder on the distant wind;
Yet could I seat me by this ivied stone
Till I had bodied forth the heated mind
Forms from the floating wreck which Ruin leaves behind.
(*Childe Harold*, IV, 104)

'Tone' again, a 'music' like 'dying thunder', which corresponds to the 'far roll' of a 'departing' storm responded to by the sleep-self or spirit-self in a stanza already quoted (III, 96; p. 273). 'Dying thunder' is as the death of death, making a 'solemn', tragic yet serene, music. 'Solemn' is likewise Shakespeare's word for just such unearthly, sombre yet heavenly, themes (*The Winter's Tale*, III, i, 7; *Cymbeline*, V, iv, 29, direction; *Henry VIII*, IV, ii, 80 and 82, directions). Shakespeare's use corresponds exactly to Byron's tragic yet serene intuition, the same word for the same music to denote an indefinable serenity.

In his address to his daughter Ada, Byron thinks of his voice as communicating with her after death as 'a token and a tone'; and he believes that 'something unearthly' in him will win the love of future generations 'like the remember'd tone of a mute lyre' (*Childe Harold*, III, 115; IV, 137).

Byron likes sounds with human impact, redolent of life or scene. He found them in Switzerland:

The music of the Cows' bells (for their wealth, like the Patri-archs', is cattle) in the pastures (which reach to a height far above any mountains in Britain), and the Shepherds' shouting to us from crag to crag, and playing on their reeds where the steeps appeared almost inaccessible, with the surrounding scenery, realized all that I have ever heard or imagined of a pastoral existence.

(Journal, 19 Sept. 1816; LJ, III, 355)

In Greece and Asia Minor, he writes, there was too much of the 'sabre and musquet' mixed with their pastoralism; this was 'pure and unmixed—solitary, savage and patriarchal'; it struck the blend of virility and peace which was Byron's soul-dream. As he puts it in *Manfred*:

Hark! the note,
The natural music of the mountain reed—
For here the patriarchal days are not
A pastoral fable—pipes in the liberal air,
Mix'd with the sweet bells of the sauntering herd;
My soul would drink those echoes. Oh, that I were
The viewless spirit of a lovely sound,
A living voice, a breathing harmony,
A bodiless enjoyment—born and dying
With the blest tone which made me!

(I, ii, 47)

'Spirit', 'voice', 'tone': these Byronic identities correspond to Shake-speare's dramatic use of music as a spiritual power.

Shakespeare's stage music is humanly related and the less other-worldly for being linked to drama. For Byron too, any ideal must be human, must somehow house the natural energies. This can best happen, in two ways: either by music of human or natural association, as in the *Thyrza* poems and the Swiss pastoral, or by use of some closely human art, as in the dancing description in *Don Juan*, where grace is blended with motion (XIV, 38–40); or in visible sculpture (pp. 47–50). Now Shakespeare's last plays show a new interest in the arts of design. The move from energies to a more plastic humanism pivots on Cleopatra's 'Now from head to foot I am marble constant; now the fleeting moon no planet is of mine' (*Anthony and Cleopatra*, V, ii, 238). Henceforth Shakespeare's drama shows an emphasis on the visual arts and in *The Winter's Tale* on sculpture, elaborately described in Renaissance terms and culminating in the tragedy-reversal of Hermione's living statue (V, ii, 105–14; iii).

We have seen how Byron's tempests and thunder-lightnings, whose ruling note is sublimity, are entwisted with perceptions that render explicit the spiritual purpose embedded within all Shakespearian tragedy. Nowhere is this clearer than in his description of the Falls of Terni (*Childe Harold*, IV, 69–72). A 'hell of waters' is seen howling and hissing as in 'endless torture', but spray mounts to fall as fertilizing 'April' rain through which sunlight makes a rainbow promise, concluding with a marvellous line of plastic and spiritualized suggestion:

> Horribly beautiful! but on the verge,
> From side to side, beneath the glittering morn,
> An Iris sits, amidst the infernal surge,
> Like Hope upon a death-bed, and, unworn
> Its steady dyes, while all around is torn
> By the distracted waters, bears serene
> Its brilliant hues with all their beams unshorn:
> Resembling, 'mid the torture of the scene,
> Love watching Madness with unalterable mien.
>
> (IV, 72)

Generally Byron expands Shakespeare; here we watch the reverse. The concluding line is an amazing compression, perfect in lucidity and final in tragic conquest, of Lear's reunion with Cordelia. The meaning is also that of Pericles when reunited with Marina who appears to him

> Like Patience gazing on kings' graves, and smiling
> Extremity out of act.
>
> (*Pericles*, v, i, 140)

Such is the high peace attainable, or imaginable, beyond conflict; it may be touched for a while, *within* tragedy, as it is in *King Lear* and Byron's lines. The Augustan and figured personifications of Byron's concluding line mark no weakness, but correspond rather to his life-long devotion to Pope's poetry as a gospel of harmony (pp. 9–10).

Byron's late poetry shows a development from energies to plastic form. First there is the spiritually impregnated statuary of *Childe Harold*, IV, already observed, and that wonderful phrase on the living architecture of St. Peter's:

> Vastness which grows, but grows to harmonize—
> All musical in its immensities . . .
>
> (*Childe Harold*, IV, 156)

A key-phrase, surely, for any sense-blending aesthetic of the kind suggested variously in my *Laureate of Peace*, reissued as *The Poetry of Pope*, see p. viii (III, 'Symbolic Eternities'); *The Starlit Dome* (1959 edn., App., 318–19); *The Christian Renaissance* (1962 edn., 'Epilogue', 328–9); and *The Saturnian Quest*, 56, 87, 124. Byron's phrase is far better, more Byronic and liberating, than the reverse attempt in Goethe's definition of architecture as 'frozen music' for which Byron was anxious to discover the source (Journal, 17 Nov. 1813; LJ, II, 326). There is too the architectural emphasis and dramatically central equestrian statue of *Marino Faliero* (III, i). *Sardanapalus* shows a plastic quality in descriptive passages and general effect, the best being Myrrha depicted in fight with 'her nostril dilated from its symmetry' (III, i, 390). As I have shown in my essay 'The Two Eternities' in *The Burning Oracle*[1], *Don Juan* is throughout rich in a plastic impressionism serving, in line with the spiritualized statuary of *Child Harold*, IV (see pp. 47–50), to

---

1. This essay is to reappear in a new volume: see p. ix.

stamp humanity with eternal and transcendant sanction. So Haidée is called 'fit for a model of a statuary', but surpassing any 'stone ideal' (II, 118); and when Byron goes on (II, 119) to assert that human actuality may, despite its having to yield to time and wrinkles, surpass 'mortal thought' and the 'less mortal' (i.e. eternalizing) 'chisel', we are reminded of Leontes' 'What fine chisel could ever yet cut breath?' (*The Winter's Tale*, V, iii, 78). When in a lighter stanza the clinging forms of Juan and Haidée are felt as a sculptured 'group', or eternal perfection (II, 194), we must not be deceived by the jaunty tone. Indeed the comedy, significantly supported by sculptural impressions, of the ghostly terror replaced by an amorous lady as 'warm' as Hermione (XVI, 122; *The Winter's Tale*, V, iii, 109) at the long poem's conclusion (XVI, 117–23) corresponds (p. 139) in terms of deep humour to Shakespeare's statue-resurrection. We have recently compared Byron's 'Love watching Madness with unalterable mien' to Shakespeare's Patience 'smiling extremity out of act'. In both the transcendental is humanly limned, as again in Byron's Aurora, whose 'spirit', like Marina as 'a palace for the crown'd Truth to dwell in' (*Pericles*, V, i, 123),

> seem'd as seated on a throne
> Apart from the surrounding world, and strong
> In its own strength.
>
> (*Don Juan*, XV, 47)

Aurora's eyes are as a 'seraph's', 'all youth' but with an 'aspect beyond time' (XV, 45); she is compared to a 'gem', in the normal poetic tradition of jewels used to connote the spiritual or transcendental, in contrast to nature's 'flower' (XV, 58). She is specifically called by Byron 'Shakespearian' in that

> The worlds beyond this world's perplexing waste
> Had more of her existence, for in her
> There was a depth of feeling to embrace
> Thoughts, boundless, deep, but silent too as Space.
>
> (XVI, 48)

Byron may have been thinking of Cordelia; or of Shakespeare's later heroines. Such, then, are some of Byron's beyond-tempest

statements in terms of spatial art, corresponding to those of Shakespeare's final period.

III

Shakespeare's tragic world throws up lonely protagonists who aim to
master it; such as Brutus, Hamlet, the Duke in *Measure for Measure*,
Lear, Timon and Pericles. These have, as persons, an aura of gener-
alized and philosophic import less evident in Othello, Coriolanus,
Antony and Leontes. Politics and kingship are involved, and in
Pericles we have a neat balance of (i) the tempest-racked king and
(ii) the sage Cerimon, of seemingly miraculous powers, who says:

> I hold it ever,
> Virtue and cunning were endowments greater
> Than nobleness and riches; careless heirs
> May the two latter darken and expend,
> But immortality attends the former,
> Making a man a god.
>
> *(Pericles*, III, ii, 26)

What we want is a man who combines both worldly place, or
power, and saintly or philosophic wisdom; Pericles and Cerimon in
one. That is what Shakespeare attempts in Prospero. Prospero had
been formerly ruler of Milan and returns to his ducal office at the
conclusion: in the interim he is a magician, on an island.

In writing of Prospero I have said (*The Crown of Life*, 232) that
he appears to be 'all mind'. At Milan he had neglected state affairs
for the 'liberal arts' and for 'the bettering of my mind' (I, ii, 73, 90),
and after his 'cloud-capp'd towers' visionary speech takes a 'turn or
two' to 'still my beating mind' (IV, i, 163). In Prospero mind-power
has been developed to an extreme. It touches, even commands, the
spirit-world. Ariel, told to 'come with a thought', answers 'thy
thoughts I cleave to' (IV, i, 164–5). Now Byron too, as we have seen
(p. 277), concentrates on 'mind'. Writing of his vast, expanding,
tree in *Childe Harold*, he stated that 'the mind may grow the same'
(IV, 20; p. 220 above); and his Prometheus' aim was to 'strengthen
Man with his own mind' (p. 226).

Byron's intense activities in the objective world must not be allowed to obscure his even more intense inwardness and soul-concentration. 'His life', writes Moore, was 'one continued struggle' between external engagements and 'that instinct of genius, which was forever drawing him back into the lonely laboratory of Self'; his imagination conjured up pictures in comparison with which all else was 'cold and colourless'. So

> From the moment of this initiation into the wonders of his own mind, a distaste for the realities of life began to grow upon him.
> (Moore, I, 592–3 or XXIII, 269)

Byron with his starvation diet and mental concentration had much in common with the mystics of the east. Parry writes:

> He was more a mental being, if I may use this phrase, than any man I ever saw. He lived on thought more than on food.
> (Parry, V, 107)

Even so, Byron did not remain content with his own mental riches but was always using them for others. Manfred had devoted himself to 'philosophy' and 'science' and all 'the wisdom of the world' till his 'mind' had the 'power' to rule them as subjects (I, i, 13–16), but his instincts were also social and political:

> I have had those early visions,
> And noble aspirations in my youth,
> To make my own the mind of other men,
> The enlightener of nations.
> (III, i, 104)

Like Dante he would 'be the new Prometheus to new men' (*The Prophecy of Dante*, IV). But the will had been frustrated.

The correspondence with Prospero is interesting. Prospero's dukedom was pre-eminent in repute 'through all the signories', and 'in dignity and for the liberal arts without a parallel'; Prospero himself being, like Manfred, rapt in 'secret studies', and to this extent 'neglecting worldly ends'. So, while remaining 'all dedicated to closeness and the bettering of my mind', he had left his brother to govern (I, ii, 70–7; 89–90). But Prospero was at this period no anti-social recluse, no Timon. The lines suggest that as a Renaissance prince, his very inwardness held a social potential, and he was in fact maintaining a state of progressive and expanding importance. His brother's treachery followed.

Prospero's rejection was like Byron's in so far as its agents were simultaneously personal and communal, Prospero's 'that a brother should be so perfidious' (1, ii, 67) matching Byron's thought that he could have endured his rejection had it been activated by one 'less near' (*Childe Harold,* IV, 132). We can say that Hamlet, Duke Vincentio in *Measure for Measure,* Timon and Prospero, all variously willing to inject wisdom into society and state affairs, suffer from having instincts beyond their respective communities. And that was precisely Byron's position. Such men are naturally rejected, and the lonely hero must then retire to solitude, companioned by beasts and the elements.

Timon went to his sea-shore grave and Prospero to an island. Prospero develops the poetic radiations of Timon into a controlled magic which may also be regarded as a continuation and expansion of his earlier Renaissance studies. For these advances an island, being solitary and surrounded by the elements, is a perfect retreat; and Byron-as-Prospero himself thought of giving himself up to study on an island. In 1812 he planned to 'leave England for ever' and settle on a Grecian island;

> Neither my habits nor constitution are improved by your customs or your climate. I shall find employment by making myself a good Oriental scholar. I shall retain a mansion in one of the fairest islands, and retrace, at intervals, the most interesting portions of the East.
>
> (Hodgson, 16 Feb. 1812; LJ, II, 100)

Again, only the sale of Newstead has prevented him 'from being long ago in my isles of the East' (Lady Melbourne, 10 Jan, 1814; C, 1, 226). In writing of tempests we found some vivid touches of Byron-as-Lear. Like Byron, Lear and Prospero are both tempest dominators, one dramatically and the other in fact; and both are old. In an interesting passage concerned both with his island and his advancing years Byron naturally quotes from *King Lear*:

> Heigho! I would I were in mine island:—I am not well; and yet I look in good health. At times, I fear, 'I am not in my

perfect mind';—and yet my heart and head have stood many a crash, and what should ail them now? They prey upon themselves, and I am sick—sick—'Prithee, undo this button—why should a cat, a rat, a dog have life—and *thou* no life at all'? Six and twenty years, as they call them, why, I might and should have been a Pasha by this time. 'I 'gin to be a-weary of the sun'.

> (Journal, 27 Feb. 1814; LJ, II, 390; *King Lear*, IV, vii, 63; V, iii, 308–11; *Macbeth*, V, v, 49)

The island where he 'should have been a Pasha' is felt as a haven of peace in relation to the *King Lear* and *Macbeth* agonies: the relation to Prospero's tempest-controlling and death-negating powers when on his island is clear. Lear and Prospero were, it is true, older than Byron; but then Byron is here already in 1814 regarding himself as old, and the tendency grew upon him. His self-reflection in *Childe Harold* was one

> grown aged in this world of woe,
> In deeds, not years, piercing the depths of life.
> (*Childe Harold*, III, 5)

Manfred was 'grey-haired with anguish' (I, ii, 66). In his *Thirty-Sixth Year* Byron's 'days are in the yellow leaf', thinking of *Macbeth* (V, iii, 23); his letters provide other examples. After his death the doctors discovered a remarkable indication of old age, Dr. Bruno's report of the post-mortem examination noting that 'the bones of the head were found extremely hard, exhibiting no appearance of suture, like the cranium of an octogenarian' (quoted Gamba, VI, 271, note).

After Byron left England in 1816 he settled in Venice, which he called 'next to the East' the 'greenest island of my imagination' (Moore, 17 Nov. 1816; LJ, V, 7). Venice held for him a magic born of poetry:

> I lov'd her from my boyhood; she to me
> Was as a fairy city of the heart,
> Rising like water-columns from the sea,
> Of joy the sojourn, and of wealth the mart;
> And Otway, Radcliffe, Schiller, Shakespeare's art
> Had stamp'd her image in me . . .
> (*Childe Harold*, IV, 18)

The magic was simultaneously a poetic magic and a sea magic. A similar intuition made Shakespeare put his magician, who is also a personification of both poetry and magic—perhaps we could call it 'poetic magic'—on an island.

Sometimes Byron quotes *The Tempest*. Apropos of Moore's government post in Bermuda he refers to a deputy's embezzlement of money as gathering 'dew from the still *vext* Bermoothes' (Moore, 19 Sept. 1818; and see 14 Dec. 1814; LJ, IV, 258; III, 163; *The Tempest*, I, ii, 228–9). If money is lost in Government funds this 'will not only be like the loss of Trinculo's bottle "disgrace and dishonour, but an infinite loss"' (Kinnaird, 18 Sept. 1822; C, II, 230; *The Tempest*, IV, i, 210–11). That *The Tempest* really was in Byron's mind when he thought of his island seems clear from Trelawny's record of a remark of his in Ithaca:

> You will find nothing in Greece or its islands so pleasant as this. If this isle were mine, 'I would break my staff and bury my book'. What fools we all are!
> (Trelawny, XIX, 189; *The Tempest*, V, i, 54–7; for 'what fools', *A Midsummer Night's Dream*, III, ii, 115)

The Juan and Haidée romance was set on an island, and its idyllic quality following sea-tempest corresponds very exactly to Ariel's 'Come unto these yellow sands' and its thought of stilling the 'wild waves' with kisses (*The Tempest*, I, ii, 375). One of Byron's most famous lyrics equates islands with love and poetry:

> The Isles of Greece, the Isles of Greece!
> Where burning Sappho lov'd and sung . . .
> (*Don Juan*, III, 86)

Both Shakespeare and Byron responded to the magic of islands. They are magical because they are surrounded by the lighter yet alien element of water. In *The Tempest* Shakespeare imagines the sea-depths as a wonderland of new dimension where, fathom-deep, dead 'bones' become 'coral', and where there is nothing that 'doth fade' but undergoes a transformation 'into something rich and strange' (I, ii, 394–9). In 1823 Byron published his Melvillian—I am thinking of *Typee*—poem, *The Island*, of the young lovers,

Torquil and Neuha (pp. 256-7, 263), islanded in idyllic seas, where,

> . . . every flower was bloom, and air was balm,
> And the first breath began to stir the palm . . .
>
> (II, 6)

The lovers are sea-adepts, and when Torquil is in danger they escape by plunging deep, like a 'corpse-light' leaving a grave (IV, 4), and reach a mysterious submarine cavern, a 'Chapel of the Seas' where love may rule 'though buried strong as in the grave' (IV, 7, 9): the descriptions are heavily loaded with 'supernatural (IV, 4) sug- gestion and the word 'eternity' recurs. To both Shakespeare and Byron—we may recall Clarence's dream in *Richard III* (I, iv, 2-63) —the ocean depths hinted marvels—as again in *Cain*—beyond mortality.

Byron based *The Island* in part on *An Account of the Natives of the Tonga Islands* by William Mariner (ed. John Martin, 1817). In his Introduction to *The Island* Hartley Coleridge notes:

> According to George Clinton (*Life and Writings of Lord Byron*, 1824, p. 656), Byron was profoundly impressed by Mariner's report of the scenery and folklore of the *Friendly Islands*, was 'never tired of talking of it to his friends', and, in order to turn this poetic material to account, finally bethought him that Bligh's *Narrative* of the mutiny of the *Bounty* would serve as a framework or structure 'for an embroidery of rare device'—the figures and foliage of a tropical pattern.
>
> (P, v, 581)

So too Shakespeare seems to have been imaginatively drawn by stories of southern sea-adventures to create *The Tempest*.

Prospero's island-life is a culmination of the return to nature dramatized earlier in *The Two Gentlemen of Verona, As You Like It, King Lear, Timon of Athens* and Belarius and the royal boys in *Cymbeline*. In such stories animals are likely to be involved, directly or indirectly. We have already, when writing of *Timon of Athens*, noticed the part they played for Byron, from youth on. In a Timon- like letter to Augusta of 9 September 1811 he describes his hermit's life at Newstead, saying that he likes no one since the death of the

Newfoundland Boatswain but his Dutch mastiff and Greek tortoises (LJ, II, 30–1). In Italy, after his rejection, his extraordinary menagerie of animals and birds meant much to him; a similar instinct perhaps made Shakespeare bring a bear on to the stage in *The Winter's Tale*; and beasts are even more important in *The Tempest* than in *Timon of Athens*. Prospero's island has many life-forms from animals to spirits, and there are spirits 'in shape of hounds' (IV, i, 257; direction). Animals and spirits are personified in Caliban and Ariel; the one a gorilla-reptile, half-man half-beast, and close to earth and all its earthy creatures (II, ii, 9–13; 180–5; IV, i, 194–5); and the other a nature-sprite, called a 'bird' and singing of bees, birds and bats (IV, i, 184; V, i, 316; 88–91). They have other connotations, corresponding roughly to (i) earth and water and (ii) air and fire; or to (i) flesh and (ii) spirit (*The Crown of Life*, 232–5).

They are, to this extent, symbolical; and it may be observed that in Timon's list of beasts in conversation with Apemantus (IV, iii, 329–51) the animals are as much emblematical as naturalistic. The best summing-up of the function of elemental beings in respect to a hermit-existence in Shakespeare and Byron—and Defoe too, for Robinson Crusoe is another—is given in Nietzsche's 'The Song of Melancholy' in *Thus Spake Zarathustra*:

> As Zarathustra thus discoursed he stood nigh unto the entrance of his cave; but with the final words he slipped away from his guests and fled for a brief while into the open air.
>
> O clean odours around me! he cried. O blessed stillness around me! But where are my beasts? Draw nigh, mine Eagle and my Serpent!
>
> Tell me, my beasts—all these Higher Men, *smell* they, perchance, not sweet? O clean odours around me! Now only do I know and feel how I love you, my beasts!
>
> (*Thus Spake Zarathustra*, Everyman translation, 74; or IV, 14)

We remember *Gulliver's Travels* (p. 222 above). This is exactly how Byron regarded *his* beasts when in a Timon mood. Zarathustra's Eagle and Serpent correspond—though inexactly—to Ariel and Caliban as spiritual and sexual principles. More generally, Caliban and Ariel symbolize the diverse strains evident in Byron and Shake-

294

speare ranging from animality to the seraphic. The first, as we found in writing of Falstaff, blends naturally with comedy, and that is why Caliban has comic associates in Stephano and Trinculo. As for Ariel, we may remember Byron's identifications of himself with lightning (pp. 273, 279). We might suggest that he found in Shelley a peculiarly Ariel-like companion.

Prospero admits that Caliban is part of himself: 'This thing of darkness I acknowledge mine' (v, i, 275). But he sternly controls both Ariel and Caliban, like the Soul as Charioteer in Plato's *Phaedrus* controlling his two horses docile and fierce. It is exactly this control of diverse instincts and elements for which Manfred is labouring:

> It is an awful chaos—light and darkness—
> And mind and dust—and passions and pure thoughts
> Mix'd, and contending without end or order.
>
> (III, i, 164)

Byron himself retained a remarkable control of his varied selves, never finally subdued to any, and riding them as a ship in storm; his greater self maintaining an assurance as firm as Prospero's.

Besides Ariel and Caliban, both of whom may be regarded as aspects of the human soul, Prospero, signifying the controlling mind, or judgment, has also Miranda; and this having-of-a-daughter is important. Many ageing dramatic persons in Shakespeare have daughters. We remember Capulet, Shylock and Polonius, all regarded as old, yet with very young daughters, over whom they tyrannize. In Lear and Cordelia the relationship begins to assume a semi-philosophic importance; and this importance is mystically developed in Pericles and Marina, and given final shape in Prospero and Miranda. The archetype in Greek drama is Oedipus, in the *Oedipus Coloneus* a mystical Lear-like figure guided by his daughter Antigone, and bound for a wondrous and blessed death, or rather ascension. What is our meaning? Clearly, somewhere within the ambit of the word 'creativity'. The daughter is in the human, earthly-creative order; related to, yet not coloured by, the sexual principle; and suffused with a love drawing towards mysticism, as in Lear's reunion with Cordelia and Pericles' with Marina. The distilled

295

essence of this particular intuition is captured by T. S. Eliot's poem *Marina*.

So much granted, what of Byron? Juan's rescuing of Leila (*Don Juan*, VIII, 99–100) and his own similar care for the little Turkish girl Hato witness his love for girl-children (see LBCV, 75–78). To his illegitimate child Allegra he was devoted and acted as he thought right, though she died (LBCV, 78–80). His daughter by Lady Byron he loved deeply and his last words were of her (LBCV, 80–1). He addressed her in these lines:

> My daughter! with thy name this song begun;
> My daughter! with thy name thus much shall end;
> I see thee not, I hear thee not, but none
> Can be so wrapt in thee; thou art the friend
> To whom the shadows of far years extend:
> Albeit my brow thou never shouldst behold,
> My voice shall with thy future visions blend,
> And reach into thy heart, when mine is cold,
> A token and a tone even from thy father's mould.
>
> (*Childe Harold*, III, 115)

His daughter is, like Pericles', and perhaps Prospero's, to be felt as a visionary being; one of 'far years' and futurity; and in these dimensions one with his own poetry. Since the spirit-word 'tone' recurs, Byron may be thinking of his spirit-self speaking beyond death. He is certainly thinking too of his poetry; but when he prophecies in his Promethean stanzas of Canto IV that 'something unearthly' in him will speak to future generations 'like the remember'd tone of a mute lyre', awaking love (*Childe Harold*, IV, 137), there is, as the word 'unearthly' implies, more than that.

Prospero controls spirits, of which Ariel is only one, though the only one dramatically developed. References to them are continual (I, ii, 193, 'quality'; 326, 'urchins'; 406–8; II, ii, 3, 68; III, ii, 105; iii, 17, direction, 'shapes'; IV, i, 149; 257, direction; 261, 'goblins'). How is his magic to be placed in regard to contemporary Elizabethan and Jacobean beliefs? In *Hamlet* and *Macbeth* the supernatural is dark, fearsome, and related to evil; and so it is in Marlowe's *Doctor Faustus* at the start of the Faust tradition, as black magic. But in *The Winter's Tale* Paulina explicitly distinguishes Hermione's

296

apparent resurrection from 'wicked powers' (v, iii, 91); it is to be related rather to art, to the 'eternity'-imitating skill of 'that rare Italian master, Julio Romano' (v, ii, 108–9; *The Crown of Life*, 118, 120–5). Prospero's magic, descending from the 'liberal arts' for which his dukedom was famous (I, ii, 73), is of similar, Renaissance, quality. In *English Literature in the Sixteenth Century* C. S. Lewis has drawn attention to the belief held by the Florentine Platonists in descent from ancient wisdom that beneficent spirits could be contacted direct, without the mediumship of the Church (see *The Golden Labyrinth*, 43–4); and he considers that *The Tempest* would have been so received; received, that is, in terms of what was later called 'white magic' and would today be called 'spiritualism'.

Shakespeare's magician symbolizes the Renaissance, not perhaps as we know it but as future ages will know it when its creative adventure has been consummated. He is, as I have elsewhere argued (*The Crown of Life*, 242–4), Renaissance art, occultism and science in one. He has spirits at his command; he dominates nature, making tempests and earthquakes at will; and he can raise the dead:

> Graves at my command
> Have wak'd their sleepers, op'd, and let 'em forth
> By my so potent art.
>
> (v, i, 48)

What conceivable realism is there in all this? Well, science itself is moving from wonder to wonder; and since the birth of organized spiritualism in the last century many of the more miraculous happenings in the Bible and literature take on new colourings and a new realism.[1] That Prospero's powers can hold a meaning for us may be seen from the way Bernard Shaw's most carefully developed personage, Captain Shotover in *Heartbreak House*, aims to control others, not by weapons but by mind and magnetism, just as Prospero controls his enemies (*The Golden Labyrinth*, 348; *The Tempest*, I, ii, 461–90; v, i; 60–1); and also by the life and work of John Cowper Powys, whose life-dream was to be a magician and who showed, as

---

1. Probably the best full account of Spiritualism and its relation both to the Bible and the modern world is the Rev. Charles L. Tweedale's *Man's Survival after Death* (1909; expanded 1925; I am thinking of the expanded edition).

I have explained in *The Saturnian Quest* (62, 83, 128), many of Prospero's qualities and even powers.[1]

To turn to Byron. Our key is *Manfred*, wherein he first developed his more occult speculations. Byron had for long, as we have seen (pp. 75–87), been obsessed with death, graves and ghosts. So was Manfred. Here he is, speaking to the Witch, or Spirit, of the Alps:

> And then I div'd,
> In my lone wanderings, to the caves of Death,
> Searching its cause in its effect; and drew
> From wither'd bones, and skulls, and heap'd up dust,
> Conclusions most forbidden. Then I pass'd
> The nights of years in sciences untaught,
> Save in the old-time; and with time and toil,
> And terrible ordeal, and such penance
> As in itself hath power upon the air,
> And spirits that do compass air and earth,
> Space, and the peopled infinite, I made
> Mine eyes familiar with Eternity,
> Such as, before me, did the Magi, and
> He who from out their fountain-dwellings rais'd
> Eros and Anteros, at Gadara,
> As I do thee;—and with my knowledge grew
> The thirst of knowledge, and the power and joy
> Of this most bright intelligence . . .
>
> (ii, ii, 79)

Manfred had, as we have seen (p. 289), studied normal science; but he is also a seer of comprehensive knowledge, using arts—like the Renaissance Platonists—known to the ancient world, but temporarily obscured and forgotten. He is a Faust-figure whose magic is felt as justified. He is called a 'Magian' who aims to 'pervade the world invisible' (iii, iv, 105–6). The 'magi' were Persian seers; the surrounding mythology of *Manfred*, with Arimanes (Ahriman) as a

---

1. Prospero's control of nature has a parallel in a suggestion occurring in a work of some authority that the psychic powers of a perfect 'master' such as those claimed in the New Testament should indeed be able to 'dominate nature' and control the winds as did Christ (Geraldine Cummins, *Beyond Human Personality*, writings purporting to be from F. W. H. Myers; edn. of 1952; 181). Compare Byron's statement on the powers of mind quoted on p. 304 below.

minor, more or less evil, deity, is Zoroastrian; and probably Byron's use of this mythology prompted Nietzsche's use of Zarathustra (Zoroaster).

Byron, like both Macbeth in the Cauldron scene and Prospero, and Powys too (*The Saturnian Quest*, 62), *commands* his drama's various spirits and even refuses to kneel to the dark and dangerous deity Arimanes. His humanity, like Prospero's, dominates.

The Cauldron scene in *Macbeth* is a dramatic exploitation of the spiritualistic fact that spirits may be, with a medium's help, contacted, as when Samuel is brought by the Witch of Endor in the Old Testament. Such activities may often be darkly toned; and in spiritualism, as in other matters, Manfred is set half-way between the dark and the light. He asks the Witch of the Alps to use her 'power' to wake the dead. She cannot, but promises all possible help provided that he will 'swear obedience' to her (II, ii, 150–6). Scorning to be the 'slave' of one whom he can 'command' (II, ii, 159), he determines to use other powers:

> I have one resource
> Still in my science—I can call the dead,
> And ask them what it is we dread to be,
> The sternest answer can but be the Grave,
> And that is nothing. If they answer not—
> The buried Prophet answered to the Hag
> Of Endor; and the Spartan monarch drew
> From the Byzantine maid's unsleeping spirit
> An answer and his destiny . . .
>
> (II, ii, 176)

Manfred solicits the aid of Arimanes, and Astarte, said rather enigmatically to be 'one without a tomb' (II, iv, 82), is called up. The phantom rises.[1]

We also have an Abbot who sternly disapproves:

> 'Tis said thou holdest converse with the things
> Which are forbidden to the search of man;

1. Astarte is, in so far as we seek a biographical reference, to be regarded as a comprehensive symbol of Byron's loves: see LBM, 128. The term 'one without a tomb' recalls the opening of *To Thyrza*: 'Without a stone to mark the spot'. Since the *Thyrza* poems are almost certainly about the chorister John Edleston, Manfred's 'the voice which was my music' (II, iv, 134) may have a similar reference.

That with the dwellers of the dark abodes,
The many evil and unheavenly spirits
Which walk the valley of the Shade of Death,
Thou communest.

(III, i, 34)

The charge is usual enough: the powers of Prospero could be regarded as demoniac. To Antonio's 'The Devil speaks in him'
Prospero's abrupt 'No!' (v, i, 129) marks simultaneously annoyance
and an explosive reserve that speaks volumes. For a more extended
defence against a similar charge we may turn to that of Joan of Arc
in the First Part of *Henry VI*:

First, let me tell you whom you have condemn'd:
Not me begotten of a shepherd swain,
But issu'd from the progeny of kings;
Virtuous and holy; chosen from above,
By inspiration of celestial grace,
To work exceeding miracles on earth.
I never had to do with wicked spirits:
But you—that are polluted with your lusts,
Stain'd with the guiltless blood of innocents,
Corrupt and tainted with a thousand vices—
Because you want the grace that others have,
Ye judge it straight a thing impossible
To compass wonders but by help of devils.

(v, iv, 36)

It is an old story; as old at least as the New Testament, wherein we
hear that Christ was charged by the authorities of his day with the
use of demoniac powers (Matthew XII, 24; Mark III, 22; Luke XI,
15). The battle has to be fought again and again. Manfred is fighting
it. He addresses the Devils who claim his soul:

I do not combat against Death, but thee
And thy surrounding angels; my past power
Was purchas'd by no compact with thy crew,
But by superior science—penance, daring,
And length of watching, strength of mind, and skill
In knowledge of our Fathers—when the earth

Saw men and spirits walking side by side,
And gave ye no supremacy: I stand
Upon my strength—I do defy—deny—
Spurn back, and scorn ye!

(III, iv, 112)

The speaker might be Rudolf Steiner, or a modern Spiritualist.

As for the evil in Manfred, that will be answered not by Hell, but by his *own* self-condemnation:

The Mind which is immortal makes itself
Requital for its good or evil thoughts—
Is its own origin of ill and end,
And its own place and time: its innate sense,
When stripp'd of this mortality, derives
No colour from the fleeting things without,
But is absorb'd in sufferance or in joy,
Born from the knowledge of its own desert.

(III, iv, 129)

This is the teaching implied by Shakespearian tragedy, wherein salvation comes not from repentance but simply from self-recognition (*The Sovereign Flower*; 249); it is also the teaching of spirit-communications today. Manfred is shown as on the brink of some high, Prospero-like achievement. As we have seen (p. 217), he is of no common order; he is searching beyond the Tree of Knowledge to the Tree of Life (I, i, 12), 'the golden secret' (III, i, 13). Like Cerimon he is all but a man-god (*Pericles*, III, ii, 31; p. 288).

Manfred, on 'the power of Thought, the magic of the Mind' (*The Corsair*, I, 8), condenses Shakespearian drama, political, amatory and spiritualistic, from *Hamlet* to *The Tempest*.

IV

Byron's thought dwells again and again (e.g. Blessington, VII, 165; XIII, 307–8) on a future life. In the early *Childe Harold*, though the stanza's first version was less assured (P, II, 103–5, note), we have

Yet if, as holiest men have deem'd, there be
A land of Souls beyond that sable shore,
To shame the doctrine of the Sadducee
And sophists, madly vain of dubious lore;

How sweet it were in concert to adore
With those who made our mortal labours light!
To hear each voice we fear'd to hear no more!
Behold each mighty shade reveal'd to sight,
The Bactrian, Samian sage, and all who taught the right!
(II, 8)

He continues, with thought of Edleston:

There, Thou!—whose love and life together fled,
Have left me here to love and live in vain—
Twin'd with my heart, and can I deem thee dead
When busy memory flashes on my brain?
Well—I will dream that we may meet again,
And woo the vision to my vacant breast:
If aught of young remembrance then remain,
Be as it may futurity's behest,
For me 'twere bliss enough to know thy spirit blest!
(II, 9)

In the two later Cantos the enquiry is loaded with darker emotions
and more complex thinking. In the third, expectance is vivid:

And when, at length, the mind shall be all free
From what it hates in this degraded form,
Reft of its carnal life, save what shall be
Existent happier in the fly and worm—
When elements to elements conform,
And dust is as it should be, shall I not
Feel all I see, less dazzling, but more warm?
The bodiless thought? the Spirit of each spot?
Of which, even now, I share at times the immortal lot?
(III, 74)

In the Fourth Canto, a darker analysis on the fading of his fictional
hero, Harold, develops into a general survey of man's mortality built
very obviously on Prospero's 'cloud-capp'd towers' speech. Destiny
is seen as 'Destruction', a vast cosmic principle creating life-forms
and dissolving them into ghosts. It

gathers shadow, substance, life, and all
That we inherit in its mortal shroud,

And spreads the dim and universal pall
Through which all things grow phantoms . . .

(IV, 165)

We attempt to penetrate what we shall be 'when the frame shall be resolved to something less than this, its wretched essence'; but even if 'less', we shall, he says, be *different*, and without 'these fardels of the heart'. Shakespearian references cluster: 'inherit' from 'all which it inherit' in *The Tempest* (IV, i, 154); 'essence' from man's 'glassy essence' in *Measure for Measure* (II, ii, 120); and 'fardels' from *Hamlet* (III, i, 76). The passage expands the negative element in Prospero's 'cloud-capp'd towers' speech (IV, i, 148–58), which is nevertheless, at least in terms of Indian philosophy, far from negative.[1]

Even here Byron expects survival. The ghost incident of *Don Juan* is preluded by an explicit acceptance. His 'belief' is 'serious', being based on personal experience (xv, 95):

I said it was a story of a ghost—
What then? I only know it so befell.
Have you explor'd the limits of the coast
Where all the dwellers of the earth must dwell?

(XVI, 4)

His most explicit prose comment occurs in his 1821 *Detached Thoughts* (96–101; LJ, v, 456–9):

Of the Immortality of the Soul, it appears to me that there can be little doubt, if we attend for a moment to the action of Mind. It is in perpetual activity. I used to doubt of it, but reflection has taught me better. It acts also so very independent of body: in dreams for instance incoherently and madly, I grant you: but still it is *Mind*, and much more *Mind* than when we are awake. Now, that *this* should not act *separately*, as well as jointly, who can pronounce? The Stoics, Epictetus and Marcus Aurelius, call the present state 'a Soul which drags a Carcase': a heavy chain, to be sure; but all chains, being material, may be shaken off.

How far our future life will be individual, or, rather, how far it will at all resemble our *present* existence, is another question;

1. Compare my remarks and note on 'Nirvana', p. 222–3 above.

but that the *Mind* is *eternal*, seems as probable as that the body is
not so. Of course, I have ventured upon the question without
recurring to Revelation, which, however, is at least as rational a
solution of it as any other.

A 'material resurrection' with hell-torments he rejects as immoral
and irrational, and continues:

Man is born *passionate* of body, but with an innate though
secret tendency to the love of Good in his Mainspring of Mind.
But God help us all! It is at present a sad jar of atoms!
Matter is eternal, always changing, but reproduced, and, as
far as we can comprehend Eternity, Eternal; and why not *Mind?*
Why should not the Mind act with and upon the Universe? as
portions of it act upon and with the congregated dust called
Mankind? See, how one man acts upon himself and others, or
upon multitudes? The same Agency, in a higher and purer
degree, may act upon the Stars, etc., ad infinitum.

That is, if my mind can activate my finger, mind may also be
acting upon the external cosmos. In one of Powys's finest metaphysical statements human wills are said to be co-creators in the
universal scheme (*The Saturnian Quest*, 98). Byron's words may hold
the further suggestion that the human mind itself might, by what is
today known as 'telekinesis', act directly upon external matter.[1] As
we have seen (p. 298), Manfred had 'power upon the air'. Byron's
thought of some great and pure 'Agency' acting as Mind upon the
elements may have been drawn from *The Tempest*, for such precisely
was Prospero's art, his link or medium being 'spirits', under the
command of his mind,

by whose aid—
Weak masters though ye be—I have bedimm'd
The noontide sun, call'd forth the mutinous winds,
And 'twixt the green sea and the azur'd vault
Set roaring war: to the dread-rattling thunder
Have I given fire, and rifted Jove's stout oak

1. Compare the contention of J. Gaither Pratt in *Parapsychology, etc.* (p. 277
above, note) that, to quote from the review in *T.L.S.*, 28 January 1965 (71), 'mind' is
sometimes capable of 'acting on the material world without the mediation of the
senses'.

With his own bolt: the strong-bas'd promontory
Have I made shake, and by the spurs pluck'd up
The pine and cedar. Graves at my command
Have wak'd their sleepers, op'd, and let them forth
By my so potent art.

(v, i, 40)

What Shakespeare's furthest flight of poetic imagination surveys as humanly conceivable, Byron's considered prose ratifies. The New Testament provides obvious analogies.

Byron rejects Priestley's 'Christian Materialism', remarking:

Believe the resurrection of the body, if you will, but *not without* a *Soul*. The devil's in it, if, after having had a Soul (as surely the *Mind*, or whatever you call it, *is*) in this world, we must part with it in the next, even for an Immortal Materiality. I own my partiality for *Spirit*.

He records that he feels 'most religious upon a sun-shiny day', as if there was 'some association between an internal approach to greater light and purity, and the kindler of this dark lanthorn of our external existence'; but the viewing of moon and stars through a telescope affects him too (LJ, v, 458).

He proceeds to speculate on the origins of creation, wondering if troubled Mankind is the relic of some higher, once 'wrecked', order of pre-Adamite creation; and of these there must have been a Creator 'for a *Creator* is a more natural imagination than a fortuitous concourse of atoms'. He concludes with an enigmatic image blending height and expanse (see p. 271 above): 'All things remount to a fountain, though they may flow to an Ocean.' I take it that the re-mounting is subsequent to the 'flow'. Man has been 'wrecked'; but that is not the end (LJ, v, 459).

We are now in the world of *Cain* (1821), which introduces us to this pre-Adamite creation. Here the key problem is throughout Death (pp. 81, 84); the death incurred by man for disobedience to God's arbitrary will. *Cain* is a natural successor to *Manfred*. In *Manfred* we have a fusion of the Prometheus, Faust, and Don Juan myths; and, as we have seen, it poses the main questions aroused by occult and spiritualistic engagements, from ancient times to our own day. Now there is one great mythology being neglected: the official mythology of the western world, housed in the Bible. The Old Testament was Byron's treasured reading; and his strong sense of the immediate and the actual did not allow him to remain content with literary and pagan myths, however authoritative. For better or worse, the Bible *is* our main mythology. He accordingly entwines his adventuring speculations with the story of Cain.

He does not write as an orthodox devotee, but he does write with full respect for the myth. Here we shall be concerned mainly with his own additions, centring on Lucifer. Lucifer is conceived as God's antagonist, but not as the tempter of Eve, which both Byron and his Lucifer insist was simply, as *Genesis* itself tells us, 'the serpent' (Preface; I, i, 218–33; and see P, v, 208, note). Lucifer—the name means 'Light-bringer'—represents the light of reason—the 'most bright intelligence' of *Manfred* (p. 298)—from the Renaissance onwards in opposition to past teachings of theological condemnation. He only tempts man, like all science, 'with the truth'; the forbidden tree *was* the 'Tree of Knowledge', and had the choice been his he would have allowed it to make men, as *Genesis* puts it, 'gods' (I, i, 196–205). Thoughts are man's 'immortal part' (I, i, 103), and his advice is that man trust his own 'mind':

> Nothing can
> Quench the mind, if the mind will be itself . . .
>
> (I, i, 213)

Lucifer, who introduces himself as 'Master of spirits' (I, i, 99), may be said to cover the positive aspects of the Faust tradition, the spirit beliefs of Florentine Platonists (p. 297), Prospero's white magic, and the spiritualistic interests and experiences of Defoe, Swedenborg and Blake, leading to the organized spiritualistic movements of the nineteenth and twentieth centuries. But he *also* covers modern science, in the accepted sense. The split of what we know as 'science', previously called 'natural philosophy', from occult investigation has only really come about since the seventeenth century. The researches of Glanvill and also much of seventeenth-century drama, as I have shown in *The Golden Labyrinth*, indicate a strong and often scientific tendency to accept, without theological inhibitions, the spiritualistic knowledge that has existed beneath the surface of culture since history began. But science was quick to assert itself in isolation, and was eventually to prove a stronger antagonist than religion. After the divergence there were, philosophically, two main Renaissance challenges to medievalism: (i) science and (ii) spiritualism. Both are dramatized in *Cain*.

Lucifer takes Cain on a grand tour which has two purposes, corresponding to Science and Spiritualism. He (i) takes him on a space-flight, rather like that in Shelley's *Queen Mab,* to show him the stellar universe, with the earth now as a small circle 'swinging in far ether' (II, i, 29),[1] and the myriads of heavenly bodies magnificent around:

> Oh thou beautiful
> And unimaginable ether! and
> Ye multiplying masses of increas'd
> And still-increasing lights! What are ye? What
> Is this blue wilderness of interminable
> Air, where ye roll along . . .?
>
> (II, i, 98)

Is it, asks Cain, bounded or endlessly expanded? Is it all mortal or immortal? Lucifer replies that it is in part mortal, in part immortal. When asked what he most desires to see, Cain replies 'the mysteries of Death' (II, i, 140). So we next (ii) pass to the world of death, of the occult, of vast pre-Adamite beings, giants and beasts, swimming in a new dimension. Our quests involve (i) space and (ii) time; they also, by juxtaposition, raise the excruciatingly difficult question of the relation of the spiritualistic, etheric, dimension to the infinities of the apparently material universe explored by science. It is enough for our present purpose to note that Byron's imaginative excursion covers these two concerns pressing on us today in (i) space-travel and (ii) contemporary spiritualism. These trace their descent from the discoveries of Copernicus, Galileo and Newton on the one side and the various carriers of spiritualistic knowledge already discussed—to which we should add the name of John Dee—on the other. As for Shakespeare's Prospero, he may

---

1. For an important manuscript variation from the Oxford text in the following line (30), see P, V, 234, and note.

be best regarded as a rough but comprehensive personification of *all* to which Renaissance man is moving. True, he does not himself engage in space-travel, but Ariel does; and Ariel is part of him.

The pre-historic giants and monsters of Byron's Hades exist in a spiritualized medium of what appears liquidity, both size and ocean, the latter Byron's main symbol of eternity in *Childe Harold* (iv, 183), serving to realize Death's majesty and expanding his normal interest in the ancestral and the numinous past so well already summed up in *Manfred* in the lines

> The dead, but sceptred, Sovereigns, who still rule
> Our spirits from their urns
>
> (*Manfred*, iii, iv, 40)

and in the equestrian statue of *Marino Faliero* (iii, i). It is a fearsome experience, without sun or moon:

> The very blue of the empurpled night
> Fades to a dreary twilight—yet I see
> Huge dusky masses . . .
>
> (ii, i, 179)

We are among 'swimming shadows and enormous shapes' (ii, ii, 31). Lucifer, who has already (i, i, 116–20) told Cain that his material covering is not existence, and that he will 'live for ever', being after death 'no less', and perhaps more, than he is at present, now tells Cain who, confronted by Hades, has asked what Death is, that God will perhaps one day reveal that secret; despite all earthly agonies, it may be that 'death leads to the highest knowledge'; and though 'matter' can never 'comprehend spirit wholly', it is yet something to know that 'there are such realms', indeed 'many states', beyond man's experience; and these, though necessarily at present 'dim and shadowy', will yet 'seem clearer to thine immortality' (ii, ii; 35–8, 164–77). We now watch an ocean of 'glorious azure', looking like water and yet of an 'ethereal hue', and like 'a liquid sun' (ii, ii, 178–87). This is what would today be called the 'astral' or 'etheric' dimension, or plane. Note that the shadowed depths are succeeded by an etheral blue-ness.

That the extra-temporal dimension should be watery matches

Shakespeare's intuition of Macbeth's 'bank and shoal of time' where earthly existence is being conceived as an island (I, vii, 6; the reading is generally accepted); Clarence's dream of death housing riches won from life under ocean in *Richard III* (I, iv, 24–33); and, on a more optimistic note, Ariel's

> Nothing of him that doth fade
> But doth suffer a sea-change
> Into something rich and strange . . .
>
> (I, ii, 397)

The suggestions are obvious: the whole action of *The Tempest* shows a wreck and its drowned occupants miraculously saved, their garments even 'fresher than before' and the ship in perfect trim (I, ii, 217–19; V, i, 236–7). Ibsen likewise, in both *The Lady from the Sea* and *Little Eyolf,* uses the sea for an other-dimensional purpose. In *Little Eyolf* the dead boy's open eyes seen through the translucent depths match well the 'rich and strange' intuition of Ariel's song; and in both *Little Eyolf* and *Emperor and Galilean* we find a *transition* from ocean to ethereality similar to that in *Cain* (see my *Ibsen,* 'Writers and Critics' Series, 69–83; 'Sea and Death', 35).

In *Manfred* and *Cain* Byron imagines an advance from the Faust and Biblical traditions to a new order resembling that to which Shakespearian drama also points. We have seen that Manfred's self-reliance, which is simultaneously self-recognition and self-condemnation and self-endurance, corresponds to the implied 'ethic', if ethic it be, of Shakespearian tragedy. Lucifer expresses a similar gospel. External and arbitrary prohibitions do not determine good and evil; the essences in question are far too subtle for such external rulings; and on this issue Lucifer will oppose the God of *Genesis* throughout all eternity (II, ii, 431–58). Therefore Cain must replace 'faith' by 'reason':

> Think and endure—and form an inner world
> In your own bosom—where the outward fails;
> So shall you nearer be the spiritual
> Nature, and war triumphant with your own.
>
> (II, ii, 463)

That Cain becomes a murderer does not discount Lucifer's teaching. The murder is prompted largely by Cain's own gentleness and horror of animal slaughter. The paradox is Byronic: Byron too saw himself as suffering by reason of his goodness of heart; like the hero of his *Prometheus* (p. 226), whose 'Godlike crime was to be kind'.

In covering so much Biblical, occult and scientific material *Cain*, called by Shelley 'a revelation never before communicated to man' (quoted P, V, 204), is a comprehensively modern work. *Manfred* and *Cain* define the evolving Renaissance powers symbolically adumbrated in *The Tempest*. Difficult categories are involved. Prospero was a man-god; Manfred of an 'order' beyond normal man (p. 217); and Lucifer's purpose would have been, and perhaps still is, to have men as gods (I, i, 202). Ibsen, Nietzsche, Shaw and Powys followed on with their related conceptions of the superhuman, or at least of some new and greater human state, with new faculties in play. Whatever all this means, we cannot deny the place held in this development by *The Tempest, Manfred* and *Cain*.

V

But what of Byron as a man? Did he not often write facetiously of both poetry and mysticism? Was he merely playing at magic and prophecy? Were these real constituents of his nature? Can we not here, once again, establish some more direct link with his life?

Obviously, it will not be easy. Any occult or thaumaturgic powers which Byron actually possessed would not normally have been accepted and reported, perhaps least of all by himself. But of his magnetic personality we have evidence enough. Graveyards and skulls fascinated him in youth; he felt the pressure of ghosts (pp. 77, 107, 153). None of this means that he was exceptionally sensitive, but there may have been more, and that 'more' may have had its part in the 1816 terrors.

We have discussed Byron's poetic equation of himself with 'lightning' (p. 273), a trend summed in Manfred's lines to a spirit:

> The Mind—the Spirit—the Promethean spark,
> The lightning of my being, is as bright,
> Pervading and far-darting as your own . . . .
>
> (I, i, 154)

Of such spirit-agility Ariel was a direct personification:

> I come
> To answer thy best pleasure; be't to fly,
> To swim, to dive into the fire, to ride
> On the curl'd clouds: to thy strong bidding task
> Ariel and all his quality.
>
> (I, ii, 189)

The words suggest what in *The Crown of Life* (233) I referred to as Ariel's 'electric, ubiquitous presence'. We have also already discussed the thought of astral travelling in both *Childe Harold* and Shakespeare's Sonnets[1] (pp. 39, 54). Of such intuitions the space-flights in *Cain* may be called imaginative extensions:

> Cain: I tread on air, and sink not—yet I fear
>   To sink.
> Lucifer: Have faith in me, and thou shalt be
>   Borne on the air, of which I am the Prince.
>
> (II, i, 1)

Hartley Coleridge compares Ephesians, II, 2: 'According to the prince of the power of the air.' For 'air' we might perhaps better use the time-honoured poetic and esoteric term 'ether'; but whatever the medium, there is a mystery here for all of us. In *The Saturnian Quest* (20) I had occasion to relate Coleridge's claim (in *France: an Ode*) to have 'shot my being through earth, sea and air' to Powys's obsession with the thought of soul-projection or astral travelling. Powys, who may be regarded as a modern Prospero, had, like Shaw's Captain Shotover, strong magnetic and thaumaturgic powers, and on one occasion exercised them in a deliberate act of soul-projection reported by Theodore Dreiser (*The Saturnian Quest*, 128–9, quoting W. E. Woodward, *The Gift of Life*). Powys had told Dreiser that he would appear to him at a certain time, though physically at a distance; and to Dreiser's amazement, he fulfilled his promise. A similar story is told of Byron. Metaphysical and romantic poetry is packed with suggestions of soul-flight, and astral travelling is a well-known phenomenon, especially at the moment of death;

1. For modern introductions to the subject, see below, pp. 313, note, and 316.

but I know of only two great writers of whom an example of soul-projection has been objectively reported: Powys and Byron. Though Byron, so far as we know, offers nothing so deliberated as Powys, he remains the only great writer of whom our records offer anything at all. The account is given by Byron himself in a letter to John Murray of 6 October 1820:

You will have now received all the acts, corrected, of the *MF* [*Marino Faliero*]. What you say of the 'Bet of 100 guineas', made by someone who says that he saw me last week, reminds me of what happened in 1810. You can easily ascertain the fact, and it is an odd one.

In the latter end of 1811, I met one evening at the Alfred my old School and form-fellow (for we were within two of each other—*he* the higher, though both very near the top of our re-move), *Peel,* the Irish Secretary. He told me that, in 1810, he met me, as he thought, in St. James's Street, but we passed with-out speaking. He mentioned this, and it was denied as im-possible, I being then in Turkey. A day or two after, he pointed out to his brother a person on the opposite side of the way; 'There', said he, 'is the man whom I took for Byron': his brother instantly answered, 'Why, it *is* Byron, and no one else.' But this is not all: I was *seen* by somebody to *write down my name* amongst the Enquirers after the King's health, then attacked by insanity. Now, at this very period, as nearly as I could make out, I was ill of a *strong fever* at Patras, caught in the marshes near Olympia, from the *Malaria.* If I had died there, this would have been a new Ghost Story for you. You can easily make out the accuracy of this from Peel himself, who told it in detail. I suppose you will be of the opinion of Lucretius,[1] who (denies the immortality of the Soul, but) asserts that from the 'flying off of the Surfaces of bodies perpetually, these surfaces or cases, like the Coats of an onion, are sometimes seen entire when they are separated from it, so that the shapes and shadows of both the dead and absent are frequently beheld'.

But if they are, are their coats and waistcoats also seen? I do not disbelieve that we may be *two* by some unconscious process, to a certain sign; but which of these two I happen at present to

1. See *De Rerum Natura*, IV, 35 ff.

be, I leave you to decide. I only hope that *t'other me* behaves like a Gemman.

I wish you would get Peel asked how far I am accurate in my recollection of what he told me; for I don't like to say such things without authority.

I am not sure that I was *not spoken* with; but this also you can ascertain. I have written to you such lots that I stop.

(LJ, v, 86)

That is Byron's account.

The story interested Moore who wrote of it in his diary, after consulting Peel himself. The entry appears in the *Memoirs, Journal, and Correspondence of Thomas Moore*, ed. Lord John Russell, 1853, vol. VI, 14, at the date 20 February 1829. Moore records:

The circumstance mentioned by Byron was, that Peel, in the year 1810, I think, had met (as he thought) Lord Byron in the streets of London at a time when the latter was actually lying ill of a fever at Patras. The fact was, Peel said (though he did not like his name to be quoted seriously as an authority for a ghost story), he was really under the impression, and still continued so, that he had not only seen, but talked with Lord Byron at that time.

A fever might facilitate the freedom in question.[1]

Of such a possibility we have direct evidence, from Byron himself. During the attacks leading to his death at Missolonghi he enjoyed supernal intuitions, or experiences. He felt himself, as it were, breaking the limits of his personality into some greater and

---

1. In *The Saturnian Quest* (129, note), when comparing this incident with the account of astral projection in the life of John Cowper Powys, I was unable to trace the Byronic reference, which I wrongly attributed to the period of Byron's last days —when he also had fever and other illnesses—at Missolonghi. I am indebted to Dr. Joseph Wallfield whose aid, in view of his great stores of period learning, I solicited. He replied at once, putting me on the right track.

Dr. Wallfield attributes the incident to 'bi-location' rather than 'astral projection'. For astral projection, see Sylvan J. Muldoon and Hereward Carrington, *The Projection of the Astral Body*, 1929, etc.; Robert Crookall, *The Study and Practice of Astral Projection*, 1961; and Horace Leaf, 'Extrusion of the Psychic Double', *The Spiritualist* (Spiritualist Association of Great Britain, 33 Belgrave Square, London, S.W.1); 1965; III, 5. For bi-location, see Charles Richet, *Thirty Years of Psychical Research*, trans. Stanley De Brath, New York 1923; 552–9. See also the books noted on p. 316.

more comprehensive existence beyond human understanding. Parry
records his words:

> You have no conception of the unaccountable thoughts which
> come into my mind when the fever attacks me. I fancy myself a
> Jew, a Mahommedan, and a Christian of every profession of
> faith. Eternity and space are before me; but on this subject, thank
> God, I am happy and at ease. The thought of living eternally, of
> again reviving, is a great pleasure. Christianity is the purest and
> most liberal religion in the world, but the numerous teachers
> who are continually worrying mankind with their denuncia-
> tions and their doctrines, are the greatest enemies of religion. I
> have read with more attention than half of them the book of
> Christianity, and I admire the liberal and truly charitable
> principles which Christ has laid down. There are questions
> connected with this subject which none but Almighty God can
> solve. Time and space, who can conceive—none but God, on
> him I rely.
>
> (Parry, V, 122)

Byron's chameleon personality in life may here be felt as drawing
towards its proper sphere within the richer dimensions of death.

Byron's many faculties might seem to have included precogni-
tion. Moore reports in his Diary an account given him by John
Cowell, as follows:

> Told me a curious anecdote of Byron's mentioning to him, as if
> it had made a great impression on him, their seeing Shelley (as
> they thought) walking into a little wood at Lerici, when it was
> discovered afterwards that Shelley was at that time in quite
> another direction. 'This', said Byron, in a sort of awestruck
> voice, 'was about ten days before his death' (LJ, II, 98, note;
> quoting Moore's *Memoirs, Journal etc.*, entry for 11 June, 1828).

However, pre-cognition need not have been involved, since the
incident could presumably have been of the same nature as Byron's
appearance to Peel.

We have other evidence that Byron had enjoyed experiences of a
clairvoyant kind to be distinguished from the poetic imagination.

Once in *Childe Harold,* after writing of the immortal qualities of 'the beings of the mind' in poetic fiction, he continues:

> Such is the refuge of our youth and age,
> The first from Hope, the last from Vacancy;
> And this worn feeling peoples many a page,
> And, may be, that which grows beneath mine eye:
> Yet there are things whose strong reality
> Outshines our fairy-land; in shape and hues
> More beautiful than our fantastic sky,
> And the strange constellations which the Muse
> O'er her wild universe is skilful to diffuse:
>
> I saw or dream'd of such—but let them go—
> They came like truth, and disappear'd like dreams;
> And whatsoe'er they were—are now but so:
> I could replace them if I would; still teems
> My mind with many a form which aptly seems
> Such as I sought for, and at moments found;
> Let these too go—for waking Reason deems
> Such overweening phantasies unsound,
> And other voices speak, and other sights surround.
>
> (IV, 6)

This must mean that Byron thinks that he has *seen* ('saw') some unearthly 'reality' distinct from the 'fairy-land' of poetry; and though he could turn his remembrance of these visions too into poetry, yet Reason persuades him that such 'overweening phantasies' may be delusions. He is afraid of *claiming too much.*

We begin to understand what Galt meant when he wrote, 'He was as a mystery in a winding sheet crowned with a halo. The influence of the incomprehensible phantasma which hovered about Lord Byron has been more or less felt by all who ever approached him' (Galt, VIII, 63). We may even begin to understand the appalling thunder-storm that occurred at Byron's death (p. 279). Whatever 'spirit' and 'electricity' may be, we have it on the authority of Byron's poetry that they are close, if not identical. Therefore, since Byron obviously had in him enough spirit-electricity for a number—I refrain from hazarding exactly how many—ordinary men, the sudden

315

releasing, like the unbottling of the djinn in Anstey's famous story, of so much power, might well be supposed to affect the upper atmosphere; as when at the death of Bishop Nicholas in Ibsen's *The Pretenders* (III), 'the powers of evil have broken loose' and demonvoices are heard. We find it easier to imagine such mysteries in terms of evil; but that evil need not be involved we know from Byron's life, and also from the New Testament, where a similar occurrence is recorded.

Additional Note, 1966

During Byron's illness at Patras (p. 312) he 'looked upon death' as a 'relief' and was so 'indifferent' to his 'bodily situation' that he refused assistance (Miss Milbanke, 26 Sept. 1813; LJ, III, 402–3. See also Hodgson, 3 Sept. 1811; LJ, II, 21).

Reviewing an American reissue of Oliver Fox's *Astral Projection* (recent edition, New York, 1965) in *Two Worlds* (Dec. 1965; No. 3863; 427–8) Mr. W. H. Mackintosh writes: 'During full waking consciousness the physical and astral bodies normally coincide, but in dreams and in states of trance and catalepsy there is separation of these bodies. Involuntary projection of the astral body can happen whenever the physical organism is weakened, or its ascendancy over the psyche diminished in any way. It can be caused by illness, shock or exhaustion. It can be induced by drugs or hypnosis'.

Another recent publication to be noted is Susy Smith's *The Enigma of Out-of-Body Travel*, New York, 1965. I should add that Charles Richet's book (p. 313, note) appeared first from Paris as *Traité de métapsychique*, in 1922.

IX

HENRY VIII

I

PROSPERO decides to renounce his 'rough magic', break and bury his magician's 'staff', or wand, and drown his 'book' (v, i, 54–7). He determines to return to Milan and resume his ducal responsibilities. Similarly his creator, Shakespeare, proceeded to compose his last play, *Henry VIII*, returning from the lonely self-sufficient and self-directed quest of the dramas from *Hamlet* to *The Tempest* to a contemporary theme; submitting his genius *for the first time* to the established religion of his day; and for the first time offering explicit honour, in Cranmer's concluding prophecy over the royal child, to the monarchs Elizabeth I and James I under whose reigns he had lived. There is some evidence that he had formerly been less willing to honour the Queen (p. 5), and if so *Henry VIII* reads as an act of self-surmounting and humility. It contains however no philosophizing; there is no obvious propaganda for 'royalism' or 'order'; there is nothing abstract about it. It is written less from the philosophic or imaginative consciousness than from an honesty that faces the near-distance facts of existence, in the author's own place and—roughly—time: an honesty that accepts and respects King and Church, balancing, as I have shown in *The Crown of Life*, their stately rituals; shows a full awareness of the robust King's all-too-human sexual drive in replacing one queen by another; and engages a Falstaffian exuberance in the seething masses of raw humanity that dominate towards the close.

The time comes, when, whatever our personal powers, we do well to focus the context within which they function; to recognize life as it is for each of us, here and now. Under such a recognition the pacifist may realize that he relies on the police, and therefore on the army too; and the militant atheist that he would not decide *today*, were the choice his, for the destruction of all the churches in the world. Personal convictions are maintained: but they are simultaneously recognized as provisional in comparison with the here and now of actual and immediate decision, and of common-sense; all of which *come first*; or, in the life work of a major poet, last.[1] This is why Aeschylus in the *Oresteia* brings his grand cosmic dramaturgy of good and evil to the bar of the Court of the Areopagus in contemporary, or near-contemporary, Athens, with a ritual conclusion bearing directly on the life of the community before which the drama was being performed. Here, as in *Henry VIII*, there is an emphasis on (i) law and (ii) ritual. The first signifies a practical necessity without which neither the boldest thought-adventures nor even the criminal class itself could pursue their vocations steadily. The second is a way of self-surmounting. We all know that society, in every age, is miserably inadequate; but ritual, like good manners, the good manners of Hamlet in his fifth act, being less than fact and more than fiction, assists an imaginative self-adjustment to what is greater than ourselves.

And what, now, of Byron? There are correspondences at every point. No great poet was more willing to 'drown' his 'book': on 6 April 1819 he wrote to Murray that had he 'wanted to book-make' he could have expanded the contents of *Childe Harold* into twenty cantos (LJ, IV, 284). He regularly refused to rate poetry high (LBCV, 103–6). Byron wrote for personal relief; but poetry as poetry he was always ready to scorn, with the exception of Pope's, because that had a more direct bearing on life (*Laureate of Peace*, reissued as *The Poetry of Pope*, p. viii above; 'The Book of Life', 155). As for his more occult poetry, he could write objectively enough of *Manfred*, as in his letter to Murray of 15 February 1817:

Almost all the persons—but two or three—are spirits of the earth and air, or the waters; the scene is in the Alps; the hero a kind of

1. Misunderstanding here is so easy that I may be forgiven a personal reference. Though my own work often constitutes an attack on the tenets of our academic and literary-critical establishments; though I find their unawareness of the occult significances of literature baffling and their tendency to discount my high-lighting of such significances by misconception or silence disturbing; yet I cannot deny that without

magician, who is tormented by a species of remorse, the cause of which is left half unexplained. He wanders about invoking these spirits, which appear to him, and are of no use; he at last goes to the very abode of the Evil principle in *propriâ personâ*, to evocate a ghost, which appears, and gives him an ambiguous and disagreeable answer; and in the third act he is found by his attendants dying in a tower where he studied his art. You may perceive by this outline that I have no great opinion of this piece of phantasy . . .

(LJ, IV, 55)

Later he described it mockingly in his *Epistle from Mr. Murray to Dr. Polidori* (1817):

> There's Byron, too, who once did better,
> Has sent me, folded in a letter,
> A sort of—it's no more a drama
> Than *Darnley*, *Ivan*, or *Kehama*:
> So alter'd since last year his pen is,
> I think he's lost his wits at Venice.
>
> (LJ, IV, 160; P, VII, 48)

At the outcry against *Cain* he claimed, or pretended, that it held no particular argument. He wrote to Murray on 8 February 1822:

If Cain be 'blasphemous', *Paradise Lost* is blasphemous; and the very words of the Oxford Gentleman, 'Evil be thou my Good', are from that very poem, from the mouth of Satan; and is there anything more in that of Lucifer in the Mystery? *Cain* is nothing more than a drama, not a piece of argument: if Lucifer and Cain speak as the first Murderer and the first Rebel may be supposed to speak, surely all the rest of the personages talk also according to their characters—and the stronger passions have ever been permitted on the stage.

(LJ, VI, 15)

---

our educational institutions and literary journals my own books would have had neither publication nor readers. It would therefore be reasonable were I at some subsequent hour to conclude my life-work in praise of both.

That scarcely covers the matter. But Byron was sincere enough in what follows:

> I have even avoided introducing the Deity, as in Scripture (though Milton does, and not very wisely either); but have adopted his Angel as sent to Cain instead, on purpose to avoid shocking any feelings on the subject by falling short of what all uninspired men must fall short in, viz. giving an adequate notion of the effect of the presence of Jehovah. The Old Mysteries introduced him liberally enough, and all this is avoided in the New one.
>
> (LJ, VI, 16)

Byron's reverence for the 'Deity' was throughout his life consistent; but Cain's questioning of his ways, at least as they are reported in scripture and interpreted by orthodoxy, are of the drama's essence. What happens is this: by a typical act of self-surmounting Byron can provisionally develop the Manfred and Lucifer thrusts to the limit whilst simultaneously recognizing that they fall within a human context wherein age-old reverences dominate which are beyond Byron's power or desire to overthrow. As for any dangerous influence, 'Who,' he asks, 'was ever altered by a poem?' (Murray, 3 Nov. 1821; LJ, V, 470). Poetry, he told Gamba, is a pursuit only for the 'idle'; 'in more serious affairs it would be ridiculous' (Gamba, I, 48).

That was, anyway, the mood in which he went to Greece. When shown some Homeric sites in Ithaca he is reported by Trelawny to have remarked that he detested 'antiquarian twaddle' and that he had not come to Greece to 'scribble more nonsense'; he wished that he had never written a line and meant to show the world that he could do 'something better' (Trelawny, XIX, 186). Nor was he prepared to accept the more mystical attributes and radiations of his own personality, and the halo with which he was now in danger of being crowned. His arrival at Missolonghi was as 'the coming of a Messiah', a 'delivering angel' (Stanhope to Bowring, 31 Dec. 1823; LJ, VI, 296, note; Gamba to Teresa, 8 Jan. 1824; Origo, IX, 374). When at a monastery in Cephalonia he had been greeted by the community with the Abbot's words 'Christ has risen to elevate the cross and trample on the crescent in our beloved Greece', together with a ritualistically intoned eulogium on the English lord, while boys swung censers of incense before him, we have our only precise report of the thunderous temper with which he himself and others credited him (Trelawny, XIX, 187–8; Edgcumbe, 61–3; Nicolson, VI, 130–3; LBCV, 276–7). The association with Christ caused him intense suffering. The truth is, Byron was *afraid* of such adulation, since though he knew well enough that there was in him 'something unearthly' (*Childe Harold*, IV, 137), he was loath to lay claim to it. For that matter, in the depths, he knew that he respected poetry, or he would not have written so much of it; and in his poetry he did, directly and indirectly, lay claim to high status; but all this he now —the process is dramatized in *The Deformed Transformed* (p. 156)— rejects, leaving poetry and metaphysics for *action* in the cause of Greece.

In treating of Byron and Hamlet we have shown how Byron on his last adventure corresponds to Hamlet after his return to Denmark. *Hamlet* forecasts Shakespeare's future development; for Hamlet, like the Shakespeare of *Henry VIII*, ends by showing a new and well-mannered, ritualistic, respect for royal authority; and it is paradoxically only when he attains this respect that he is able to kill the king. His own courteous bearing and other ritual touches throughout the play's last act may be said to correspond to the royal rituals of *Henry VIII*. Now in moving from writing to direct action in Greece Byron shows qualities correspondent to Hamlet's final behaviour and Shakespeare's composition of *Henry VIII*.

There is evident in him a newly obvious—it was not really new— humility. This humility had too main aspects, as in *Henry VIII*: (i) religious and (ii) political.

We have already, in writing of *Hamlet*, pointed to Byron's daily conversations on religion with the proselytizing James Kennedy at Cephalonia, at a time when one might have expected him to be concentrating on his political and military plans; and he was, in fact, criticized for his apparent delay. It was as though he were being impelled to a fourth-act, Gethsemane, preparation (p. 113) for his self-sacrifice. The outcome was, as he said, in 'the hands of Providence, as indeed are all things' (p. 113 above); but like Hamlet in his words to Horatio on 'providence' (V, ii, 222–38), or Prospero whose 'every third thought' *after* his return was to be his 'grave' (*The Tempest*, v, i, 311), he expected to die.

These conversations, reported by Kennedy in his book, were undertaken in an earnest mood:

> His patience, however, in listening to me, his candour in never putting captious objections, his acknowledgment of his own sinfulness, gave hope that the blessing of religious truth might be opened to his understanding. . . .   (Kennedy, 321)

He showed, we are told, an 'occasional levity', though not enough to matter; and we may be sure that the merest hint of 'levity' would be enough to worry the anxious Kennedy.

Kennedy's account of the conversations is fascinating. Of it he wrote in a letter to Parry:

> It will prove that his Lordship, if not a *real Christian,* was not a *confirmed infidel;* that he wished to believe in the truth of Christianity if he could; that he was not happy in the unsettled opinions which he had respecting religion; and that latterly he studied the subject more than he was accustomed to do.
> (Parry, IX, 208–9, note)

'Latterly': all our sources suggest that at this last period religion in its accepted sense meant more to Byron than it had done before; or at least that there was more external evidence of his concern. Religious and Christian phrases were more ready in his talk. At Missolonghi he discussed religion with Parry, saying:

> All men believe in the great first cause, which we call Almighty God. Love of life is fear of death, or of annihilation, and therefore we hope to enjoy eternal life. The liberal principles of Christianity, what Christ taught—mind, I say what Christ taught—I have no doubt would be conducive to the happiness of the world; but the system of ramming opinions down our throats does harm to the cause which the fanatical preachers endeavour to support.   (Parry, IX, 208)

This was Byron's attitude always; he believed in the spirit of Christianity and often acted as though deliberately copying Christ's example. But, as his conversations with Kennedy show, he was ill-at-ease with dogma and found a vicarious sacrifice hard to accept.

Of his general religious and Christian qualities we have good accounts in a letter by William Fletcher (Byron's servant) to James Kennedy (19 May 1824; Kennedy 369–75); and in the chapter 'His Religious Opinions' in Teresa Guiccioli's *Recollections*.

Though Byron's approach witnesses no personal submission to orthodoxy, the tone is often now one of an impersonal respect, and even reverence, as though he were accepting the traditional religion as an objective reality independent of personal viewpoints. He could, quite dispassionately, see the Greek campaign as a crusade. According to Gamba he defined the conflict as one 'between barbarism and civilization' or 'Islamism' and 'Christianity' (Gamba, v, 210; and see Parry, VIII, 170, 'Christians contending against Turks'). He would have Greece 'enter into all her rights, as a member of the great commonwealth of Christian Europe' (Parry, VIII, 185). The campaign had in everyone's eyes a Christian aura: was not his sacrifice, asked Gamba 'the most generous and beneficent action which could be undertaken by a Christian?' (Gamba to Kennedy, 21 May 1824; Kennedy, 382). In his funeral oration Spiridion Tricoupi recalls how on Easter Sunday 'the happy salutation of the day "Christ is risen"' remained among the towns-folk 'but half spoken'; and as they met, 'before even congratulating one another on the return of that joyous day, the universal question was, "How is Lord Byron"?' (Edgcumbe, 185). The name of Christ seldom appears in Byron's writings and was probably seldom on his lips. But that the inspiration was there, there seems little question, and at the end of his life he was more ready to acknowledge it. Certainly it seems not unfitting that Parry should report among his dying words the invocation, in Italian style, '*Ah Christi*' (Parry, v, 127).

I am not suggesting that there was anything strange in all this: much of it was forced by the situation. But that is just the point, for I am arguing that Byron attuned himself to what was in fact forced by the situation. He was an Englishman in the nineteenth century engaged in an action concerned deeply with the Western tradition, which involved Christianity. Besides, despite his questioning of orthodoxy in matters of damnation and lack of metaphysical charity, he was a deeply religious man, revering the Bible, a chapter of which he read every day (Parry, IX, 207); which was always by his bed-side and of which his intimate knowledge exceeded Kennedy's. His life shows Christ-like qualities and a willed and Christ-like sacrifice; and, though he did not believe in putting Christ before the Almighty (Parry, IX, 207), his calling on him at death had a certain, dramatic, relevance.

To pass to Byron's outlook as soldier-statesman. Here again we find a new, or at least a newly emphatic, humility. In the self-reflection of *The Deformed Transformed* (see pp. 156, 259) Byron pictured himself as renouncing claims to a Caesar's leadership and the semi-divine honours of a Demetrius Poliorcetes for the purer ideal of service to Greece, symbolized by a *mild* Achilles, chosen to designate prowess newly subdued to humility, the very strangeness of the choice of Achilles being organic to the meaning. In Greece Byron shared the privations of an ordinary soldier: Parry tells us that he 'submitted' to live on the coarsest and meanest rations and allowed himself to be 'drilled' as a common soldier, going through the various exercises (Parry, IV, 79–80; Gamba, IV, 177). His attitude was summed up in words reported by Gamba: 'I should be perfectly ready to serve as a common soldier, under any body, if it be thought of any good to the "cause"' (Gamba, IV, 162).

In reading the various accounts of Byron in Greece we are also aware in him of a new statesmanship and a new respect for Great Britain, both for the home government and for British authority abroad, quite unlike his early uncompromising attacks. At Cephalonia 'it was generally supposed', writes Kennedy, 'that his lordship would shun his countrymen, as he had done in Italy'; but on the contrary, he delighted in their society (Kennedy, 3–5). Circumstances had forced a change. Being now in the arena of action, impinged on from all sides by the forces of world politics, he *had* to compromise. Statesmanship demands caution. Gamba writes:

Those who have studied the character of Lord Byron in his writings will easily believe that prudence was not in the catalogue of his virtues. Lord Byron knew that this prejudice was entertained against him, and, therefore, feeling the necessity of such a virtue in his situation, no one could have more scrupulously endeavoured to attain it.

(Gamba, I, 35)

At every turn of Byron's negotiations and plans we can apply Drinkwater's words: 'It was, in fact, the careful rhythm of a real statesmanship that was quite beyond Trelawny's intelligence' (VI, 369).

The most obvious example is his disagreement with Colonel
Stanhope as to the running of the journal of the liberation, *The Greek
Chronicle*. Stanhope was all for violent leftish propaganda, Byron for
caution. To Samuel Barff he wrote, on 19 March 1824:

> Col. Stanhope and myself had considerable differences of
> opinion on this subject, and (what will appear laughable
> enough) to such a degree, that he charged me with *despotic*
> principles and I *him* with *ultra radicalism*.

Stanhope's editor, Dr. J. J. Meyer, given 'the freedom to exercise an
unlimited discretion' was, says Byron, a danger:

> He is the Author of an article against Monarchy, of which he
> may have the advantage and fame—but they (the Editors) will
> get themselves into a scrape, if they do not take care. . . . Of all
> petty tyrants, he is one of the pettiest, as are most demagogues,
> that ever I knew.
>
> (LJ, VI, 355)

Though of all contemporary world powers Byron most hated the
Austrians, this hatred was irrelevant to his present engagement. I
quote from an editorial footnote to the *Letters and Journals:*

> In the 20th number of the *Greek Chronicle* Meyer published so
> violent an attack on the Austrian Government, that Byron
> suppressed the whole edition.
>
> (LJ, VI, 355, note)

No action could have been more significant. In normal Byronic
terms Meyer was justified; but 'Byronic terms', being abstract, faded
into insignificance before the immediate and compelling task.
Millingen writes of the preliminary 'prospectus' of another paper of
Stanhope's, *The Greek Telegraph* (for this journal see LJ, VI, 355,
note):

> The sentiments imprudently advocated in this prospectus in-
> duced the British authorities in the Ionian Islands to entertain
> so unfavourable an impression of the spirit which would guide

its conductors, that its admission into the heptarchy was inter-
dicted under severe penalties. The same took place in the
Austrian States, where they began to look upon Greece as 'the
city of refuge', as it were, for the Carbonari and discontented
English reformers. The first number appeared on 20th March;
but it was written in a tone so opposite to what had been expected, that it might, in some degree, be considered as a protest
against its prospectus. Lord Byron was the cause of this change.
More than ever convinced that nothing could be more useless,
and even more dangerous, to the interests of Greece, both at
home and abroad, than an unlimited freedom of the press, he
insisted on Count Gamba becoming Editor. Byron cautioned
him to restrict the paper to a simple narrative of events as they
occurred, and an unprejudiced statement of opinions in respect
to political relations and wants, so as to make them subjects of
interest to the friends of Greece in the western parts of Europe.
                                    (quoted Edgcumbe, 113–14)

The cause came first. A statesman cannot always be a Timon, or a
Cain, ranging the inter-stellar spaces of good and evil.

It is not surprising that Byron's most explicit statements regarding
his respect to the constitution of his own land appears in Parry's
reports of his conversations in Greece:

I am still so much attached to the constitution of England
personally, that were it to be attacked—were any attempts made
by any faction or party at home to put down its ancient and
honourable aristocracy, I would be one of the first to uphold
their cause with my life and fortune.
                                          (Parry, VIII, 173)

The report may not be exact; but it is consistent with what we have
called (p. 202) Byron's 'middle course'; there is a new emphasis, that
is all. In another conversation Byron's reported words are: 'There is
not on earth a more honourable body of men than the English
nobility, and there is no system of government under which life and
property are better secured than under the British constitution' (Parry,
IX, 205). However, in planning a constitution for Greece, Byron did
not advise the British pattern, thinking America a better model. But
Greece must choose for herself; it must be an organic growth (Parry,

VIII, 174–5 etc.). Byron knew that he could, had he so wished, have made himself the leader, even the king, of Greece; but, he said, 'I came here to serve the Greeks on their own conditions and in their own way'; and to that determination he remained firm (Parry, VIII; 179–81, note).

I am arguing for a comparison with *Henry VIII*. But it may be objected that Shakespeare's drama honours the royal and ecclesiastical establishment of his day without apparent question, whereas Byron is supporting a movement of liberation. Is this not an obvious contrast, politically, of 'right' and 'left'? To ask such a question is to fail in understanding of the nature of Shakespeare's drama. It is not, as I have often emphasized (*The Crown of Life*, 336; *The Shakespearian Tempest*, 1953, etc; xxiii; *The Sovereign Flower*, 253; and elsewhere), propaganda for 'order', 'nationalism' or 'even 'royalism', or for any *abstract* category whatever, but an acceptance of the actualities of his time and place leading to a dramatization of near-distance events concluding with an act of devotion to the reigns of Elizabeth and James. What is right in one period and for one place may be wrong in another. We could even, following *Hamlet*, say that the soul of Britain had to learn to honour the Tudor and Stuart monarchies in Shakespeare's day before it won the right to execute Charles I in Milton's.

Byron too was thinking in vital rather than 'abstract' terms:

> There is no abstract form of government which we can call good. I won't say with Pope that 'whate'er is best administer'd is best'; but I will say, that every government derives its efficiency as well as its power from the people.
>
> (Parry, VIII, 174)

Byron went to Greece neither as a 'revolutionary' nor as a propagandist for the British constitution, but simply to right what he regarded as in the circumstances, of which the historic and religious traditions of Europe were part, a great wrong. Gamba tells us:

> Lord Byron's view of the politics of Greece was, that this revolution had little or nothing in common with the great struggles with which Europe had been for thirty years distracted, and that it would be most improvident for the friends of Greece to mix up

their cause with that of the other nations who had attempted to change their form of government, and by so doing to draw down the hatred and opposition of one of the two great parties that at present divide the civilized world. Lord Byron's wish was to lay it down for granted, that the contest was simply one between barbarism and civilization—between Christianity and Islamism —and that the struggle was in behalf of the descendants of those to whom we are indebted for the first principles of science, and the most perfect models of literature and of art. For such a cause, he hoped that all politicians of all parties, in every European state, might fairly be expected to unite.[1]

(Gamba, v, 209)

Categories both secular and religious are involved, but they are all firmly presented in historical and contemporary terms.

The point I wish to establish is simply this: just as Shakespeare, like his own Hamlet, leaves his more personal and esoteric quests and questionings for a common-sense and realistic embracement, both secular and religious, of his here and now, so does Byron, each acting according to his lights and the period concerned. In both instances we may note that it is of the very essence of the matter that both State and Church should be at one, and in harmony. In *Henry VIII* the balance is emphatic, especially vivid in the ritual processions of Anne Boleyn's coronation as Queen and the culminating christening of Elizabeth. For Byron our best record occurs in Spiridion Tricoupi's funeral oration. In it he addresses Byron's daughter:

As in the last moments of his life you and Greece were alone in his heart and upon his lips, it was but just that she [Greece] should retain a share of the precious remains. Missolonghi, his country, will ever watch over and protect with all her strength the urn containing his venerated heart, as a symbol of his love towards us. All Greece, clothed in mourning and inconsolable, accompanies the procession in which it is borne; all ecclesiastical, civil and military honours attend it; all his fellow-citizens of Missolonghi and fellow-countrymen of Greece follow it, crowning it with their gratitude and bedewing it with their tears;

1. That Byron was aware that the Greeks of his day were a mixed race not all biologically descended from those in the ancient world need not here concern us. See Appendix ii to Note on *Childe Harold*, ii, 73; P, ii, 192–6.

it is blessed by the pious benedictions and prayers of our Arch-
bishop, Bishop, and all our clergy. Learn, noble lady, learn that
chieftains bore it on their shoulders, and carried it to the church;
thousands of Greek soldiers lined the way through which it
passed, with the muzzles of their muskets, which had destroyed
so many tyrants, pointed towards the ground, as though they
would war against that earth which was to deprive them for
ever of the sight of their benefactor;—all this crowd of soldiers,
ready at a moment to march against the implacable enemy of
Christ and man, surrounded the funeral couch, and swore
never to forget the sacrifices made by your father for us, and never
to allow the spot where his heart is placed to be trampled upon
by barbarous and tyrannical feet. Thousands of Christian voices
were in a moment heard, and the temple of the Almighty re-
sounded with supplications and prayers that his venerated remains might be safely conveyed to his native land, and that his
soul might repose where the righteous alone find rest.

(Edgcumbe, 190)

The expression may be over-decorative for modern British reading,
but the record, in all its ritualistic splendour, stands.

II

Shakespeare's *Henry VIII*, as I have shown in *The Crown of Life*,
counters Crown, Church and Law and their attendant dignities
with a very different emphasis on the raw elements of human creation.
King Henry himself has much of it in his bluff personality, and we
are left in no doubt as to the part played in the developing pattern by
the sexual instincts which prompted him to divorce one queen and
marry another, leading on to the birth of Elizabeth. Apart from all
ideals and all morals, nature itself has its own, unethical, methods,
without which we can have no kings and queens.

That is why we find here so curious a concentration on crowds.
After the Field of the Cloth of Gold, celebrating the amity of
England and France, we are told that

> Every man,
> After the hideous storm that follow'd, was
> A thing inspir'd; and, not consulting, broke

Into a general prophecy: That this tempest,
Dashing the garment of this peace, aboded
The sudden breach on't.

(I, i, 89)

There was an actual storm, and the crowd prophecied as with a
single voice ('aboded' = 'boded'): there is a strange unity born of
diversity. The effect here is a spiritual, Pentecostal effect; but at Anne
Boleyn's coronation the crowd is more physically apprehended. Its
sounds are like those of a ship's sails in storm, of many 'tunes', and
yet there is again a unity, a communal welding into an undiffer-
entiated mass:

Great-bellied women,
That had not half a week to go, like rams
In the old time of war, would shake the press,
And make 'em reel before them. No man living
Could say, 'This is my wife', there; all were woven
So strangely in one piece.

(IV, i, 76)

Notice the violent sexual, fertility, emphasis; and the fusion, the
mass.

At the final christening the Crowd is as a vast sea flooding into
the Palace yard. The Porter addresses his man:

Porter: . . . Keep the door close, sirrah.
Man: What would you have me do?
Porter: What should you do, but knock 'em down by the
dozens? Is this Moorfields to muster in? or have we some
strange Indian with the great tool come to court, the
women so besiege us? Bless me, what a fry of fornication
is at door! On my Christian conscience, this one
christening will beget a thousand: here will be father,
godfather, and all together.

(V, iv, 31)

The impressions are violent; humanity is shown in the raw; but we
are aware of a vast fertility, of men and women in appalling, challenging, fertile, creative power, a single vast unit; an ocean in comparison with which State and Church, the King, Cranmer, and
the child Elizabeth, are as fragile steersmen.

We may seem far from Byron; but in both we find, at the last, the same honesty; before and beyond all ideals whatsoever, there is this soil of rough humanity without which no such ideals could come to flower.

At Missolonghi many of Byron's cherished interests were paling. His *Macbeth* intuitions had for long, except for occasional interruptions, been giving way before sun and humour; his anti-social Timon extravagances were left behind in Venice; and he had parted with his last Cleopatra, Teresa. Even Loukas Chalandritsanos, who was by him as a tormenting sweetness, appeared, as we have seen, unresponsive, while Byron blamed himself for his weakness. His destiny was calling him, and that he knew it is clear from what is probably his finest lyric, *On This Day I complete my Thirty-Sixth Year*. These lines we have already (p. 69) quoted. The 'beauty' referred to in them is Loukas'. In 'Think through whom thy life-blood tracks its parent lake' Byron is thinking of his own claim to royal ancestry. When Moore wrote of the poem, 'There is perhaps no production within the range of mere human composition round which the circumstances and feelings under which it was written cast so touching an interest' (Moore, II, 719 or LIV, 615), he was presumably thinking, with all due diffidence, of the New Testament.

The beau, the aristocrat, the lover, the superman-dream, were fading. Byron had by him a natural companion of equal social status in Count Gamba, Teresa's brother; and such natural man-to-man companionships were normally life-breath to him. And yet his one sheet-anchor in these last days was not Gamba. After a life of distracting ideals and passions, now, near death, Byron felt most at home, and safe, with the rough and simple honesty of the 'sort of hard-working Hercules' (Kinnaird, 30 March 1824; LJ, VI, 363), Parry. The record of their association in Parry's admirable account shows that he understood Byron perhaps better than anyone; especially he understood that in Byron which had always rejected insincerity and cant; and his reported conversations ring true. In one of these Byron expressed his approval of a proposed school for the 'working classes', saying 'It gives me pleasure to think what a mass of natural intellect this will call into action' (Parry, IX, 205). Probably Byron had said as much on other occasions, though we have no record of it. Perhaps only a Parry would have reported such a remark which in that period of revolution held a threat, though Byron himself regarded the education of the masses as a safeguard for the constitution, and even for the aristocracy (Parry, IX, 205). To Byron, the aristocracy was there to lead, raise and enlighten; his dislike of radicals was motivated by fear of tyrannic demagogues and unruly mobs; but his remark to Parry witnesses his conviction as to the unmined riches awaiting development in the humbler, proletarian, orders.[1]

In Byron's last engagement Church and State and Soldiership are accordingly countered by his ingrained at-home-ness with the raw Falstaffian material of human creation. This we have already discussed; at Missolonghi, in Parry, it became a final, *the* final, support; and it is perhaps dramatically fitting that Parry should have been the one to report Byron's 'Ah Christi' at death and the fearful thunderstorm at his passing.

1. In my *Lord Byron: Christian Virtues* the reference for this remark is at one point incorrectly given. On p. 232, '211-14' should read '204-14'.

X

THE GOLDEN THREAD

I

SHAKESPEARE'S world is royal; Byron is great. Once again, we ask—what is the exact relation of Byron's greatness to the Shakespearian royalty? What *is* royalty? Let me again quote, as I have quoted in other contexts before, Gordon Craig's apt statement in *On the Art of the Theatre* (1957; 45):

> I use the word 'Kingdom' instinctively in speaking of the land of the Theatre. It explains best what I mean. Maybe in the next three or four thousand years the word Kingdom will have disappeared—Kingdom, Kingship, King—but I doubt it; and if it does go something else equally fine will take its place. It will be the same thing in a different dress. You can't invent anything finer than Kingship, the idea of the King.

Craig is obviously thinking of some eternal human necessity, outspacing, though including, politics. The King links earthly affairs to that which encloses and surpasses them: he—or, as Craig says, some equivalent—is a human necessity.

What of Byron? He knew himself to be great and he was proud of his title. On his early travels he engaged in a dispute regarding priority in an official ceremonial (C, I, 8–9). Stendhal said that his 'noble birth' was often 'uppermost in his thoughts' (LJ, III, App. viii, 440). And yet we know that Byron was naturally a humble man, and liked mixing with his social inferiors. His statement in one of his lyrics that he was 'stern to the haughty, but humble to thee' (*Stanzas for Music*, 'I speak not . . .'; the addressee is unknown) may be regarded as a central and correct self-diagnosis. How then shall we place his respect for his own title? Surely we shall find that it had for him a *poetic* aura, like his swimming of the Hellespont and the Mermaid crest on his carriage (LBCV, 108). We have to attune ourselves to the aristocratic tradition if we are to understand what even a minor baronetcy could, in that period, mean. We may also suggest that the royal essence so powerful in Shakespeare, and existing poetically independent of the failings of its various human representatives, had after the failure of the Stuarts been housed less in the monarch than in the great aristocracies of the eighteenth century. On these had fallen the responsibility of leadership; more, on these had descended the lustre; for we are thinking of an essence, a spiritual quality, an aura, not limited by political categories. Byron accordingly believed in his country's 'ancient and honourable aristocracy' (p. 326); but he also felt that it had fallen lamentably from grace. It had not fulfilled its task of serving and raising those less wealthy and less gifted. Content to rule, it had failed to lead, to enlighten.

In this sense, Byron's title had, under the new system, royalistic affinities and responsibilities. But Byron also knew that he was descended through his mother from the Stuarts; that he had, in this more direct sense, royal blood. In his long reply to the attack in *Blackwood's* he wrote of Southey:

> What is there in such a man to 'envy'? Who ever envied the envious? Is it his birth, his name, his fame, or his virtues, that I am to 'envy'? I was born of the aristocracy, which he abhorred; and am sprung, by my mother, from the kings who preceded those whom he has hired himself to sing.
>
> (LJ, IV, App. ix, 483)

Othello's

> I fetch my life and being
> From men of royal siege . . .
>
> (*Othello*, I, ii, 21)

is recalled by Byron's self-admonition in *On This Day I Complete my Thirty-Sixth Year:*

> Think through *whom*
> Thy life-blood tracks its parent lake,
> And then strike home!

On leaving England in 1816 he left for his daughter a ring containing 'the hair of a King and of an ancestor' (Lady Byron, April, 1816; LJ, III, 281; p. 93 above).

Byron liked playing with the thought of himself as a king's equal:

> Buonaparte has lost all his allies but *me* and the King of Wirtemberg. Do you remember Wolsey, 'I and my king?' No matter, my alliance is quite as useful as that of Bavaria.
> (Lady Melbourne, 4 Nov. 1813; C, I, 214)

The phrase appealed to him. Writing to Hobhouse on 11 November, 1818, after referring to the styles of his own *Beppo* and the Italian poet Pulci, he remarks: 'Forgive me for putting Pulci *second*, it is a slip—"Ego et Rex meus"' (C, II, 89). In the Bowles Controversy he blames Bowles for a similar fault: 'Courtesy requires, in speaking of others and ourselves, that we should place the name of the former first—not "*Ego et Rex meus*"' (LJ, V, App. iii, 568). These are light touches, but they are symptoms of an instinct that on occasion could rise to the statement that he had no ambition unless it were a case of '*Aut Caesar aut nihil*' ('either Caesar or nothing'; Journal, 23 Nov. 1813; LJ, II, 339). Bearing a title from his father and royally descended from kings who were at least *real* kings, as the Hanoverians were not (p. 93 above), he seems to have felt himself by nature called to be 'the enlightener of nations' (*Manfred*, III, i, 107) and guide history back into nobler channels than those in which its present course was set. But he did not find collaboration easy, could not make terms with contemporary politics and their devious ways (*Manfred*, III, i, 116–23; LBCV, 136–8). He was by nature proud to the mighty, though humble in other respects (p. 333 above). When, and only when, he had power, as he had at Missolonghi, his life-long chafing against his surroundings fell from him; given authority he proved himself a superb leader. There was talk of his being offered the crown of a re-born Greece (Parry, VIII, 179–81, note); but he rejected the thought, wanting Greece, in democratic style, to choose her *own* way (p. 327).

Two of Byron's most powerfully created heroes, the Doge in *Marino Faliero* and Sardanapalus, are royally conceived. The Doge stands for the royal essence as against an effete ruling clique.

Sardanapalus refuses to remove his royal insignia before the rebels. Warned that he will be recognized, he replies tersely 'I go forth to be recognized' (III, i, 143). The six plain words do no less than Claudius' famous lines in *Hamlet* (IV, v, 123):

> There's such divinity doth hedge a king,
> That treason can but peep to what it would,
> Acts little of his will.

My claim that Byron is a great royalistic poet may seem strange, but it is supported by his having penned *the* finest poetic statement on true royalty which our literature affords. I refer to the sonnet to the Prince Regent *On the Repeal of Lord Edward Fitzgerald's Forfeiture* (1819):

> To be the father of the fatherless,
> To stretch the hand from the throne's height,
> and raise
> *His* offspring, who expir'd in other days
> To make thy Sire's sway by a kingdom less—
> *This* is to be a monarch, and repress
> Envy into unutterable praise.
> Dismiss thy guard, and trust thee to such traits,
> For who would lift a hand, except to bless?
>
> Were it not easy, Sir, and is't not sweet
> To make thyself belovéd? and to be
> Omnipotent by mercy's means? for thus
> Thy sovereignty would grow but more complete:
> A despot thou, and yet thy people free,
> And by the heart, not hand, enslaving us.

That constitutes the distilled essence of Byron's mature political poetry. It is something Shakespeare could do, and did, in *The Merchant of Venice* (IV, i, 184–97) and Isabella's speeches on justice in *Measure for Measure* (II, ii, 58–63; 72–9). It is something that Blake and Shelley could never have done; nor Wordsworth, though for a different reason. It is too true to the facts of power and leadership for Blake and Shelley; and too true to the equally compelling demands of Christian softness, for Wordsworth, whose own later sonneteering was given to support of the death-penalty.

Byron stands alone in having lived that fusion for which our world so agonizedly strives, of the heroic, aristocratic, values and the Sermon on the Mount; accepting both and making within himself, making *of* himself, the fusion, almost an identity (p. 114). How this was done I have attempted to explain in *Lord Byron: Christian Virtues* (IV and VI).

The interest of such a man in titles and what I have called 'the royal essence' had, obviously, little to do with externals; it was one with a profound recognition of both the responsibilities of leadership in a period of social transition and a recognition of emotional and spiritual values of Christian quality: 'and by the heart, not hand, enslaving us'. Nor was royalty in Shakespeare an external; kings could be, and usually were, fallible, even disastrous; but the *royal essence* remained *poetically* invulnerable. We may, moreover, note that the independence of this essence can be seen from Shakespeare's tendency to put his final personal trust in *princes* rather than *kings*. In the Sonnets his adoration is given to a youth of gentle, but it would seem not noble, blood, who nevertheless is given an aura of royalistic poetry.[1] In those dramas where a single person assumes a peculiarly high degree of spiritual authority, that person is not a king: Hamlet is a prince set in contrast to a king; the Duke in *Measure for Measure* and Prospero in *The Tempest* are minor sovereigns only, devoted to learning; Timon and Cerimon (in *Pericles*) are lords. There is a clear forecast of the eighteenth century, but there is more than that. What Shakespeare is driving towards is a *saintly aristocrat;* the strangeness of the phrase denotes the greatness of the conception. Now this was, as I have shown throughout *Lord Byron: Christian Virtues,* exactly what Byron was driving at throughout his life, as a man and as a poet. The royal essence is a power, in its own right, able to function under any system. It is, as it were, the *leaven* of politics; it endows them with grace. Byron came near to approving Pope's apothegm 'Whate'er is best administer'd is best' (Parry, VIII, 174; *An Essay on Man,* III, 303). At the limit, he could regard all

1. For my views on the theory recently advanced by Leslie Hotson regarding the identity of the Youth, see my book on the Sonnets, *The Mutual Flame,* 8–9; also my article 'New Light on Shakespeare's Sonnets' in *The Listener,* LXXI, No. 1831; 30 April 1964; to be included in a volume of collected essays entitled *Shakespeare and Religion,* at present in preparation.

men as royal (LBCV, Index A; xii, Politics; *Theory*. See p. 347 below).

Crown, aristocracy and hero-worship are close to the soul of drama. Today they survive, for some of us, only there, though we must also recognize the extraordinary part hero-worship has in fact played, for good or for evil, in our day, over world affairs. We must also recognize the extraordinarily important part played by the sovereign in our own constitutional monarchy, acting as a dramatic conception, an accepted make-believe like drama, housing none the less a—or *the*—central political truth, if only because it denies royalty to upstart leaders; and its radiations, both at home and abroad, are potent. Shakespeare's kings are inadequate to the poetic royalty they represent. Royalty is, has always been, a symbol of a higher kind of Man as yet unknown, though poetry is his language and Byron his forecast, if not more. We can say that Byron's interest in royalty, titles and heroes is really one with his interest in poetry; and also one with his instinctive will not merely to read or write poetry, but to be, and act, it. He is a human gesture towards something we cannot, any more than he could, fully define; of the distant future, or maybe of some other dimension altogether. From time immemorial the hero-god and priest-king, the patron, the aristocrat, the leader—or their poetic simulacra of stage, film or gramophone within the mind or soul—have been necessities. No actual representations may suffice; but neither will abstractions serve in their stead.

I have heard Byron's generally accepted descent from James I of Scotland (Marchand, I, 16) questioned. But if the claim be doubted, the blend accruing of imaginative lustre and genealogical uncertainity will only the better serve, as it does with Christ's reputed descent from King David, to pose the *tertium quid* on our horizon.

II

Byron is cosmopolitan and international; he is not, in any usual sense, English. He told the Count D'Orsay on 22 April 1823 that he was only in part English; his mother was Scottish; 'my name and my family are both Norman'; and he himself 'of no country' (LJ, vi, 195). What he perhaps meant was that his personality was not to be confined by any normal limitation. Such a conviction was, as we have seen (p. 314), powerfully experienced by him on his death-bed. Byron is an archetypal and universal figure; and being so humanly comprehensive, his life cannot be profitably discussed in moral terms: the subject is too big. If man were perfected it might be for us all to conform; but he is not; he is travailling and awaking. Byron would be less important if his life were more moral. Without some challenge, especially in our era some erotic challenge, it would lack ignition and detonation. We must not therefore wish him blameless; the blame is from the immorality and that the measure of a disloca-tion more vital than words. Byron's life was a satire on his com-munity, not merely because he was better but because he was bigger; and he was bigger because he was more honest; he let himself be, as few of us dare to, his own whole, and therefore vast, self. He was, certainly, better also, though from a purely moral valuation there were also difficulties. Drinkwater (256) wrote: 'Less admirable but more blameless men have been canonized for half his virtues'.

Granted this reading, we can begin to understand his life in Italy in all its sensuous extravagance and poetic comprehension. Re-member that at its core and heart was a gentleness, a sweetness, a love and generosity which, rightly or wrongly, he felt to have been repaid by calumny and slander. The crash of his domestic life, to us a pass-ing excitement and a pleasing mystery in his spectacular career, was to him an agony, an extension of the Ishmael-anguish of his youth and his physical deformity. How easy it is, in view of such a man's later fame, to forget the sensitivity of genius, the inferiority, the dread of abnormality, of being seen and known as a negative, a deformity. This dread made his rejection a crucial test. There was only one way for him, other than suicide, which he contemplated: to mask his Timon love by cynicism and attack, and gain what solace he could from monastery[1] and mistress; and, further, to assert super-status and justify it; in his letters, his greater work, and his death. This he did, directly or indirectly; and throughout all he maintained his golden humour.

1. For Byron's visits to the Armenian monastery on the island of St. Lazzaro near Venice, see LJ, IV, 9, note. Byron was taking lessons in Armenian. For Byron's interest and accomplishments in foreign languages see again LJ IV, 9–10, note.

On the moral issue much of Byron is contained in one of Shakespeare's Sonnets (121):

> Tis better to be vile than vile esteeméd,
> When not to be receives reproach of being;
> And the just pleasure lost, which is so deeméd
> Not by our feeling, but by others' seeing:
> For why should others' false adulterate eyes
> Give salutation to my sportive blood?
> Or on my frailties why are frailer spies,
> Which in their wills count bad what I think good?
> No, I am that I am, and they that level
> At my abuses reckon up their own:
> I may be straight though they themselves be bevel;
> By their rank thoughts my deeds must not be shown;
>   Unless this general evil they maintain,
>   All men are bad and in their badness reign.

My extended paraphrase is given in *The Mutual Flame* (p. 51). The thought is: 'I am being true to myself and moral criticism only bears witness to the lusts of lesser ('frailer') men who cannot accept, as I do, what is basic to human nature. I act as a unit, they criticize from an indirect, twisted, and evilly-impregnated consciousness.'

Byronic comparisons cluster. For 'I am that I am' we have Byron's 'I am myself alone', quoting *Henry VI* (Journal, 27 Feb. 1814; LJ, II, 389; *3 Henry VI*, v, vi, 83). The thought is repeated by Cain (*Cain*, III, i, 509). For the Sonnet's sense of integrity, we may adduce Byron's reported 1816 statement that, were the charges against him revealed, he would 'glory in it' (Sir John Fox, *The Byron Mystery*, 108). For 'I may be straight' we have his words reported by Parry: 'My conduct has been like the arrow's flight compared to their sinuous serpent-like track' (Parry, IX, 204). That is not to deny what are called vices, but it does deny hypocrisy, in Byron's eyes—as in Christ's—'of all crimes the worst' (Parry, IX, 204). We are all, in our degree, hypocrites. Byron was impelled to the opposite course, living from his total self.

As we have already seen (pp. 62–3 above), the Shakespearian, Byronic and Nietzschean psychology seems to announce a certain plenitude, a fulness, which is itself so abnormal that it becomes a kind of sickness; and in this state the subject is drawn *down* towards the lower level of ordinary mankind, for relief, the strain having become unbearable. Vices may be involved, Shakespeare's poisoning 'drugs' (Sonnet 118; p. 63). Byron's words are 'I plung'd amidst mankind' (*Manfred*, II, ii, 145). It may, of course, well be that the best course for any of us in this or some similar state is to gain physical release through sexual fantasy rather than external action, as counselled by John Cowper Powys (see *The Saturnian Quest*, 119–20; 125–6). But Byron on every front tended to live and act what he imagined, and whatever our own opinions as to the constituents, the result was a personality of staggering range and power. He was, in fact, Ibsen's man 'who wills himself' in *Emperor and Galilean*, who is to bring in the Third Empire (*The Emperor Julian*, III, iv).[1]

He was himself baffled. In his more confident moods he annoyed Stendhal 'by an absurd vanity, which urged him to pretend to everything' (LJ, III, App. viii, 444). When driven to it by what he considered slander and injustice, he could, in certain powerful letters and his denunciation in *Childe Harold*, (IV, 132–7), suddenly assume, as by natural right, an almost superhuman status which, as we read, tends to carry its own conviction; and from that Timon-like height pours his scorn on the lesser beings who have wronged him. No one can be forced to take him, on these occasions, at his own valuation; but it is the purpose of my studies to make it easier for us to do so. It was not easy for him to find words for the kind of superiority he felt in himself. He could think of ancient heroes, of Napoleon, of his royal descent, of his title; but none were quite what he meant, or wanted, while in the depths his contemporaries recognized, as surely as did he, an indefinable superiority. Society was antagonized. Poetic genius in writing we can—some of us—accept; but the other, more indefinable, assertion of poetic-genius-in-action is less widely tolerable, and easily leads to revulsion or ridicule in those around. We must therefore guard against our own natural

1. See my *Ibsen*, Writers and Critics Series, 42; on Byron and Ibsen, 6, 107. For a further discussion of Byron's influence on Ibsen, see Peter Simonsen, 'Om *Hedda Gabler, Lille Eyolf*, og Lord Byron'; *Edda* (Oslo), 1962; 176–84.

hostility. In his own life, in his day, Byron knew that superiority arouses hatred:

> He who surpasses or subdues mankind
> Must look down on the hate of those below.
> *(Childe Harold,* III, 45)

After listing the number of famous names he has been compared to, he says:

> The object of so many contradictory comparisons must probably be like something different from them all; but what *that* is, is more than *I* know, or anybody else.
> *(Detached Thoughts,* 1821; Int.; LJ, V, 408)

Sardanapalus, speaking as a Byronic reflection, likewise wonders what he himself, the enlightened and pacifist emperor at odds with all convention, *is (Sardanapalus,* II, i, 489). Our most important evidence comes at the heart of his life's drama when he is reported by Augusta Leigh to have claimed to be the greatest man alive and to have answered his cousin George Byron's query whether he excluded Napoleon with the reply: 'God—I don't know that I do except even him' (LBM, 270–1; also p. 102 above). There was no pleasure in the thought; it was a responsibility and an agony, like Hamlet's

> The time is out of joint. O cursed spite,
> That ever I was born to set it right!
> *(Hamlet,* I, v, 188)

He saw man and society disjointed, religion a hypocrisy, and cruelty, to men and animals, abounding. His own natural gentleness had been thwarted; its centre was a love-instinct regarded by society as an appalling vice; and yet his instincts simultaneously told him that he was, as a man, the solution to the human enigma.

III

He felt in himself a new reality which was like poetry but more than poetry: his image for it was, as we have seen, 'lightning'; and its personification in myth was Prometheus.[1] It could be referred

[1]. Of Byron's status as super-hero I have already written at some length in my chapter 'The New Prometheus' in *Lord Byron: Christian Virtues* and in the final chapter of *Lord Byron's Marriage.*

both to spiritual categories and to scientific advance. In talking to Medwin he grouped Prometheus and science. The passage is fascinating:

'Who would not wish to have been born two or three centuries later?' said he, putting into my hand an Italian letter. 'Here is a *savant* of Bologna, who pretends to have discovered the manner of directing balloons by means of a rudder, and tells me that he is ready to explain the nature of his invention to our Government. I suppose we shall soon travel by air-vessels; make air instead of sea-voyages; and at length find our way to the moon in spite of the want of atmosphere.'

'*Caelum ipsum petimus stultitia*', said I.

'There is not so much folly as you may suppose, and a vast deal of poetry, in the idea', replied Lord Byron. 'Where shall we set bounds to the power of steam? Who shall say, "Thus far shalt thou go, and no farther?" We are at present in the infancy of science. Do you imagine that, in former stages of this planet, wiser creatures than ourselves did not exist? All our boasted inventions are but the shadows of what has been—the dim images of the past—the dream of other states of existence. Might not the fable of Prometheus, and his stealing the fire, and of Briareus and his earth-born brothers, be but traditions of steam and its machinery? Who knows whether, when a comet shall approach this globe to destroy it, as it often has been and will be destroyed, men will not tear rocks from their foundations by means of steam, and hurl mountains, as the giants are said to have done, against the flaming mass?—and then we shall have traditions of Titans again, and of wars with Heaven.'

(Medwin, 226–8)

Byron would no doubt have been only the more excited to know that fire and electricity had a greater future than steam; for on these his own poetic concentration was fixed; and they were more directly forecast by the myth of Prometheus. We have a neat instance of myth and poetry proving more exact forecasts than deductions drawn from contemporary fact. The passage may be related to the space-flight in *Cain*.

On every level, and at every turn of his life and thought, Byron directs us to a sense of the poetic as the central reality; the life, the essence, the being, of creation and of man. It was from what may be called the 'poetic' or 'dramatic' dimension that Byron, in this summing up so much of western drama, could come so near to a fusion of State and Church, of Renaissance heroism and the Sermon on the Mount. The fusion cannot be *explained* outside drama; its consummate literary expression is Ibsen's *Emperor and Galilean;* and Byron was, in himself, this drama, this fusion. In *The Prophecy of Dante* (IV) he is at pains to define this state of *poetic being:*

> Many are poets who have never penn'd
> Their inspiration, and perchance the best:
> They felt, and lov'd, and died, but would not lend
> Their thoughts to meaner beings; they compress'd
> The god within them, and rejoin'd the stars
> Unlaurell'd upon earth, but far more bless'd
> Than those who are degraded by the jars
> Of passion, and their frailties link'd to fame,
> Conquerors of high renown but full of scars.
> Many are poets but without the name,
> For what is poesy but to create
> From overfeeling good or ill; and aim
> At an external life beyond our fate,
> And be the new Prometheus of new men,
> Bestowing fire from heaven, and then, too late,
> Finding the pleasure given repaid with pain,
> And vultures to the heart of the bestower,
> Who, having lavish'd his high gift in vain,
> Lies chain'd to his lone rock by the sea-shore?

After all, if written poetry were not in some way pointing us to a living, a *tao* or way, or state of being—definitions cannot be easy—why do we so value it?

Some message is involved, psychological, social and political. Byron's personal centre touches with equal intimacy the widening circles of his own family relationships, mother and wife; sexual encounters, both homosexual and heterosexual, London and Italian society; politics, national and inter-national affairs; nature, the universe, religion. It is in this, Shakespearian, sense that he exerts a royalty. Royalty is the attunement of human affairs to some higher dimension. It is not, like religion, a concentration mainly *on* that dimension; it is apparent wherever earthly affairs or beings are shot through with a mysterious light. There is a splendour luring man onwards and upwards; kings and queens exist to symbolize it.

There is a golden thread which runs through the Western imagination from Plato onwards. Its gleam is present whenever human creation is shot through with spiritual glory: there must be a sense of physical presence; but there must be more than that. Plato, or Socrates as Plato reported him, saw this glory in male youth; so did the Middle Ages, in drama, pageantry and emblem, presenting angels in boy-forms. Our dramatic tradition is rich in such figures, as I have shown throughout *The Golden Labryinth,* either as boys or as girls in boy-disguise. Where such loves, or visions, are our concern, I follow Byron, Shelley and Tennyson in using the word 'seraphic' (p. 50 above), which preserves a greater human warmth than 'angelic', and has stronger spiritual connotations.

The relation of such visionary eroticism to royalty is close. The blend of strength with charm which arouses a poet's adoration of male youth corresponds to the blend of power with grace which constitutes the royal principle. The adorations are of similar tone. Shakespeare compares a lover's experience to that of a subject before 'a beloved prince' and 'vassalage' almost paralyzed before 'the eye of majesty' (*The Merchant of Venice,* III, ii, 176–84; and see *Troilus and Cressida,* III, ii, 36–9). His Sonnets are for the same reason royally impregnated: the wondrous youth is the lover's sovereign. Byron was not only himself a magical personality, but he was peculiarly and at all times responsive to the magic, the essential 'thou', of other personalities. Of this characteristic I have already written in my *Lord Byron: Christian Virtues* (226), relating it directly to the instinct in man which responds to the royal categories (226. See also Index A, XII, Politics, 'Approach personal, the "thou"'; LBCV, 295). Perhaps as good a summation of the whole matter as any comes in a love-lyric of Byron's already (p. 333) noticed, where he writes that he is 'stern to the haughty, but humble to thee'. Love and royalty exert the same, authoritative, magic.

Because the love-vision must be the heart of all best human endeavours, we must have our kings or king-equivalents; neither politics alone, nor religion alone, nor both, can give us the royal and golden quality which we want. Plato's philosophy is royal as well in its demand for rulers of philosophic wisdom as in its sense of spirit-beauty known through youth. Christ himself loses his power over the imagination if he is reduced to terms of theology on the one side or ordinary mankind on the other. 'Christ' means the 'anointed one'; and the Messiah was an earthly conception, a king. His life, whatever its further extensions, flowers from the Messianic beliefs of his time and race, and the royal quality of it must, as I have elsewhere insisted (*The Christian Renaissance*, 1962 edn.; Epilogue, 300–1, 337), be preserved.[1] Poetry demands it. Dante in his *De Monarchia,* though what he laboured for was a just balance of powers, was, in the conflicts of his day, the supporter primarily of Emperor as against Pope (*The Golden Labyrinth*, 25–6). Shakespeare's is a royal world. Milton was a royal poet, his earliest revolutionary impulses, in Dantesque fashion, arguing that ecclesiastical authority was wronging the majesty of the King (*Chariot of Wrath,*[2] III, 99); and despite his puritanical allegiances, *Paradise Lost* is loaded with royalistic tonings. As we have already noted, the royal powers, which must not, and cannot, be in any period subdued—if we slight them, we shall find them having a terrible revenge—were lodged during the eighteenth century in the aristocracy (*The Dynasty of Stowe*, IV, especially 61–3; VI, 91–2).

We may suppose that our whole poetic tradition, whatever the superficial variations, is in reality maintaining a single concentration. Differences in period and person with corresponding changes in politics, sociology and morality will necessitate differing emphases; each emphasis must be read in terms of its age; but each in turn, poets Greek, Roman, Renaissance, Augustan, Romantic, Victorian and modern, are trying to keep us on the one, communal and spiritual, middle path, the golden path; in politics neither right nor left, but both, and in matters religious neither of body or spirit, but of body spirit-infused or, conversely, what St. Paul called the 'spiritual body' of other-dimensional manifestation. This is, from

1. See also Robert Graves and Joshua Podro, *The Nazarene Gospel Restored,* 1953, especially Introduction and Parts II and III; also Robert Graves, *King Jesus,* 1946.
2. To be reissued in a larger volume: see p. ix.

Plato on, the golden path, Flecker's golden journey to Samarkand:

> *White* on a throne or *guarded in a cave*
> There lives a prophet who can understand
> Why men were born: *but* surely *we* are brave,
> Who take the *Golden* Road to Samarkand.

I italicize crucial words; the opposites of white and shadow are of good and evil, of morality, prophecy, and metaphysics; *but* the golden path is a path of living and of action, experienced immediately and transcending the other categories. Its symbol in the body communal is the crown; in personal vision, the seraphic.

Byron inherited this tradition; and he was true to it. He sees glory in the human form, male or female, living or as statuary (p. 97); and throughout he labours for the kind of spiritualized and love-impregnated royalty defined in the *Fitzgerald* sonnet (p. 336); and he could see all men 'fit for the society of kings'; as, potentially, royal (Mrs. Byron, 1 July 1810; LJ, 1, 284). Because the golden thread is of body and spirit, or shall we say of body-spirit, actual affairs and action are involved; and Byron was a man of action. He is eminent among those great ones such as Dante in whom spiritual power compelled action in the contemporary arena. Such men will to infuse poetry into politics; and their cause is generally, as with Swift—or in our time Lawrence of Arabia—some kind of 'liberation' or 'freedom'. Christ himself was such a man; the freedom he stood for will be by some discussed as freedom from Roman domination;[1] while others will concentrate on that freedom from the Law announced by St. Paul. Freedom is no easy concept. Both Milton and Byron knew this, and for both it involved poetic and spiritual categories.

The romantic period was one of (i) revolution and (ii) individualism. New depths were being upturned in the body social and the psychology of man. They were not all pleasant, as that archetype of the period, the Marquis de Sade, reveals. Byron, and other romantics and so-called 'Gothic' writers, wrestle with a new self-consciousness, working the Shakespearian impulses into a conscious

1. I am thinking of Joel Carmichael's *The Death of Jesus*, 1963. Mr. Carmichael gives a reference list of other relevant works.

awareness and a conscious artistry. And a discovery was simultaneously revealed: the discovery of what Nietzsche was to call the 'over-
man'. That is, the new depths, grim though they often seemed, were
also felt as new powers; and new powers meant new strength for both
good and evil. A greater kind of man—the gigantic figure of
Napoleon served as a sign—was glimpsed. Byron's torment was that
he had good reason to think himself such a man; or, at the least, a
step towards such a man; towards a far greater than Napoleon.
Greater, because more poetic, and so more golden. Gold is sun-
fire and precious worth; the alchemists dreamed of some higher state
attainable by man, and gold was its symbol. For Nietzsche's Zarathustra gold symbolized his furthest human vision, as in 'the Golden
Wonder, the boat of freewill and its Master' in *Thus Spake Zarathustra* ('Of the Great Longing', III, 58; other references, *Christ and
Nietzsche*, 193–5). Gold is more lovely than theology and of more
worth than reason; it is of the middle way, the interfusion, comprehensive, nature and man divine in beauty and power. That is
why we find Byron's Manfred saying that he has all but known

> The golden secret, the sought 'Kalon', found,
> And seated in my soul.
>
> > (*Manfred*, III, i, 13)

'Soul'; he might as well have said 'heart'; for, as in the *Fitzgerald*
sonnet, the softer, the un-Napoleonic, qualities, are present. There
is in it love, and gentleness. Otherwise it would not be golden.

Of Byron's pre-eminence his contemporaries were well aware. In
his preface to *Julian and Maddalo* Shelley wrote of him:

> But it is his weakness to be proud: he derives, from a com-
> parison of his own extraordinary mind with the dwarfish intel-
> lects that surround him, an intense apprehension of the nothing-
> ness of human life.

The thought is repeated in the poem itself (50):

> The sense that he was greater than his kind
> Had struck, methinks, his eagle spirit blind
> By gazing on its own exceeding light.

In his *Sonnet to Byron* Shelley could see himself as a worm offering
'homage' to 'the God', and in a three-line fragment *To Byron* wrote:

O mighty mind, in whose deep stream this age
Shakes like a reed in the unheeding storm,
Why dost thou curb not thine own sacred rage?

Again, in an interesting sonnet which must be referring to Byron
(LBCV, 254–5), Shelley sees him, as so many of our recent analyses
have shown him, as one who has penetrated beyond all superficial
manifestations into a disturbing dimension beyond normal insight:

Lift not the painted veil which those who live
Call Life: though unreal shapes be pictured there,
And it but mimic all we would believe
With colours idly spread—behind, lurk Fear
And Hope, twin Destinies; who ever weave
Their shadows, o'er the chasm, sightless and dread.
I knew one who had lifted it—he sought,
For his lost heart was tender, things to love,
But found them not, alas! nor was there aught
The world contains, the which he could approve.
Through the unheeding many he did move,
A splendour among shadows, a bright blot
Upon this gloomy scene, a Spirit that strove
For truth, and like the Preacher found it not.

That was how Byron struck a great contemporary. Goethe's reaction, though he never met Byron, was similar. His like, he wrote
to Crabb Robinson in August, 1829, 'would never come again'
(quoted Lovelace, *Astarte,* expanded 1921; 14).

He felt, without being able to define, his own stature. On
28 February 1817 he wrote to Thomas Moore:

If I live ten years longer, you will see, however, that it is not over
with me—I don't mean in literature, for that is nothing; and
it may seem odd enough to say, I do not think it my vocation.
But you will see that I shall do something or other—the times
and fortune permitting—that, 'like the cosmogony, or creation
of the world, will puzzle the philosophers of all ages'.[1] But I
doubt whether my constitution will hold out. I have, at inter-
vals, exorcised it most devilishly.

(LJ, IV, 62–3)

1. For the reference to *The Vicar of Wakefield* see LJ, IV, 63, note.

His life, as a whole, has justified his words, which recall Lear's

> I will do such things—
> What they are, yet I know not, but they shall be
> The terrors of the earth.
>
> (*King Lear*, II, iv, 283)

If Byron's words be egotism, they are the necessary egotism of the tragic protagonist; of the same sort, on the same gigantic scale. Byron's comparison suggests a marvel of *creation*, as though he were on the brink of some new evolutionary advance. The language of that advance is poetry. 'What is Poetry?' wrote Byron, and continued: 'The feeling of a Former world and Future' (Journal, 28 Jan., 1821; LJ, v, 189). It speaks from a dimension including both. His story, as truly Hamlet's or Timon's, is touched with gleams of that 'something unearthly '(*Childe Harold*, IV, 137) darkly symbolized by the greatest art. At his death a great peal of thunder sounded, like the thunder-tempests of a Shakespearian tragedy; like the rending of the Veil of the Temple at the death of Christ.

Byron foretold that this 'something unearthly' would live on and gradually attune mankind to respond to him, that is to his royalty, with the 'love' that was its right (*Childe Harold*, IV, 137). The prophecy is coming true: for today what is most strange about Byron is that he arouses the responses, of both antagonism and devotion, that we are accustomed to in a *living man of genius,* fighting for acceptance. With Byron all this is *still going on;* his challenge lives, eternally new, feared and loved, but deathless. Gradually the fear will melt, and the love remain.

We have not yet plucked out the heart of his mystery. Much of it is written into *Manfred,* especially the many phrases describing the protagonist as a man of some new 'order' (pp. 217, 301 above). 'All my madness', Byron wrote in his 1816 *Fare Thee Well* (p. 115 above), 'none can know'; he is referring to that 'deeper' madness of *The Dream* (p. 106), which lies beyond the boundaries of reason. If we want a crisp definition to conclude on, we may point to the Doge's reply to his accusers in *Marino Faliero:* 'The secret were too mighty for your souls' (v, i, 285).

APPENDIX

THE SEPARATION CONTROVERSY

SINCE the publication of my *Lord Byron's Marriage* in 1957 the issues in question appear to have been confused rather than clarified by subsequent works. Censorship and inhibitions have been active, and the public fogged. Evidence regarding the obstacles at present hampering investigation I have lodged in the Brotherton Collection in the University of Leeds; and other relevant papers, including cuttings of the reviews and press-correspondence used in this appendix, will eventually be stored there.

On 22 March 1957 I printed in *The Times Literary Supplement* a letter dated 29 November 1920 written by the 10th Lord Byron to the late F. Farrer, which had been shown me by Mrs. V. Hancock Nunn. The letter states that Lord Lovelace's *Astarte* deliberately put forward a false account of the Separation, which had nothing whatsoever to do with incest. The original, which contains some erratic spelling not followed in my version, and a word-variant of slight consequence ('fairly' for 'faring' in 'I hope you are both faring well') which I misread from the hand-script, is lodged in the Brotherton Collection.

In *Essays in Criticism* of October 1958 (VIII, 4) I answered a review which, while more or less accepting my account of the marriage relationship, opposed my arguments in respect to homosexuality, by showing that Prof. Leslie Marchand's quotations from certain of Byron's letters containing the code-phrase 'Plen. and optabil.—Coit' had direct homosexual connotations, thus indicating that his engagements were frequent and continuous. The letters concerned were written from Falmouth on 22 June 1809, and from Greece on 23 August and 4 October 1810 (Marchand, 181–2,

351

258, note[1]). Prof. Marchand was the first to decipher the mysterious code-phrase from the manuscripts in the Murray collection at Albemarle Street, London, and Prof. Gilbert Highet traced the reference for him to Petronius (Marchand, 181, note). Marchand gives his readers no direction as to its exact meaning, which I would not myself have recognized without the assistance of a friendly correspondent.

After a favourable review of my *Lord Byron's Marriage* by Mr. Cyril Connolly in *The Sunday Times*, Mrs. Doris Langley Moore contributed two letters to that journal, on 27 January and 10 February 1957, discounting my emphasis on homosexuality and my general approach to the problems raised by Byron's destroyed *Memoirs* and the *Don Leon* poems. To the first letter I replied on 3 February 1957, but my reply to the second was unfortunately not printed. After reading Mrs. Moore's letters Lady Wentworth decided to offer her the chance of viewing and working extensively on the Lovelace, that is Lady Byron's, papers, so long with-held except to those who enjoyed favour, with a view, as Mrs. Moore tells us, to the writing of a book 'on certain lines which we often discussed'. This was recorded on 8 March 1959 in Mrs. Moore's full account of the offer and of her viewing of the papers in four long articles in *The Sunday Times* of 15 and 22 February and 1 and 8 March 1959. Mrs. Moore incorporated her reading of the Lovelace Papers into her *The Late Lord Byron*, published in 1961.

Meanwhile Lady Lovelace had died, and possession of the papers and much of the copyright had passed to Lord Lytton, who, while granting Mrs. Moore permission for the use of material needed for the completion of *The Late Lord Byron* then in process of publication, with-held from her any further permissions and decided instead on a long-range plan of publication involving some seven volumes (letter, *T.L.S.*, 22 Sept. 1961) under the editorship of Mr. Malcolm Elwin. Mr. Elwin's first volume, *Lord Byron's Wife*, appeared in 1962.

It will be evident that the challenging expositions of my own book had, as I had suggested in my preface that I hoped that they

1. The numeral 258 was wrongly given as 248 in my article (*Essays in Criticism*, as above, 455).

might, blasted the way for what seemed a new freedom of inspection and approval. But the results have been far from satisfactory. My reasons for saying this will shortly appear.

Since my own study, three major works have now appeared: Professor Leslie Marchand's three-volume biography in 1957 and those by Mrs. Moore and Mr. Elwin, in 1961 and 1962. In all three I find signs of a reluctance to face and explain the facts.

In reviewing Prof. Marchand's *Byron: a Biography* in *The York-shire Post* of 13 March 1958 I wrote, referring to Byron's love for his half-sister Augusta Leigh:

> He believes that incest occurred, and he may be right: but his presentation of the evidence is scarcely just. In quoting from the two most telling pieces of incriminating suggestion (Byron's letters of 30 April 1814 and 17 May 1819; Marchand, 448, 785–6; discussed in my *Lord Byron's Marriage*, 40, 135–44) he omits the very phrases which are known to counter the evidence.

The points omitted are (i) Byron's use in the first letter of 'senseless' as 'non-sensuous' in respect to his love for Augusta (I quote the sentence below); and (ii) the assertion in the second that he had recently met a Venetian of the same name as its addressee, which suggests that she may *not* have been Augusta. Prof. Marchand appeared to be once again following the old tradition of *pretending* that incest was the central trouble, when it was not. We have yet more direct evidence of it. I wrote further:

> The process reaches an extreme when, at the crucial incident of Lady Byron's visit to Dr. Lushington at which she divulged the secret which made him insist on a separation, Prof. Marchand's text simply tells us that there is evidence enough 'to indicate quite clearly that she then for the first time fully confessed her suspicion of the incest' (582). She may have done so, but it certainly was not this that turned the scales. We have only to look up the reference given in Prof. Marchand's own footnote regarding this particular 'secret' (The Bathurst Statement, printed in Sir John Fox's *The Byron Mystery*, 57–8; discussed in LBM, 238–40) to discover that it was not incest at all.

Here we have a truly extraordinary example of a well-reputed scholar giving for a crucial statement a reference which firmly contradicts it on the specific issue on which we know that biographers are regularly misleading. Why? I repeated my charges in *The Times Literary Supplement* of 21 March, 1958. There was no reply.

My present conclusion is that Prof. Marchand, like Sir John Fox, who in *The Byron Mystery* was the first to print the Bathurst Statement which he subsequently proceeded to contradict (LBM, 239–40), succeeds in veiling the truth from the public while simultaneously putting the expert, who may be expected to read footnotes, look up references, and see the more glaring contradictions, on the right track.

Prof. Marchand had been refused permission to inspect the Lovelace Papers which the publication of my own book laid open —for a while—for Mrs. Moore's use. Her *The Late Lord Byron* was reviewed by me in *The Yorkshire Post* of 13 July 1961. Contact with the private papers had now shown Mrs. Moore that Lady Byron's suspicions of homosexuality had indeed played their part at the Separation period[1]; and Mrs. Moore, like Prof. Marchand, related, as my own study had already done, Byron's Missolonghi love-poems to the boy Loukas. So much was of value; but I would complain that, though her investigations had thus tended to support my own earlier arguments concerning which she had written so scornfully in *The Sunday Times*, her book contained no retraction on her part nor salute to my researches, even though it was these which had opened to her view the papers which she was being privileged to use.

I had other complaints. In my review I wrote:

> Referring to Lady Wentworth, Mrs. Moore tells us that 'It was by now fully agreed between us that I was to write a book on certain lines which we often discussed' (*The Sunday Times*, 8 March, 1959).

Whatever that may mean, her technique of quotation and omission is certainly confusing. Her *Sunday Times* quotation from John Buchan's *Memory Hold-the-Door* on 22 February 1959

---

1. In *Lord Byron and his Detractors* by Sir John Murray, published in 1906, Lord Ernle (R. E. Prothero) contributed a section 'Lord Lovelace on the Separation of Lord and Lady Byron' in which he asked, on page 98, 'Did the cause mentioned by Lady Byron to Mrs. Leigh in her letter of September 1816, have no influence on the separation?' The letter is that of 21 September, 1816 (LJ, III, 328) discussed in *Lord Byron's Marriage*, 210).

omitted the one really embarrassing phrase,[1] and comparisons of her quotation from the Bathurst Statement with my use of it and of her quotations from Campbell's article with mine (*The Sunday Times*, 1 March 1959; *The Late Lord Byron*, 328; *Lord Byron's Marriage*, 239, 228–30) will serve as pointers in regard to her methods.

At the crux of the separation problem the evidence is, as it was by Prof. Marchand (see *T.L.S.* 21 March 1958), curiously handled, for how could the appalling secret which made Dr. Lushington on 23 [22] February 1816, finally insist on a separation have been incest (304, 310) when on that very day Lady Byron reports that he 'was far from thinking that the suspicions are any good to me' (305, note)? They were, as Mrs. Moore knows and elsewhere emphasizes, 'suspicions' only (81, note, 233, 244–245; also 'I very much fear that She may be supposed the cause of the separation by many, and it would be a cruel injustice', 304, note; and see *Lord Byron's Marriage*, 75, 88–9, 238–9).

The words 'I very much . . .' were Lady Byron's. I repeated my main charges in the columns of the *Literary Supplement* (*T.L.S.*, 28 July 1961). I found Mrs. Moore's answers, in both journals, unsatisfactory.

She had, it is true, avoided inconsistency, but only at the cost of discounting Dr. Lushington's statement regarding the decisive secret revealed to him by Lady Byron as caused by a 'lapse of memory'; she asserts that Lady Byron had revealed no more than those suspicions of incest which Lushington had thought of no use (Mrs. Moore, 304; 310; 305, note). During the correspondence developing from my *Literary Supplement* letter, which ran from 4 August to 3 November 1961, I wrote, on 11 August 1961, with reference to this statement of Dr. Lushington as reported by H. A.

---

1. Buchan wrote: 'So, during a summer week-end, Henry James and I waded through masses of ancient indecency, and duly wrote an opinion. The thing nearly made me sick, but my colleague never turned a hair. His only words for some special vileness were "singular"—"most curious"—"nauseating, perhaps, but how quite inexpressibly significant"' (VI).

Both Mrs. Moore and Marchand (582, note; Marchand is quoting a secondary source) omit 'The thing nearly made me sick', using dots. However, Prof. Marchand's study is more daring in its footnotes than in its text. His notes constitute an underworld of suggestion contrasting with the chastity of the pages to which they are appended.

Bathurst, which I had regarded as central evidence in *Lord Byron's Marriage* (238–40):

> Any full-length treatment of the Separation that does not openly quote and discuss this our one piece of all but irrefragable evidence as to what was Lady Byron's central charge must be regarded as to that extent invalidated.

Admirable letters by Lord Lytton and Mr. Keith Walker were contributed in my support, on 25 August and 1 September, 1961. Lord Lytton had already stated in *The Sunday Times* of 16 July 1961 that he had not 'authorized' any of Mrs. Moore's 'writings' except by giving copyright assent for material already being used in *Lord Byron's Marriage*, and that he was for the future entrusting the papers to Mr. Elwin, who was to begin by producing a 'scholarly and non-partisan book'. It was reasonable to expect a major clarification.

The first volume of Lord Lytton's projected series, entitled *Lord Byron's Wife*, appeared in 1962, and it turned out to be constricted, on the crucial issues, in much the same fashion as its predecessors. True, it was not ostensibly concerned with the Separation controversy; it merely concentrated on Lady Byron's letters and notes during and after the Separation. But since the sequence of Separation letters certainly *appeared* to be telling the story of the Separation, it would surely have been helpful to inform the readers of Lady Byron's crucial visit to Dr. Lushington on 22 February 1816, at which we have reason to suppose that she revealed a secret which changed the course of the proceedings. Many reviewers, who were obviously quite unversed in Byronic studies, regarded the book as a striking contribution tending to show that there was, as I myself had thought in the early stages of my investigations, no especial cause behind the Separation beyond incompatibility of temperament; but, despite the value of the book's material and the care of its presentation, there was nothing bearing on the *controversy* of central importance—not even the emphasis on Byron's drinking (p. 130 above)— that was new to anyone who had read the letters of the section 'The Separation' in *Letters and Journals* (LJ, III, 287–329), the account given in the second volume of Lord Broughton's (i.e. J. C. Hobhouse's) *Recollections of a Long Life*, or the letters printed by Ethel Colburn Mayne in her *Life of Lady Byron*. Many of Mr. Elwin's letters had already appeared, in abbreviated form, in Miss Mayne's study. The reviewers were, in fact, in the position that I myself had been after reading these works; but I had found that they did not cover the problem.

Here are some specific complaints. Mr. Elwin follows Prof. Marchand in most unfortunately omitting, perhaps by inadvertence though dots appear, that phrase in Byron's letters that so firmly counters the charge of incest. In my review in *The Yorkshire Post* of 29 November 1962 I wrote:

> On the incest, Mr. Elwin is reserved. Only one complaint may be recorded. Our strongest evidence for incest occurs in Byron's enigmatic letters to Lady Melbourne, and yet one (30 April 1814) might seem to contain a denial: 'You, or rather *I*—have done *my A——*much injustice. [The expression which you recollect as objectionable meant only 'loving' in the *senseless* sense of that wide word, and it must be some selfish stupidity of mine in telling my own story, but] really and truly—as I hope mercy and happiness for her, by that God who made me for my own misery, and not much for the good of others—*she* was not to blame, one thousandth part in comparison.'
> The letter is ambiguous, but in replacing (194) by dots, as did Prof. Marchand also, the words which I have bracketed, Mr. Elwin turns an ambiguous disclaimer into apparent admission.

The omitted passage raises important and difficult questions; to omit it obscures the problem; and that our leading authorities should do this is unfortunate. (My 'replacing' was poor English.)

Mr. Elwin appears to be writing from a bias against those who attribute homosexuality to Byron. He refers to 'sophisticated modern critics' who relate Byron's ideal love for Edleston to 'homosexual practices' (127). If he is referring to me, the statement is untrue; if he is not, to whom *can* he be referring? He appears to be unaware of my *Essays in Criticism* article (p. 351 above) on Byron's sexual engagements in Greece in 1810, leaving his readers to suppose that they were heterosexual, whereas my article had given proof that they were not. Moreover, while letting Lady Byron's *private* papers at least *appear* to tell the story of the Separation proceedings, he omits, as I have already stated, all mention of Lady Byron's *public* revelation that there had been a secret which made Dr. Lushington on 22 February 1816 change his first opinion that a re-union was possible. Mrs. Moore thought Dr. Lushington's subsequent statement regarding this visit was due to weak memory (p. 355 above); Mr. Elwin thinks that he was lying (p. 361 below).

Three major works had now appeared veiling, if not distorting, the crux of the matter. Since it had become by now clear that the reviewers and their public were not properly aware of the issues, I composed a long letter which was printed in *The Times Literary Supplement* of 7 December 1962, as follows:

In the course of his impressive study of Lady Byron, *Lord Byron's Wife*, Mr. Malcolm Elwin complains that some of Byron's biographers have 'jumped to the conclusion that only revelations of inquities' could account for the separation (419). This is a dangerous simplification, and since some of Mr. Elwin's reviewers appear to have regarded the unhappy controversy as settled, may I remind your readers of the facts?

The ground was prepared by the burning of Byron's defence at Albemarle Street in 1824 and the controversy proper was started by Lady Byron's 'Remarks Occasioned by Mr. Moore's notices of Lord Byron's Life', privately printed in 1830 and then included as an appendix to Moore's second volume. After a lull, controversy was reawakened by Mrs. Beecher Stowe's *Lady Byron Vindicated* in 1869 [1870], which contained an accusation of incest that was afterwards given strong family support by Lord Lovelace in *Astarte* in 1905, the book [*Astarte*] being reissued with new material by his widow in 1921.

Lady Byron's 'Remarks' had included a letter written to her for the occasion by Dr. Stephen Lushington, her chief legal adviser, dated 31 January 1830:

I can rely upon the accuracy of my memory for the following statement. I was originally consulted by Lady Noel on your behalf, whilst you were in the country; the circumstances detailed by her were such as justified a separation, but they were not of that aggravated description as to render such a measure indispensable. On Lady Noel's representation, I deemed a re-conciliation with Lord Byron practicable, and felt most sincerely a wish to aid in effecting it. There was not on Lady Noel's part any exaggeration of the facts; nor, so far as I could perceive, any determination to prevent a return to Lord Byron: certainly none was expressed when I spoke of a reconciliation. When you came to town in about a fortnight, or perhaps more, after my first interview with Lady Noel, I was for the first time informed by you of facts utterly unknown, as I have no doubt, to Sir Ralph and Lady Noel. On receiving this additional information, my opinion was entirely changed: I considered a reconciliation im-possible. I declared my opinion, and added, that if such an idea should be entertained, I could not, either professionally or other-wise, take any part towards effecting it.

I continued:

That is the keystone of the controversy. Later in the century Mr. H. A. Bathurst, Registrar of the Admiralty Court from 1879 to 1890, and designated by Sir John Fox 'the surviving trustee' of Lady Byron's 'sealed papers', set down a memorandum of a conversation with Dr. Lushington held on 27 January 1870. This memorandum, which is in the Lovelace collection and was printed by Fox in *The Byron Mystery* in 1924 (57–8), contains the following paragraphs:

After what had passed in the papers and Reviews of late he said it would be some relief to tell me what follows:—
That he was first consulted by Lady Noel, Lady Byron's mother, and that she did not know all or the most serious of the causes of Lady Byron's complaints against her husband. He (Dr. L.) only learnt them at a subsequent period from Lady Byron herself (referred to [in] his letter in the *Remarks*).
He considers that the real cause of Lady Byron's separation, when it was ascertained that there was no adequate ground in the opinion of the medical men for supposing him insane, was his brutally indecent conduct and language to her . . .
Dr. L., speaking with much feeling and emotion, described Lord B.'s conduct as most foul and gross, but of this there could hardly have been any evidence; and I gathered that Lady B. would have been most reluctant or positively unwilling to

359

charge him with such offences if legal proceedings became necessary—she would naturally shrink from doing so.

At the time of her leaving his house she was not convinced of any incest having taken place.

This was the statement referred to by Prof. Marchand's footnote in support of his conclusion that incest was the secret that made Lushington change his mind!! My letter continued:

The passage covered by Fox's dots was printed from the Lovelace Papers by Mrs. Doris Langley Moore in *The Sunday Times* of 1 March, 1959, and is in the nature of a qualifying statement suggesting that Byron's brutality consisted in forcing Lady Byron to listen to detailed accounts of his behaviour with loose women.

That the determining revelation of 22 February 1816 was not incest is, quite apart from the Bathurst Statement, established by Lady Byron's letter to her mother of 23 February 1816 (Elwin 417); and in claiming that it was incest that made Lady Byron's advisers insist on a separation (Lovelace, 181-2), Lord Lovelace misled his readers. Biographers now have three choices: (i) to admit alternative explanations; (ii) to attempt, at the cost of convolutions unprecedented in scholarship, to pretend that it *was* incest; and (iii) to neglect Lushington's statements. The first course was taken by myself in *Lord Byron's Marriage*; the second, as I have demonstrated in your columns on 21 March 1958, and 28 July 1961, by Prof. Marchand and Mrs. Moore; and the third, though I am prepared to believe that the scheme of his book did not force this discussion, by Mr. Elwin.

What the Bathurst statement says may be less or more than the truth, or false; and it admits of divergent interpretations; but it remains our only objective evidence. I am not here arguing that the solution put forward by the *Don Leon* poems is correct. The seeming embarrassment aroused by these documents in authoritative biographers has become *in itself evidence*; and, if grouped with the late Lord Tweedsmuir's reaction as reported in his *Memory Hold-the-Door* and the letter by the tenth Lord Byron which you printed for me in your issue of 22 March, 1957, may point towards a rarer, though related, trouble, at once less criminal and more embarrassing. If this is so, admission and a Greek name would leave a clear field for the future investigation of Byron's towering genius.

Mrs. Moore did not exactly regard incest as a determining issue, but she did state (310) that it was the 'additional information' of 22 February 1816 (her date 23 February seems to be an error). I was not rejecting the *Don Leon* hypothesis, but assuming that there must be something else as well. Nor was I attacking the main substance of Mr. Elwin's book. I was rather opposing those reviewers and members of the public who regarded it as a full account of the Separation. My purpose was to indicate why the kind of material contained in Mr. Elwin's volume had not in the past proved satisfying. I wished: (i) to show the public exactly what was the cause, I will not say of the *Separation,* because of that the causes were probably multiple, but of the *Controversy*; and also (ii) to force anyone anxious to discount the argument of my *Lord Byron's Marriage* into an open denial of Lushington's reliability.

Though there was no real need for their involvement, my letter produced on 14 December 1962 replies from both Mr. Elwin and Mrs. Moore, as well as a valuable contribution from Mr. Michael Joyce. Mr. Elwin argued that Lushington 'was from the first against a reconciliation', and that he only 'pretended in recollection' that his views were changed by Lady Byron's visit; in other words that he was a liar. Mrs. Moore attributed Lushington's statement to 'an honest or dishonest lapse of memory'; while also discounting my reference to Lord Tweedsmuir's (John Buchan's) book (pp. 354–5 and note, above) by suggesting that he also was suffering from temporary amnesia.

On 21 December I (i) drew attention to Dr. Lushington's career as Fellow of All Souls, D.C.L., Member of Parliament, and of the Privy Council, judge of the High Court of Admiralty, and ecclesiastical judge. I also (ii) while agreeing that on the visit of 22 February 1816 Lady Byron seems to have mentioned her suspicions of incest, yet once again reminded my readers that Lushington dismissed them as irrelevant, Lady Byron reporting that he 'was far from thinking that the suspicions are any good to me' (Mrs. Moore, 305, note; Elwin, 417; Mrs. Moore's version of the letter differs from Mr. Elwin's, with which it should be compared). I suggested that the more important revelation was being referred to in Lady Byron's letter to Lushington of 17 February 1816:

> I feel confident that if I were in London I could put in action some resources which would prevent the ultimate necessity of legal proceedings—and besides, there are things which I, and I only, could explain to you in conversation, that may be of great importance to the thorough understanding of the case.
>
> (Elwin, 412)

This is a clear corroboration of Lushington's 1830 statement.

I also (iii) referred to the omitted passage in the Bathurst Statement, where there are dots or asterisks. In *The Sunday Times* of 1 March 1959 Mrs. Langley Moore had, while pouring scorn on my suggestion in *Lord Byron's Marriage* that the omission might be of something important, quoted from the Lovelace Papers the words concerned, so that the passage (of which I had already seen her version in a note to me of 29 November 1958) ran

> indecent conduct and language to her—compelling her to listen, when he returned from his profligate revels at a late hour, to the most disgusting descriptions of his adulteries and indecencies with loose women, toying with more than one at the same time naked.

Mrs. Moore significantly omitted the sentence containing the words 'most foul and gross'. However, in order to assure honesty I had, despite, or rather because of, its countering of my own arguments, quoted this addition of hers during the earlier correspondence (*T.L.S.*, 28 July 1961); moreover on 7 December 1962 (p. 360 above) I had noted it as 'in the nature of a qualifying statement suggesting that Byron's brutality consisted in forcing Lady Byron to listen' to these accounts. But I had subsequently become aware, from Mr. Elwin's quoting of the same passage in his answer (*YP*, 5 December 1962) to my *Yorkshire Post* review, that Mrs. Moore's version, which countered, or at least softened, some of my own arguments, might not be correct. Mr. Elwin's version ran:

> indecent conduct and language to her—and compelling her

The words are no longer a qualifying addition to 'conduct'; 'con-

362

duct' now stands by itself; the significance of the dash is completely changed from a link to a break; Byron's actual 'conduct' to his wife, apart from any stories he told her, is being called first 'indecent' and, subsequently, 'most foul and gross'. So I wrote: 'Since the one version states "indecent conduct" towards Lady Byron herself and the other does not, it is important to know which transcription is correct.' I was aware that Lord Lytton had, during the earlier correspondence, complained of Mrs. Moore's inaccurate transcriptions (*T.L.S.*, 6 Oct. 1961); though I should record that Mrs. Moore replied that the typescripts viewed by Lord Lytton were unchecked versions (*T.L.S.* 13 Oct. 1961).

On 4 January 1963 Mr. Elwin, after insisting that Lushington had *never* from the start been in favour of a re-union, gave us his assurance that his version of the omitted lines was correct. Mrs. Moore now retired from the combat; but Mr. Elwin's discounting of Lushington remained.

As I have said, I welcomed this view of Lushington as a straight issue on which clarification was eventually certain. My thoughts were running on Sherlock Holmes' principle that when you have rejected the impossible what remains must be the truth. Now it was, quite simply, *impossible*—or as near impossible as makes no matter—that a man of Dr. Lushington's professional status should lie publicly, and once with Lady Byron's knowledge, about a scandal of national, and even international, reverberations in which he had played the leading legal part; and that he should do this on two separate, and formal, occasions during his long and distinguished career, the second being a deliberated statement for posterity made near death to quiet his conscience. Peers, Bishops, Members of Parliament, Vice-Chancellors and Headmasters, Doctors, Scholars—all may, when it seems professionally or personally advisable, lie in public; but the one man who cannot, on a professional or public issue, lie, is a judge. He is the only man whom it *cannot pay to lie*; for honesty is, whatever may be his other vices, his most cherished life-illusion, his stock-in-trade, his bread-and-butter. Nor could a man of Lushington's intellectual calibre have forgotten what had happened twice over a period of forty years in precisely the same way in regard to this perhaps the most dramatic incident of his career. Even if Bathurst were lying, we still have Lushington's first, 1830, statement. This must have been basically true: nothing else is possible.

When, in an argument of this kind, you know that you are on the side of the truth, it will generally be only a question of time before corroborating evidence turns up. In this instance I did not have to wait long. Turning over the pages of Mr. Elwin's book expecting evidence that Lushington had been, as he said, in favour at first of a reunion, my eye fell on a letter which constituted the needed evidence. On 11 January I wrote:

> Moreover on 4 February a letter of Mrs. Clermont's to Lady Noel shows that Lady Byron was then being offered from what Mr. Elwin calls 'an unlikely source'—why so 'unlikely'? [1]—'a last opportunity for retraction'. Mrs. Clermont enclosed a copy of a letter 'which has been agreed upon by Dr. Lushington and Colonel Doyle' for Lady Byron to send to Byron 'if she determines to persevere'. She continues: 'but Colonel Doyle is most anxious that she should not be pressed to pursue the course *legally* pointed out if she is not quite certain of having sufficient strength to persevere in it . . .' She might prefer to leave things 'more open to reconciliation at a future period' (original italics; Elwin, 392–3).

> Doyle and Lushington were working together in unison as Lady Byron's advisers. The letter corroborates Lushington's 1830 statement.

The argument was at an end. What appears to have deceived Mr. Elwin is that Lushington had probably explained, with full professional assiduity, what should be Lady Byron's *legal* course *if* she insisted; he had no doubt pointed out assiduously all the facts in her favour; but this does not prove that he *advised the course*. I might also have referred to Lady Byron's letter of 23 February 1816 directly *after* her crucial interview with Dr. Lushington: 'Dr. L. wishes to try one more expedient (Ld. Holland's mediation) before the Process is commenced. Of the success of which I have great doubts . . . At least I shall be justified to the world' (Elwin, 417). Though the question here probably concerns less the Separation itself than its

1. Only, of course, because of Mr. Elwin's theory that Lushington was from the start against a reconciliation.

method, the general tone ('one more') is unmistakable: Lushington has been cautious and pacific, Lady Byron on the attack. Mr. Elwin's last letter on 18 January 1963 did not again dispute the central issue.

That a powerful censorship is constricting Byronic studies will be obvious; if more exact evidence of its nature is wanted, it will be found among the private papers I have lodged in the Brotherton Collection at Leeds. It is a pity that such seemingly authoritative books as those we have been reviewing should mislead the public. Apart from all questions of suppression no transcriptions by a single scholar can be trusted with any finality. I know well enough that my own could not be; inaccuracy is ingrained in the human psyche, motivated sometimes by unconcious prejudice. Mrs. Moore's inaccurate transcription of a key-passage served by the simple omission of an 'and' so to oppose my reading and boost her own that my thoughts on the Bathurst Statement were, over a period of four years (from 1958 on; p. 362), deflected; and had Mr. Elwin not, by a lucky chance, quoted the correct version in *The Yorkshire Post*, I should have remained in ignorance.

My Byronic investigations are now, I hope, at an end. I do not wish, and may not have the time, to be involved in further controversy. I could wish that some other scholar might shoulder the responsibility of watching what happens and indicating where Byron is being misrepresented and the public misdirected. Help is perhaps more likely to come from America than from Britain. I am already grateful to Dr. Morton D. Zabel for pointing out to me what appears to be the first open reference, under the date 9 November 1829, to Byron's homosexual interests in *The Greville Memoirs* (ed. Lytton Strachey and Roger Fulford, 1938; 1, 326; the passage is unlikely to be found in the earlier editions); and I look with confidence to the learning and insight which Dr. Joseph Wallfield will bring to his edition of the *Don Leon* poems and his investigation of the problems which they raise.

For an additional note, see p. 366

Additional Note, 1966

In her recent *John Buchan*, Appendix A, Miss Janet Adam Smith quotes, presumably in full, the written 'opinion' of Buchan and James referred to in Chapter VI of *Memory Hold-the-Door* (p. 355 above, note). This is found to relate simply to copies made by Lord Lovelace of Byron's well-known and subsequently published letters to Lady Melbourne, which touch on nothing more embarrassing than Byron's ambiguous relations with Augusta, one of the most powerful phrases being quite urbanely quoted in the 'opinion'. This cannot be what made Buchan, who was no prude, feel 'sick'.

The text of *Memory Hold-the-Door* (U.S.A. *Pilgrim's Way*), which was according to the 1964 wrapper posthumously printed from his typescript, is vague. After referring (VI) to Lady Lovelace's 'archives' and the marriage 'quarrel' it passes directly to 'those particular papers'. The style is loose for an experienced writer, and it may be that a sentence has been inadvertently dropped or intentionally suppressed.

Both Miss Adam Smith (175-6) and Mrs. Moore (p. 361 above) think that Buchan subsequently confused the 'Lovelace Papers' and the comparatively innocuous Melbourne letters, thus leading his readers to suppose that what he examined for his 'opinion' were the former. But Buchan's text says nothing at all about the 'Lovelace Papers', that is the ancestral Lady Byron papers, as such, but merely that he was invited to 'examine' Lady Lovelace's 'archives', where Lord Lovelace's copies of the Melbourne letters were, in fact, lodged; and he might be simply saying that he examined these letters. What troubles us is that he might seem also to be saying that his written 'opinion' referred to what made him feel 'sick', whereas it obviously does not. There would consequently have been no need for Mrs. Moore and Miss Adam Smith to suppose any lapse of memory at all unless they were themselves assuming that the phrases of disgust, being inapposite to the Melbourne letters and the 'opinion', refer to *other* material among what Buchan calls the 'masses of ancient indecency' which he and James inspected. Miss Adam Smith is aware of the difficulty, remarking (176) that, in view of Buchan's known 'Rabelaisian' turn, it is hard to see why the Melbourne letters should be referred to 'in terms that suggest obscenity'.

The words of the formal 'opinion' indicate that it was wanted by Lady Lovelace as a support for her late husband's thesis in *Astarte*, and that it should have been confined strictly to the Melbourne letters, which are presumably 'those particular papers' of Buchan's account, was in accord with her known policy.

INDEX

OF NAMES AND TITLES

Material in footnotes is indexed simply under the page numeral where it occurs. Names occurring in references to correspondence are not necessarily indexed. Artists are listed on p. xv.

367

INDEX
OF BYRONIC THEMES (SELECTED)

Material in footnotes is indexed simply under the page numeral where it occurs.

378